# THE MIGHTY ACTS OF GOD

# THE MIGHTY ACTS OF GOD

## Arnold B. Rhodes

*Revised by W. Eugene March*

Geneva Press
Louisville, Kentucky

*Book design by Sharon Adams*
*Cover design by PAZ Design Group*
*Cover illustration: Scala/Art Resource, NY*

*First edition*
Published by Geneva Press
Louisville, Kentucky

This book is printed on acid-free paper that meets the American National Standards Institute Z39.48 standard. ∞

PRINTED IN THE UNITED STATES OF AMERICA

**Library of Congress Cataloging-in-Publication Data**

Rhodes, Arnold Black, 1913-
    The mighty acts of God / Arnold B. Rhodes; revised by W. Eugene March.
      p. cm.
    Includes bibliographical references and index.
    ISBN 0-664-50076-5 (alk. paper)
    1. Bible—Textbooks.   2. Presbyterian Church (U.S.)—Doctrines.
  I. March, W. Eugene (Wallace Eugene), 1935-   II. Title.

BS605.2 .R46 2000
220.6'1—dc21                                       00-039345

# Contents

PART SIX: GOD'S TRANSFORMING ACTS
THROUGH THE CHURCH

# Foreword

*A*rnold B. Rhodes's *The Mighty Acts of God* is a book that influenced in a significant way a whole generation of Presbyterian and Reformed church readers. The opportunity to revise it and make it available once again in an updated form is a great honor. The confidence that the author and the publisher have placed in me is gratifying as well as humbling.

My work is intended to provide for the church a version of the original work that I hope will be as helpful as the original. The book is still intended for a lay readership and is written in that style and with that readership in mind. It is my sincere hope that this book will enable its readers to become as excited and as informed with respect to scripture as happened with the original edition.

While the basic structure of the original book has been followed, there have been significant revisions. First, the language has been made inclusive. This has been done in light of the commitments of the Presbyterian Church (U.S.A.) to present our educational material in an inclusive style as best we are able. Second, the New Revised Standard Version of the Bible has been used as the source for biblical quotations. Third, the notes have been updated to include later editions whenever possible and supplemented by newer materials as necessary. The Study Aids section presents a set of materials that are available for use at the present and deletes some of those originally presented that are no longer in print. Fourth, the revision tries to honor commitments currently in place in the Presbyterian Church (U.S.A.) that recognize a different relationship between Christianity and Judaism from that which prevailed at the publication of the original version. Thus, some language and some images that could be read as suggesting that the church has replaced Israel as God's people have been removed and different imagery and language put in their place. Finally, the promise-fulfillment theme that was especially prominent in the first edition has been supplemented by other approaches to the relationship between the Old and New Testaments. The aim has been to emphasize the continuity between the Testaments and to avoid any idea that the Old Testament is primarily or only an "introduction" for the New Testament.

There is one person especially who is due a special word of thanks and appreciation. Without the help of Melissa Nebelsick this project would have gone much more slowly and certainly not as smoothly. Melissa showed uncommon patience and diligence in helping to prepare the manuscript. She made suggestions, did research, prepared the biblical citation index, and in other ways as well assisted in the production of this work. Melissa, thank you for your assistance and encouragement.

There are others who also assisted in this project. Martha Gilliss at Geneva Press guided the manuscript through the publication process. And my good wife, Margaret, put up with me graciously and lovingly through the many hours I devoted to this project. Finally, a word of thanks to Lela and Arnold Rhodes for their confidence in me and their willingness to have this classic work refashioned for a different generation.

W. Eugene March

# Witness to God's Mighty Acts

*T*he pilgrimage that we are about to take through the Bible can be the most exciting trip of your entire life—even more exciting than a visit to old Jerusalem or to St. Peter's in Rome. Actually it is a pilgrimage from the Garden of Eden to the new Jerusalem. But this is a trip that you cannot take as a tourist. Your camera will do you no good. You can make the trip only as a participant.

Or to change the metaphor, this is a story and we are characters in it. True—it is primarily God's story. True—it is the story of those who lived long ago. But it is also true that it is our story. This means that the biblical story is still going on. We are, historically speaking, living in that part of it that extends from the ascension of our Lord to his coming in glory. All of us were intended by the Author of the story to be actors in it. If the world stands, our children and our children's children will be a part of it too. "Were you there when they crucified my Lord?" Yes, we were there. Were you there when Moses cleft the sea in two? Yes, we were there. The more the story becomes our story, the more effectively will we be able to tell it and live it. Never minimize the part you play in the divine program. As a Christian, you have a distinctive witness to give.

Of course there are many discouragements and threats to life in these days. But when have God's people not been threatened? Indeed, as a people they were born in crisis. They have always lived in crisis. The Bible was penned in the blood of martyrs and saints.

## The Witness of God

The Bible is not only "the greatest story ever told"; it is the greatest drama ever enacted—and its chief Actor is God. The Bible centers on God's mighty acts: what God has done, is doing, and will do for us human beings and our salvation through Jesus Christ. God provides self-witness by mighty acts, which are interpreted and appropriated by people of faith. This is not the whole of revelation, but it is its heart.

Of course, the person who thinks he or she can explain how God's self-revelation becomes known to us is as naive as the one who thinks he or she can explain God. In spite of all the volumes written on the subject, human beings cannot comprehend revelation; but they can apprehend it. That is, we can get hold of the matter, or rather, by faith we can know ourselves to be grasped by God. Obviously this kind of knowledge is faith-knowledge, the kind that characterizes interpersonal relations. For example, you may know that someone loves you, but you cannot give a scientific demonstration of this fact to anyone else. It is not that kind of knowledge; it *is* the kind of knowledge by which you can live richly. After all, what would nuclear physics be worth without faith and love in interpersonal relations? Not a dime. This means that the tangibles of life receive their deepest meaning from the intangibles.

How do we know God? We know God through divine acts, primarily through specific events of history as presented and interpreted in the Bible. The basic unit of revelation is the event interpreted and appropriated by people of faith. The circuit of revelation is God → event(s) → interpreter → interpreted event(s) → God:

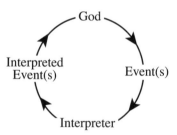

Of course any such representation is an oversimplification, but so is any human attempt to express God's relation to humankind, whether it be done in words or in other symbols. Human language and thought are always "in part"—not absolute. Once the interpreter responds to God's initiative, a dialogue is carried on between human and God, in which God's self and God's will are known. Such a meeting includes specific content. For example, it made it possible for John to say, "God is love."

God does not come to an individual as if that person lived in splendid isolation from others. Rather God comes to each through a historical event or a series of events. Individuals respond to God's action, interpreting it and understanding it through faith. And by God's grace they appropriate the meaning of the event(s) by changed lives. They become coworkers with God and other persons as they undertake the will of God where they live. For Christians, the supreme event through which God has been and is revealed is Jesus Christ. Christ gives all other revelatory events their real meaning in relation to God's saving purpose in history. In a sense Jesus Christ *is* the meaning of all revelatory events past, present, and future.

But humans do not receive God's revelation unaided. Inspiration accompanies revelation. In revelation God's self and will become known to humans. Inspiration is the Holy Spirit's preparation of human beings to receive revelation and to communicate it (2 Peter 1:20–21). The Holy Spirit so worked, for instance, in prophets, wise teachers, psalmists, and apostles. Moreover, this inspiration did not stop with these writers but was carried over to writings when they were declared "scripture" by the community. "All scripture is inspired by God and is useful for teaching, for reproof, for correction, and for training in righteousness, so that everyone who belongs to God may be proficient, equipped for every good work" (2 Tim. 3:16–17). While the reference here is primarily to what we know as the Old Testament, by implication it includes those writings that came to be known as the New Testament. Not only did the Holy Spirit inspire the authors of the Bible, the Spirit enables us to interpret these scriptures aright in our own day. Indeed, apart from such help we cannot interpret them properly (2 Peter 1:20–21).

While in divine providence God is in sovereign control of all things, God did not do violence to the personalities of the writers of scripture. Rather God established what we know as "secondary causes." In relation to the Bible this means that its writers were moved and guided by the Spirit, but not in such a way as to prevent them from using their abilities and resources. The Spirit enabled them to use such abilities and resources in accord with the divine purpose. Furthermore, God has remained in control of the whole process by which the Bible has come to us today.

It may be helpful for us to think a bit further about the idea of event and interpretation. First we take an example from the Old Testament. The exodus from Egypt was an event in history. By faith, Moses and his people interpreted this event as a mighty act of God through which God was revealed as their Redeemer. Their privilege of freedom carried with it the undertaking at Sinai to be the covenant people of God. Subsequent generations of Israelites heard God speaking to them through the retelling of the Exodus story, and in turn undertook the covenant responsibility as God's people.

A second example comes from the New Testament. The crucifixion of Jesus was an event in history. Even an atheist will admit this. But by faith the earliest Christians and all subsequent Christians have held that Christ died for our sins. This is interpretation, which the nonbeliever rejects. The unit of revelation is the event of the crucifixion and its interpretation in faith. As God has come to us through this interpreted event, we have found ourselves confronted by the living God and have committed ourselves to Jesus Christ as Savior and Lord in the fellowship of the covenant. Our contact with God in the reality of revelation is no less direct than our contact with electricity that is mediated through a wire. This encounter with the living God is the ultimate of all ultimates in human experience.

The believer is not simply caught up in general human history. Believers are members of the chosen people, the covenant community. This places them within a particular history, which we know as biblical history that relates the story of God's redeeming love. Chronologically each of us as a Christian stands within this biblical history, between the ascension of Jesus and the consummation of the full reign of God. Theologically we take our stand with the people of God in all generations. The Bible was destined by God to be that book by which believers are to interpret history. This does not mean that every book in the Bible is, from a literary point of view, strict history. It does mean that the various literary forms tend to center more closely on the mighty acts of God. For example, the writers of the New Testament considered the book of Isaiah more important than the book of Obadiah; they quote from Isaiah repeatedly but never once from Obadiah.

Just as God by creative word-deed called a special people into being, so God called a particular book into being as a witness in times past and as an instrument of revelation in each succeeding generation. The Bible has proved itself to be such and is also rightly received as "the word of God written." As the original biblical events are re-presented to us, we become involved in them and God speaks to us through them as we live in this flesh-and-blood, time-and-space world.

## The Witness of the Bible

We engage in this study in the faith and with the prayer that the Spirit will make God and God's will known to us today and enable us to respond to God in faith and obedience. Before considering the biblical narrative in some detail, it will be helpful to get a brief preview of the witness of the Bible.

## The Words of the Bible

The very words of the Bible keep us reminded of God's mighty acts. In fact, the title of this book was taken almost verbatim out of the Bible.[1] In the Old Testament there are four chief Hebrew words that express the idea of the mighty acts of God directly, and in the New Testament each of these words finds its counterpart in Greek. The following table will make this clear. In the left-hand column the Old Testament words are listed, and in the right-hand column the corresponding New Testament words. Under each basic word the translations of the New Revised Standard Version are given.

OLD TESTAMENT

NEW TESTAMENT

BASIC HEBREW WORD—"MIGHT"
mighty acts (Deut. 3:24; Ps. 145:4)
mighty deeds (Pss. 145:12; 150:2)
mighty doings (Ps. 106:2)
mighty power (Ps. 106:8)

BASIC GREEK WORD—"POWER"
deeds of power (Matt. 11:20–23;
   Mark 6:5)
miracles (Acts 8:13; 19:11)

OLD TESTAMENT

NEW TESTAMENT

BASIC HEBREW WORD—"PORTENT"
miracles (Pss. 78:43; 105:5, 27)
wonders (Exod. 4:21)
glorious deeds (Ps. 78:4)
portent (Isa. 20:3)
sign (1 Kings 13:3–5)

BASIC GREEK WORD—"PORTENT"
wonders (John 4:48; Acts 2:43;
   7:36; 15:12)

OLD TESTAMENT

NEW TESTAMENT

BASIC HEBREW WORD—"WONDER"
miracles (Ps. 78:11)
wonderful deeds (Judg. 6:13)
wonderful works (Pss. 105:5; 107:8)
wondrous deeds (Ps. 26:7)
wondrous works (Job 37:14)

BASIC GREEK WORD—"WONDER"
amazing things (Matt. 21:15)

OLD TESTAMENT

NEW TESTAMENT

BASIC HEBREW WORD—"SIGN"
sign(s) (Exod. 4:8–9; Josh. 24:17;
Isa. 66:19)

BASIC GREEK WORD—"SIGN"
sign(s) (Matt. 16:1; John 2:11; 4:54)
portent (Rev. 12:1, 3; 15:1)

*Read each of the passages listed in this table within its biblical setting, and write down the particular mighty acts of God referred to in each instance.*

*How would you define "miracle" from the biblical point of view?*

*We shall consider the subject of miracle again in the latter part of the book in relation to the ministry of Jesus. If you are interested in pursuing the matter now, see pages 274–79.*

At the heart of the Old Testament stand specific confessions of Israel's faith (for example, Deut. 26:5–10a and Josh. 24:2–13). These confessions place special emphasis on the mighty acts of God that are associated with the exodus from Egypt. Corresponding to the Old Testament confessions of faith in God's mighty acts are the affirmations of the apostles as they preached the mighty acts of God in Jesus Christ (see especially Acts 1–10). Much of both Testaments is an expansion of these proclamations of God's mighty acts.

The concept of revelation is also presented in the Bible by the phrase "the word of the LORD" and other expressions having the same meaning: for example, "Thus says the LORD," "The LORD has spoken," and "God said." This concept does not contradict that of the mighty acts but is at one with it. The word of God has a dynamic, not a static, meaning. For God to say something is for God to do something. For God to do something is for God to say something.

The word of God is sometimes clearly God's *creative and redemptive act(s)*. For example, "Then God said, 'Let there be light'; and there was light" (Gen. 1:3). God's word in creation was no mere utterance of sound or mark of ink on paper; it was a mighty deed. God spoke, and it was done (compare Heb. 11:3). In Psalm 33:4 the Hebrew parallelism makes it clear that the "word" and "work" of God are synonyms. Another way of expressing a similar idea is found in Psalm 107:20—"He sent out his word and healed them, and delivered them from destruction." In this case God's mighty word issues in a mighty act of healing and delivering. God as Great Physician is made clear by divine healing. God's speaking and acting cannot be separated, for there is no insincerity in God.

On other occasions God's word *is a message: of promise (Gen. 15:1), or of hope (Ps. 130:5), or of judgment (Jer. 1:13).* Nevertheless, such a message is related to the acts of God. When the prophets delivered God's message to the people, the message was clearly related to what God had done in the past, what God was doing in the present, and what God would do in the future. We read in Isaiah 40:8, "The grass withers, the flower fades; but the word of our God will stand forever." The word of God here was God's message of comfort through the prophet to the exiles of the Babylonian captivity. A part of that message was that God was going to deliver them from that captivity in a second exodus, this time from Babylon rather than Egypt. This promise was interrelated with God's mighty acts in the first exodus, the current events of the Persian empire (Isa. 41:2; 44:28; 45:1–4), and the coming acts of deliverance.

God's word is also associated with *the covenant and the law* (Ps. 119:11, 17). According to Psalm 105:8–10, God's covenant with our forebears is founded on God's words of instruction. The making of the covenant was an event in the life of the people of God. The Ten Commandments are set in the context of the Exodus events (Exod. 20:2; Deut. 5:6). Israel's Torah (Law) was given after the mighty act of God's deliverance.

The supreme Word of God to humanity is *a person, Jesus Christ.* "In the beginning was the Word, and the Word was with God, and the Word was God. . . . And the Word became flesh and lived among us. . . ." (John 1:1, 14; compare 1 John 1:1–2; Rev. 19:13). All of God's other words find their fulfillment in Jesus Christ. This supreme Word is at one and the same time God's supreme Act. All that Jesus was and did was a revelation of God. His miracles were mighty acts of God. It is Jesus Christ to whom the scriptures bear witness (John 5:39).

"The word" in the preaching of Jesus (Mark 2:2) and the apostles (Acts 4:4) was *the gospel.* When we come to examine the apostolic preaching, we shall find that it consisted of the announcement of God's mighty acts in Jesus Christ. To preach Jesus Christ is not to repeat his name five hundred times without interruption, but to preach the mighty acts of God's salvation as they are focused in Jesus. Revelation is the word-deed of God.

Since "the word of God" has various meanings in the Bible itself and since no biblical writer ever speaks of our canon (recognized scripture) of sixty-six books as "the word of God," why do people today often call the Bible "the Word of God"? Of course the answers to this question will vary. Why not write down your own understanding in your notebook before reading any further? Obviously, on the basis of our study of the scriptures themselves, the Bible is not the only word of God. Our forebears in the faith thought of it as "the word of God written" (The Westminster Confession of Faith, Ch. I, Sec. II ). One reason for thinking of the Bible as the written word is the fact that it bears witness to God's mighty acts in times past and to Jesus Christ, the Word of God Incarnate (John 5:39). Another is the fact that by the Holy Spirit, who breathed the life-giving message into the scriptures (2 Tim. 3:16), God uses these same scriptures as an instrument of revelation and salvation today. That is, by the working of the Holy Spirit within us we accept the Bible as authoritative for our lives.

## The Bible as a Whole

The Bible as a whole, with all its diversity of form and content, tells one story of redemption. The following hourglass diagram has proved helpful to many.[2]

Jesus Christ is the focal point of biblical history and of the Christian's

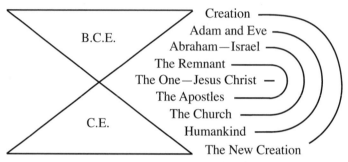

*In this volume, Before Common Era replaces B.C. and Common Era replaces A.D.*

personal history. The Christian takes a stand with Christ at the crossroads of history and looks backward from Christ to creation and forward from Christ to the new creation. The biblical story also moves from creation to Christ and from Christ to the church. The earliest confessions of Israel's faith (Deut. 26:5–10a; Josh. 24:2–13) do not mention creation. But the time came when creation began to play an important role in Israel's expressions of faith (see Ps. 124:8). Eventually creation became the first event in the biblical story. The hourglass representation, therefore, begins at the broad base of creation and moves in ever narrowing fashion to the human family; to the covenant people; to the preserved remnant; and to Jesus Christ, the One in whom the purpose of God is fulfilled. Then out from the One the story moves in ever expanding fashion to the apostles, to the church, to humanity, and finally to the broad base of the new creation.

The parallels between the events B.C.E. and the events C.E. are not accidental. As God created in the beginning and the creation was good, so God will create a new heaven and a new earth. As there was a beginning, so will there be an end; and it will not be a dead end but a new beginning. All evil will be put down, and God will reign forever. As the story of Adam and Eve clearly shows the involvement of all people in the problem of evil, so the gospel is directed to all people, for their predicament is essentially the same in every generation. As God called into being a special people, Israel, as the instrument of divine saving purpose, so God called into being the church as the body of Christ. Jesus Christ is the One who is the key to the whole story of redemption.[3]

> *For your study, compare and relate the outline found in the Table of Contents of this book with the hourglass diagram of the biblical narrative.*
>
> *Perhaps you would like to draw a diagram of the one story of the Bible yourself.*

## The Witness of the Church

### The Book and the People

The Book of God and the people of God go together; they are inseparable. God has elected both to be witnesses to divine revelation and instruments of God's continuing confrontation of humankind. By the living word God called the old covenant people into being before there was a written word. God also called the new covenant church into being before the New Testament was written. The books of the Bible were not written by atheists or agnostics but by believing members of the covenant community. In the Bible is a record of those mighty word-deeds through which God called both the Bible and the church into being. The Bible keeps the church in contact with that original revelation, without which its covenant life would become impossible. On the other hand, it is the church that witnesses to God's message found in the Bible. Without it there would be no present-day human witness to the word of God. Israel as God's servant was called to be witness to God's revelation (Isa. 43:10). Likewise Christians are called to be Christ's witnesses (Acts 1:8). The church bears witness to the gospel by all it is and does. For God did not die with the close of the New Testament; God is still mightily at work in the church and through the church in the world.

The story of the Bible is in a sense the story of the people of God, and we are "God's own people"—therefore, the story of the Bible is our story: the story of our sin and need, yet the story of God's grace working in us and through us. We, the church gathered for worship and study and the church scattered in the common vocations of life, have the privilege and responsibility of joining our witness to that of "all the saints who from their labors rest."[4]

There is nothing really comparable to the biblical story in all the world. Parts of it were recorded at many different times over more than a millennium. For the most part it was written in Hebrew and Greek (with a few chapters in Aramaic) and includes a multitude of literary forms. Some writers did not know what other writers were writing or had written. Yet together their various and varied contributions tell one story. Through this story we find our true security, for it is God's story. God's redemption places on us a corresponding responsibility—to be God's witnesses. For "to whom much has been entrusted even more will be demanded" (Luke 12:48). But the responsibility of sharing the good news is itself a glorious privilege. Indeed, it is one of the most inexpressible joys known to us.

*How is the church making its witness today?*

*Can you think of ways this witness may be made more effectively?*

*Write down, if you will, the ways you yourself are witnessing to the gospel.*

## The Use of the Book by the People

In order for the people of God to bear their witness most effectively, they must use the Bible rightly. This brings us to a consideration of principles of biblical interpretation.

The first principle suggested is this: *Interpret the Bible in expectant prayer.* Such prayer is opening one's heart to the guidance of the Holy Spirit. It involves the recognition that, alone, one is inadequate for the task of interpretation. Many will testify that the most fruitful study of the Bible is impossible apart from active waiting for God.

The second principle: *Interpret the Bible in its historical context or setting.* This means, first of all, that the Bible or any part of it should be studied to determine what the writer meant to say to the writer's own contemporaries. It includes an honest dealing with the facts of history and with literary forms. The truth of the Bible is not presented in abstractions but through concrete events and particular literary forms. To treat literal history as though it were allegory or to interpret a parable as though it were literal history or to read poetry as prose is to be careless in handling the word of truth. This principle of interpretation requires one to raise such questions as these: Who wrote this book or passage? When was it written? Why? To whom and against what background? In what literary forms? Is it possible to enter into the writer's thought and situation in such a way as to catch the emotional overtones of this message? How is this message related to other parts of the Bible and to the Bible as a whole?

The third principle: *Interpret the Bible in the covenant community.* This principle is implicit in everything that has been said in this introductory chapter, but it is made explicit here because it is so important. Many things of which we read in the Bible actually come alive for us in the fellowship of God's people. For example, a person who has never experienced Christian love in human relationships finds it next to impossible to respond to the love of God heard only by the utterance of the voice or through ink on paper. When that person, however, experiences the love of God in Christian fellowship, these words about love take on new meaning.

Furthermore, as we interpret the Bible we need to take seriously what the church says in creed, worship, and life—not because the church is infallible but that we may consider the collective wisdom of our brothers and sisters in Christ. Although God's people are to be examined in the light of God's Book, the interpretation of the Bible should not be separated from the fellowship of the body of Christ. God ordained that the Bible should be written by members of the community; that it should be canonized (accepted as authoritative) by the community in the process of church history; that it should be translated, transmitted, and interpreted especially in the fellowship of believers. Of course we must not overlook the fact that God by the Spirit also uses the Bible in the work of evangelism.

The fourth principle: *Interpret the Bible in Christian faith.* The Bible was written by people of faith to people of faith, and faith is essential for its proper interpretation. One can listen to what God has to say only with the ears of faith. Faith does not mean believing what one knows is not true. It does not make the study of the facts involved unnecessary. Indeed God often speaks in the midst of mental sweat. Faith is taking an affirmative stand with the biblical message and with God's people. At the core, it is commitment to Jesus Christ as Savior and Lord. Jesus is not only a historical person who lived years ago; he has become our Lord and Savior in the here and now. The objective elements in the gospel remain, but "the" gospel has become, in a vital sense, "our" gospel—good news to us in our sin, and glad tidings that we willingly share with others.

The fifth principle of interpretation: *Interpret the Bible in obedient action.* This principle is implicit in the preceding principle, but for the sake of clarity it needs to be stated separately. We have seen that God reveals through the divine word-deed. God also calls us to bear witness through word and deed to the message of the Bible. Faith without works is a dead faith; it is not the real article. From the biblical perspective faith is trust-faithfulness—that is, it includes trust in God and faithfulness to God. Interpretation is complete only when it bears fruit.

In our interpretation of the Bible we sometimes begin with the Bible and seek to hear God speak to us. Through this process we have received God's word of judgment and mercy many times. At other times we begin with an issue or problem and go to the Bible to seek for light on it. In either case we make use of the words of others; we consider what the church has said in creed and life; and we seek the guidance of the Holy Spirit; but we know that God holds us responsible for the decisions we reach. In seeking a solution to a particular problem, it is well to remember that Jesus summarized the written word of his day in the two great commandments: Love God with all your being and your neighbor as yourself. Any interpretation worthy of the name Christian must pass the searching examination of these two commandments as Jesus presented them.

These five principles of interpreting the Bible operate simultaneously, not independently.

## Individual and Group Bible Study

This book has been designed to be used as a guide in individual Bible study and as a help in preparing for participation in group study.[5] The presupposition on which it has been written is that those who use it are interested in doing serious work. The Bible is the primary textbook, and the suggestions for study are made with this fact in mind. The aim is to survey the story of the whole Bible in the period of one year. Thus, it will be possible to treat only selected parts of the biblical text in depth. However, this guide will fill in the story and prevent unnecessary fragmentation. You will want to put your individual systematic Bible study into your *daily schedule*. You will also want to keep a large notebook, in which you record your findings as you study, questions that you wish to have discussed by the group of which you are a part, decisions that you reach, and areas in which you desire to do further work. Nothing can take the place of *conscientious work* in the study of the Bible.

To be most effective, individual Bible study must be carried on in connection with the group learning process. This process is dynamically conceived as a fourfold one: listening, participating, exploring, and undertaking. *Listening* means carrying on an internal conversation with the Bible and other study materials, with the group leader, with other members of the group, and especially with God. It requires a mood of high expectancy.

*Participating* means becoming involved in the biblical narrative itself by putting oneself in the biblical situation insofar as that is possible and hearing God speak. It also means participating in the give-and-take of the study group and of the worship and mission of the larger church family. *Exploring* involves an attempt to analyze the contemporary world in which we live and relate the gospel to the specific situations that confront us. *Undertaking* means that one accepts the demands of Christ and the gospel in every aspect of life as these demands are made known. This fourfold process is a means of putting into effect the principles of biblical interpretation stated above and applies to student and teacher alike.

## Selected Aids to Bible Study

The only tools essential for participating in this study are the Bible, this book *The Mighty Acts of God,* and a notebook. The Bible is the basic text; by all means read it and study it as requested. Nothing can take the place of coming to grips with the biblical text itself. It is not anticipated that a chapter of *The Mighty Acts of God* will be covered at each class session. On the average it will take two class sessions and sometimes more. Your group leader will make assignments as the study proceeds. Moreover, it is not expected that you will necessarily agree with everything in this book. You are encouraged to think through issues for yourself.

For those who are interested in doing additional study, a brief set of study aids is included at the back of the book.

# PART ONE

# GOD'S MIGHTY ACTS OF CREATION

2

## Creation

*W*e now begin our journey through the Bible with a study of creation. Some who tell the one story of the Bible begin with Abraham and Sarah or with the exodus from Egypt because the accounts of creation in Genesis 1–2 were actually formulated in the light of these mighty acts of God in behalf of the chosen people. It is better for our particular purpose, however, to begin with God's mighty acts of creation, as did the psalmist so eloquently in Psalm 136.

Genesis 1 and 2 were not placed at the beginning of the Bible by accident. It is highly fitting to have accounts of the beginning of all things at the very beginning of the Bible itself. Creation, as the initiation of the whole universe by God, antedates the events of Israel's history. Furthermore, in the theology of Israel creation came to be regarded as the first event in the story of redemption. Both Jews and Christians of all denominations place Genesis 1 and 2 first in their canon. Though the sequential order of some biblical books varies, the order of the books of the Pentateuch remains constant from manuscript to manuscript and from denomination to denomination. The Apostles' Creed begins, "I believe in God the Father Almighty, *Maker of heaven and earth. . . .*"

However, we must not forget that all the references to creation in the Bible were made in the light of at least some of God's mighty acts of deliverance. Deliverance is a far more dominant theme in the Bible than creation. At the same time, we must remember that our biblical forebears also took creation seriously. No doctrine of redemption could be complete apart from a doctrine of creation. God could not be our Savior if the universe were in the control of someone else.

As Christians, we recite our faith in creation in the light of Good Friday and Easter morning, just as the Israelites recited their faith in creation in the light of the exodus from Egypt. This means that we want to know what Genesis 1 and 2 mean to us as Christians in our present situation. In other words, we read these accounts of the initial creation as those who are themselves new creations in Christ Jesus. Creation is viewed through the eyes of saving faith. Such a faith is not a casual unthinking acceptance but an interpersonal relationship with God the Creator.

## Literary Considerations

The most important thing about the first chapters of Genesis is what they tell us about God, ourselves, and our world, not how they tell it. It will help you to get at what they really mean, however, to understand something of the Hebrew literary patterns this book uses. There are two accounts of creation in Genesis 1–2, which differ in literary form, vocabulary, and purpose. It is widely held that the first account (Gen. 1:1–2:4a) reached its present form later than the second (Gen. 2:4b–25), but surely Genesis 1:1–2:4a is appropriately placed at the beginning of the biblical story: "In the beginning when God created the heavens and the earth. . . ."

> As you read these two accounts, jot down in your notebook your answers to the following questions:
>
> What repeated formulas (such as "And God said," "And it was so") do you find in the first account? Can you find anything comparable in the second?
>
> Do you notice any difference in the names of God and the verbs used to express God's creative acts?
>
> What do you think is the main purpose of Genesis 1:1–2:4a? of Genesis 2:4b–25?

With this background, we now concentrate on Genesis 1:1–2:4a, one of the most majestically beautiful passages in all literature. Mighty act ("God created," "God blessed") and mighty word ("And God said") are woven together as the mighty word-deed of God. As one reads it in reverence and appreciation, one can almost hear the heavenly chorus singing the song of creation. The passage is a creed of mature faith that has put a song into the hearts of many who have found the universe a domed cathedral in which they have bowed to confess their own faith in the Creator of the heavens and earth. The creed begins with a preamble, or general introductory statement. Next comes the body of the confession, which is set in the sequence of the Jewish workweek of six days; and within this body there is a parallelism of days (one and four, two and five, three and six). The creed is concluded with a seventh-day summary. This literary framework can be seen clearly in the following outline:

Preamble (Gen. 1:1–2)

1. Day One: Light (Gen. 1:3–5)
4. Day Four: Luminaries (Gen. 1:14–19)
2. Day Two: Firmament; Waters Separated (Gen. 1:6–8)
5. Day Five: Fish and Birds (Gen. 1:20–23)
3. Day Three: Dry Land and Vegetation (Gen. 1:9–13)
6. Day Six: Land Animals and Humans (Gen. 1:24–31)

7. Day Seven: Rest (Gen. 2:1–4a)

When a person grasps the fact that this account of creation is neither a fairy tale nor the kind of history that is literally viewed in process by human eye, but a theological confession placed in the literary framework of the Jewish week, many worries about the so-called conflict between science and religion will vanish into thin air. There is no need to try to make everything in the biblical account square with present-day scientific theory or evidence, for the "scientific" view of the universe at any given moment may differ from that of previous ages. In fact, it is only recently that we have learned that the earth is not spherical but pear-shaped.

The biblical writer used the worldview and thought-forms of the time to express faith in God as Creator for all days. The worldview and vocabulary of the twenty-first century C.E. would not have been understood by the writer's contemporaries and the beautiful theological statement would have been lost to posterity. The writer's view of the physical world was similar to that held by Babylonians and others outside the fold of Israel, just as Christians and non-Christians alike accept many of the same things in the worldview of the space age. The drawing on p. 18 approximates the conception of the universe as held by people in ancient Mesopotamia and Palestine.

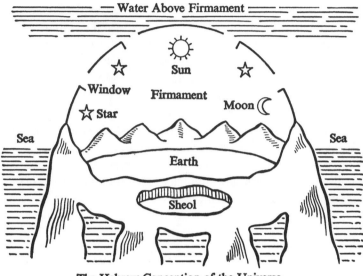

**The Hebrew Conception of the Universe**

In connection with Genesis 1 and with this drawing, read Genesis 7:11; 8:2; Isaiah 24:18; Psalms 24:1–2; 104:1–35; 148:4. Obviously, the conception of a solid firmament above the earth was not an article of faith to the ancient Israelite any more than the distance from the earth to some other planet is an article of faith to us. But it was and is an article of faith that the One True God created all there is. The ancient writer was not writing to make the study of biology, botany, geology, astronomy, and nuclear physics unnecessary. Many devout Christians are able simultaneously to accept the fundamentals of biblical faith and a carefully documented theory of evolution because they have distinguished between framework and faith. Other equally devout Christians have not found it possible to do this.

In the seventeenth century C.E. Archbishop Ussher, on the basis of a literalistic interpretation of biblical dates, calculated that the creation took place in 4004 B.C.E. Yet anyone who has studied archaeology, to say nothing of geology, knows that this date is grossly inaccurate. Unfortunately, it has been included as a statement of fact in the chronological schemes of some editions of the Bible. But this date is not the kind of information that ought to be made into an article of faith. Scientists today generally agree that the universe came into being billions of years ago. Neither is such a theory as this an article of faith. It is the type of thing that one examines on the basis of the evidence presented in its behalf.[1]

Another consideration that underscores the necessity of distinguishing between literary form and biblical faith is the parallel between "the Babylonian Genesis" (*Enuma elish*) and Genesis 1:1–2:4a.

How different the Bible is from the pagan myths of creation! Yet there are certain similarities in the forms of the stories. In brief, the *Enuma elish* tells the story of how Marduk, the elected champion of certain of the gods, met the "dragon" goddess Tiamat in mortal combat. As they came together Marduk enmeshed Tiamat in his net. When Tiamat opened her mouth to swallow him, Marduk drove in the wind and thereby stretched her body. Then he shot an arrow through her open mouth, which pierced her heart and killed her. He split her carcass in two: out of one half he formed the heaven and out of the other he made the earth. Finally, he created humankind from the blood of Kingu, the consort of Tiamat. Humans were given the responsibility of feeding the multitude of deities.

Both accounts of creation (that in Genesis and that in *Enuma elish*) mention a watery chaos. The Hebrew word *tehom* ("the deep") is usually regarded as the linguistic equivalent of the Babylonian *Tiamat*. The basic concept of heaven and earth is essentially the same in both accounts, and the sequence of creative acts is essentially the same: light, firmament, dry land, luminaries, and humankind, with God or the deities resting at the end of creation. These parallels are too precise and too numerous to be denied. In fact, students of all types of theological outlooks readily admit them. They indicate that Israel was acquainted with literary ideas and forms that did not originate among the covenant people.

However, we must remember that the likenesses referred to above are in the realm of form, not faith. The differences that are in the realm of faith are far more significant. For example, the Babylonian "Genesis" is crassly polytheistic and degrading, while the biblical Genesis is monotheistic and elevating. According to the Babylonian account, creation takes place in a struggle of competing deities, while according to the biblical account it takes place by the mighty word of the One True God. Tiamat is depicted as a goddess, but *tehom* ("the deep") is not regarded as a person. In the *Enuma elish* the creation of humanity is relatively unimportant, but in Genesis 1 the creation of humankind is the climax of the acts of creation—only humans are made in the image of God.

The whole matter of literary relationship and difference in faith can be illustrated rather clearly by an examination of our English word "Easter." This word comes from the old Anglo-Saxon word *Eastre*, the name of the Teutonic goddess of spring. But in the process of Christian history it was baptized into Christian usage in such a way that to us it stands for the resurrection of Jesus Christ from the dead. In a similar manner, ancient Israel borrowed words, worldviews, and literary forms from her neighbors, and so purged them of paganism as to make them vehicles of biblical revelation.

## The Creed of Creation

We have already introduced Genesis 1:1–2:4a as the creed of creation. We now examine it part by part. You will find it interesting and informative to read Psalm 104 and compare its divisions with those found in this passage.

### The Preamble (Gen. 1:1–2)

"In the beginning when God created the heavens and the earth" is a summary statement that includes all the specific acts of creation mentioned later in the chapter. "The heavens and the earth" is the Hebrew way of saying "the universe." The meaning of the rest of this verse, however, is not as easily determined. The Hebrew of this verse in its original form may be read in connection with verse 2 as follows: "When God began to create the heavens and the earth, the earth was without form and void. . . ."

Did the author intend to say that God created the world out of nothing? Or is the point that God used formless stuff (chaos) as building blocks? There is no doubt that the word "create" (*bara'*) bears distinctive theological significance in the Old Testament. Humans are never said to "create" anything. Only God can "create." It would probably beg the question to ask, Did God make chaos (see Isa. 45:18)? There is a mystery in the universe which suggests that, save for the power of God, all would turn into chaos.

In any case, God brought order out of chaos, which implies that God is always able to bring order out of any chaos. Creation out of nothing versus creation out of something or vice versa was apparently not a conscious issue when Genesis 1 was written. But the writer's statement of the sovereignty of God in such a distinctive and forceful way would of necessity be translated into the out-of-nothing doctrine when it was brought into contact with a philosophical approach to life. In other words, Genesis 1 may be regarded as the theological womb out of which this doctrine was to be brought forth in the fullness of time. The doctrine of creation out of nothing is important because it affirms the *absolute* sovereignty of God. No devil and no thing is God's equal. The One True God brings into being, and controls, all there is.

## Day One: Light (Gen. 1:3–5)

Here is the first mention of God's creative word (see vv. 6, 9, 14, 20, 24, and 26). God is not the universe as in pantheism; God is not confined to the universe as in naturalism; God stands over against the creation as its sovereign Creator and Lord. Light heads the list of specifics in creation as being of primary significance. One was to say many years later, "God is light" (1 John 1:5) and "The true light, which enlightens everyone, was coming into the world" (John 1:9). What is the meaning of each of these statements from the New Testament, and how are they related to Genesis 1:3–5? We read, "And God saw that the light was good." Statements similar to this recur throughout the chapter. How do you account for this emphasis?

The evening is mentioned before the morning in verses 5, 8, 13, 19, 23, and 31 because the Jewish day began in the evening; in fact, it still does. For example, among Jews Sabbath begins on Friday evening at sunset. The alternation of night and day reminds us of the divine ordering of rest and work. Our time belongs to God.

## Day Two: Firmament (Gen. 1:6–8)

The ancient worldview is clearly reflected in the mention of the firmament and the waters above and below it. Rain, it was thought, came from the heavenly water supply when the windows in the solid dome or firmament were opened.

## Day Three: Dry Land and Vegetation (Gen. 1:9–13)

The dry land appears when the waters are collected into the encompassing ocean. The three-storied universe, which we represented earlier by a diagram, is referred to in Exodus 20:4—"You shall not make for yourself an idol, whether in the form of anything that is in *heaven above*, or that is on the *earth beneath*, or that is in the *water under the earth*" (compare Pss. 24:2; 136:6). Vegetation is associated with the earth on which it grows.

## Day Four: Luminaries (Gen. 1:14–19)

Light in its elemental nature was mentioned as the first of God's creative acts; here the heavenly bodies are referred to as "lights." "Signs" may signify unusual appearances in the sky, such as comets and eclipses. "Seasons" are the fixed times in the agricultural and religious calendars.

## Day Five: Fish and Birds (Gen. 1:20–23)

The verb "create" was used in verse 1. It is used for the second time in verse 21 in relation to the sea animals and the flying creatures. In other words, there is something distinctive about the creation of animal life. Though we think of fish as the chief sea animals, all water animals are included. Similarly, birds are the most prominent flying creatures, but the writer includes all flying creatures. Here also the blessing of God is first introduced, for God gives the capacity of procreation to these creatures.

## Day Six: Land Animals and Humans (Gen. 1:24–31)

Recall that on the third day the dry land appeared, and the earth put forth vegetation at God's command. On the sixth day the earth brought forth land animals at God's command, and God created humans in the divine image. The land animals are classified in three groups: "cattle" or domestic animals, "creeping things" or small animals, and "wild animals of the earth of every kind."

The creation of humans is of climactic importance. The amount of space as well as the development of the subject indicates this. "Let us make humankind in *our* image" suggests that the heavenly King of creation involves the heavenly council of angels in this decision. The idea of the heavenly court occurs frequently in the Old Testament (see, for example, Gen. 3:22; 1 Kings 22:19–22; Isa. 6:1–2, 8; Job 1; Ps. 82:1). To say that the biblical writer was consciously speaking of the Trinity would be to undercut the distinctiveness of the biblical revelation as given through history, for the triune nature of God was to be recognized only many centuries later. Presumably the angels were thought of as already in the image of God. But the creed does not stress humankind's likeness to angels but rather to God alone (see v. 27). Psalm 8 is Genesis 1 set to music.

The identification of the "image of God" in humankind is a very important, though very difficult, undertaking.

> *Before reading further, jot down in your notebook your present understanding of what the image of God is. Then, after you have completed your study of the subject, reexamine your statement to see if you desire to change it in any way.*

It is agreed that *adam* (Hebrew) in Genesis 1:26 embraces humankind. "Adam" has a "likeness" to God that other creatures on the earth do not have. But this similarity does not mean that humankind is in any sense deity. The Hebrew word that is translated "image" has the basic meaning of "something cut out." Occasionally it refers to an idol (Num. 33:52) or a painting (Ezek. 23:14). Therefore, it is sometimes held that the image means that the physical appearance of human beings looks like God's (compare Gen. 5:3). In support of this view is the fact that humans are said to see the form of God in visions (Isa. 6:1; Exod. 33:23; Ps. 17:15). But more to the point, the term is used of "images" set up by kings of themselves or the deity they served to indicate their sovereignty over a particular area.

There are at least three implications of humankind's likeness to God. First, humans have a *relationship* to God that other creatures do not have. Humans may have communion with God. Moreover, they cannot be human in absolute isolation. Humankind was created male and female and therefore must stand in relationship with other human beings as well as with God. Second, humankind is the *representative* of God. A literal image might be manufactured to represent a person, an animal, or a so-called god. Sometimes in the ancient Near East the image of an animal or bird was used to represent a deity. But humans, not things or animals, represent the Most High God. Third, humankind has a *responsibility* to God. To represent God requires the exercise of a responsible stewardship and presupposes the capacity of moral choice. You cannot try a parrot in a law court, but you can try a person. Humankind's superiority to the animals and the responsibility as the under-sovereign of the sovereign God are set forth clearly by these words: ". . . and let them have dominion over the fish of the sea, and over the birds of the air, and over the cattle, and over all the wild animals of the earth, and over every creeping thing that creeps upon the earth."

In other words, humans are as kings over a kingdom for which they are accountable to the heavenly King.

> *What does this dominion mean to a farmer? To a homemaker? To a student in school?*
>
> *How is the idea of the image of God related to racial, national, and international problems today? (Compare Acts 17:22–31.)*
>
> *What does the freedom and responsibility of human beings inherent in the teaching about the image of God have to do with the so-called determinism of heredity and environment? That is, how free are you?*

Some Christians, in the light of what they consider overwhelming evidence, believe that humankind was created by God through a long evolutionary process; that is, that at a particular point in the process of life a mutation occurred, when the creatures who are characterized by the image of God appeared for the first time on this planet. This change is thought to have taken place 100,000 to 200,000 years ago or earlier. Other Christians maintain that God created humankind altogether apart from any evolutionary process. They point out that there are links missing in the so-called family tree of human life. Is either of these groups necessarily more Christian than the other? Why or why not? Can a view of evolution be held that leaves room for the doctrine of the image of God?

The image of God as found in Genesis 1 constitutes a part of the background of the incarnation. When God was ready for the supreme self-revelation, God did not send an animal, a plant, or a stone as divine representative. Rather, God became incarnate in Jesus Christ. According to Paul, Jesus Christ is "the image of the invisible God" (Col. 1:15; compare 2 Cor. 4:4); that is, he is the true revelation of the unseen God. By implication Jesus is also the one true human through whom the intent of the Creator, as expressed in Genesis 1, is fully realized.

There is a sense in which God's image in a human being can never be lost, for humans are always responsible to God. In another sense, however, it can be lost or defaced, for through sin human fellowship with God is broken.[2] This is implied by the fact that human beings as sinners need to be transformed into the image of Christ (1 Cor. 15:49; 2 Cor. 3:18; Rom. 8:29; Col. 3:10).

God endowed humans with the capacity to procreate and gave them the command to reproduce their kind. This fact is written into the very constitution of human life. In the context of biblical revelation as a whole it is obvious that this is a command that is to be fulfilled *responsibly*. Some persons do not receive the vocation of marriage and the propagation of the race. Those who do receive it are confronted with the question of what responsible propagation means. In fact, all of us today are confronted by the fact of "the population bomb." This bomb has already exploded in many parts of our world and is resulting in disease, early death, political unrest, war, and the mounting threat of totalitarian dictatorship. It is threatening to explode all over the world in the near future unless the issue is faced with intelligence and dedication. In ancient times there was no danger of overpopulating the earth. A large family was an advantage in many ways. But in our particular situation, how are we as Christian citizens to understand the command "Be fruitful and multiply"?

The account of the sixth day of creation includes God's provision for the needs of both people and animals and concludes with the statement "And God saw everything that he had made, and indeed, it was very good." It was good because it corresponded to the intent of the Creator.

## Day Seven: Rest (Gen. 2:1–4a)

The Sabbath is here rooted in creation, for God "rested on the seventh day from all the work that he had done." For God to rest does not mean that God lies down and goes to sleep, leaving creation to take care of itself, but that God enters into the joy of the divine accomplishment. God gave the seventh day a special place in the divine economy. If a person's Sabbath rest is truly patterned on the divine rest, there must always be the entering into the joy of accomplishment. There yet remains a Sabbath rest for the people of God (Heb. 3:7–4:10), which will be more the joy of an accomplishment received than of an accomplishment achieved.

"These are the generations of the heavens and the earth when they were created" summarizes and concludes the first account of creation. The word "generations" is used as a formula to introduce the sections of the book of Genesis. Here, however, it is used to conclude the first section. Ordinarily it refers to the begettings or generations of human beings. Here it refers to the origins of the heavens and the earth.

> *Now that you have studied the creed of creation rather carefully, without reproducing its framework, list in brief form the articles of faith that you find in it. For example, one such article of faith, might be stated, God is the sovereign Creator of all.*

> *After you have completed your list, try to state briefly the present-day relevance of each of the affirmations. For example, to say, "God is the sovereign Creator of all" is very much like saying, "The earth is the LORD's and all that is in it, the world, and those who live in it" (Ps. 24:1). Ask yourself the question, What does this mean to me in relation to my money, my property, my talents, and my opportunities?*

## Man and Woman in the Garden (Gen. 2:4b–25)

Already it has been noted that this account of creation is usually regarded as written earlier than the first account. The differences in the two accounts have also been noted. The name for deity in chapter 1 is "God" (Elohim); in chapter 2 it is "LORD God" (Yahweh Elohim). The distinctive word for God's activity in chapter 1 is "create"; in chapter 2 it is "form." In chapter 1 the series of creative acts begins with light and ends with humankind; in chapter 2 the series begins with man and ends with woman. In chapter 1 God speaks the mighty word; in chapter 2 God plants a garden. The first account is a formalized creed in the literary framework of a week; the second is a down-to-earth story with heavenly meaning. The second also expresses a confession of faith, but not in so formal a manner. The person who placed these accounts side by side could see the differences as well as we but was not disturbed by them. They are in the realm of form, not in the realm of faith. This means that the ultimate meaning of the two accounts is not to be found in a mechanically literal-istic or superficial interpretation.

## God's Dust Creature (Gen. 2:4b–7)

The creation (making) of "the earth and the heavens" is mentioned only briefly, for this is not the point of the author's emphasis. The earth is pic-tured as a desert waste, to which the chaos of Genesis 1:2 roughly corre-sponds. The ground is first watered, not by rain, but by a subterranean water supply. The desert land of much of the Near East was no doubt in the author's mind.

"Then the LORD God formed man from the dust from the ground." The participle of the verb "to form" means "potter." God is pictured as a pot-ter who molds clay from the ground into the desired shape. In Hebrew there is a play on the words "man" (*adam*) and "ground" (*adamah*). This is a way of saying that humans are related to the ground (compare 1 Cor. 15:47). While we must never forget that we are made in the image of God, we must also remember that we are dust.

God "breathed into his nostrils the breath of life; and the man became a living being." It is not said with regard to the animals that God breathed the breath of life into them. In other words, "man" is different from the animals, although, like them (v. 19), akin to the ground. The word trans-lated "being" is literally *nephesh* (Hebrew). "Man became a living *nephesh*." *Nephesh* has often been translated as "soul," but "being" is bet-ter. The words sometimes translated as "soul" in both Testaments have many different meanings, but they are used to describe a human as a uni-tary being who thinks, feels, and wills. In Genesis 2:7 *adam* did not receive a "soul" but "became a living being."

## The Garden of Eden (Gen. 2:8–17)

The divinely fashioned human was placed in the garden that the LORD God planted. God caused both beautiful trees and food-producing trees to grow there. Note God's concern for meeting the human's needs. God also caused to grow in the garden the tree of life and the tree of the knowledge of good and evil. The tree of life would impart immortality to those who ate of its fruit. The human was given permission to eat of any of the trees of the garden (including the tree of life) but was forbidden, on pain of death, to eat of the tree of the knowledge of good and evil. This tree stands for a kind of omniscient knowledge that is the prerogative of God alone. In other words, the human was given real freedom, but a freedom within limits. Our freedom is not the equivalent of God's freedom, for we are not God's "size."

The opinion is often expressed that work is evil. Yet we read, "The LORD God took the man and put him in the garden of Eden to till it and keep it."

> *In the light of this statement, what is wrong with the foregoing opinion?*

> *How does the apparent purpose of this story help us to see the difficult details in proper perspective?*

## The Creation of Animals and Woman (Gen. 2:18–25)

The placing of the creation of the animals in the same context with the creation of woman was not intended to low-rate woman, but rather to exalt her. "It is not good that the man should be alone; I will make him a helper as his partner." To be alone is to be helpless. In God's gracious purpose the human was not meant for utter solitude, but for companionship with an equal, a counterpart. Therefore, God brings the various divinely fashioned animals before the human, that the human might name them. This process of naming shows humanity's superiority to the animals and dominion over them. The determination of the position and function of the animals is assigned to the human by God. But among the animals there is found no helper.

The statement about the rib is one of the most beautiful in all the Bible: "So the LORD God caused a deep sleep to fall upon the man, and he slept; then he took one of his ribs and closed up its place with flesh. And the rib that the LORD God had taken from the man he made into a woman and brought her to the man." It was not intended as a lesson in anesthesia, surgery, or anatomy. Rather, it is a lesson in love—woman taken from the rib of man. It is a marvelous way of saying that man and woman belong together, that sex is the gift of God, and that God has established and sanctified marriage.

The man's response to his God-given bride is one of pure delight. The

Hebrew idiom is here freely rendered into contemporary American idiom:

> This is the moment I've been waiting for!
>     She was made just for me!
> She shall be called Woman,
>     because she was taken out of Man.

Anyone who has ever really loved another knows at once what this exclamation means. The Hebrew word used here for "woman" is *ishshah* and that for "man" is *ish*. This play on sounds is well represented by the English words "woman" and "man." A man's relationship with his parents is modified when he marries by the relationship he establishes with his wife: "They become one flesh." The arithmetic of marriage is a very extraordinary kind of mathematics: $1 + 1 = 1$. This is the only formula that will really work. It entails a total psychophysical union: thinking together, feeling together, believing together, and working together. "I," "my," and "me" are replaced by "we," "our," and "us."

*Does Genesis 2:24 imply monogamy? If so, how do you account for the practice of polygamy by some in Israel?*

*How do you explain the Old Testament law concerning divorce (Deut. 24:1–4) in the light of the teaching of Jesus on the subject (Mark 10:2–12; Matt. 19:3–12)?*

*According to Genesis 2:4b–25, what are the purposes of marriage? In the light of your knowledge of the Bible as a whole, does marriage serve any other purposes?*

*What makes a marriage a Christian marriage?*

*Summarize briefly the explicit and implicit teachings of Genesis 2:4b–25.*

*At what points do the two accounts of creation supplement each other?*

*With both of these accounts in mind, how would you answer the question, What is humankind? (We recognize that there are other statements about humans elsewhere in the Bible.) How does your answer to this question help you to answer the more personal question, Who am I?*

*How do you answer the perennial questions of little children: Who made God?*

*How did God make me? How do you help a child warm up to the idea that God is the Creator?*

# The Fall

We human beings are not only creatures made in the image of God but also suffering and dying sinners standing in the need of a salvation that we ourselves cannot provide. We remind ourselves again that we read the Bible as believers who are members of the covenant community. Because we have already experienced redemption from sin, we are in a preferred position for studying the Fall of humankind. We do this as those who know both the first Adam and the last Adam. Indeed we know the first Adam aright only as we know the last Adam, Jesus Christ. That is, we know ourselves for what we really are only when we know Christ for what he really is.

## Adam and Eve

The story of the man and the woman in the Garden of Eden (Gen. 2:4b–25) is continued in the story of the Fall (Gen. 3). In the former we saw the man (*ish*) at peace with God, with nature, and with the woman (*ishshah*). In the latter we see them in the disruption caused by sin. Often the deepest truths are set forth in picture language. Jesus often employed this form. Students of the scriptures have placed Genesis 3 in many different literary categories, but it defies all of our usual pigeonholes. Through a graphic and dramatic representation it gives a profound theological diagnosis of the predicament not only of the first man and the first woman but also of every man and every woman and of the whole human family. It is not the kind of picture that you could take with your camera, but the kind an artist might capture with brush.

The English word "Adam" is a transliteration of one of the Hebrew words for "man," which we encountered first in Genesis 1:26, where it has the meaning "humankind"; "Eve" is a rendering of a Hebrew word for "life" or "living." The understanding that these names refer to the first man and woman, to every man and woman, and to the entire human race is suggested by the story itself and is altogether in harmony with Hebrew psychology, in which the person and the group often blend. For example, "Jacob" is both the ancient patriarch and also the people of Israel (Ps. 46:7, 11), and every Israelite is considered as an extension of the forebears of the people.

> *Read Genesis 3 with the following question in mind: What does this story tell me about myself? Jot down these things in your notebook.*
>
> *Then reflect a bit on this question: What does this story tell me about my neighbor?*

## The Temptation (Gen. 3:1–6a)

The serpent had a reputation in antiquity for a subtle kind of wisdom (Matt. 10:16). Not yet associated with Satan in Genesis 3 as in such later writings as the Apocryphal Wisdom of Solomon (2:24) and the book of Revelation (12:9; 20:2), the serpent is represented as one of the wild creatures that God had made, in no sense as a god who rivals the LORD. Still, the serpent depicts very forcibly the mystery of evil and the subtlety of temptation. The presence of the serpent in the narrative suggests that temptation is in some way connected with what is outside humankind (see pp. 246–49, 379–82).

The serpent's question, "Did God say, 'You shall not eat from any tree in the garden'?" is calculated to plant the seed of doubt of God's goodness in the woman's mind. It succeeds, and in her reply the woman exaggerates God's prohibition by adding to what God had said (2:16–17) "nor shall you touch it" (that is, the tree of the knowledge of good and evil). This exaggeration seems to indicate the woman's increasing awareness of God-imposed limitations. Then the serpent comes in for the kill: "You will not die; for God knows that when you eat of it your eyes will be opened, and you will be like God, knowing good and evil." The first part of verse 6 shows that the temptation here is based on three desires: the desire to eat, the desire to see the beautiful, and the desire to know (compare 1 John 2:16). Temptation, therefore, is presented as an appeal through natural desires (which are fundamentally good) to go beyond limits set by God.

> *Compare and contrast the temptation of Jesus as found in Matthew 4:1–11 or Luke 4:1–13 (see Heb. 4:15) with the temptation of Adam and Eve.*

*How are we as Christians to face temptation? You will find help in answering this question in Mark 14:38; 1 Corinthians 10:13; and Hebrews 2:18.*

## The Fall (Gen. 3:6b–8)

The man and the woman ate of the fruit of the forbidden tree. They yielded to the temptation. They wanted to be "like God, knowing good and evil." That is, they wanted a kind of omniscient knowledge that is the prerogative of God alone. The word "to know" in Hebrew often includes the meaning of "to choose." Adam and Eve wanted to decide for themselves what is right and what is wrong. They became traitors to the Kingdom of God by attempting to set up a rival sovereignty of their own. They did not want a freedom within law, but a license without limit. They wanted to be like God. This is also our story. We are guilty of pride, rebellion, and idolatry. We have worshiped the creature rather than the Creator (Rom. 1:23).

Sin is both a personal affair and a social affair. The woman disobeyed, and so did the man. But this means the whole human family. All of us have gone astray and fallen short of the glory of God (Rom. 3:10–18). We are sinners born of sinners (Ps. 51:5; Rom. 5:12–14). How do you account for the fact that every person rebels against God? That is, what makes sin universal?

The eyes of the man and woman were opened all right, but the knowledge they received was not the knowledge they expected: "They knew that they were naked." The guilt and shame of sin are expressively portrayed as the sense of nakedness. Not only did they make aprons for themselves; they even hid from God among the trees of the garden. The happy fellowship they had enjoyed with God was interrupted. They now felt like strangers before God. Did you hide from your father or mother as a child when you had done wrong? Have you felt like trying to hide from God as an adult when you have sinned?

## The Interrogation (Gen. 3:9–13)

The language used with reference to God in chapter 3 is very anthropomorphic (that is, it speaks of God as if God were a human). In verse 8 God is pictured as taking a walk at the breeze-time of the day. In verse 9 the LORD calls on the man, who is hiding, to reveal his whereabouts. The interrogation of the man and woman shows clearly that "passing the buck" is nothing new. When God interrogates the man about his disobedience, the man "passes the buck" in a double-dealing fashion to God and to his wife: "The woman whom *you gave* to be with me, *she gave* me fruit from the tree, and I ate." Then, when God interrogates the woman, she places the blame on the serpent. What does Genesis 3:9–13 say about the tendency to blame all of one's bad choices on others?

It is interesting to note that the sin that the man and the woman committed together did not bind them closer to each other. Instead it brought disharmony and recrimination. When you "pass the buck" to your wife or to your husband, what happens? Persons who unite in committing a crime will often turn against one another. This is to say, sin is not a cohesive force in life. It is also interesting to note that God does not question the serpent. The origin of evil remains a mystery.

## The Sentence (Gen. 3:14–19)

In the divine sentence the word "cursed" is used with reference to the serpent but not with reference to the woman and the man. However, serpent, woman, and man all stand under God's judgment. Of course the perennial hostility between snakes and human beings is reflected in the judgment on the serpent (see Isa. 11:8), but more than that the writer depicts the conflict between the forces of evil and humankind. Human existence is a life-and-death struggle. Although the writer does not tell us how the struggle will end, we as Christians already know the sequel to the Genesis story in which one "born of woman" bruises the serpent's head.

The sentence on the woman involves the pain associated with pregnancy and childbirth and that associated with male dominance. One of the greatest desires of woman has been to be a wife and mother, but even life's greatest joys are fulfilled under the shadow cast by sin. It seems that human suffering is somehow related to sin in the human race. This does not mean that every experience of suffering can be traced to some particular sin: Job and Jesus set the record straight on that score (John 9:3). But in both Testaments suffering is regarded basically as an evil that will have no place in the new creation (Isa. 65:16–17; Rev. 21:4).

In thinking of the woman's sentence, we recognize that the pain associated with motherhood and the subservience to one's husband are not regarded by the biblical writer as desirable. They are illustrations of the consequences of sin. From our vantage point we know that the solution to all pain is found in the one who "has borne our infirmities and carried our diseases" (Isa. 53:4). Jesus healed men, women, and children in the days of his flesh and still works in many ways his wonders to perform.

Furthermore, the ultimate resource for dealing effectively with disharmony in marriage is the same Christ, in whom "there is no longer male and female" (Gal. 3:28). Recall Paul's injunction: "Husbands, love your wives, as Christ loved the church and gave himself up for her" (Eph. 5:25). The husband who loves his wife just as Christ loved the church provides a climate of self-giving love in which no one could ever be a slave. Marriage is, in a sense, human society in miniature, and self-giving love is desperately needed in all human relationships.

The man's sentence takes the form of a curse on the ground (*adamah*) from which the man (*adam*) was taken. This means that the human's close bond with nature is broken. Human work, assigned as a blessing of God in Eden (Gen. 2:15), is now hampered by frustration as a consequence of sin. It is not the pure joy that it ought to be. How is the doctrine of Christian vocation related to this problem?

Humans will die, but the man and the woman did not literally die on the very day of their disobedience (see Gen. 2:17; 3:3). Perhaps the writer means to say that by relaxing the warning God showed his mercy. Certainly it is an evidence of God's mercy that each one of us is not struck dead on the occasion of our first act of rebellion. But the writer may well intend something more profound than commentators ordinarily think, namely, that the broken relation with God is the real death of which the later physical death is the sign and seal. Genesis 3 certainly indicates that there is a connection between human sin and death (compare Ezek. 18; Pss. 41; 107). Death, as humans experience it, is what it is because humans are sinners. "The sting of death is sin" (1 Cor. 15:56). Death in its deepest dimension, however, is not the opposite of biological life but of eternal life (see Eph. 2:1, 5; Col. 2:13; Rev. 3:1). How would you explain the relation between sin and death?

## The Grace of God (Gen. 3:20–21)

The story of humanity's fall includes a word about the grace of God. Eve can be called "the mother of all living" only because God is gracious to the sinful creatures and permits them to propagate the race. Furthermore, God clothes the man and the woman and covers their shame and nakedness. This they did not deserve.

## The Expulsion (Gen. 3:22–24)

The man and woman have now created the fiction that they are their own god. They seek to determine what is right and what is wrong by their own standards. To prevent them from taking of the tree of life and living forever as fallen creatures, God in a merciful judgment sends them forth from the garden into the world of hardships.

The sequel to *Paradise Lost* is *Paradise Regained*. Though the story of the Fall is seldom, if ever, referred to directly in the remainder of the Old Testament, it is used in the New Testament letters of Paul (1 Cor. 15:21–22; 2 Cor. 11:3; Rom. 5:12–14; 1 Tim. 2:14) and in the book of Revelation (12:9; 20:2). Moreover, the message of the Bible as a whole is addressed to sinful humanity, and the solution to Adam's "fallenness" is the mighty act of God in the second Adam. And the fruit of the tree of life will one day be available again in the new Jerusalem (Rev. 2:7; 22:2).

## The Malignant Growth of Sin[1]

Sin is a malignancy that continues to spread until it issues in the death of its victim. The estrangement from God set forth in the story of Adam and Eve manifests itself in various forms in all their posterity. A large part of Genesis 4–11 is devoted to telling this sad tale. It is usually agreed that these chapters are a combination of different traditions that were handed down in oral form before they were put into written form. Within the diversity of form and content is a unity of faith. In Genesis 1–11 Israel sees God in relation to humanity, of which Israel is but a part. The universality of sin was clearly recognized. Though the stories reflect specific memories and cultural phenomena (for example, the life of the shepherd and that of the farmer), they are really speaking to the condition of humankind in all ages.

> *Before reading any further in this book, open your Bible and read Genesis 4:1–16; chapters 6–9; and 11:1–9. Record in your notebook what you have learned about sin from each of these passages.*
>
> *If you have the time now, read the whole of chapters 4–11.*

### Cain and Abel (Gen. 4:1–16)

In the Adam and Eve narrative, humanity's basic malignancy took the form of disobedience to God. Here it takes the form of violence against one's sibling. Abel is a shepherd, and Cain is a farmer. Each of the brothers makes an offering to the LORD from the fruit of his own labors. Abel's is acceptable to God, but Cain's is not. Evidently Cain's is rejected because his heart is not right with God (4:6; Heb. 11:4). Therefore, Cain kills Abel in jealous resentment.

When Adam sinned, God's question to him was, "Where are you?" In the case of Cain, it is, "Where is Abel your brother?" At this point, Cain is afforded the opportunity of confessing his sin and seeking forgiveness. But instead he lies as he answers, "I do not know," and compounds his lie with insolence as he adds, "Am I my brother's keeper?" Sin has a way of encouraging further sin. To what extent and in what way is each of us responsible for our neighbors?

In the case of Adam and Eve, sin issued in estrangement from the soil, from God, and from each other. In this story Cain's sin issues in estrangement from the soil, from God, and from his community (vv. 12–13). Symbolically Cain represents the attempt of humans to secede from the universe, from the reign of God, and from human society. Sin has its devilish effects on all relationships. The sinner who holds on to sin is no longer at home with God in God's world and with God's people.

*What are the implications of the Cain and Abel account when it is read in the light of Jesus' statement in Matthew 5:21–26?*

Just as God showed grace toward Adam and Eve by clothing them, so the Lord shows grace to Cain by placing a mark of protection on him. Here in these early narratives it is already clearly seen that humankind not only stands under the judgment of God but also under God's mercy. Can you bear witness from personal experience and observation to this same judgment and mercy?

## The Flood (Gen. 6–9)

Humankind's malignancy is described in connection with the Flood in terms of inner depravity: "The LORD saw that the wickedness of humankind was great in the earth, and that every inclination of the thoughts of their hearts was only evil continually." The total inner self (thinking, willing, and feeling) is included in the Hebrew word for "heart." To express the seriousness of the situation God speaks in very human terms: "I am sorry that I have made them [human and animal]."

It should be noted in passing that stories of a great Flood or floods in primeval times are almost universal among the peoples of the world. This seems to indicate the human memory of a catastrophe that occurred many millennia ago. The story to which the biblical narrative has its closest known parallels in form is found in a Babylonian document known as the

Gilgamesh Epic. Although the chief theme of this epic is not the Flood but Gilgamesh's search for immortality, the flood story is told by Ut-napishtim (the Babylonian Noah) to Gilgamesh. The biblical account draws on the same general tradition as the Babylonian but is not directly based on the Babylonian. As in the case of the parallels between the Babylonian "Genesis" and Genesis 1, so here the parallels are only in the realm of externals, not in the realm of faith. Looking at the Babylonian story one sees all the more clearly the differences between the Babylonian gods and our God.

As you read Genesis 6–9 you were probably aware of certain repetitions in the narrative and of variations in the content.[2] As an illustration of repetition: There are two statements of the entrance of Noah and his family into the ark (7:7 and 7:13). As an illustration of variation in content: According to 6:19 Noah is instructed, "And of every living thing, of all flesh, you shall bring two of every kind into the ark"; while according to 7:2 he is instructed, "Take with you seven pairs of all clean animals . . . and a pair of the animals that are not clean." Such repetitions and variations are usually accounted for on the basis of the theory that different Israelite traditions were combined to form the present narrative. In any case, the story achieves its purpose of presenting the judgment and mercy of God in a distinctive way. Repetitions and variations do not impede the word of God.

Though God's judgment on the wicked through the Flood is terrible, the Lord preserves alive a remnant of humans and animals. And in spite of continuing human sin after the Flood, God promises a dependable world: "As long as the earth endures, seedtime and harvest, cold and heat, summer and winter, day and night, shall not cease"(8:22). Such dependability sinful humanity does not deserve; it is an evidence of pure grace. Furthermore, through Noah and his family, the human race is given a new start with the same injunction to "be fruitful and multiply, and fill the earth" (9:1–7) as that given in Genesis 1:28. Here (9:1–7) humans are first allowed to eat the flesh of animals, but not with blood, because the life is in the blood and life belongs to God alone (compare Lev. 17:11 ). Above all, humans are not to shed the blood of one another in violence, for humans are made in the image of God.

> The following statement has sometimes been taken to settle the issue of capital punishment for all time: "Whoever sheds the blood of a human, by a human shall that person's blood be shed; for in his own image God made humankind" (9:6). Is this a valid interpretation?
>
> Does Genesis 9:5 throw any light on the question?

God's covenant with Noah established a consistent relationship with all humans and animals just as was later established with the chosen people. The Noahic covenant is unconditional, universal, and perpetual. Indeed it is a promise of God's faithful care. It is highly significant that the rainbow is made the sign of this covenant, because the Hebrew word for "bow" literally refers to a weapon of war. Lightnings were regarded as God's arrows, shot from a divine bow (Pss. 7:12–13; 18:14). Therefore, that which was ordinarily associated with war and divine judgment is made into the very sign of mercy itself. What relation do you see between God's covenant with Noah and Jesus' statement, "He makes his sun rise on the evil and on the good, and sends rain on the righteous and on the unrighteous" (Matt. 5:45)?

## The Tower of Babel (Gen. 11:1–9)

This is the last of the Genesis stories that depict the sinfulness of humanity. In a sense, it is the climax of the series. Here human malignancy expresses itself in pride, arrogance, and self-sufficiency as humans develop cultural patterns. This is to say, the deepest motivations of humans in pursuit of civilization are perverted, and all human achievements stand under God's judgment. This is not to say that humans and human achievements are as bad as they could be, but that both are tainted from beginning to end with sin and stand in need of transformation.

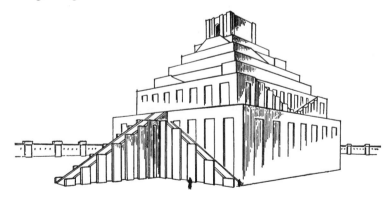

**ZIGGURAT OF BABYLON (Tower of Babel)**

The story of the Tower of Babel does not fit perfectly into any known literary category. Its primary purpose is not to explain how human languages arose. The land of Shinar, where Babel (Babylon) is located, is regarded as the cradle of civilization, and archaeology confirms this testimony. But the biblical writer is not primarily interested in Babylon as such; rather, the Babylonians represent all people in their typical pride and arrogance. The writer is speaking to our universal condition as human beings.

The migrants to Shinar said, "Come, let us build ourselves a city, and a tower with its top in the heavens, and let us make a name for ourselves; otherwise we shall be scattered abroad upon the face of the whole earth." Of course "a city" is a composite of human culture and contains within itself many cultural achievements. But the people do not seek God's guidance and help in building the city. The city is to include "a tower with its top in the heavens."

On the basis of archaeological and historical evidence many have identified this tower with one of the pyramidal ziggurats, which were temples in the ancient Mesopotamian world. "With its top in the heavens" simply means that it was very high. On page 37 you will find a drawing of the probable appearance of such a tower as the Tower of Babel. Originally the shrine at the top of the tower was thought to be a meeting place of the deity who came down from heaven and the worshiper who climbed up from the earth. In time, however, these temple-towers became the symbols of the pride and oppression of the great Mesopotamian empires (see Isa. 13:19; Jer. 51:6–10). This is the background against which the Hebrew author used the Tower of Babel as the symbol of humankind's pride and arrogance in the construction of civilization.

On such sin God comes in judgment. The confusion of language and the scattering of the people mean that people and nations will not come together in harmony but will erect hostile barriers between themselves. The scientific etymology of the word "Babel" is "gate of God," but the biblical writer plays on the popular etymology, which is based on sound. In this way "Babel" is related to the Hebrew word *balal,* "confuse." When people try to build a city, a nation, or a world apart from God, their result is confusion.

> *What do you think God is saying to us about national and international crises through this ancient story?*
>
> *How may we put ourselves in the path of God's word in such a way as to be used by it?*
>
> *How is the account of Pentecost in Acts 2 related to the story of the Tower of Babel?*

We have seen the operation of both judgment and grace in the stories of Adam and Eve, Cain and Abel, and the Flood. In the story of the Tower of Babel we see judgment but no grace. Why? Because God brings Abraham onto the scene of human need with the promise "in you all the families of the earth shall be blessed" (Gen. 12:3). In fact, the thrust of the Bible as a whole is a message of God's grace addressed to human need.

# PART TWO

# GOD'S COVENANT ACTS OF REDEMPTION

4

# God's Election of the Patriarchs and Matriarchs

*T*he biblical story, which thus far has been largely concerned with the human race in relation to God, narrows to a concern with a particular people. This does not mean, however, that God's purpose is confined to this people, but that through them the divine purpose for all may be realized. In other words, God selects a minority through which to reach the majority with the message of salvation. The election of the patriarchs and matriarchs is that mighty act by which God inaugurated the history of the covenant people. God's dealings with Abraham, Sarah, Isaac, Rebekah, Jacob, Leah, and Rachel speak to us, who are the heirs of the promises, about how God may deal with us.

## The World of Our Forebears

The world of our forebears included the territories known to us as Mesopotamia, Asia Minor, Syria, Canaan [Palestine], and Egypt. The Fertile Crescent, which is within this area, is the semicircle of fertile land extending from the Persian Gulf on the east to the southern border of Canaan on the west.

*As you study this lesson, the use of the map, below, will add much to clarify this period in the history of the covenant people.*

Abraham and Sarah and their successors did not create the setting for the biblical drama. The Near East of their day was the heir of highly developed civilizations characterized by written records, mighty empires, irrigation systems, wide commercial relations, art, and literature. Moreover, they lived among a large variety of peoples who contributed to their culture and customs. In other words, they did not live in a vacuum. For example, the great Hammurabi, emperor of Babylon, who was made famous by his code of laws still studied in law schools today, lived during this era (1728–1686 B.C.E.).

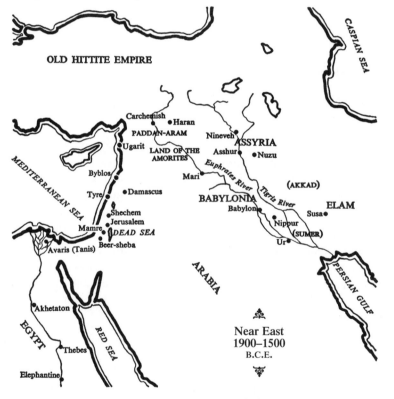

The original home of Abraham and Sarah was Mesopotamia, the land between the Tigris and Euphrates Rivers, roughly identified with modern Iraq. The land in which he sojourned was Canaan, the bridge between the great empires of the ancient Near East, which is now shared by modern Israel and the Palestinian Authority. Egypt, the country of the famous pyramids, which unto this day has remained the land of the Nile, also hosted various of the patriarchs and matriarchs and their families.

## The Forebears as a Group

### The Patriarchal and Matriarchal Narratives

The patriarchal and matriarchal narratives constitute Genesis 12–50. It is recognized by persons of varying theological persuasions that these narratives were not written down in their present form until long after the exodus from Egypt. Many students think they are composed of two, perhaps three, principal documents from much later periods. In any case, the traditions that compose Genesis had to be shaped, passed on in oral form, and then handed down in both oral and written form. But this is what we would expect, since the ancient Near Easterner habitually transmitted much of the cultural heritage by word of mouth. Moreover, the material was transmitted accurately. Obviously these narratives reflect Israel's faith and interpretation. Here again this is something to be expected, since the unit of revelation is event plus interpretation (see Chapter 1). Biblical narrative is largely "theological history," not the chronology of events for the sake of a record as many think of "history" today.

### Hebrew Origins

Where did the Hebrews come from? According to ancient records there was a group of people known as the Habiru. It seems that these people were not a particular racial or national group but were a landless, disenfranchised social class of individuals throughout the Near East. They cannot be identified with the Hebrews in a simple equation, but it is possible that the Hebrews were a specific group within the larger group of the Habiru.

According to the Table of Nations in Genesis 10, the nations of the earth are divided into three major groups after the three sons of Noah: Shem, Ham, and Japheth. Furthermore, according to Genesis 10:25 and 11:10–17, Eber (or Heber) is a descendant of Shem, and according to 11:26 Abraham (Abram) is a descendant of Eber. In other words, Abraham was a Semite and a Hebrew, and his descendants came to be known as Hebrews. We have already noted some of the relationships of the Hebrews to their most ancient neighbors. "The language of the patriarchs had presumably been a form of Northwest Semitic not greatly different from that spoken at Mari; but as ties with the homeland grew weaker they assimilated the Canaanite language, of which Hebrew is but a dialect (just as their kinsmen in Mesopotamia ultimately adopted Aramaic)."[1]

The composite origin of the Hebrew people is not only suggested by what has already been said; it is categorically stated in the Old Testament itself. In Genesis 14:13 Abraham is referred to as "Abram the Hebrew," while in Deuteronomy 26:5 Jacob is called "a wandering Aramean." Moreover, we read in Ezekiel 16:3, "Thus says the Lord GOD to Jerusalem: Your origin and birth were in the land of the Canaanites; your father was an Amorite, and your mother a Hittite." Of course, Abraham's descendants through Hagar and Keturah, as well as those through Sarah, were Hebrews. Joseph married Asenath, an Egyptian, who became the mother of Manasseh and Ephraim (Gen. 41:50–52). These and many other data mean that we cannot correctly speak of a Hebrew race. The Hebrews were a mixture of many biological and cultural streams.

The geographical origin of our forebears is Mesopotamia. The biblical record is emphatic at this point, and archaeological evidence confirms it. There is good reason for maintaining that the patriarchs and matriarchs brought with them Mesopotamian customs, laws, and stories. According to the Hebrew text of Genesis 11:28, 31, and 15:7 (compare Neh. 9:7)—which is followed in the English versions—Abraham's original home was Ur; but in the Greek translation (the Septuagint) the name Ur does not occur at all. On this account, and because early traditions were so closely associated with Haran (Gen. 24; 28; 29), some have claimed that "Ur" was not a part of the original text. In either case our forebears came from Mesopotamia.

## The Date of the Patriarchal and Matriarchal Era

While the time of the forebears cannot be identified with absolute precision, a comparison of archaeological and biblical data places them in the Middle Bronze Age (2000–1500 B.C.E.). Such biblical names as the following have been found from this period in extrabiblical documents of Mesopotamia and Canaan: Abraham, Jacob, Benjamin, and others. Moreover, ancient records from a place called Nuzu (located southeast of Nineveh) contain customs and laws that throw light on certain events of this time. For example, according to Nuzu custom a childless couple could adopt a son who would care for them, bury them, and inherit their estate. But if the couple should have a child by natural means, the adopted son surrendered the rights of inheritance. In the light of this Hurrian custom, Genesis 15:1–6 can be more easily understood. Because Abraham had no child of his own at that time, he thought that his slave Eliezer would be his heir.

Marriage contracts at Nuzu required a childless wife to provide her husband with a handmaid who could bear children. Apparently such a law as this lay behind Sarah's giving Hagar to Abraham as a concubine (Gen. 16:1–4) and behind Rachel's giving Bilhah to Jacob (Gen. 30:1–8). The fact that Nuzu law forbade the expulsion of the handmaid and her son may well be a part of the reason for Abraham's reluctance to cast out Hagar and Ishmael (Gen. 21:11).

Among the contemporaries of some of our forebears were the Hyksos, "rulers of foreign lands," a northwest Semitic people who ruled Syria-Canaan and Egypt about 1710–1550 B.C.E. When they conquered Egypt, they set up their capital at Avaris in the Delta not far from the land of Goshen, where Jacob and his sons were to sojourn. It is not difficult to see how Joseph, also a foreign Semite, could have become prime minister of Egypt under the Hyksos. Apparently the patriarchs and matriarchs wandered in the hill country and the Negeb of Canaan between 2000 and 1700 B.C.E., and the family of Jacob entered Egypt about 1700 B.C.E. Under the leadership of native Egyptians, the Hyksos were expelled from Egypt about 1550 B.C.E. It is altogether possible that some of the Hebrew people were among the Hyksos who were expelled at that time.

## Matriarchal and Patriarchal Religion

Our primary interest in the matriarchs and the patriarchs is religious and theological. Joshua made it clear to the Israelites of a later day that their ancestors were pagans and insinuated that there was still a remnant of polytheism among those to whom he was speaking: "Put away the gods that your ancestors served beyond the River, and in Egypt, and serve the Lord" (Josh. 24:14; compare 24:2).

In these early times there was a close covenant relationship between the deity, the clan leader, and the clan. The deity gave the wandering patriarch and matriarch guidance and promised them land and offspring. The deity was not thought of as confined to one place, for the clans were seminomadic, wandering from place to place. Moreover, the covenant God was quite distinct from the gods and goddesses of the Canaanites, whose religion centered in fertility and the cycle of the changing seasons. Our forebears' religion left more room for a genuinely historical perspective and the dimension of the ethical.

One of the chief names for deity was Shaddai or El Shaddai, "Mountain

One," usually translated into English as "God Almighty." This name has association with the power of the storm. But the term "Shaddai" also has etymological relationship with the term for "breast" and the name might provide a strong feminine image. Other divine names associated with the early religion are El Elyon, "God Most High" (Gen. 14:18–20); El Olam, "the Everlasting God" (Gen. 21:33); and El-bethel, "the God of Bethel" (Gen. 35:7). There are those who also regard the following expressions as names for deity as well: "the Shield of Abraham" (Gen. 15:1), "the Fear of Isaac" (Gen. 31:42, 53), and "the Mighty One of Jacob" (Gen. 49:24). In the tradition God came to be known as "the God of Abraham, the God of Isaac, and the God of Jacob" (Exod. 3:6). Furthermore, this God was identified with "the LORD" (Yahweh), the God of Israel (Exod. 3:13–17).

In the early religion there was no hierarchy of priests. The head of the clan offered animal sacrifice at various holy places, such as Shechem (Gen. 12:7), Bethel (Gen. 13:4), Hebron (Gen. 13:18), and Beer-sheba (Gen. 26:25). The patriarchs and matriarchs made a real contribution to the later Mosaic faith, especially in relation to the family nature of the covenant between God and the people. It is a thrilling experience to see at least a bit of how God worked through the very concrete circumstances and persons of the ancient Near East to initiate the covenant acts of redemptive history.

## The Patriarchs and Matriarchs as Individuals

Thus far we have considered the early forebears as a group; now we look at them as individuals. In doing this, however, we remember that the individual patriarch or matriarch cannot be wholly separated from the clan. Indeed, sometimes the person and the group seem to merge, just as events and their interpretation tend to merge.

### Abraham and Sarah (Gen. 12:1–25:18)

The first of the mighty acts of God recited by Joshua on the occasion of covenant renewal at Shechem was God's election, guidance, and blessing of Abraham (Josh. 24:3). Throughout the Abraham/Sarah cycle of stories and, for that matter, throughout all the biblical narratives, God is the chief Actor. At the same time, the patriarchs and matriarchs are called on to respond to God in faith and obedience. This does not mean that every unit of the narratives will fit readily into such a simple pattern.

*Read Genesis 12:1–25:18, and, as you complete each unit of the narrative, write down in your notebook what you learn of God's activity, and in a parallel column write down what you learn of the patriarch's/matriarch's response. If you cannot do this much reading, read at least chapters 12, 15, 17, and 22. In each instance ask the question, What does this story say about God's relation to me and my relation to God?*

The call of Abraham (Gen. 12:1–9) marks a major transition in the biblical narrative. Up to this point the emphasis has been on the creatureliness and sinfulness of humankind. In Abraham we see God's election of a particular people within the larger whole as the instrument of the divine blessing. In Abraham's call the universal and the particular meet. Why did God call Abraham? Why not call someone else? This is like asking, Why was I so favored as to be born into a Christian home? The call is from God and is hidden in the mystery of divine wisdom. Abraham's call was to break with the familiar and to adventure into the unknown in faith. Furthermore, a promise was coupled with the call. God promised to make of Abraham a great nation, to bless him, and to make his name great; God also promised, "in you all the families of the earth shall be blessed" (Gen. 12:3). The promise of the land of Canaan was made a little later (Gen. 12:7). In other words, the election of one family was for the benefit of all families (compare Acts 3:25; Gal. 3:8, 16; Rom. 4:13).

We read, "So Abram went, as the LORD had told him" (Gen. 12:4). A New Testament writer comments, "By *faith* Abraham *obeyed* when he was called to set out for a place that he was to receive as an inheritance; *and he set out*, not knowing where he was going" (Heb. 11:8). It is God who calls; it is humans who must respond. Abraham responded in faith and obedience, or obedient faith. The kind of faith exhibited in this instance is pioneering faith, that which enables a person to break new ground, tread new paths, adventure into the unknown for the sake of the one who calls. Where is pioneering faith especially needed today? How can we know when God is calling us to a particular task?

Abraham's behavior during his sojourn in Egypt (Gen. 12:10–20; compare 20:1–18) stands in contrast to his response to the call of God. In order to protect himself from the Egyptians, he conspired with Sarah to identify herself as his sister. Pharaoh took her into his harem and dealt well with Abraham on her account. Of course Sarah was Abraham's half-sister (Gen. 20:12); but the point of Abraham's conspiracy was deception, and there's no lie so attractive as a half-truth. In other words, Abraham showed a lack of faith in God on this occasion. But God remained faithful. Plagues came upon Pharaoh and his house that the truth might be known and that Sarah might be restored to Abraham. (Although the details concerning the keeping of God's promise to Abraham had not yet been revealed, Sarah obviously had a very important role to play.) What makes it so hard even for persons who are basically honorable to tell the truth? Can one be a successful doctor, lawyer, businessman, politician, husband, or wife and consistently tell the truth? Should one always tell the whole truth under all circumstances? Is the truth all or nothing?

In the account of the separation of Abraham and Lot (Gen. 13:1–18), Abraham appears in a better light. It seems that he and Lot were seminomads with small animals that lived on the leftovers in fields owned by others and already harvested. There simply was not enough food for the flocks and herds of both men. Abraham, the older man, generously gave the younger Lot his choice of the land.

Up to this point the story is largely about human relationships. But in verses 14–18 we are reminded of the providence of God. Although Lot had chosen the best land for himself, God promised the whole land (including Lot's choice) to Abraham and his seed—a startling reminder that destiny is ultimately in the hands of God.

According to Genesis 15:1–6 God renews the promises to Abraham and specifies that Abraham will have a son through the normal biological process and through that son will have innumerable descendants. Abraham "believed the LORD; and the LORD reckoned it to him as righteousness" (v. 6). Faith is here the basis of a right relation with God, and righteousness is the name for that right relation.

> *How did Paul use this passage in developing his doctrine of justification by faith? (See Rom. 4:1–25; Gal. 3:6–9; compare James 2:23.)*

> *In what respects are Abraham's faith and Christian faith alike? In what respects are they different?*

Without the word "covenant" much of the essential nature of covenant has already been described in God's relation with Abraham and Sarah (Gen. 12:1–9; 15:1–6). God has already undertaken promises on behalf of the two and through them on behalf of all the families of the earth, and Abraham and Sarah have responded in faith and obedience. This relationship is first described as "covenant" when God renews the promise of the land of Canaan in Genesis 15:7–21. The covenant is confirmed according to one ancient form of covenant making. According to this ancient form, the corresponding halves of slain animals were placed opposite each other and the contracting parties passed between the two rows. This procedure not only symbolized the agreement of the parties but also indicated that if one of them should violate the agreement, that one would be slain like the animals (Jer. 34:18). No mention is made of Abraham's passing between the rows; perhaps it is implied. Rather, the emphasis is on God and the divine promise of the land. Though Abraham will not literally possess it in his own lifetime, his descendants will. God initiates the covenant, and its ultimate security depends on God.

Abraham's faith was not always up to par. It moved in something of an up-and-down or zigzag fashion. The story of Hagar and Ishmael (Gen. 16:1–16) shows that even so great a man as Abraham had clay feet. To an ancient oriental woman, childlessness was one of life's worst tragedies; indeed this is true for some even today. How was God going to keep the promise to Abraham if Sarah had no child?

In accord with the customary law of the time, Abraham acquiesced in Sarah's plan for him to have a child by Hagar, Sarah's Egyptian maid. This can hardly be construed as an act of faith on the part of either Abraham or Sarah. Sarah is taking the issue into her own hands. The child that was born of such a union was to be regarded as the child of the first wife. When Hagar learned that she had conceived, however, she seems to have repudiated this custom and displayed contempt for Sarah. Therefore, Abraham permitted Sarah to reduce her status to that of a slave again. In her distress Hagar fled, but was commanded by an angel of the LORD to return home. She was also promised numerous descendants. In this episode were Abraham and Sarah attempting to snatch providence from the hands of God? Do we ever make such an attempt ourselves?

The account of God's making a covenant with Abraham in Genesis 17 records the changing of the name Abram to Abraham and Sarai to Sarah. This time the emphasis is on the two-way nature of the covenant, for Abraham and his descendants are to bind themselves to God by circumcision. Yet when God promises a child to Abraham by Sarah, Abraham laughs, because both he and Sarah are very old. Later in the narrative (18:12) Sarah also laughs. In other words, both faith and lack of faith played a part in the life of Abraham and Sarah. This was Israel's understanding also of the ongoing relationship with God. How do you account for a lack of faith in the life of a person who is fundamentally committed to God?

Reluctantly we pass by some very rich and instructive chapters in the

Abraham/Sarah narrative. We stop, however, to consider one of the most beautifully told and deeply moving stories in all Holy Writ, God's test of Abraham (Gen. 22:1–19). In chapter 12, verses 1–3, Abraham had to cut himself off from his past; here he is called to give up his future.[2] Abraham had been confronted by many tests in his earlier pilgrimage. Some he had passed, and others he had failed. On which occasions would you say he passed? On which did he fail? Now he is confronted by the most severe test of all.

Among the Canaanites child sacrifice was a well-established practice. The sacrifice of Isaac is best understood as reflecting a knowledge of this practice. Abraham, "the friend of God," could not withhold his best from God, the very child of promise himself. He seems to have responded at a depth of faith he had not known before. The story is told with deeply moving pathos. As Abraham and Isaac journeyed to the place that God had designated for the sacrifice, Isaac said to his father,

> "Father!" And he said, "Here I am, my son." He said, "The fire and the wood are here, but where is the lamb for a burnt offering?" Abraham said, "God himself will provide the lamb for a burnt offering, my son." So the two of them walked on together. (Gen. 22:7–8)

This journey was Abraham's *Via Dolorosa* (Sorrowful Way), as the path Jesus trod to Calvary is called. He obeyed the word of God without a murmur, and God taught him that he did not approve of child sacrifice but wanted his son to be "a living sacrifice."

Abraham's surrender was now complete. To trust God to fulfill divine promises, when the very instrument of the fulfillment is about to be destroyed, is the kind of faith that accepts God as the only ultimate security. No longer did Abraham seek to snatch providence from the hands of God and seek to fulfill the promise himself. We can see why people in Old Testament times, in New Testament times, and throughout all succeeding generations have praised the God of Abraham. And it is no accident that our New Testament begins, "An account of the genealogy of Jesus the Messiah, the son of David, the son of Abraham" (Matt. 1:1).

> *How has the rhythm of alternating promise and fulfillment been developed in the Abraham narrative?*
>
> *Can you illustrate this theme from other parts of scripture also?*
>
> *Have you experienced it in your own life?*

There are times when we need the faith of pioneering adventure. There are occasions when we must renew our trust in the grace of God. And there are those times when it seems the sun will never shine again, when all the evidence seems to be against us. We face an impregnable wall: it is too high, we cannot go over it; it is too deep, we cannot go under it; it is too broad, we cannot go around it; it is too thick, we cannot go through it. It is then that we come to know at the deepest level of our being the friendship and power of the Shield of Abraham: God alone can provide.

The story of Abraham is quickly brought to its close. With the purchase of the Cave of Machpelah as a burial plot for Sarah (Gen. 23), Abraham "receives" the Promised Land in token. Further, securing Rebekah as wife for his son Isaac, he has fulfilled his last responsibility in relation to the covenant promise.

## Jacob (Gen. 25:19–36:43)

*Read all of these eleven chapters if possible, and make the same kind of study that you were asked to do in relation to the Abraham story. If it is impossible to undertake this much reading, omit chapters 34 and 36. Who is the chief character so far as the narrative itself is concerned, God or Jacob?*

The account of the birth of Esau and Jacob (Gen. 25:19–26) is highly theological. Rebekah, like Sarah, was barren, and the birth of Esau and Jacob, like the birth of Isaac, was a mighty act of God. The birth of Joseph was also considered to be miraculous (Gen. 29:31; 30:22–24). This means that the history of redemption is altogether a matter of the grace of God. The struggling of the twins in Rebekah's womb is interpreted as a foreshadowing of the rivalries between Edom and Israel, since Esau was to be the patriarch of Edom and Jacob the patriarch of Israel. In popular thought, the name Jacob was associated with the Hebrew word for "heel," and the biblical account suggests, perhaps with a touch of humor, that even before birth Jacob was a heel-grabber or supplanter. Scientific study of the name suggests the meaning, "May [God] protect."

Jacob's "heel-grabbing" nature shows up clearly in his purchase of Esau's birthright (Gen. 25:27–34). Esau represents the life of the typical hunter of that day, while Jacob represents that of the shepherd. The life of the hunter was more precarious. Esau was the favorite of his father, and Jacob the favorite of his mother. When Esau the hunter comes in famished and begs food of Jacob the shepherd, the heel-grabber takes advantage of his brother's extremity, and the "bread alone" Esau (see Matt. 4:4) sells his birthright for a mess of pottage (bowl of soup). So far as this unit of the Jacob narrative is concerned, neither of the brothers is pictured in a favorable light. God's election of Jacob as bearer of the covenant certainly did not rest on Jacob's merit.

> *Genesis 26 is the only chapter in the Bible where the chief human character is Isaac. Note the renewal of the Abrahamic promise to Isaac.*

> *Compare verses 6–16 with Genesis 12:10–20 and 20:1–18. What conclusions do you draw from this comparison?*

Jacob's stealing of the blessing intended for Esau (Gen. 27:1–45) adds nothing to the moral stature of Jacob. He is still a heel-grabbing supplanter (v. 36). To understand this story, it is necessary to remember that it was assumed that a father's blessing conveyed the potent word of God and therefore could not be withdrawn. But recognizing that assumption, what is the real purpose of this story? A conniving wife and mother, a son's callous deception of his blind father, a son's brazen lie and his scornful disdain for his brother—what do all these things mean? Even in those times such things were known to be reprehensible and wrong. And the biblical writer does not condone them. They were not written for our imitation. The writer makes it plain that God is able to rule and overrule with sovereign majesty the affairs of men and women. Even human sin is made to praise God. Clearly the covenant is in the final analysis the gift of God's amazing grace. Accepting this truth, how do we relate it to personal and international dilemmas in our own time?

On the occasion of his departure to the ancestral home in Aram (Gen. 27:46–28:9), Jacob spent the night in "a certain place." It was at Bethel that he had the revelatory dream (Gen. 28:10–22) of angels, ascending and descending a ladder that reached to heaven. This "ladder" was hardly the kind with which we are best acquainted today. It probably refers to the steps leading from the ground to the shrine on the top of an ancient ziggurat (tower). In the ancient Mesopotamian world the deity was thought to meet with humans at the top of the ziggurat (see Chapter 3, p. 37). As Jacob awakens, he realizes in awe that he has received a revelation of God and calls the place Bethel, "house of God." The revelation comes from the God of Abraham and Isaac, who now becomes also the God of Jacob. Secondhand religion now gives way to firsthand encounter.

The threefold divine promise, which was made to his forebears, is now made to Jacob: land, numerous descendants, and himself as a universal source of blessing. In addition God promises, "I am with you." Thus in spite of his previous duplicity Jacob receives the gracious work of God as bearer of the covenant. Yet even his response to the divine revelation shows that the old Jacob has not been fully conquered. In response to God's promise Jacob sets up a sacred pillar and makes a vow that sounds like a bargain. When God promises to be with him, Jacob can only say, "If God will be with me. . . ."

*What is the difference between a bargain and a covenant?*

*Do you feel that at least a part of the meaning of Jacob's experience at Bethel was that God took the initial step in the transformation of Jacob?*

*What is the dominant message of the story for you?*

The account of Jacob's marriages to Leah and Rachel (Gen. 29:1–30 ) is a fascinating story. When Rachel comes to the well to water her sheep, it seems that for Jacob it is love at first sight. It was customary for the shepherds arriving at the well early to wait for all the other shepherds to arrive before uncovering the well. Apparently this unwritten agreement had two reasons behind it: (1) Adequate water might not be left for late-comers. (2) The stone that protected the well required the combined strength of all the shepherds to move it. But when Jacob sees Rachel, he casts the unwritten law to the wind and removes the stone with extraordinary strength. He even kisses Rachel before he identifies himself. To say the least, there is nothing slow about Jacob.

Laban's welcome is most gracious. But in Laban, Jacob meets his match. Jacob agrees to work seven years for Rachel, whom he loves, but under the cover of night and of the bride's heavy veil Laban treacherously gives the weak- or pale-eyed Leah to Jacob. When the treachery is discovered, Laban makes it clear that the younger cannot be given in marriage before the older. Perhaps the writer means to hint that the retributive justice of God was at work. Jacob, the younger twin, had through treachery swindled Esau out of his father's blessing. Yet beyond all of this we see the hand of God working out the divine purpose and turning the deepest treachery into praise of God. Indeed, apart from Leah (the unwanted bride) there would have been no Reuben, Simeon, Levi, or Judah—or, for that matter, Moses, David, or Jesus. The works of God are profoundly mysterious. Jacob accepts his predicament and agrees to work another seven years for Rachel, though he is able to marry her in a week.[3]

Although Laban had tricked Jacob into marrying Leah, the time came when Jacob returned the "compliment" (Gen. 30:25–43). As long as he worked for Laban, he was not altogether free. He requested Laban to let him go back home and take with him his wives and children. But because

Jacob had proved an economic asset, Laban did not want him to leave. Moreover, there was some question as to Jacob's right to take his wives and children with him (see Gen. 31:43). Therefore, the two tricksters worked out a mutual agreement. The "biological" ideas associated with breeding lying behind Jacob's chicanery were typical of the times.

Finally, under divine direction and with the agreement of his wives, Jacob flees from Laban (Gen. 31:1–55). When Laban learns of the flight, he seeks to overtake Jacob. He is most disturbed about the loss of his household gods, which Rachel has stolen without Jacob's knowledge. The possession of these teraphim was connected with clan leadership and inheritance. But Rachel, daughter of the tricky Laban and wife of the devious Jacob, is fully competent to deceive them both.

Before they part, Jacob and Laban make a covenant, and Laban says, "The LORD watch between you and me, when we are absent one from the other" (v. 49). This so-called Mizpah benediction was a threat to either of these men if he transgressed the covenant. A sacred pillar was erected, and neither man was to cross that boundary with the intention of harming the other. The covenant was sealed with oath taking, sacrifice, and the eating of a sacred meal.

> *From your reading of Genesis 31, would you say that Jacob believed in the existence of only one God?*
>
> *What likenesses do you find between human-human covenant making and divine-human covenant making? What differences?*
>
> *What is the difference between covenant making inside the church and covenant making outside the church?*

The time came when Jacob knew that he must face Esau again (Gen. 32:3–21). He knew that he had wronged his brother and that Esau had a right to be angry. Therefore, he sent messengers ahead to greet Esau. When the messengers returned with their report about Esau and his four hundred men, Jacob was all the more disturbed. In his extremity, the old heel-grabber prayed a very unusual prayer, especially as he confessed, "I am not worthy of the least of all the steadfast love and all the faithfulness that you have shown to your servant" (v. 10). Furthermore, he showed a real concern for "the mothers with the children," as well as for God's fulfillment of the covenantal promise. The way in which Jacob sent gift after gift ahead in an attempt to appease Esau's anger is amusing, but it also indicates the deep distress in Jacob's own heart. The old proverb "Human extremity is God's opportunity" is clearly illustrated in this experience of Jacob.

The story of Jacob's all-night wrestling bout (Gen. 32:22–32) is most significant, although the meaning of some of its details eludes us. Jacob was tortured by a guilty conscience and the fear of meeting Esau. Getting right with his brother somehow involved getting right with his God. Jacob's struggle with God is depicted as the struggle with a man; yet it is really God's struggle with Jacob. Jacob is made weak and is partially crippled, and yet, through his weakness, is made strong. Jacob the heel-grabber is changed to Israel. The original meaning of the word "Israel" is not definitely known. It seems to have been "Let God strive." The popular meaning here seems to have been "He who strives with God" (v. 28). The change in name signifies a change in Jacob. The change had already begun to take place (Gen. 32:9–12). Heretofore God had been the God of Abraham and Isaac, and the God of the Bethel dream, but here Jacob met God in a head-on encounter and was never quite the same again. This encounter is recalled by the place-name Penuel or Peniel, which means "the face of God."

> *Do you think that what is often referred to as "conversion" today is applicable to Jacob's Penuel experience?*
>
> *Can a person be right with others without being right with God?*
>
> *Can someone be right with God without being right with their human brothers and sisters?*

After facing God, Jacob had to face Esau (Gen. 33). He arranged his family in such a way as to protect those dearest to him, but he himself took the lead. The sevenfold prostration with which he greeted Esau seems to have been a widespread practice. In contrast to Jacob's formality, Esau reacted spontaneously and freely, embracing Jacob warmly with tears of joy and forgiveness. In the conversation that followed, the most gripping statement came from the lips of Jacob: "To see your face is like seeing the face of God" (v. 10).

> *How is this related to Jacob's experience at Penuel?*
>
> *Is there a sense in which a reconciliation between others with whom one is alienated can confirm a wrestling with God?*
>
> *According to the remainder of the account, Jacob excused himself from accompanying Esau to Edom but promised to meet him there later. According to the narrative, he failed to keep his promise. How would you account for this failure?*

After the encounter with Esau, the Jacob story proper (not the life of the patriarch) is quickly brought to an end (see chaps. 34–36).

## Joseph (Gen. 37:1–50:26)

*Read all of these chapters if possible. If you are unable to read all of them, you will probably want to concentrate on those that are specifically about Joseph (37; 39–47; 50). As you read, note especially the relation of the providence of God to human activity.*

From the very outset (Gen. 37) Joseph is placed over against Jacob's other sons. Moreover, as Jacob himself had been the favorite son of his mother, Joseph was the favorite son of his father. To show his favoritism Jacob gave him a luxury item of the day, a long cloak with long sleeves. The King James "coat of many colors" was derived from ancient translations, not from the Hebrew text. Joseph's two dreams did not improve the family situation. The modern interpretation that maintains that Joseph should not have told his dreams does not take into account the ancient Near Eastern view of divine communication: "A vision was for the ancients so important and obligatory that a demand to keep it tactfully to oneself would not have occurred to them."[4] Most of the account of how Joseph was sold into slavery is very clear. Jacob, who had deceived his blind father and had robbed his brother, was himself deceived by his own sons.

Joseph was sold to Potiphar, an officer of the Egyptian Pharaoh (Gen. 39). In this menial capacity God was with Joseph, and Joseph was made overseer of Potiphar's house. Potiphar's wife did her best to seduce Joseph, but Joseph replied by setting forth his relation to his master, to his master's wife, and to God. He concluded with the question, "How then could I do this great wickedness, and sin against God?" (Compare Psalm 51:4.)

*How does this question throw light on the nature of sin?*

But Potiphar's wife was the kind of person who would not take "no" for an answer. She bedeviled Joseph "day after day," until one day she caught his garment and tore it from him. He fled, and she used the garment in her false accusation of Joseph before the other men of the household and later before her husband. Therefore Joseph was thrown into prison. But even in prison God was with Joseph, and he was placed in charge of other prisoners.

*In what way does the temptation of Joseph throw light on the nature of temptation and how to resist it?*

*In what way does this story go beyond the teachings and implications of Genesis 3?*

After Joseph's interpretation of the dreams of the butler and the baker in prison (Gen. 40:1–23), he was eventually brought to the attention of Pharaoh and interpreted his dreams (Gen. 41:1–57). In each case, however, Joseph made it clear that the interpretations he gave came from God. When Joseph had interpreted Pharaoh's dreams, he was made "prime minister" of Egypt with the power to execute the counsel he himself had given to Pharaoh. God had now placed Joseph in a position where he could be an instrument in preserving alive the chosen people in time of famine. Through his interpretation of Pharaoh's dreams, Joseph stressed God's providence through the plenteous years and the lean years, and then he undertook the human responsibility consistent with such a conviction.[5] Can you find examples of the combination of divine sovereignty and human freedom from other parts of the Bible?

The first visit of Joseph's brothers to Egypt (Gen. 42) was the beginning of the process of reconciliation. Because of famine in Canaan, Jacob sent ten of Joseph's brothers to Egypt to buy grain. While Joseph recognized them at once, they did not recognize him. After accusing them of being spies, Joseph put them in prison for three days. Then he held Simeon as a hostage and sent the others home to bring their youngest brother as a proof that they had told Joseph the truth. The details of the story make it clear that the crisis in which the brothers found themselves opened the old sore of their guilt. In fact, Joseph heard them confess their sin to one another. They were now forced to go back to their father a second time without one of their number. Joseph was testing them to see if genuine reconciliation were a possibility.

The famine made it necessary for the brothers to return to Egypt for more food (Gen. 43). Judah made the "prime minister's" position clear to Jacob by quoting his exact words: "You shall not see my face unless your brother is with you." Finally, Jacob allowed the brothers to take Benjamin with them, because Judah became surety for him. They took a present to the governor (Joseph). The details of the story gain in suspense as they build up toward the climax. Joseph was so moved by the sight of his brother Benjamin that he had to go aside to weep.

The time had come for Joseph to give his brothers the final test (Gen. 44). This is one of the most powerfully beautiful scenes in all literature. Nothing can take the place of reading the biblical text itself. On orders from Joseph, his steward places Joseph's divining cup in Benjamin's sack.

Then he overtakes the brothers as they begin their homeward journey and accuses them of stealing the cup. Out of a sense of innocence and corporate responsibility, they reply, "Should it be found with any one of your servants, let him die; moreover the rest of us will become my lord's slaves." After the cup is found in Benjamin's sack, they return to Joseph disconsolate, and confess, "God has found out the guilt of your servants."

The word "guilt" here has a double meaning. It refers to the fact that the cup has been found in the sack of one of their number. But it also points by way of a guilty conscience to their treatment of Joseph years ago. Joseph refuses the penalty set by the brothers on themselves, and in so doing presses the testing to its focal point. He will keep Benjamin as his slave and let the others return home. In other words, the examination question is this: Have the brothers changed, or will they sacrifice Benjamin as they once sacrificed Joseph in selfishness? Judah's reply indicates that the brothers have passed the examination. In this reply he rehearses the whole story leading to their present predicament. Further, he shows genuine concern for his aged father who cannot survive the loss of another son. And then he speaks of his promise to his father that he himself would be surety for Benjamin. Finally Judah says, "Now therefore, please let your servant remain as a slave to my lord in place of the boy, and let the boy go back with his brothers."

Now that Joseph is convinced that his brothers are capable of reconciliation, in an atmosphere fraught with deep emotion he makes himself known to them (Gen. 45). For reconciliation is more than a one-way feeling of forgiveness; it is forgiveness as a genuine transaction. Without attempting to explain how God overrules human sin to serve the divine purpose, Joseph makes his great affirmations of faith: "God sent me before you to preserve life"; "God sent me before you to preserve for you a remnant on earth"; "So it was not you who sent me here, but God." Through the brothers, both Joseph and Pharaoh extend the invitation to Jacob and his family to move to Egypt. Wisely Joseph cautions his brothers not to quarrel on the way home, for it would be so easy to try to blame one another for their evil. When Jacob hears the good news that Joseph is alive, he says, "I must go and see him before I die."

*How is forgiveness related to reconciliation? What light do the following passages throw on this question: Matthew 5:21–26; 6:12–15; Luke 6:35–38; 2 Corinthians 5:16–20; Ephesians 4:31–32; and 1 John 4:20?*

*Think back over the Joseph story from the beginning and list in your notebook the various occasions on which God used human sin to accomplish the divine purpose.*

Jacob settled in the land of Goshen (Gen. 46:1–47:12), and Joseph carried out his responsibilities as the food administrator of Egypt (Gen. 47:13–27). Before his death Jacob blessed Joseph's two sons, Ephraim and Manasseh, and adopted them as his own (Gen. 47:28–48:22). After his blessing of the twelve sons (Gen. 49:1–27), Jacob died and was buried by Joseph in the Land of Promise (Gen. 49:28–50:26). After Jacob's death the brothers became afraid of Joseph and begged his forgiveness. They still had not understood fully that which had already transpired. Therefore, Joseph reassured them: "Do not be afraid! Am I in the place of God? Even though you intended to do harm to me, God intended it for good. . . . So have no fear" (Gen. 50:19–21). In other words, forgiveness is not only a person-to-person affair; it is a God ↔ human ↔ God ↔ human affair. God had justified the brothers; Joseph would not presume to play a role superior to God. If he should seek vengeance on them now, he would be doing just that.[6]

In the stories of Abraham, Isaac, and Jacob there is frequent divine-human encounter on a very personal basis, while in the stories of Joseph emphasis is placed on the overruling providence of God. Have not both of these factors been a part of the life of God's people throughout the ages? Through the patriarchs and matriarchs, God was working out the divine purpose of redemption.

# Exodus and Sinai

*I*n our pilgrimage from creation to the new creation, we have now arrived at the bedrock foundation of Old Testament faith—the exodus from Egypt and the covenant at Sinai. The exodus is the most celebrated of all of God's mighty acts in the Old Testament. Through the redemption of God's people from literal slavery, they came to look to the LORD as the Redeemer from suffering, sin, and death. Therefore, they made the exodus redemption central in their confessions of faith, saying, for example, "the LORD brought us out of Egypt with a mighty hand and an outstretched arm, with a terrifying display of power, and with signs and wonders" (Deut. 26:8). Moreover, they never ceased to sing about it in their psalms of praise:

> When Israel went out from Egypt,
> the house of Jacob from a
> people of strange language,
> Judah became God's sanctuary,
> Israel his dominion.
> (Ps. 114:1–2)

In this connection we study about the great Moses—prophet, lawgiver, and statesman; about the covenant at Sinai, where the people of Israel became the people of God; and about the Ten Commandments, whose influence through the centuries has been immeasurable. Exodus and Sinai are focal points of our study, marking the birth of Israel as a people.

## The Mosaic Era

More than one thousand years before the time of Moses (the latter part of the Late Bronze Age, 1500–1200 B.C.E.), Egyptian pharaohs had already built the great pyramids as tombs for themselves. Moses was the heir of a civilization then quite old. When he was introduced to the Egyptian court, the sights were dazzling. Such splendor and displays of wealth have not been overdone even in Hollywood motion pictures. The palaces and temples and tombs were magnificent, characterized by decorated columns and ceilings. After all these centuries the tombs of the pharaohs still amaze us with the brilliance of their colors. These monuments were erected through the use of a labor force composed largely of slaves. Education, commercial wealth, and political status were available to the privileged few. The boundaries of the Egyptian empire included Canaan.

Several of the pharaohs come in for special attention. Among them is Amenhotep IV (ca. 1364–1347), who is known as "the heretic king" because he forsook the popular religion of his time. Because his father was very ill in his old age, Amenhotep reigned with him as coregent for a time and then succeeded him as king. He became a devotee of the cult of Aton, or the solar disk—he worshiped the sun. Furthermore, he changed his name from Amenhotep ("Amen is satisfied") to Akhenaton ("the one who is beneficial to Aton"). As another expression of his religious zeal, he moved his capital from Thebes, the center of Amen worship, to Akhetaton, a city that he himself built. Some think that Akhenaton believed in only one God. Others have challenged this assertion. Because of his preoccupation with religion and art, to the exclusion of military exploits, the Egyptian empire became increasingly weak. Letters on clay tablets found at the site of Akhenaton's capital (Tell el-Amarna is the modern site name) were written by vassals of Akhenaton and his father from Canaan, requesting aid against attackers, including some Habiru (see Chapter 4).

## The Oppression in Egypt (Exod. 1:1–12:36)

The book of Exodus may be briefly outlined as follows: the oppression in Egypt (1:1–12:36), the deliverance and march to Sinai (12:37–18:27), and the covenant at Sinai (19:1–40:38). At the outset we concentrate on the oppression of the descendants of Jacob by the Egyptian Pharaoh.

*Before reading any further in this book, read Exodus 1–2. What is the overall impact of these chapters dealing with the oppression?*

### Pithom and Rameses

The new king "who did not know Joseph" (Exod.1:8) cannot be identified with certainty. But by the mention of this king, the biblical writer prepares the reader for what is to come—the oppression of God's people by the Egyptians: "Therefore they set taskmasters over them to oppress them with forced labor. They built supply cities, Pithom and Rameses, for Pharaoh" as slave laborers (Exod. 1:11). Pithom is probably to be identified with Tell er-Retabeh, which is located south of Avaris and west of Succoth. Rameses is another name of Avaris, the delta capital of Egypt in the Hyksos period. Seti I undertook the reconstruction of this capital. His son, Rameses II, continued the reconstruction and named the city the "House of Rameses." According to Egyptian documents the pharaohs used Habiru as slave labor. No doubt within this group of slaves were some of the biblical Hebrews. These data, along with other considerations, suggest a probable date for the exodus about 1280 B.C.E.

## The Early Years of Moses

The story of the baby Moses (Exod. 2:1–10) is a moving story of God's providential care of the future deliverer. The daughter of Pharaoh is used by God in preserving the life of the very person who will one day save his people from their bondage to Pharaoh. God prepared Moses well for his future ministry. Through his natural family he received his Hebrew heritage, and as a son of Pharaoh's daughter he "was instructed in all the wisdom of the Egyptians" (Acts 7:22). When there is a big job to be done, God has a way of calling forth a person who has a solid preparation.

Although Moses was brought up in Pharaoh's court, he was still a Hebrew at heart. This is forcibly brought out by his killing of the Egyptian (Exod. 2:11–15a). In his flight from Pharaoh, Moses made his way to Midian, where he married Zipporah, a daughter of Reuel (Jethro), the priest of Midian (Exod. 2:15b–22).

## The Call of Moses

But God was not aloof from the people's distress; God heard their groaning and remembered the covenant with the ancestors (Exod. 2:23–25). Indeed the LORD called Moses from tending the flock of his father-in-law to be the shepherd of God's afflicted people (Exod. 3:1–4:31). This call took place in the form of a divine-human dialogue. As Moses stood on holy ground before God, we too stand there when we read this account reverently. No doubt the fugitive Moses was burdened with the suffering of his people, and God spoke to and through his burdened heart to call him to his appointed task. But Moses was reluctant to assume so great a responsibility and began to raise objections.

*Read Exodus 3:10–4:17, recording in your notebook each objec-
tion and God's response to the objection. Why was Moses so
reluctant?*

*Of what relevance is this series of objections and responses for
us?*

## The Revelation of God's Name

The personal name of God was revealed to Moses at the burning bush
(Exod. 3:13–22). The English versions usually translate the Hebrew text
"I am who I am," or "I am what I am," or "I will be what I will be." This
translation takes the root of the Hebrew verb to mean "to be." On this
basis, the abbreviated form of the name in Exodus 3:14 is "I am" or "I will
be." In harmony with this understanding, many construe the name "the
LORD" in verse 15 and throughout the Old Testament as the third person
of the verb "to be" with the meaning "He is" or "He will be." The third
person verb would have the consonants YHWH. Because the first syllable
is thought to be "Yah" (Hallelujah in Hebrew means "praise Yah"), the
name might be pronounced *Yahweh.* This latter name is translated in both
the King James Version and the New Revised Standard Version with capital letters, "the LORD," to distinguish it from other words that are translated "the Lord." It is rendered "Jehovah" in the American Standard
Version and "the Eternal" in Moffatt. Some who accept the above derivation of the name take it to refer to God's absolute being and existence, but
this understanding is more Greek than Hebrew. Others who accept the
same derivation take the name to refer to God's presence with the people
as the One who is always adequate to every situation (see v. 12). More
plausible is the suggestion made by many able scholars that the term has
the meaning "He causes to be," thereby placing the emphasis on God's
creative activity.

The fact is we cannot assert the original meaning of this name of God
with certainty, but we do know that the name "Yahweh" was associated
with all of God's activity in relation to the people. In Jewish tradition, and
reflected in the Hebrew text, the name YHWH was not to be pronounced.
The four consonants are written without vowels and are known as the
tetragrammaton, representing God's holy and unspeakable personal name.

Not only is there a question about the meaning of this name, there is
also one concerning the time and circumstances of its origin. In Exodus
6:3 we read, "I appeared to Abraham, Isaac, and Jacob, as God Almighty,
but by my name, 'The LORD' [YHWH] I did not make myself known to

them." Yet we read in Genesis 21:33, "Abraham planted a tamarisk tree in Beer-sheba, and called there on the name of the LORD [Yahweh], the Everlasting God" (compare Gen. 4:26; 9:26; 12:8). How are these two statements to be understood in relation to each other?

The relationship is usually explained in terms of different literary sources. But even when such sources are recognized, the question still arises, who first worshiped God by the name YHWH? We do not know. Exodus 6:3 seems to be a statement of historical fact: the ancestors did not worship God under the name YHWH. Genesis 21:33 is a statement of the truth that the God of Israel was also the God of Abraham. But was God worshiped under the name YHWH by anyone before Moses? Here again we do not know.

Many have held that Moses was introduced to the worship of YHWH by his father-in-law Jethro, "the priest of Midian"(Exod. 3:1). It was while he tended Jethro's flocks that he was called by YHWH to deliver his people from slavery. Moreover, when Moses and Jethro met after the exodus, Jethro presided at the sacrifice to the LORD (Exod. 18:10–12). Yet, there are still other theories, and we cannot give a conclusive answer to our question. We do know, however, that with Moses the name YHWH came to have a new significance. The LORD became known as the God of Redemption and the God of the Covenant People.

## The Contest Between God and Pharaoh

Much of the material in Exodus 5:1–12:36 is concerned with the contest between the LORD and Pharaoh. Of course the LORD is in complete control of the whole situation but works through Moses and Aaron.

*List each plague as you come to it.*

*A dominant theme in these chapters is the hardening of Pharaoh's heart. As you reread this section of the book of Exodus, underline every reference to this subject.*

The word "heart" refers to a person's inner decision-making center. Three different Hebrew verbs are used to describe the process of hardening. The most frequently used means "to hold fast, be strong, make obstinate"—that is, it suggests an unyielding disposition. The second word means "to be heavy or dull, or to make heavy or dull," suggesting moral and spiritual insensitivity. The third, which is used only once (Exod. 7:3), means "to stiffen or make severe"—that is, it suggests stubbornness and harshness. In other words, Pharaoh is characterized as unyielding, insensitive, and stubborn.

Sometimes God is said to harden Pharaoh's heart; at other times Pharaoh is said to harden his own heart; and on still other occasions it is stated that Pharaoh's heart was hardened. This kind of paradox is typical of biblical thought. To say God hardened Pharaoh's heart means that God's sovereignty permeates the whole of life. To say Pharaoh hardened his own heart means that humans are free and responsible creatures. Human freedom is not the equivalent of God's sovereignty, but it is real within the limits set by God. We ran into this kind of expression in the story of Joseph (Gen. 45:8). We also find it elsewhere. For example, in Luke 22:22—"For the Son of Man is going as it has been determined, but woe to that one by whom he is betrayed!" At Pentecost, Peter maintained that "this man, handed over to you according to the definite plan and foreknowledge of God, you crucified and killed by the hands of those outside the law" (Acts 2:23).

Biblical people were not given to our modern bent on analysis. They spoke whole mouthfuls, not half or quarter mouthfuls. For example, in Romans 9–11 Paul first writes as if nothing matters except the sovereignty of God. Then he goes on immediately to hold Israel responsible for rejecting the gospel only to conclude in doxology for the mystery of divine grace. God's sovereignty and human responsibility are set side by side without an attempt to harmonize them. For after all, humans could live by knowledge if they could put these two things together perfectly. In spite of all our attempts at logical consistency, we Christians do not live by logic alone. When we do something good, we do not pat ourselves on the back and say, "What good people we have been!" Rather, we thank God for divine grace. On the other hand, when we sin, we do not say to God, "You made us do it." We confess our sins and ask for forgiveness. Yet, even in our sin we often see the hand of God ruling and overruling to the divine purpose and glory. Though we cannot fully explain the relation between God's sovereignty and human responsibility, Christians are satisfied that they are both real. Can you not illustrate this relationship from your own Christian experience?

## The Meaning of Passover

The institution of Passover is placed appropriately in the midst of the exodus narrative (12:1–36) because this festival commemorates Israel's redemption from the Egyptian bondage. It is possible that a pre-Mosaic seminomadic festival was "baptized" into the exodus faith and thereby given a new meaning, just as at a later time Passover itself served somewhat as a model for the Lord's Supper. As God's ancient people celebrated the Passover from time to time, the events of the exodus deliverance were re-presented by word and act in such a way that Israelites long centuries after the exodus received God's revealing and redemptive word. A similar work of God's grace takes place in the sacrament of the Lord's Supper. Indeed the exodus, Passover, Calvary, and the Lord's Supper are all brought together by Paul in 1 Corinthians 5:7—"For our paschal lamb, Christ, has been sacrificed."

## The Deliverance and March to Sinai (Exod. 12:37–18:27)

*As you read these chapters in your Bible, mark the names of the places and follow the route of the exodus as shown on the map on page 67.*

### The Beginning of the Journey

"The Israelites journeyed from Rameses to Succoth, about six hundred thousand men on foot, besides children. A mixed crowd also went up with them, and livestock in great numbers, both flocks and herds" (Exod. 12:37–38). The estimate of 600,000 men is startling and has caused interpreters great trouble (compare Num. 1:46; 26:51). If this figure were accepted literally, it would mean that the total number of escapees would be from two to three million persons. In such a case they would have had no need to fear Pharaoh at all. The Egyptians may not have numbered that many themselves. Obviously only two midwives (Exod. 1:15–16) could not have served so great a population: "Such a host even if marching in close order (as it did not) would more than have extended from Egypt to Sinai and back!"[1] It has been estimated that such a multitude would need "900 tons of food (two train loads) per day, 2,400 tons of firewood daily for cooking."[2] Clearly some explanation must be sought for the number 600,000.

Several explanations have been proposed. Some maintain that this number represents a misplaced census from the time of David, when Israel would probably have numbered about two and a half million. Others prefer to translate the word "thousand" as "clan," thereby reducing the total to a plausible number. Finally, it is also held that the biblical writer was

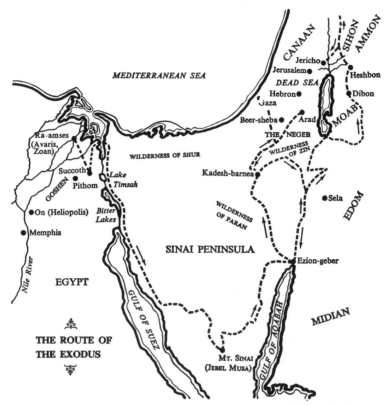

MEDITERRANEAN SEA

CANAAN

Jericho
Jerusalem
DEAD SEA
Hebron
Gaza
Beer-sheba    Arad
THE  NEGEB
WILDERNESS OF ZIN

SIHON

AMMON

Heshbon
Dibon

MOAB

Kadesh-barnea

WILDERNESS OF PARAN

Sela

EDOM

Ra-amses
(Avaris,
Zoan)

WILDERNESS OF SHUR

Succoth
Pithom

GOSHEN

Lake
Timsah

On (Heliopolis)   Bitter
Lakes

Memphis

Nile River

EGYPT

GULF OF SUEZ

SINAI PENINSULA

Ezion-geber

MIDIAN

THE ROUTE OF
THE EXODUS

MT. SINAI
(JEBEL MUSA)

GULF OF AQABAH

not thinking literally but in anticipation; that is, that all Israel of a later day were in a sense redeemed at the exodus by God, just as the Negro spiritual implies that the Christian of today was present "when they crucified my Lord." Whatever explanation appeals most to you, it is certainly true that biblical history is no superficial chronicle—it is history with the dimension of the word of God.

Earlier we saw that there was a Hebrew people but no Hebrew race. It is equally true that those who participated in the exodus were not confined to the Children of Jacob: "A mixed crowd also went up with them" (compare Num. 11:4). No doubt this mixed multitude included quite a variety. It is probable that some of them were from among other groups of Habiru (see Chapter 4).

"The time that the Israelites had lived in Egypt was four hundred thirty years" (Exod. 12:40). This figure tallies well with the date (ca. 1700 B.C.E.) that we accepted for the beginning of the sojourn in Egypt and with the date (ca. 1280 B.C.E.) that we accepted for the exodus. The biblical text (Exod. 12:40–13:16) kept the people of Israel reminded of the relation of Passover, unleavened bread, and the consecration of the first-born to God's act of deliverance.

Though the exact route of the exodus is uncertain, some things should be noted about it. "When Pharaoh let the people go, God did not lead them by way of the land of the Philistines," lest they be discouraged by war (Exod. 13:17). "So God led the people by the roundabout way of the wilderness toward the Red Sea" (Exod. 13:18). The Hebrew text says nothing about "the Red Sea." Instead it speaks of the *Yam-Suph*, which means "Sea of Reeds" and probably refers to the marshy area in the vicinity of Lake Timsah in the northern part of Egypt. There are no reeds in the Red Sea. Furthermore, Lake Timsah borders the Land of Goshen where the Children of Jacob had been living. Translators of the Bible have followed the Greek Septuagint in their use of "Red Sea" rather than the wording of the Hebrew Bible. This means that wherever you find the translation "Red Sea" in the Old Testament, the Hebrew has "Sea of Reeds." More important, however, than the body of water that was crossed is the fact that God led the people both day and night.

## The Crossing of the Sea

The hardening of Pharaoh's heart continued even after the Israelites were on their way. Pharaoh pursued them to the sea. Hemmed in by the forces of Pharaoh and the waters of the sea, the people began the complaining that was to characterize them in the wilderness wanderings. But God protected them throughout the night. "Then Moses stretched out his hand over the sea. The LORD drove the sea back by a strong east wind all night, and turned the sea into dry land; and the waters were divided" (Exod. 14:21). Read again the heart of the account of deliverance (Exod. 14:21–31). The people crossed the sea on dry land and their pursuers were destroyed in the returning waters.

The fact that God "drove the sea back by a strong east wind" did not make the event of the crossing of the sea any less a miracle. The biblical writers did not have any concern with the modern notion of "breaking natural law." God was God, and that was sufficient. A miracle was a demonstration of the power and purpose of God, a sign pointing beyond itself to God, an event calling forth wonder—received as such by people of faith. The strong wind, the dividing of the waters, the dry land, the crossing of the sea, and the destruction of the Egyptians were not a mere coincidence. They were the mighty acts of God by which the LORD's people were delivered from bondage to a new freedom.

The most significant word in the salvation vocabulary ("save") is derived from a term that means "to be wide, spacious, free." This word is used for the first time in Exodus 14:30. Both language and the Exodus events define this word as the gift of freedom by the hand of God. Such salvation was not something the people deserved; it was the gift of God, to be received by faith (v. 31). The exodus keeps us reminded that God is concerned with the physical as well as the spiritual needs of humans—that salvation is a great and broad concept in the Bible. We are well aware that people are oppressed in many parts of the world today. Ask yourself, are there oppressions or manipulations of other persons of which I am guilty or for which I am in part responsible? What forms do our contemporary injustices take? What does Exodus say to us in relation to both grace and wrath? Do we stand with Moses and the oppressed, or do we stand with Pharaoh and his taskmasters?

## Songs of Victory

The theme of the Song of Moses (Exod. 15:1–18) and that of the Song of Miriam (Exod. 15:21) is the same: God's victory over the Egyptians. Verse 1 of the former is almost identical with the whole of the latter. Perhaps the Song of Moses is simply a longer form of the same poem. Verses 13–16 recount God's guidance of the people in the wilderness. Does verse 17 refer to the Temple in Jerusalem, or is the reference to God's heavenly sanctuary? In any case, the song belongs to the literary category of the hymn and should be compared with those psalms that celebrate the mighty acts of God (68, 78, 105, 106, 111, 114, 149). In fact, it may be called "The Star-Spangled Banner" of Israel. The salvation mentioned in Exodus 14:30 is defined in verse 13 of the song as redemption. And the hymn ends with an affirmation of the continuing sovereignty of God: "The LORD will reign forever and ever." There was something final about the revelation of the sovereignty of God at the exodus that assured people of faith in all generations of God's relevance and adequacy in every situation.

## The March to Sinai

*In the march to Sinai the people undergo several severe tests. List in your notebook all the tests you can find in Exodus 15:22–17:16 (see also Num. 11:1–35; 20:2–13) and note the people's response in each case.*

*Compare and contrast these tests in the wilderness with those of Jesus in his wilderness experience (Matt. 4:1–11; Luke 4:1–13).*

We have already thought together about the hardening of Pharaoh's heart. The author of Psalm 95 maintained that the ancestors of Israel had hardened their hearts at Meribah by putting God to the test (see vv. 7b–11). They mistrusted God in spite of the fact that they had witnessed God's mighty acts of deliverance. In other words, it is possible for members of the church to harden their hearts also. The author of Hebrews used the verses of the psalm to warn the Christians against hardness of heart (3:12–4:13).

A word should be said about the miracles of the manna and the quails. Through the years various explanations have been attempted. One growing out of detailed research is that proposed by F. S. Bodenheimer of the Hebrew University in Jerusalem who has identified the manna (Exod. 16; Num. 11) with honeydew-like excretions of certain insects that feed on wilderness tamarisk trees.[3] These particles have the appearance of hoarfrost and contain three basic sugars with pectin. Since sweet food was hard to come by in the desert, this delicious manna was all the more memorable.

Through the centuries, quails have been accustomed to migrating over the territory in large numbers. They often fall exhausted in their long flight and are easily caught. The fact, however, that the manna and the quails have been so understood by many in no way detracts from their significance as miracles. God provided them at the very time they were so desperately needed, and they were received as special acts of God. The Bible itself tells us in the miracle of the crossing of the Sea of Reeds that "the LORD drove the sea back by a strong east wind" (Exod. 14:21). Of course, there are miracles for which no such explanation can be offered.

## The Covenant at Sinai (Exod. 19:1–40:38)

While you are encouraged to read all of the chapters listed in this section of the book of Exodus, we shall have to limit ourselves in our thinking together primarily to chapters 19–24.

*At this point read these chapters and make your own outline of them.*

*Then continue your reading, following the additional suggestions for study.*

### The Covenant Enacted

We know more about the covenant at Sinai than we do about the exact location of the sacred mountain. At least four different sites have been suggested. Jebel Musa, at whose base the Monastery of St. Catherine is located, is the "popular" site identification (see map on p. 67).

A brief statement of the covenant is found in Exodus 19:4–6a:

> You have seen what I did to the Egyptians, and how I bore you on eagles' wings and brought you to myself. Now therefore, if you obey my voice and keep my covenant, you shall be my treasured possession out of all the peoples. Indeed, the whole earth is mine, but you shall be for me a priestly kingdom and a holy nation.

Clearly, the covenant rested on God's gracious deliverance of Israel from the Egyptians, and the keeping of the covenant by Israel meant obedience to God's will. A covenant is a binding of persons in a special relationship. In the ancient Near Eastern world, covenants were frequently made. Sometimes the contracting parties were equals; at other times they were not. The covenant of God with Israel was of the latter type.

God and Israel were not equal parties. God as the Sovereign King was the initiator of the covenant and stipulated all its requirements. God's gracious commitment to the people was the basis of the divine call for them to commit themselves to the Lord. This meant that they could not enter into a covenant relationship with other gods. It also meant that they had a covenant relationship with one another. In the case of the ancestors the covenant rested on God's unconditional promises for the future, which were received by the ancestors in faith. At Sinai the covenant rested on God's mighty acts already executed and was to issue in grateful obedience.[4]

The binding of God and Israel together is one of the chief facts that bind the two Testaments (covenants) together. Israel, as the covenant people, was to be "a kingdom of priests and a holy nation." While not every Israelite was called to serve at the altar, all Israel had a vocation to worship and serve God as a people set apart to a special task, a task that was to be made clearer in the process of time.

The covenant is rightly understood in the context of election, God's choice of a people. Election is implicit throughout the history of Israel, but it is particularly emphatic in Deuteronomy and in Isaiah 40–55. One of the clearest statements of it is found in Deuteronomy 7:6–15, where it is evident that God elected Israel and entered into covenant strictly in the mystery of divine love. Moreover, God maintains the covenant in faithfulness and steadfast love. When the themes of election and covenant are examined throughout the Old Testament, it becomes clear that Israel was elected to privilege, obedience, and service as the covenant people.

Election was given the form of covenant. The covenant relationship is dynamically set forth in the Old Testament under several metaphors and similes:

| GOD | | ISRAEL |
|---|---|---|
| Redeemer | Exod. 20:2; Deut. 7:8; Isa. 43:1 | Redeemed |
| King | Exod.19:5–6; Isa. 41:8–9; 43:15 | Servant |
| Father | Exod. 4:22; Hos. 11:1; Isa. 63:16 | Son |
| Husband | Hos. 1–3; Jer. 2–3; Ezek. 16; Isa. 54 | Wife |
| Mother | Isa. 66:12–13; Deut. 32:18; Hos. 11:1–4 | Child |
| Vinedresser | Isa. 5; Ezek. 15:1–6; 19:10–14; Ps. 80:8–19 | Vine |
| Shepherd | Ezek. 34:11–31; Isa. 40:11; Pss. 23:1–3; 80:1 | Sheep |

*Copy in your notebook each metaphor or simile in turn and make a study of it by looking up the appropriate scripture passages and then writing down in your own words the meaning of the covenant relation depicted thereby.*

*What is the current relevance of each of these pictures of the covenant relation for the church? for the family? for the individual?*

The people at Sinai responded to God's word concerning the covenant: "Everything that the LORD has spoken we will do" (Exod. 19:8; see 24:3). After the account of the giving of the Law (to which we shall return in a moment), the sealing of the covenant is described in Exodus 24. Sacrifices are made, and half of the blood is thrown against the altar. The book of the covenant is read, and the people respond, "All that the LORD has spoken we will do" (24:7). Then Moses throws the other half of the blood on the people. This throwing of the blood on the altar (representing God) and on the people seals the covenant. This close association of blood (the bearer of life) with covenant is carried over into the New Testament (1 Cor. 11:25; Mark 14:24; Heb. 9:15–22). The eating of the sacrificial meal by the leaders of Israel is also a sealing of the covenant (Exod. 24:9–11). The Lord's Supper includes the symbolism of both blood and meal.

## The Law of the Covenant

One of the chief expressions of the covenant was law. In Exodus this is indicated by the placing of the Ten Commandments (20:1–17) and the Covenant Code (20:22–23:33) in the midst of the covenant ceremony itself. Many think that the Mosaic form of the Ten Commandments was briefer than the forms found in Exodus 20:1–11 or Deuteronomy 5:6–21. Several reasons are given for this opinion: (1) In the Hebrew text of Deuteronomy 4:13 and 10:4, the Decalogue is called "the ten *words*"; (2) there are differences between the version of the Decalogue found in Exodus and that found in Deuteronomy, with reference to commandments 4, 5, and 10; and (3) half of the commandments are still in the short "word" form: 1, 6, 7, 8, and 9. This is not a matter of paramount importance, however, since the longer forms of five of the Ten Words simply elaborate on their basic idea. In fact, we sometimes see the commandments listed in a short form similar to the following:

> I am the LORD your God, who brought you out of the land of Egypt, out of the house of slavery:
> 1. You shall have no other gods before me.
> 2. You shall not make for yourself a graven image, or any likeness.
> 3. You shall not take the name of the LORD your God in vain.
> 4. Remember the Sabbath day to keep it holy.
> 5. Honor your father and your mother.
> 6. You shall do no murder.
> 7. You shall not commit adultery.
> 8. You shall not steal.
> 9. You shall not bear false witness against your neighbor.
> 10. You shall not covet your neighbor's house.

We begin with the prologue, which is even more basic than the commandments themselves: "I am the LORD your God, who brought you out of the land of Egypt, out of the house of slavery." By this, God is identified as the God of the exodus. We see that law operates within grace and is founded on it. God redeemed the chosen people from slavery before the commandments were given. This was an act of pure grace. Then God gave them the commandments to tell them how to live as God's special possession. In other words, it was no accident that Sinai followed the exodus: The redeemed people needed to know how to live in distinction from those who worshiped false gods. Their relationship to God and others was to be motivated by gratitude for what the LORD had done for them.

This passage and others in the Bible teach us that ethics should spring from gratitude to, and trust in, the God of grace. As Christians we recognize that we are created in Christ Jesus, not by good works, but for good works (Eph. 2:10). Although we were not literally present at the exodus from Egypt, neither were subsequent generations of Israelites. Yet theologically both Israelites and Christians were present in their ancient religious ancestors. The church is a new Israel and rightly claims the Old Testament as a part of its heritage. Christians interpret the Ten Commandments not only as those who share in the exodus from Egypt but also as those who share in the exodus from sin through Jesus Christ. We, of necessity, interpret the commandments in the context of the gospel. The Ten Commandments are relevant for all, since they are expressions of the unchanging character and will of God. They help to make us conscious of our need of a Savior, for no one except the Savior has ever kept them perfectly. They teach us God's better way. We are justified only by grace.

While various religious groups agree that there are ten commandments and that the ten are to be divided into two groups, they disagree concerning the exact numbering and organization. The numbering and organization followed here is that ordinarily found in the Reformed tradition. The first four commandments set forth a person's relation to God, and the last six, a person's relation to other persons. It is well to remember that Jesus summarized the Law and the Prophets in terms of love for God (Matt. 22:37; see Deut. 6:5) and love for neighbor (Matt. 22:39; see Lev. 19:18). "Love is the fulfilling of the law" (Rom. 13:10).

The First Commandment prohibits polytheism (that is, belief in more than one God) and insists on the worship of the LORD alone. In a society where people are, for the most part, not tempted to commit themselves to supernatural rivals of God, how does this commandment apply? Are there "other gods" that take priority in the life of the individual, in marriage, in the home, in the church, in business, in politics, and in world affairs?

The Second Commandment prohibits the making and worship of images and thereby implies the spiritual character of God. An image of God would limit God in the eyes of the worshiper and tend to identify the divine with human-made images. To make images of other gods would be a transgression also of the First Commandment. When we remember that the ancient world was full of polytheism and images, the radical nature of this commandment can be appreciated. How is God's jealousy like our jealousy? How unlike our jealousy? In the light of this injunction, how are we to distinguish between the right and wrong use of art and symbols in Christian life and worship?

The Third Commandment prohibits blasphemy and by implication enjoins reverence for God. God's name stands for God's Person as revealed. Therefore, God's name (all that through which God's self-revelation is known) is to be revered. The use of the divine name in the practice of magic and perjury is specifically forbidden. Moreover, any light or irreverent use of God's name is also prohibited. How is God's name blasphemed today? Is there any connection between this commandment and the common variety of swearing and cursing? Positively speaking, how is reverence for God to be shown (Matt. 6:9)?

The Fourth Commandment enjoins the sanctification of the Sabbath and thereby teaches that all time belongs to God. In Exodus 20:8–11 the Sabbath is rooted in creation (compare Gen. 2:2–3), while in Deuteronomy 5:12–15 it is rooted in the exodus redemption. After the resurrection of Jesus on the first day of the week (Sunday), the early Christians worshiped on both the Jewish Sabbath and the Lord's Day. In time, the Lord's Day supplanted the Jewish Sabbath. To Christians the resurrection of Jesus was evidence of the new creation. Theologically, therefore, the Lord's Day symbolizes both creation and redemption. In his interpretation of the Sabbath according to Deuteronomy 5:15, J. Coert Rylaarsdam said, "It is, in short, a weekly reminder of Passover, just as for Christians Sunday is a weekly reminder of Easter."[5] From a very practical standpoint the Lord's Day is needed for rest—such a need is written by God into the very fiber of our beings—and for Christian worship and education.

> *Read Romans 14:5–9. How do you relate what Paul says to our present-day understanding of the Fourth Commandment?*
>
> *It is sometimes claimed that the issue of the Lord's Day is ceremonial and not ultimately moral and spiritual. Would you accept this in whole or in part? Why?*
>
> *How do you deal with Sunday observance in relation to public transportation, drugstores, filling stations, other businesses, movies, sports . . . ?*
>
> *What positive approach would you suggest for the Christian's use of Sunday? Does Jesus' statement in Mark 2:27–28 help in formulating your answer?*

The Fifth Commandment requires the honoring of parents and implies the sanctity of the family. Such honoring included respect, obedience, and care in old age. Yet, in Jesus' day there were those who would set aside as *corban* ("devoted to God") goods that should have been used to aid parents. They would then use the goods for themselves. Jesus made it clear that they were transgressing the Fifth Commandment (Mark 7:10–13). In our day of increased life span, how does one both forsake father and mother (Gen. 2:24) and honor father and mother? Under what conditions should a couple take aged parents into their own home? Paul called the Fifth Commandment "the first commandment with a promise" (Eph. 6:2). How did Paul reinterpret the promise for Christians?

The Sixth Commandment forbids murder and all other unauthorized killings and upholds the sanctity of human life. Life is the gift of God in a special sense, and it must therefore be highly respected and valued. In Israelite society, capital punishment was designated as the penalty for some crimes, and war was an accepted means of settling disputes. Obviously this commandment did not, in that setting, prohibit either of these kinds of killing.

However, in light of the teachings of Jesus (for example, Matt. 5:21–26, 38–48) and of the total impact of the gospel, there are those who feel that Jesus has reinterpreted this commandment in a way that makes it impossible for them to sanction either capital punishment or war under any circumstances. On the other hand, there are equally conscientious Christians who feel that both capital punishment and war are justifiable under certain circumstances. Still others repudiate capital punishment but support the preparation for war as the lesser of two evils. As a result of the frightful possibilities of nuclear warfare, some have become "nuclear pacifists." Have you worked your way through these issues? Perhaps your pastor can supply you with additional help. The Sixth Commandment has further ramifications. How does it apply to the failure to save human life through food, clothes, medical care, and the like? What is its relation to suicide and "mercy killing" and abortion?

The Seventh Commandment forbids adultery and upholds the sanctity of marriage. In the Israelite world, adultery involved sexual intercourse between a married person and one who was not the legal spouse. Jesus said that "every one who looks at a woman with lust has already committed adultery with her in his heart" (Matt. 5:28). Many Old Testament laws deal with various types of sexual offenses. The New Testament writers condemned all kinds of sexual abuses (1 Cor. 5:9; 6:9; 2 Cor. 12:21; Rom. 1:24–27; Eph. 5:5; Col. 3:5; 1 Tim. 1:9–10; Heb. 13:4; Jude 7; compare Acts 15:20, 29).

*How do you account for so much sexual license in our society?*

*Where does the responsibility lie for changing the situation?*

The Eighth Commandment forbids stealing and upholds the right to own property. It may have originally been a prohibition against kidnapping that has been generalized (compare Exod. 21:16). We know from personal experience that honesty and the respect for the property of others is critical for harmony in the life of society.

*What constitutes stealing? What forms may it take?*

*What are the positive implications of this commandment? Does Matthew 5:42 help to answer this question?*

*How would you describe an honest person?*

The Ninth Commandment forbids false witness and undergirds the integrity of the court. While the chief emphasis is the prohibition of false witness in court, the smearing of someone's reputation was also included.

*How truthful are we as a people in court, in advertisement, in church disputes, in everyday conversation?*

*What is the best way to teach a child to tell the truth?*

*Paul says we are to speak the truth in love (Eph. 4:15; compare John 3:21 and 1 John 1:6). How does love affect the telling of the truth?*

The Tenth Commandment forbids coveting what belongs to another and encourages the integrity of the heart. The word "house" is the general word and includes all else. This has been called the most spiritual of all the commandments. It gives a greater depth of meaning to commandments six through nine. Jesus said, "It is from within, from the human heart that evil intentions come: fornication, theft, murder, adultery, avarice, wickedness, deceit, licentiousness, envy, slander, pride, folly" (Mark 7:21–22). Paul placed the covetous or greedy among the spiritual reprobates (1 Cor. 5:10–11; 6:10; Eph. 5:5). On the positive side, Jesus commanded his disciples to seek first God's Kingdom and God's righteousness (Matt. 6:33). Likewise Paul counseled the Corinthians to covet or desire earnestly the higher gifts (1 Cor. 12:31).

*How may a person best do battle with the temptation to covetousness? (See Romans 13:8–10.)*

## Symbols of the Covenant

Because of their lack of faith, the covenant people wandered in the wilderness until a new generation should arise; their life was characterized by murmuring and rebellion. A large part of Numbers 10:11–22:1 is devoted to the telling of this sad tale. All the while, however, God's presence in the midst of the people was represented by the Ark of the Testimony (Exod. 25:10–22) and the Tabernacle (Exod. 26:1–37). The

Ark was a portable box or chest, symbolizing also the guidance of God in peace and war (Deut. 31:9; Josh. 6:4–11). After the wilderness wanderings and invasion of Canaan, it was left at Shiloh (Josh. 18:1). Although it was captured by the Philistines (1 Sam. 4), it was later returned (1 Sam. 5–6). At first it was kept in the Holy of Holies of the Tabernacle. When David brought the Ark to Jerusalem, he placed it in a temporary sanctuary (2 Sam. 6). Later it was placed in Solomon's Temple. It disappeared on the occasion of the fall of Jerusalem in 587 B.C.E., and no one knows exactly what happened to it.

The Tabernacle was a movable sanctuary, established in the wilderness, where prayers were said and where the people assembled. The religious significance of the Tabernacle was carried over into the New Testament. John 1:14 may be translated, "And the Word became flesh and *tabernacled* [dwelt] among us." As God's presence among the ancient people of Israel was associated with the Tabernacle, so God *tabernacled* among the people at a later time in the uniqueness of the incarnation.

## The Law of Moses

We now come to a very difficult subject to present briefly, namely, that of Moses' relationship to the Torah or Pentateuch (Genesis, Exodus, Leviticus, Numbers, and Deuteronomy). Scholars have been debating the question for years, but many laypeople have been unwisely shielded from questions of authorship and date in their study of the Bible. As Protestants, we believe in the priesthood of all believers and of each believer, and this means that we all must take responsibility for the decisions we make.

There is no attempt here to sell a bill of goods. The two major theories concerning the authorship and composition of the Pentateuch are presented: the Mosaic and the documentary. Suggestions are made in footnotes for further reading on both sides of the subject. You are invited to pursue the matter as far as you like and make up your own mind on the basis of the evidence available.

Regardless of what conclusion you reach, you can still use this book and agree with it where you think it is right and disagree with it where you think it is wrong. You are simply requested to consider the evidence carefully and fairly.

### The Documentary Hypothesis

Until the eighteenth century C.E., Christians for the most part accepted the tradition that Moses wrote the Torah/Pentateuch. In that century, however, a type of study began that was to result during the latter part of the nineteenth century in what has been called the Graf-Wellhausen or documentary hypothesis. K. H. Graf and Julius Wellhausen did much to bring the theory to its classic formulation. But today many who hold to some form of this hypothesis have modified it considerably—often in a more wholistic direction. The following is a brief general statement of the hypothesis as it is held by many in our time.

Mosaic authorship is denied, and the Pentateuch is considered a compilation of four major documents written down over a period of centuries. These documents incorporated many ancient traditions handed down orally (some in written form) for centuries before the documents themselves were written. Here are some of the reasons ordinarily given for denying the authorship of the Pentateuch to Moses or to any other one person:

1. Moses' obituary is found in Deuteronomy 34:1–12, and, to say the least, it would be rather odd for Moses to write his own obituary. Moreover, the language of the chapter suggests someone other than Moses wrote it.

2. The Pentateuch contains anachronisms (errors in chronology that place people or events incorrectly earlier in time). For example, Genesis 36:31 reads, "These are the kings who reigned in the land of Edom, before any king reigned over the Israelites." In other words, the point of view of the writer was that of one living after Israel had had kings, and this took place long after the time of Moses. For other anachronistic statements see Genesis 12:6; 14:14.

3. The same author would not have used the various names of God as they are sometimes used. Exodus 6:3 states, "I appeared to Abraham, Isaac, and Jacob as God Almighty, but by my name 'the LORD' I did not make myself known to them." Yet according to Genesis 21:33, "Abraham planted a tamarisk tree in Beer-sheba, and called there on the name of the LORD, the Everlasting God" (see also Gen. 12:8; 15:2, 8; compare 4:26; 9:26). In the first account of creation (Gen. 1:1–2:4a) the name God is used; but the name LORD God suddenly appears with the beginning of the second account (Gen. 2:4b).

4. In the Pentateuch Moses is said to write something only occasionally, the implication being that he did not write everything contained therein.

5. There are certain narratives that can best be explained as duplications. For example, according to Genesis 32:28 Jacob's name was changed to Israel at Peniel, but according to Genesis 35:10 it was changed at Bethel. Compare also Genesis 21:31 with Genesis 26:33; Genesis

12:10–20 with Genesis 20:1–18 and Genesis 26:6–11; Genesis 6:19–20 with Genesis 7:2–3.

6. The codes of law reflect a settled life rather than the seminomadic life of the desert wanderings (Exod. 22:5, 29; 23:10).

7. The law of the sanctuary varies. According to Exodus 20:24 an altar may be set up in various places, while according to Deuteronomy 12:14 sacrifice is to be offered at only one place.

8. The law concerning slaves also varies (Exod. 21:2–11; Deut. 15:12–18; Lev. 25:39–55).

9. There are differences in language and style that cannot be accounted for simply in terms of the differences in subject matter. The mountain of the covenant is sometimes called Sinai, at other times Horeb. Moses' father-in-law is variously named Reuel, Hobab, and Jethro. The pre-Israelite occupants of Canaan are called both Canaanites and Amorites. Both prophetic and priestly emphases are present.

The four major documents in the classic form of the hypothesis are usually referred to as JEDP and are characterized as follows. J is dated as a written document somewhere between 950 B.C.E. and 850 B.C.E. It is found chiefly in Genesis and Exodus, and receives its name from the divine name Yahweh or Jahweh, because in this document this name is used from the earliest times. The style is simple and powerful, exhibiting a fondness for anthropomorphism (that is, speaking of God as if God were a human). The primary interest of the writer is in the South (Judah).

E is dated between 850 B.C.E. and 750 B.C.E. It also is found chiefly in Genesis and Exodus, and receives its name from the divine name Elohim, because this name is used for God prior to the time of Moses. The language is less anthropomorphic than J's, and the writer demonstrates a special interest in the northern tribes (Ephraim) and in dreams and angels.

D is dated in the seventh century B.C.E. and is essentially synonymous with Deuteronomy. It places great stress on the purity of Israel's religion. Simultaneously it is very anti-Canaanite and deeply humanitarian. Sacrifice is permitted at only one sanctuary. All members of the tribe of Levi are admitted to the altar to serve as priests. The doctrine of God's electing love is especially strong. D sets forth the blessing-and-curse view of history; that is, obedience to God's commandments issues in the divine blessing, and disobedience in the divine curse.

P is dated between 600 B.C.E. and 500 B.C.E., and is found in Genesis, Exodus, Leviticus, and Numbers. It is a priestly document, emphasizing priestly concerns, genealogies, and the greatness of God. The style is rather formal and repetitious. Like E, it does not employ the name YHWH ("the LORD") until after it has been revealed to Moses. No sacrifice is mentioned prior to the time of Moses, and only priests descended from Aaron are permitted to officiate at the altar. Within P is the Code of Holiness (Lev. 17–26), which is usually designated H. The Law, Torah, or Pentateuch reached its full form (JEDP) between 500 B.C.E. and 400 B.C.E.[6]

In recent years the hypothesis has been challenged radically with respect to the existence of J and E as freestanding documents. Many scholars consider P to have started with traditions from Israel's earliest history (those formerly assigned to J and E) as well as the so-called "priestly" materials. P then created what we now know essentially as Genesis through Numbers sometime after the Babylonian exile (ca. 500 B.C.E.). D, on the other hand, late in the seventh century B.C.E., reflecting on the same early traditions, developed the book of Deuteronomy as a summation of Mosaic teaching for the purposes of theological and political reform.[7]

## The Mosaic Tradition

Here are some of the statements often made in behalf of the Mosaic authorship of the Pentateuch:

1. In Jewish tradition Moses has been considered the author since pre-Christian times.
2. The kind of references made to Moses throughout the Bible support this position. He is mentioned over and over again in every book of the Pentateuch except Genesis. In certain passages of the Law he is said to write particular materials (Exod. 17:14; 24:4–8; 34:27; Num. 33:1–2; Deut. 31:9, 22, 24). The witness of the remainder of the Old Testament presupposes the Mosaic authorship of the Pentateuch (for example, Josh. 8:31; 1 Kings 2:3; Ezra 6:18; Dan. 9:11–13). Jesus and the writers of the New Testament accepted Moses as the author of the Torah (for example, see Mark 10:4–5; Luke 24:27, 44; Acts 15:5, 21; Rom. 10:5).
3. Writing was available; Moses was well educated; and we know of no one better qualified to produce this work. The unity of the Pentateuch presupposes a great mind.
4. It is unnecessary to contend that Moses wrote his own obituary.
5. Discrepancies in the narratives may be textual errors. The laws concerning slaves deal with different kinds of slaves.
6. So-called duplications are not doublets but separate events.
7. Differences in style and language are best accounted for by differences in subject matter.

8. If Deuteronomy originated in the seventh century B.C.E., what is the point of exterminating the Canaanites?

9. If Moses did not write the Pentateuch, how could such a strong tradition that he did have ever arisen?[8]

## A Summary Word

Today the authorship and composition of the Pentateuch or Torah is more of an open subject than it was some years ago. There are many versions of the documentary hypothesis. Much more attention is being paid to oral tradition (that is, the handing down of biblical materials by word of mouth before they were written down). The fact that certain materials are assigned to P, for example, does not necessarily mean that they originated late on that account. People of antiquity depended on oral tradition far more than we do. There were both oral and written traditions, some of them very ancient, prior to the writing of any major part of the Pentateuch.

Although any form of the documentary hypothesis is theoretical and not proved fact, the cumulative force of the evidence suggests strongly that there is some truth in it. Some duplications may be separate events, but it is highly improbable that they all are (see, for example, Gen. 6:19–20 and 7:2–3). The differences in style and language are too great to be accounted for by any simple formula. The unity within the Pentateuch can be accounted for by the skillful editing of the history of the one people of God. The books of the Law do not everywhere profess to be written by Moses. The fact is that Moses is never mentioned a single time in the fifty chapters of Genesis. It should also be remembered that the title "The First Book of Moses" and similar titles do not belong to the Hebrew text. At least a part of the answer to the question about the Canaanites in Deuteronomy is that the whole of the content of this book did not originate in the seventh century. The writing down of documents does not necessarily coincide with the origin of material.

But there is also some truth in the contention that Moses wrote at least parts of the Pentateuch. The Mosaic tradition did not arise out of nothing. Moses was the human founder of Israel's religion. He made it clear that the LORD is known through history, that the LORD is the redeeming and covenanting God, Sovereign over all, not to be represented by images, and without female counterpart. Moses was the human instrument of the exodus deliverance and the covenant at Sinai. He was the great pioneering lawgiver of Israel. There probably is a Mosaic nucleus in the Pentateuch, which was expanded and adapted to meet the changing conditions of the people of God. For subsequent generations of Israelites to attribute all their Torah to Moses is fully understandable.

Israel thought collectively. All Israelites were the Children of Jacob, even those who were not related by blood; indeed all Israelites were Jacob. Furthermore, all Israelites were delivered from Egyptian bondage, even those who were not born until generations later. Since David was the father of psalmody within Israel, the entire Psalter came to be synonymous with his name, although everyone agrees that some of the psalms were written long after David's time. Solomon's name became almost a synonym for wisdom literature, even connected to some books like the apocryphal Wisdom of Solomon written long after Solomon's day. When Jesus and the writers of the New Testament spoke and wrote of Moses in the manner of Jewish tradition, we can understand where they are coming from without ignoring the evidence that points to a multiplicity of traditions and "authors."

Regardless of how few or how many the human authors of the Pentateuch may have been, the Law is a part of God's written word. To see even a little bit of how God worked through real people of old in bringing it into being fills one with awe and gratitude, and enables one all the more to see its relevance for real people today. Even so traditional a scholar as Edward J. Young says, "When we affirm that Moses wrote or that he was the author of the Pentateuch, we do not mean that he himself necessarily wrote every word. To insist upon this would be unreasonable. . . . Also, under divine inspiration, there may have been later minor additions and even revisions."[9]

If it can be admitted that there could be "later minor additions and even revisions," the principle is established that Moses did not have to write the whole Pentateuch in order for it to be known as "the law of Moses." Moreover, if God could take care of minor additions and revisions, God could surely take care of a far more complicated process of composition. The quality of one's Christian faith should not be judged on the basis of one's attitude toward the authorship and composition of the Pentateuch. There are good Christians on both sides of the issue and some in between.

# The Promised Land

$W$e can imagine that hope and expectation were running high in the hearts of many Israelites as they left the wilderness and stood on the threshold of the Promised Land. Surely they must have felt that many hardships had been left behind and that great opportunities lay ahead. Undoubtedly this land would be a pleasant place with fertile soil, cooling breezes, and adequate water supply for humans and beasts. Thoughts of great bunches of grapes and of "milk and honey" must have made a tasty appeal after the rations of the desert. God had promised a land to Abraham's descendants, and now at last the day of fulfillment had arrived. In the books of Joshua and Judges this story is told, but not as a time of easy prosperity. Instead it was a time of life-and-death struggle—both military and religious. The marvel is not that Israel was shaken and tempted, but that faith survived. Yet it had to survive, for God had so ordained. After all, we are concentrating on the mighty acts of God, not on the prideful accomplishments of human beings.

## The Setting of Joshua and Judges

Joshua crossed the Jordan about 1250 B.C.E., and the period of the Judges ended about two hundred years later. Before the conquest of Canaan by Joshua, the kingdom of Edom had been established south of the Dead Sea. To the east of the Jordan were the kingdoms of Moab, Sihon, Ammon, and Og ( see map on p. 87). On the west side of the Jordan, the Canaanites lived in city-states, without a central government. These city-states had been under Egyptian control for a long time. In the time of Akhenaton (see Chapter 5), however, this control was challenged by the invading Habiru of whom we have already spoken. The exodus under Moses probably took place during the reign of Rameses II (1290–1224). Merneptah, his successor, states in his famous stele (inscribed stone),

| | |
|---|---|
| Libya is ruined, | Khatti (Hittite-land) is pacified; |
| The Canaanite land is despoiled | with every evil. |
| Ashkelon is carried captive; | Gezer is conquered; |
| Yanoam is made | as though it did not exist. |
| The people of Israel is desolate, | it has no offspring; |
| Palestine has become | a widow for Egypt.[1] |

This stele was made about 1220 B.C.E. and contains the first extrabiblical reference to Israel. It indicates that Israel was already in Canaan by the latter part of the thirteenth century, though not as a completely established people. The Pharaoh's statement is greatly exaggerated, for Israel was to have a numerous offspring. After the beginning of the twelfth century, Egyptian power declined rapidly, and Egypt's Asiatic empire was lost. This decline greatly assisted the conquest and settlement of the Israelites in Canaan.

About 1175 B.C.E. Pharaoh Rameses III repulsed an invasion of Egypt by sea peoples, including the Philistines, who subsequently settled on the coast of Canaan in the twelfth century. The Philistines' ability to make iron gave them an advantage over the Israelites in their early days of conflict. It was from the name *Philistia* that the name Palestine was eventually to be derived by the Romans and applied to the land in a spirit of disdain.

## The Gift of the Land

The gift of the land of Canaan to Israel is celebrated as one of the mighty acts of God in Israel's confessions of faith. On the occasion of offering the first fruits, the worshiper included these words in confession: "He [the LORD] brought us into this place and gave us this land, a land flowing with milk and honey" (Deut. 26:9; compare Ps. 78:54–55). In other words, God elected a land as well as a people.

### The Land Itself

In size the land of Palestine is exceedingly small, but historically and religiously it has been called "the navel" of the world. "From Dan to Beersheba" (1 Sam. 3:20) is less than 150 miles in length, and west of the Jordan the median width is about forty miles. There are extreme variations in terrain and climate. In the north, Mount Hermon reaches a height of 9100 feet above sea level, while in the south the Dead Sea is 1290 feet below sea level. Jerusalem, with a moderate climate, stands about 2600 feet above sea level, while Jericho at a distance of only fifteen miles to the east as the crow flies, with a tropical climate, is 825 feet below sea level. Winds from the west bring the rains October to April. Fortunately, cool winds blow from the northwest in the summer. Sometimes the blistering sirocco wind comes from the desert on the east.

Remember that you are making a pilgrimage as you study. You have now arrived at a land that is going to be your home for a considerable period of time. It therefore behooves you to become well acquainted with this home. The names of some of its parts are already familiar to you; other names may seem strange.

> *Make careful use of the map on p. 87 and locate on it every place mentioned in the body of the text.*

From time to time you will want to return to the map and refresh your memory. The main parts of this land are four: the Plateau of Transjordan, the Jordan Valley, the Hill Country, and the Coastal Plain. The Plateau of Transjordan is subdivided into five areas (Bashan, Gilead, Ammon, Moab, and Edom) by the four streams (the Yarmuk, the Jabbok, the Arnon, and the Zered). Bashan is famous for its grain; Gilead for its water supply; Ammon for its hostility to Israel; Moab as the home of Ruth, the ancestress of David and Jesus; and Edom as the rock fortress controlling trade from the desert to the west.

The Jordan Valley is a part of the great geological depression that extends from the plain between the Lebanons and Anti-Lebanons in the north, through Lake Huleh, the Sea of Galilee, the Dead Sea, the Arabah, and the Red Sea, to Africa.

The Hill Country is the central part of Palestine west of the Jordan, extending from Dan to Beer-sheba. It is made up of three sections: Galilee, Samaria, and Judah. The word "Galilee" comes from two Hebrew words meaning "the circle of the Gentiles." Indeed it is an appropriate name, since that area had close association with Gentiles from the days of the settlement by Israel. At its lower end, its hills are interrupted by the Plain of Esdraelon (or Jezreel). In this same general area are the River Kishon, celebrated in the Song of Deborah (Judg. 5:21); Mount Carmel, where Elijah contended with the prophets of Baal (1 Kings 18); and Megiddo, from which the name Armageddon ("Mount of Megiddo") is derived (Rev. 16:16).

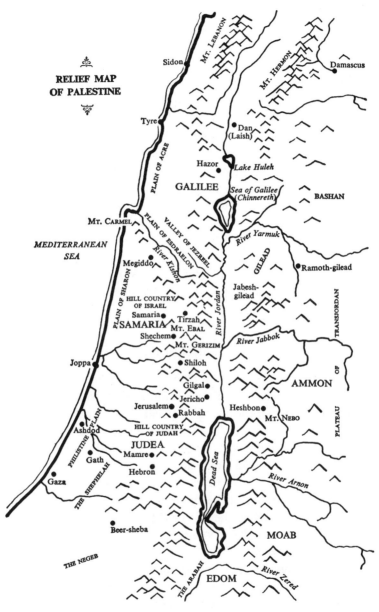

RELIEF MAP
OF PALESTINE

Within the borders of Samaria were such well-known cities as Tirzah, Samaria, Shechem, Shiloh, and Beth-shan. Its most famous mountains are Mount Ebal and Mount Gerizim, between which ran the important north-south pass. In the Old Testament period, Samaria was chiefly associated with the Northern Kingdom of Israel.

Within Judah were Jericho, Jerusalem, Bethlehem, Hebron, Beersheba, and other famous places. The eastern part of Judah is desert, while the western Shephelah or Lowland is fertile. In a sense, Judah included the Negeb, or Southland, between Beer-sheba and Kadesh-barnea. Living in the Negeb was precarious because the water supply was very limited.

The Coastal Plain along the Mediterranean is composed of three smaller plains: the Plain of Acre, north of Mount Carmel; the Plain of Sharon, between Mount Carmel and Joppa; and the Philistine Plain, south of Joppa. For various reasons (mainly Philistine occupation) the Coastal Plain did not play as large a role in the life of the people of God as did the Hill Country.

In contrast to the desert much of the land of Palestine could be described as "a land flowing with milk and honey."

The location of Palestine was not an insignificant factor in Israel's faith and life. It served as a bridge between Egypt and the great empires and cultures to the north and east. Comparatively speaking, Israel was never powerful except in the days of David and Solomon. Undoubtedly this weakness was an occasion for God's revelation of divine grace (compare 1 Cor. 1:26–29).

## The Conquest of the Land

Kadesh-barnea was one of the chief places of Israel's sojourn in the period of the wilderness wanderings. From Kadesh some of the Israelites made an abortive attempt to invade Canaan. Therefore, Moses led Israel by a circuitous route through Transjordan. Because he was refused passage through Edom and Moab, he and his people bypassed these kingdoms. However, the Israelites defeated Sihon, king of the Amorites, and Og, the king of Bashan. The territory of these kings was assigned to Reuben, Gad, and the half-tribe of Manasseh (Deut. 29:8; Josh. 12:6; 13:15–33). After addressing the people, Moses died, and Joshua became their new commander, under whom the conquest of western Canaan was undertaken.

The book of Joshua records this conquest (chaps. 1–12), the division of the land (chaps. 13–21), and the last days of Joshua (chaps. 22–24). It is widely held that Deuteronomy gives the basic interpretation of the conquest and settlement of Canaan, and that the Former Prophets (Joshua, Judges, Samuel, and Kings) were compiled and edited from the Deuteronomic point of view. According to this point of view God gave the land to Israel, but Israel had to obey the law of God to continue to possess the land. Obedience to God issues in blessing; disobedience, in curse.

*Before reading any further in this book, pick up your Bible and read Joshua, chapters 1–12, and Judges, chapter 1. Take four sheets of notebook paper and write one of the following topics at the head of each sheet: (1) A Comparison of Joshua 1–12 with Judges 1, (2) The Strategy of Joshua's Conquest, (3) Joshua as a Second Moses, and (4) Theological Issues Involved in the Conquest. As you encounter material bearing on any one of these topics, record it on the proper sheet.*

*What kind of likenesses and differences do you find between the narrative of the conquest in Joshua and that in Judges? How do you account for the differences?*

*What were Joshua's qualifications as a military strategist? A hint concerning number 3 above is found in the fact that Moses led his people across the Red Sea and Joshua led them across the Jordan River. Can you list other parallels?*

*How do you relate God's command to destroy the Canaanites to your understanding of the Christian faith?*

*After you have made your own independent study, read what is said below. Some of the questions that have been raised will be treated briefly. We may not agree at every point, but such agreement is not necessary.*

Joshua 1–12 is often referred to as an idealized account of the conquest, and Judges 1 is often called a realistic account. According to the former account, Joshua employed a threefold strategy in conquering the land: (1) a campaign against the central Hill Country where the Canaanites were weakest, (2) a campaign against the southern Amorite league, and (3) finally a campaign in the north. As one reads these chapters the impression is gained that Canaan was well under Israelite control when Joshua had finished his campaigns. On the other hand, Judges 1 calls attention repeatedly to the fact that the Canaanites were not driven out. What does all of this mean?

First of all, it should be noted that the book of Joshua also recognizes the incompleteness of the conquest in the days of Joshua (see 15:63; 16:10; 17:12, 18). Furthermore, the Gibeonites, through a stratagem, secured the protection of Joshua (Josh. 9). Nevertheless, archaeological excavations at such sites as Debir, Lachish, and Hazor have produced evidence of destruction that might coincide with the reports associated with Joshua's violent invasion of Canaan in the thirteenth century B.C.E. It seems clear from Joshua 1–12 that Joshua was seen as the first great leader in the conquest. As such he was regarded as the true conqueror of the land as a whole.

There is a problem associated with the capture and destruction of Ai (Josh. 7 and 8). Excavations indicate that this site was destroyed before the time of Abraham, not in the time of Joshua. Several explanations have been offered, but the most plausible is that of W. F. Albright.[2] He suggests that, after the destruction of Ai about 2200 B.C.E., its inhabitants built Bethel at a distance of only one and a half miles away. Bethel, composed of the people from Ai, was destroyed by Joshua in the thirteenth century (compare Judg. 1:22–26 ). Excavation shows that Bethel was built about 2200 B.C.E. and that it was destroyed in the thirteenth century.

But more significant than the historical problems of the book of Joshua are the theological issues of the conquest. God's gift and demand go together. We read in Joshua 1:2, "My servant Moses is dead. Now proceed to cross the Jordan, you and all this people, *into the land that I am giving to them.*" In verse 6 we read, "Be strong and courageous; for *you shall put this people in possession of the land* that I swore to their ancestors to give them." God still comes to us with gift and demand. Christ is both Savior (gift) and Lord (demand).

Nevertheless, the question still arises: How are we to understand the blood, sweat, and tears of the conquest in relation to the teaching of Jesus? You have just read the first twelve chapters of the book of Joshua.

> *Now read from the Sermon on the Mount, Matthew 5:38–48. Does the reading of these two passages together disturb you in any way?*

It has disturbed many people. Here are some thoughts on the subject, offered as a stimulus to you in your own wrestling with the ethical issues raised by your study.

1. The fullness of God's revelation was not made in Joshua's day. Jesus Christ had not come in the flesh. The times were hard, and any people God might have chosen would have been rough and rugged. Israel was no polished pearl, having just come out of slavery. Yet God did not wait for a people to become perfect before selecting the instrument of the divine redemptive purpose. If God had waited for such an attainment, there would have been no gospel to preach. God used the people available in the actual historical process. In Deuteronomy 9:4 Israel is warned with stark clarity against self-righteousness: "When the LORD your God thrusts them [the Anakim] out before you, do not say to yourself, 'It is because of my righteousness that the LORD has brought me in to occupy this land.'"

Indeed, the writer goes on to say that the gift of the land to Israel is rooted in the wickedness of the nations already living in the land and in God's promise to the ancestors.

2. It is impossible for us to remake the history of the past according to contemporary tastes and perspectives. In light of the wars and atrocities of the twentieth century, we are in no position to say that if we had been there things would have been different.

3. The election of a people involved the election of a land. In that day, peoples expected one another to fight for land. For us to expect Israel to secure a land peacefully would be as anachronistic as expecting Joshua to use a computer. If we are to understand biblical revelation, we must have respect for the integrity of the historical process. Revelation comes through the raw material of human history. In other words, God works through the tragic experiences of life as well as through those that are more pleasant.

4. Not only did God judge the nations of Canaan for their wickedness; God also judged the Israelites for their sins. Much of the Old Testament dwells on Israel's sin and God's judgment.

5. The Promised Land is inextricably bound up with the revelation of God as the Maker and Keeper of promises. Promise and the keeping of promises constitute a basic rhythm of the divine economy.

6. The Canaanites were never actually annihilated. In retrospect the Deuteronomic editors wished that had been the case so that Israel would not have been tempted and succumbed to idolatry, thereby losing their right to the land. The "exceptions" to such destruction mentioned in both Joshua and Judges warn against sweeping claims about the savagery of ancient Israel or the character of God.

## The Renewal of the Covenant

*The renewal of the covenant at Shechem (Josh. 24; compare 8:30–35) was a momentous occasion in the life of Israel. Read Joshua 24 and list in your notebook the mighty acts of God found in this confession of faith.*

The league of twelve tribes had its roots in the covenant at Sinai. But the covenant was renewed at Shechem after the entrance into western Canaan under the leadership of Joshua. In early Israel it is probable that the covenant was renewed at the annually recurring festival at Shiloh (Judg. 21:19; 1 Sam. 1:3, 21), where the Ark of the Covenant became enshrined. It is also probable that such renewal took place at all festal celebrations.

The covenant at Shechem, however, was of special importance. It is highly likely that groups previously unaligned with those who entered the land under Joshua joined the alliance at this time. There is no evidence that Joshua had to fight in the Shechem area, for instance. This suggests that relatives and friends willing for Joshua to come in lived there (perhaps some of the Habiru). Moreover, Shechem was an ancient religious site and therefore an appropriate place for a ceremony of covenant renewal. All of these things point to the conclusion that the full, twelve-tribe confederacy was established at Shechem. The participating groups were either initiated into, or confirmed in, the covenant community.

This confederacy did not have a central government but was definitely a covenant society, held together by its faith in the LORD. In addition to Joshua, its leaders included patriarchal elders, priests, and later the judges. Their life was governed by the covenant law.

With this background we look more directly at Joshua 24. First, Joshua rehearses the history of God's people from the ancestors to his own time in terms of the mighty acts of God. He stresses the acquisition of the land as a gift from God: "I gave you a land on which you had not labored, and towns which you had not built, and you live in them; you eat the fruit of vineyards and oliveyards that you did not plant" (v. 13). As the covenant made at Mount Sinai was based on the grace of God in the exodus deliverance, so the Shechem covenant is based on God's grace in the gift of the land. And as the Sinaitic covenant placed requirements on the people, so the covenant at Shechem calls for decision and commitment. Joshua's famous words have not lost their original power: "Choose this day whom you will serve . . . as for me and my household, we will serve the LORD" (v. 15). The rhythm of gift and demand is continued. The people respond with a promise of undivided loyalty to the LORD. And the covenant is sealed by the recording of its terms in the book of God's law and by the erection of a memorial stone.

On what occasions do we as the covenant community participate in ceremonies of covenant renewal? What part does the pattern of gift and demand have in these ceremonies? Do you think of ways in which such occasions may be enriched?

## The Gift of the Judges

God not only gave the people a land but also gave them judges. We read in Judges 2:16—"Then the LORD raised up judges, who delivered them out of the power of those who plundered them." Only one of the Old

Testament confessions of faith (Neh. 9:27) includes God's gift of the judges in the list of God's mighty acts. But Paul mentions them in his sermon at Antioch of Pisidia, saying, "He gave them judges until the time of the prophet Samuel" (see Acts 13:16–20). Though at least some of the judges arbitrated disputes (Judg. 4:4–5), the judges were primarily deliverers, who were specially endowed by the Spirit of God to meet emergency situations. Therefore they are often referred to as charismatic leaders, since the Greek word *charisma* means "gift."

## The Testing of Israel

The book of Judges is divided into three chief divisions: further conquest and settlement of Canaan (1:1–2:5), sketches of the judges (2:6–16:31), and an appendix concerning Dan and the war with Benjamin (17:1–21:25). We have already considered most of the first division in relation to Joshua 1–12. We now begin our study of the second.

*At this point read Judges 2:1–3:6 to get the perspective of the conflict between the religion of Israel and the religion of Canaan.*

In the wilderness the Israelites had been taught the high morality of the Mosaic faith, born of historical revelation. They were now living in the midst of an agricultural people whose religion centered in fertility and the changing of the cycles of nature. Furthermore, after the older generation died out, "another generation grew up after them, who did not know the LORD or the work that he had done for Israel" (Judg. 2:10). In other words, every new generation needs to be evangelized and educated. Israel's neighbors were a test repeatedly failed (Judg. 2:22–23; 3:1, 4). Indeed, the Israelites forgot the LORD, served the Baals and Ashtaroth, and intermarried with their pagan associates. This meant compromise and syncretism (that is, the introduction of aspects of Canaanite religion into Israel's religion).

A brief description of Canaanite religion is a help in understanding Israel's predicament. El was the head of the Canaanite pantheon of so-called gods and goddesses, and Asherah was his wife (see 1 Kings 18:19). Baal, the son of El and Asherah, was the god of rain and vegetation. In Judges 2:11 he is referred to in the plural, but in verse 13 (Hebrew text) he is referred to in the singular. Such variation in number is typical. The Canaanite priests regarded Baal as one, but his representations at local sanctuaries were called Baals. Anath, the goddess of love and war, was the wife of Baal. But in other texts Astarte, the goddess of fertility, is Baal's consort. In character and function Anath is so similar to Astarte, sometimes called Ashtoreth in the Old Testament, that the two seem to be identified with each other. Astartes (Judg. 2:13) is the plural form of Astarte (Ashtoreth).

Canaanite religion was characterized by a myth and ritual whose purpose it was to ensure fertility of family, flock, and field. It was thought that through sex relations between Baal and Anath the fertility of nature was revived. It was also thought that men and women could contribute to this revival by participating in the dramatization of the myth of Baal's loves and wars. This involved the institution of sacred prostitution. The Canaanites believed that they could bring about fertility by means of imitative magic. They also believed that Mot (Death) killed Baal each year, thereby causing the summer drought; and that Anath later killed Mot and caused Baal to be resurrected from the dead. With the sexual reunion of Baal and Anath in the fall, the cycle of fertility was thought to begin all over again.

Canaanite religion was similar to other ancient forms of naturalistic polytheism. It is easy to see how Baalism became a stumbling block to many Israelites through its appeal to fertility and sex desire. For years to come, the prophets were to wage a war against various forms of Baal worship. They were not willing to prostitute their faith by combining it with Baalism. Baalism was focused on the ever recurring cycles of nature; Israel's faith, on the nonrepeatable events of history. While Israel learned valuable lessons from the Canaanites in language, writing, literary forms, agriculture, pottery making, and other things, Canaanite polytheism and sexual practices provided a deadly contamination.

While we do not deliberately and formally worship more than one God as the Canaanites did, would it not be fair to say that our own culture is also polytheistic—that is, that we give our real allegiance to various things in our culture? For example, does not the overemphasis on sex in our culture have much of the same degrading effect as the concern given to sex in Canaan? Are there things that you and your class might do to correct unwholesome situations in your own community? Can you think of other aspects of our culture that pose a threat to Christian faith and life? What remedies do you propose?

## The God-given Deliverers

In the days of the Judges there was no one great leader such as Moses or Joshua. Moses had been the great pioneer, and Joshua had lived and led his people in the afterglow of the great Moses. But in the days of the

Judges there was not only no Moses or Joshua, "there was no king in Israel; all the people did what was right in their own eyes" (Judg. 17:6; 21:25). It was a period of anarchy and degeneration. Even a quick reading of Judges 17–21 will confirm this impression. Yet the judges were better than no leadership at all. The book of Ruth reminds, however, that anarchy was not total.

The period of the Judges lasted from about 1225 to 1050 B.C.E. For the most part the work of the particular judges was localized, and some of the judges worked in different areas simultaneously. Israel had no central government. Shiloh was the central religious shrine. The Israelites were undergoing military conflict and religious conflict at the same time.

Altogether there are sketches of twelve judges, if Deborah and Barak are reckoned as one. Abimelech, included in the list below, is often counted as a petty king rather than as a judge. Obviously several of the sketches are very brief.

> *As you read Judges 3:7–16:31, make a record in the words of the biblical text itself of the "philosophy" of history presented there. Compare it with Proverbs 14:34.*
>
> *Do you regard this as the total view of history found in the Bible, or would you supplement it from other parts of the Bible?*

Here is a list of the judges and the adversaries against whom they fought:

| JUDGES | | ADVERSARIES |
|---|---|---|
| Othniel | 3:7–11 | Cushan-rishathaim of Mesopotamia |
| Ehud | 3:12–30 | Eglon of Moab |
| Shamgar | 3:31 (5:6) | Philistines |
| Deborah and Barak | 4:1–5:31 | Jabin and Sisera of Canaan |
| Gideon | 6:1–8:32 | Midianites |
| Abimelech | 8:33–9:57 | His own people |
| Tola | 10:1–2 | Unnamed |
| Jair | 10:3–5 | Unnamed |
| Jephthah | 10:6–12:7 | Ammonites |
| Ibzan | 12:8–10 | Unnamed |
| Elon | 12:11–12 | Unnamed |
| Abdon | 12:13–15 | Unnamed |
| Samson | 13:2–16:31 | Philistines |

At the very outset of the sketch of Othniel, "the Baals and the Asherahs" (plural of Asherah) are mentioned. Asheroth is a plural form of Asherah. Just as Baal was represented by a stone pillar in various places, so Asherah was represented by a sacred tree or image. In other words, Israelite religion was being contaminated with Baalism.

The only time the Canaanites are specifically named as the adversary of a judge of Israel is in the accounts of Deborah and Barak.

*Compare the prose account (chap. 4) with the poetic account (chap. 5).*

It is usually agreed that the Song of Deborah is an eyewitness record of the battle in the famous Plain of Jezreel near Megiddo, where so many battles of history were yet to be fought. God's action in the battle is indicated by the reference to the storm (Judg. 5:20–21), which presumably caused the chariots of Sisera to bog down in the mud. The orientation of the song is found in the recollection of the revelation at Sinai (vv. 4–5). The account of Gideon (chaps. 6–8) presents Israel's struggle with Baalism and with the notion of monarchy as practiced by Israel's neighbors.

*How many different kinds of evidence can you find in the sketch of Gideon for the conflict between the religion of the Hebrews and Baalism?*

*In what different ways are the wonderful deeds of God accented?*

*Do you see anything in the story to suggest psychological warfare?*

Gideon's people made this request: "Rule over us, you and your son and your grandson also" (8:22). But Gideon replied, "I will not rule over you, and my son will not rule over you; the LORD will rule over you" (8:23). In other words, Gideon thought that a monarchy would be a denial of the Kingship of God.

*How is the story of Abimelech (chap. 9) related to the proposed kingship of Gideon?*

*What is the point of Jotham's fable?*

*How is the activity of God related in the Abimelech narrative?*

*Does Jephthah's vow remind you of a particular patriarchal narrative? How do you react to this vow and its fulfillment? What is the positive element in the incident?*

*Note the origin of our expression "shibboleth" (12:1–6).*

Samson (chaps. 13–16) was destined before birth to be a Nazirite, that is, one who abstained from alcoholic beverages, refused to cut his hair, did not touch dead bodies, and did not eat unclean food. One could be either a temporary or a lifelong Nazirite. Samson belonged to the latter category. Indeed his mother observed the Nazirite regulations while she carried the promised child in her womb. Probably the combination of asceticism with other aspects of Samson's life seems odd to many in our time. But we must remember the kind of society in which Samson lived and must never forget the strange combinations within ourselves. The marvel is that God chooses to use any of us.

# The House of David

$D$own through the centuries Jews and Christians have always looked at God's choice of King David as one of the mighty acts of God. For all of his faults David was seen by later generations as "a man after God's own heart." The memory of his kingdom became a symbol of the promised kingdom of God. The title of this chapter is based on 2 Samuel 7:11. David wanted to build a house for God, but instead God promised to make David a house. In his address to David, Nathan the prophet said, "Moreover the LORD declares to you that the LORD will make you a house." David used the word "house" in the sense of a place of worship; Nathan used it in the sense of a dynasty, that is, the line of kings descended from David. Here we are concerned with the establishment of the Davidic dynasty.

The earliest of Israel's confessions of faith (such as Deut. 26:5–11 and Josh. 24) were formulated before the time of David and therefore do not mention him. However, later recitals of God's covenant acts of redemption do. For example, in Psalm 78:70–72 we read:

> He chose his servant David,
>     and took him from the sheepfolds;
> from tending the nursing ewes he brought him
>     to be the shepherd of his people Jacob,
>     of Israel, his inheritance.
> With upright heart he tended them,
>     and guided them with skillful hand.

In his sermon at Antioch of Pisidia, Paul included these words:

After that he gave them judges until the time of the prophet Samuel. Then they asked for a king; and God gave them Saul son of Kish, a man of the tribe of Benjamin, who reigned for forty years. When he had removed him, he made David their king. In his testimony about him he said, "I have found David, son of Jesse, to be a man after my heart, who will carry out all my wishes." Of this man's posterity God has brought to Israel a Savior, Jesus, as he promised. (Acts 13:20–23)

These words of Paul summarize the history of the messianic hope from the covenant with David (2 Sam. 7) to its manifestation in Jesus Christ. Just as God had given Israel the Promised Land, so God gave them the house of David.

In order to enter more fully into the meaning of this gift, we must study the lives of Samuel, Saul, David, and Solomon. The accounts of these men are found in 1 and 2 Samuel and 1 Kings 1–11. Second Samuel 9–20 and 1 Kings 1:1–2:12 are usually called "the Court History of David," and are regarded as being very similar to present-day history writing. It is certainly true that these chapters are as candid as a camera.

## Samuel, Leader of Many Talents

Samuel was a leader of many talents. Indeed the times in which he lived called for such a leader. It was a period of transition from an old order to a new. Israel had been living as a tribal confederacy without a strong central government, yet united as the covenant people of the LORD, with Shiloh as the chief sanctuary. But soon Israel was to experience both the blessings and the curses of a monarchy. Samuel stood in the gap between the past and the future, and fulfilled the ministries of judge, prophet, and priest. He has been called the last of the judges and the first of the prophets after Moses.

### Samuel's Birth and Call (1 Sam. 1:1–3:21)

Samuel was born in answer to prayer and, like Samson, was dedicated before birth to be a Nazirite. Moreover, he was brought up as the servant of the old priest Eli at Shiloh. Eli's sons, Hophni and Phinehas, habitually behaved in a wicked manner at the sanctuary. It was in this situation that Samuel received the dramatic call of God.

*Read 1 Samuel 3:1–21 with the following questions in mind:*

*1. What did his call mean to Samuel himself?*

*2. What did it mean to Eli?*

*3. What did it mean to Israel?*

*4. What does it mean to us?*

Up to this time Samuel's duties as assistant to Eli had been primarily those of a priestly nature. But the content of chapter 3 makes it clear that Samuel was now being called also to the prophetic ministry. The very first verse of the chapter gives the key for understanding what follows: "The word of the LORD was *rare* in those days; visions were not widespread." That is, God's word announced by a prophet was scarce in those days. And into this spiritual desert, God called Samuel. Another clue to the prophetic nature of the call is found in verse 7: "Now Samuel did not yet know the LORD, and the word of the LORD had not yet been revealed to him." Of course Samuel could not have ministered to the LORD under Eli without knowing something about God. But up to this point in his experience he had not known the LORD in the intimacy of the prophetic word. The response that Eli counseled the young Samuel to make to God's call is profound: "Speak, LORD, for your servant is listening." The word "listening" means "to give serious attention to." This Samuel did not only on this occasion but throughout his ministry. As in the case of so many prophets who were to follow Samuel, the word of the LORD was one of judgment. The house of Eli must be punished for blasphemy. From that time Samuel began to be known throughout Israel as the man with an authentic word from God.

## The Philistine Menace (1 Sam. 4:1–7:2)

The Philistines played a major role in the area throughout the lifetimes of Samuel, Saul, and David. They settled along the southwestern coast of Palestine in the twelfth century and had already become a threat to Israel in the period of the Judges. The tribe of Dan had been forced to move north on their account, and it was against them that Samson did battle. They were organized in what has been called a "pentapolis," or league of five cities. The leaders of these cities were known as "the lords of the Philistines" (1 Sam. 7:7), and they operated with greater solidarity and military effectiveness than the Canaanites. Furthermore, they maintained military bases here and there in the land. Because of them the populace of Israel was in constant jeopardy.

Since the Ark of the Covenant was the visible manifestation of the presence of God in the midst of the people, the Israelites thought it would help them if it was brought into their camp as they prepared to engage their enemy. But it was captured by the Philistines, and Hophni and Phinehas, the sons of Eli, were slain. After the Ark was placed in the temple of the Philistine god Dagon, the statue of Dagon fell down and was broken. Moreover, the Philistines were smitten with a pestilence, perhaps the bubonic plague. Therefore, in fear they returned the Ark to Israel, and it was kept at Kiriath-jearim until David carried it to Jerusalem. Evidently the Philistines had destroyed the sanctuary where it had resided at Shiloh (compare Jer. 7:12; 26:6).

## Samuel as Prophet, Priest, and Judge (1 Sam. 7:3–17)

In these few verses Samuel's threefold ministry as prophet, priest, and judge is summarized. As prophet, he warned the people against Baalism. As priest, he interceded for them and offered sacrifice on their behalf, though intercession was also a prophetic function. As judge, he made a yearly circuit to Bethel, Gilgal, and Mizpah, settling disputes among the people. His home was at Ramah.

## The People's Demand for a King (1 Sam. 8:1–22)

Apparently Samuel had planned for his sons to carry on his work as judge. In fact, they were already serving as judges in Beer-sheba. Yet they did not walk in the ways of their father, "but turned aside after gains; they took bribes and perverted justice."

The elders of Israel as representatives of the people came to Samuel at Ramah and requested a king. The reasons for the request may be summarized as follows: (1) Samuel is getting old. (2) His sons are dishonest. (3) We want to be "like other nations." (4) We need a king to govern us and fight our battles for us.

> *What part does the desire to be like others play in our lives today? For example, do your children ever say to you, "Everybody does it"? How do you cope with such a statement?*

No doubt one of the major concerns of the elders and their people was the constant threat of the Philistines and other enemies. They knew that the Philistines were besting them. We are told that the demand for a king displeased Samuel, but that God instructed him to acquiesce in the request, with a warning that a centralized government would reduce some of their liberties.

> *Do your sympathies lie with the people or with Samuel?*

## Saul, the First King of Israel

Saul of Benjamin, son of Kish, was Israel's first king. He was the kind of person who calls forth both admiration and sympathy. His beginning was promising, but his end was tragic.

### Saul's Accession to the Throne (1 Sam. 9:1–12:25)

*Read 1 Samuel, chapters 8, 9, and 10. We have already noted that according to chapter 8 Samuel did not approve of the people's request for a king. In 9:1–10:16 we find the record of how Samuel and Saul were brought together by God and how Saul was anointed king by Samuel. Here there is no hint of Samuel's disapproval. The Spirit of God comes upon Saul, marking him as a charismatic leader like the judges before him. But then in 10:17–27 Samuel again expresses his disapproval of the kingship, saying, "But today you have rejected your God, who saves you from all your calamities and your distresses; and you have said, 'No! but set a king over us' " (compare 12:17). Then Saul is selected by lot, and Samuel explains to the people the rights and duties of the kingship. After reading chapters 8 through 10, how do you account for the positive and negative attitudes toward the kingship expressed in them?*

Saul's status as king was really confirmed in the eyes of the people by his action in behalf of the citizens of Jabesh-gilead (1 Sam. 11:1–15). Nahash, the leader of the Ammonites, threatened to gouge out the right eye of every man of Jabesh-gilead. When the news of this threat reached Saul, he summoned the men of Israel and roundly defeated the Ammonites. Saul's kingship was renewed at Gilgal.

### Saul's Rejection by Samuel (1 Sam. 13:1–15:35)

There was hard fighting against the Philistines throughout the days of Saul, and Saul's son Jonathan was of great aid to his father. Excavation of Saul's palace-fortress at Gibeah has revealed a two-storied structure of considerable size but with no evidence of luxury.

The first breach between Samuel and Saul seems to have taken place at Gilgal, when Saul offered sacrifice because Samuel was late in arriving and the Philistines were apparently ready to join battle (1 Sam. 13:8–15). But the real rejection of the king by the prophet must be associated with Israel's war against the Amalekites (1 Sam. 15:1–35).

*Read chapter 15 very carefully, for it deals with the subject of holy war, a subject that is little understood in our day.*

The Amalekites were inveterate enemies of Israel (Exod. 17:8–16; Deut. 25:17–19; Judg. 6:33; 7:12). Samuel, therefore, gave Saul the command to wage holy war on them. Such a war was regarded as a religious obligation and involved placing the enemies and their possessions under the ban of complete destruction: "Now go and attack Amalek, and utterly destroy all that they have; do not spare them, but kill both man and woman, child and infant, ox and sheep, camel and donkey" (1 Sam. 15:3). Both persons and things were regarded as devoted to the LORD and could not therefore be kept by the Israelites. Because in disobedience Saul let his people keep the best of the booty and did not put Agag, the king of the Amalekites, to death, Samuel pronounced the sentence of the LORD's rejection on Saul and hewed Agag in pieces.

On the basis of his own understanding of the meaning of holy war Saul said to Samuel, "I have sinned; for I have transgressed the commandment of the LORD and your words." This conception did not characterize all the wars of Israel. But we must try to understand such a conception in its own setting. Furthermore, God ruled and overruled in that day just as in this. From the time of his breach with Samuel, Saul became increasingly a deeply disturbed man. Can you imagine what it would be like to feel that you had been rejected by your best friend and by your God?

## Saul's Relation to David (1 Sam. 16:1–31:13)

"Samuel grieved over Saul," and this probably means that there were elements in the relationship between these two men about which the record is silent. Perhaps Saul's psychological condition made real communication and reconciliation between them impossible. In any case, Samuel anointed the shepherd lad David to be the shepherd king of Israel, "and the spirit of the LORD came mightily upon David from that day forward" (1 Sam. 16:13). David in turn became a charismatic leader, that is, one endowed by the gift of God's Spirit to do the job to which he had been appointed.

On the other hand, "the spirit of the LORD departed from Saul, and an evil spirit from the LORD tormented him" (1 Sam. 16:14). This means that Saul lost the charismatic gift of leadership that had earlier characterized him. When the Bible says that God sent "an evil spirit" on Saul, it means that even Saul's deep depression, perhaps to the point of madness, was not the product of chance.

All of us remember how the music of David soothed Saul's troubled mind and how he met the giant Goliath. When Saul was returning from battle with the Philistines, the women of Israel sang:

> "Saul has killed his thousands,
> and David his ten thousands."
> (1 Sam. 18:7)

Such an unflattering comparison only increased Saul's sense of insecurity and made him jealous of David. Yet David became Saul's son-in-law by his marriage to Michal. Nevertheless, from this point on Saul attempted to kill David, though on occasion he was friendly to him. While David had opportunity to kill Saul, he refused to harm the LORD's anointed.

Saul's son Jonathan was as emotionally stable as his father was unstable. He and David had made a covenant (1 Sam. 18:1–5), and their friendship was uncommon. Caught between his loyalty to his father and his loyalty to David, Jonathan was essentially faithful to both. In humility and fidelity he was without peer among his contemporaries.

For some time David and his bodyguards lived the life of outlaws in flight from Saul, and David was a shrewd outlaw indeed. Saul took Michal from him and gave her to another, but David married Ahinoam of Jezreel, and Abigail, the widow of Nabal. To escape the hand of Saul, David eventually became a vassal of the Philistines under Achish, king of Gath. In fact, Achish gave David the town of Ziklag. Fortunately David was not put in a position of being required to fight against his own people (1 Sam. 29). As a good diplomat he kept the lines of communication open between himself and the elders of Judah. For example, when he defeated the Amalekites, he sent booty to his friends in Judah (1 Sam. 30).

Saul's last days were tragic indeed. Depressed by his sense of rejection, jealous of the winsome David, and harassed by the warring Philistines, he resorted to the medium at Endor, begging her to call up the shade of the dead Samuel. But the word of the medium only depressed him the more. He went out from her to face the Philistines on Mount Gilboa with the word of doom ringing in his ears. And on Gilboa his army was defeated, three of his sons (including Jonathan) were slain, and he himself was wounded. Rather than die at the hands of the Philistines, he took his own life. The Philistines cut off his head and hung his body and the bodies of his sons on the wall of Beth-shan. But the men of Jabesh-gilead, whom Saul had at the outset of his career saved from the Ammonites, took the bodies of Saul and his sons to Jabesh and there cremated their bodies and buried the remains (1 Sam. 31:12–13).

*What do you feel is the central message of Saul's life?*

*Why should the Christian's attitude be negative toward spiritualism, fortune-telling, and astrology?*

## David, the Founder
## of a City and a House

### David as King of Judah (2 Sam. 1:1–4:12)

An Amalekite reported the death of Saul and Jonathan to David in Ziklag. In order to curry favor with David he claimed to have killed Saul at Saul's request. But David had the Amalekite executed for daring to kill the LORD's anointed. There is every reason to believe that David's lament over Saul and Jonathan was genuine. In spite of Saul's repeated hostility, David had never been willing to harm him. His covenant with Jonathan remained in force, and he admired the contributions of this father and son to Israel:

> Saul and Jonathan, beloved and lovely!
>   In life and in death they were not divided;
> they were swifter than eagles,
>   they were stronger than lions.
>
> (2 Sam. 1:23)

"The Book of Jashar" (2 Sam. 1:18) is the literary source from which the lament was quoted. This is one of a few notations in the Bible that roughly correspond to the modern system of footnoting.

David went to Hebron of ancestral fame and was there anointed king over the house of Judah. At once he demonstrated political diplomacy in seeking to cultivate the men of Jabesh-gilead, who had been devoted friends of Saul. Abner, who had been the commander in chief of Saul's army, attempted to establish a dynasty of Saul by making Saul's son Ishbosheth (Eshbaal) king over all the tribes except Judah, with headquarters on the east side of the Jordan at Mahanaim. Because there was no precedent in Israel for the succession of kings, a period of fighting, discord, political intrigue, and murder followed, culminating in the death of Saul's son Ishbosheth (Eshbaal).

### David as King of All Israel (2 Sam. 5:1–8:18)

After David had reigned over Judah for several years from Hebron, he was invited to become the shepherd of all Israel. If he had kept Hebron as his capital or had selected another capital in Judah, the northern tribes would have been jealous. On the other hand, if he had selected a city in the north for his capital, the Judeans would have been jealous. Therefore, he set about to capture Jerusalem (or Jebus), which came as close to being a neutral city as there was available. The Jebusites were so confident that their stronghold was impregnable that they chided David as he made preparations for his attack, saying, "You will not come in here, even the blind and the lame will turn you back" (2 Sam. 5:6). David, however, pulled a surprise attack by sending his men up a water shaft into the city.

After taking the stronghold David named it the city of David, or to use George Adam Smith's word, "David's-Burgh." In a sense, the city was David's personal property, for he took it with his own personal troops. When he captured it, it "was shaped somewhat like a gigantic human footprint about 1250 feet long and 400 wide" ,and contained no more than eight acres.[1] Archaeologists have clearly identified David's-Burgh and have excavated a part of the Jebusite wall and a Jebusite gate. David strengthened the fortress, and people lived outside as well as inside its walls. Over the years this small fortress was expanded into a great city.

The Philistines, whose vassal David had once been, now realized that as king of all Israel he was a threat to their power. They attacked. David defeated them as they had never been defeated before. In fact, he eventually brought under his control an empire extending from the Euphrates in the north to Ezion-geber in the south and including the Transjordanian kingdoms of Ammon, Moab, and Edom (see 2 Sam. 8).

Jerusalem was to be the religious as well as the political capital of David's empire, for David brought the Ark of the Covenant there. But this was not accomplished without difficulty.

*Read 2 Samuel 6:1–23 carefully.*

It is clear that David and some of his men were in process of removing the Ark from Baale-judah (probably Kiriath-jearim; see 1 Sam. 7:2) and that Uzzah died. Precisely what Uzzah did is not clear in the Hebrew text. Various explanations have been given as to why he died. Perhaps the most popular is the psychological one: Among the early Israelites holiness was thought of as a quasi-physical reality that carried the potentiality, so to speak, of "electrocution." This means that, because Uzzah thought he would die by touching the Holy Ark, he actually died. How do you explain Uzzah's death?

In any case, David's plans were temporarily interrupted, and the Ark was left in the house of Obed-edom for three months. When David did bring it to Jerusalem with great rejoicing, he girded himself in a linen ephod, a priestly garment, and performed the priestly functions of offering sacrifices and blessing the people. In other words, he regarded himself as a priestly king. From David's day, Jerusalem was to play a central role in the life of the people of God, and eventually it was to become the symbol of the Eternal City of God (see Rev. 21:1–22:5). In the final analysis we must say, God not only chose a people and a land, but also a city.

God established the dynasty of David as well as the city of David.

> *In the judgment of many, 2 Samuel, chapter 7, contains material from different historical periods. Nonetheless, it is regarded as being of great theological importance. At this point read the chapter carefully and record in your notebook what it says to you.*

This chapter (2 Sam. 7) as it now stands maintains a much needed theological tension, which may be easily overlooked. First, there is the tension between the humanity of the prophet and the deity of God. David had built a house of cedar for himself, but the Ark of God resided in a tent. Therefore, he wanted to build a house for the Ark. Nathan said, "Go, do all that you have in mind; for the LORD is with you." But overnight the LORD corrected Nathan's first word to David. That is to say, a prophet, as a human, may be mistaken. Therefore, a prophet is subject to correction by God.

Second, there is the tension between the presence of God in the midst of the people and God's presence in the Temple (which is viewed as not yet built). Certainly we must never forget the presence of God with God's people everywhere and under all sorts of conditions. God is not confined to houses built by human hands. At the same time, church buildings perform a useful function for the people of God. One fact does not negate the other.

Third, there is the tension between the grace of God and the responsibility of the Davidic kings. Yet far greater weight is placed on the grace of God. God promised to make David a house, which means a dynasty. The building of a house of worship for God was to be left to David's son. Moreover, David's son was also, in a sense, to be God's son. For he would be God's representative before the people and the people's representative before God. All Israel was God's son, and the king of Israel embodied his people before God. This sonship to God, however, was a matter of adoption on God's part, not a matter of procreation. And the establishment of the indestructible covenant with the house of David was an act of pure grace, just as the election of Israel was in the first place. This grace is emphasized especially in David's prayer (vv. 18–29). Nevertheless, the obligation of the Davidic king is not overlooked: "When he commits iniquity, I will punish him with a rod such as mortals use, with blows inflicted by human beings."

God's covenant with David was to play a great role in the hope of Israel, for the Messiah ("anointed one") was to be known as the son of David. As people thought about David, they were led to envision the Ideal King of the future. While the kingdom of God cannot be identified with the kingdom of David, the Messiah of God's kingdom was to be known as both son of David and Son of God.

## David as a Repentant Sinner
### (2 Sam. 9:1–20:26 and 1 Kings 1:1–2:12)

Because David was a man who so often acted on the highest motives, it hurts all the more to have to face the fact of his sin. For example, in fidelity to his covenant with Jonathan, he was kind to Mephibosheth, Jonathan's son. And David's fidelity to God in the end proved to be his deliverance. Nonetheless, even someone good can do bad things as David so well demonstrates.

> *Read the account of David's sin with Bathsheba and Nathan's confrontation of David with the word of God (2 Sam. 11:2–12:23). And as you read keep the following questions in mind:*
>
> *1. How did David's sin affect him, Bathsheba, Uriah, Joab, Nathan, the house of David, the nation, and God?*
>
> *2. What does this passage teach about sin, forgiveness, and the consequences of sin?*

David committed adultery, treachery, and murder. One cannot help being impressed by the contrast between David and Uriah. After David learned that Bathsheba was with child, he did everything in his power to get Uriah to go to his home in order that he might believe that the child was his own. But Uriah remained absolutely faithful to his commitment as a soldier, namely, that he would refrain from sexual intercourse in time of battle. Therefore, David ordered Joab to put Uriah "in the forefront of the hardest fighting, and then draw back from him, that he may be struck down, and die."

"But the thing that David had done displeased the LORD, and the LORD sent Nathan to David." Nathan's story of the poor man and his one little ewe lamb is one of the most powerful allegories in literature. After David had unwittingly condemned himself, Nathan said to David, "You are the man." When Nathan had finished pronouncing the judgment of God on him, David confessed, "I have sinned against the LORD." And Nathan assured David of God's forgiveness.

David's repentance was genuine, and God forgave him. But forgiveness did not wipe out all the consequences of his sin. David was reconciled to God, but he had to bear the judgment of God. If he had not repented, the judgment would have been even heavier to bear.

> *Read the words of judgment as they are found in 2 Samuel 12:9–12.*

Not only did the baby die, but respect for David sank to a low ebb within his own family and within all Israel. His son Amnon raped his half-sister Tamar. Absalom, Tamar's full brother, murdered Amnon. Later Absalom conspired to overthrow his father David as king and almost succeeded. Yet in spite of everything David loved his rebellious son. In the battle against Absalom and his men, David ordered his three commanders (Joab, Abishai, and Ittai), "Deal gently for my sake with the young man Absalom." In spite of the king's orders, however, Joab and his armor-bearers put Absalom to death. When the sad news was brought to David, he wept, "O my son Absalom, my son, my son Absalom! Would I had died instead of you, O Absalom, my son, my son!"

Intermingled with David's family problems were various problems of state. For one thing, the emotional rift between the northern tribes and southern Judah was widening, as witnessed by the revolt of Sheba (2 Sam. 20:1–26).

The last days of David were filled with turmoil (1 Kings 1:1–2:12). He was physically so weak that he could not get warm. Again because no precedent had been established in Israel for the succession of kings, there arose among David's courtiers an Adonijah party and a Solomon party. Solomon was named his successor by David and was anointed by Zadok the priest and Nathan the prophet. In his charge to Solomon, David encouraged him to be faithful to the Law of God, to remember God's covenant with his house, and to execute certain reprisals in accord with the customs of the times (see pp. 110–11). "Then David slept with his ancestors, and was buried in the city of David."

While David built on the work of Saul, his achievements cannot be attributed to Saul. He was a shepherd lad who became the shepherd king of all Israel; and in spite of his lapses he never ceased to have a pastoral concern for his people. He was endowed with a handsome physique and a winsome personality that inspired confidence. He had the capacities of a real leader. In most situations David manifested a genuine respect for covenant loyalty and friendship. In military genius and political diplomacy few have ever equaled him. He was a devoted servant of the LORD, who recognized both prophetic and priestly values in religion. David's removal of the Ark to Jerusalem was far more than a political gesture alone. He was truly concerned about the religious life of his people. His reputation as "the sweet singer of Israel" is based on solid fact. He was a musician, poet, and psalmist.

While evidence of David's sinfulness is by no means confined to the Bathsheba incident, the biblical narrative places its emphasis at this point. Certainly the consequences of David's sin were visited to the third and fourth generations. But David's despising of the LORD (2 Sam. 12:10) was only temporary; he confessed his sin and was forgiven through the grace of God. In the long run, it was God's covenant with David and the establishment of the city of David that were to play such a significant role in the memory of God's people. The basic unity of the Bible is not to be found primarily in the inconsistent behavior of mortals but in the sovereign purpose of the Eternal God.

> *In what sense was David a man after God's own heart (1 Sam. 13:14; Acts 13:22)? If you spoke of a person today in such terms, what would you mean?*

## Solomon, a King like Other Kings

The people of Israel had informed Samuel that they wanted a king to govern them like all the nations. Although both Saul and David had been kings, it was Solomon who was most like the kings of other nations. In fact, he seems to have aped the Near Eastern despots of his time. The judges and Samuel, Saul, and David had all been charismatic leaders, selected and endowed by the Spirit for particular tasks. But Solomon succeeded to the throne as David's designated heir and reigned from 961 to 924 B.C.E. Of course, the house of David could not have been a historical reality unless there had been succession to the throne.

### Solomon's Political Housecleaning (1 Kings 2:13–46)

Modern states are familiar with political "housecleaning." In our particular situation the party that wins the election fills the jobs formerly held by the other party. In Solomon's day, members of the losing side faced more severe consequences than losing their jobs.

Adonijah, Solomon's half-brother, had made a play for the kingship, and Solomon had mercifully granted him life. But at a later time Adonijah requested Abishag, a member of the royal harem. Inasmuch as it was customary for a new king to inherit the harem of his predecessor, Solomon interpreted Adonijah's request as a continuing claim to the kingship (compare 2 Sam. 3:7; 12:8; 16:20–23) and therefore ordered his execution.

Abiathar, the priest, had supported Adonijah in his first bid for the throne. However, because Abiathar was a good friend of David and a priest, Solomon refrained from sentencing him to death. Instead he banished him to Anathoth.

Bloodguilt was serious business in ancient Israel. Joab had not only supported Adonijah as successor to David, but had also murdered two of David's commanders, Abner and Amasa, thereby leaving a curse on the house of David. It was thought that this curse could be removed by putting Joab to death. Solomon's sentence was carried out by Benaiah, the new commander in chief of the army.

Shimei had cursed David (2 Sam. 16:5–14) but later apologized (2 Sam. 19:16–23). Although he did not support Adonijah, Solomon did not forget the curse that he had placed on David. A curse was thought to have devastating power. Yet, under the circumstances, Solomon did not feel justified in putting Shimei to death. Consequently he placed him under what we may call "city arrest." He was confined to Jerusalem under penalty of death if he should ever venture beyond its borders. After three years he violated the terms of his arrest in pursuit of two of his slaves. He was executed, and his curse on the house of David was considered broken. Solomon's political enemies were now either dead or impotent.

## Solomon's Achievements

Solomon had a reputation for wisdom. In a dream he prayed, "Give your servant therefore an understanding mind to govern your people, able to discern between good and evil" (1 Kings 3:9). "An understanding mind" in Hebrew is literally "a hearkening heart." This means that Solomon desired to respond to God's will in obedience from the very center of his being. And God promised to give him a wise and discerning heart, and in addition riches and honor. The story of the two harlots is given as an illustration of the kind of wisdom Solomon exercised as king (1 Kings 3:16–28). It took considerable wisdom to maintain the Davidic kingdom essentially intact (Edom and Damascus revolted; see 1 Kings 11:14–25) and to do some things that David had not attempted.

Moreover, there is good reason to believe that Solomon was a patron of literature. He had a staff of court officials (1 Kings 4:1–6; compare 2 Sam. 20:24), some of whom certainly kept official records. "The Book of the

Acts of Solomon" (1 Kings 11:41) is listed as a source of 1 Kings. It is possible that the Court History of David (2 Sam. 9:1–20:26; 1 Kings 1:1–2:12) was composed during Solomon's reign. It is also probable that Solomon not only originated proverbs and songs (1 Kings 4:29–34), but that he also sponsored their collection. In time his name came to be associated with a large part of Jewish wisdom literature. We are safe in asserting that there were great literary achievements at this time.

Solomon was a commercial genius, and Palestine was strategically located for commercial pursuits.

*Read 1 Kings 10:28–29.*

Through his merchants Solomon secured horses from Egypt and Kue (Cilicia in Asia Minor) and chariots from Egypt. He then resold horses and chariots to his neighbors to the north at a profit. But Solomon's commercial activities were not confined to overland transport, for with the aid of Hiram of Tyre he operated a fleet of ships between Ezion-geber at the northeastern tip of the Gulf of Aqabah (or Elath) and Ophir in southwest Arabia (1 Kings 9:26–28; 10:11–12, 22). The visit of the queen of Sheba (1 Kings 10:1–13) probably had as one of its purposes the concluding of trading agreements with Solomon.

Closely related to Solomon's commercial enterprises was his development of a metal industry. Archaeologists tell us that he mined copper and iron in the Arabah south of the Dead Sea. Near the mines, furnaces have been found where the first stage in the smelting process was carried out. At Ezion-geber a large tenth-century B.C.E. smelting refinery was discovered. The partially smelted ore was brought here for additional refining and shaping into ingots. The ingots were shipped to the various furnaces in Palestine and elsewhere, remelted, and made into useful implements.[2]

Solomon's reign was characterized by a tremendous building program. He built store-cities, where supplies of grain were kept (1 Kings 9:19), and chariot cities (1 Kings 9:19; 10:26), which served as fortresses.

Though Solomon spent far more time and money in building his palace and other government buildings in Jerusalem (1 Kings 7:1–12), the biblical narrative concentrates on the building and dedication of the Temple (1 Kings 5:1–6:38; 7:13–8:66), for the Temple was more crucial in the life of God's people than the other buildings. In early Israel there were various shrines, of which Shiloh was the most celebrated. While certain shrines continued, David made Jerusalem the religious capital of his people by bringing the Ark there. He also left large resources to aid Solomon in building the Temple (1 Chron. 18:5–13; 22:6–16). The Temple was built under the direction of Phoenician artisans and in part according to Phoenician architectural design.

The Temple proper was about ninety feet long by thirty feet wide and was flanked on either side by adjoining rooms three stories high, which could be entered by a door on either side of the structure. At the entrance to the center building stood the two bronze pillars, Jachin and Boaz. The Temple itself was composed of three parts: the vestibule, the Holy Place, and the Holy of Holies. In the Holy of Holies were the two cherubim and the Ark of the Covenant, symbolizing the presence of God. A cherub, it seems, was a composite figure, having the body of a lion, the wings of a bird, and a human face. East of the Temple was the altar of burnt offering, and south of the altar was the molten sea.

Solomon dedicated the Temple "at the festival in the month Ethanim" (1 Kings 8:2), which was the Feast of Ingathering or the preexilic New Year festival. Solomon's Temple for centuries served mainly as a royal chapel. After the return from the exile and rebuilding, the Second Temple became the focal point of the community's worship.

*How significant are church architecture and physical equipment in the life of a congregation today? What does the presence of a church building in a community say?*

## Solomon's Difficulties

In spite of Solomon's splendor, his reign was not without its blemishes. In place of the old tribal boundaries Solomon set up twelve administrative districts in Northern Israel, each under a governor (1 Kings 4:7–19). Each district was responsible for supplying provisions for the court and the army one month out of every year (1 Kings 4:20–28). Perhaps Solomon was seeking to abolish the original tribal loyalties and thereby to centralize more power in his own hands. It is certainly possible that this issue played a part in the subsequent trouble between North and South. The biblical text may be interpreted to mean that Judah was exempt from this requirement. If this interpretation is correct, such partiality only added fuel to the flame of resentment by the northern tribes.

In order to support his many undertakings, Solomon not only taxed his people heavily but also resorted to conscription and slave labor. It was he who inaugurated the conscription of freeborn Israelites for his building projects and for his army (1 Kings 5:13–18; 9:22). David had already used people he had conquered as slave labor (2 Sam. 12:26–31). Solomon forced the Canaanites remaining in the land to supply levies of slaves

(1 Kings 9:15–22). But it was the conscription of the Israelites themselves that was to cause trouble in the future.

That for which the biblical writer roundly pronounced the judgment of God on Solomon was his compromising support of the religions of his foreign wives (1 Kings 11:1–13). Many of Solomon's marriages were a matter of political alliance. But he built shrines for the gods of his wives and worshiped at the shrines himself.

Even before Solomon's death, Edom and Damascus had revolted, and the revolt of the northern tribes under Jeroboam was pending (1 Kings 11:14–43).

*To what extent were Solomon's difficulties inevitable?*

*To what extent was Solomon responsible for creating them?*

*How did the relation between religion and state in Solomon's time differ from that relation in the time of David?*

*What do you think is the ideal relation between religion and state? Why?*

# GOD'S RIGHTEOUS ACTS OF JUDGMENT

8

# The Judgment of Division

*T*hus far in our study of the one story of the Bible we have considered "God's Mighty Acts of Creation" and "God's Covenant Acts of Redemption." Among the covenant acts of redemption we included God's election of the ancestors, the deliverance at the exodus and covenant at Sinai, the gift of the Promised Land, and the establishment of the house of David.

We now begin our study of Part Three of the course, which we have entitled "God's Righteous Acts of Judgment." This part will be composed of three chapters respectively entitled "The Judgment of Division," "Judgment on Northern Israel," and "Judgment on Southern Judah." Of course the theme of God's judgment does not begin with the divided monarchy, for we have already had occasion to deal with the subject of judgment. Nevertheless, at this point in Israel's history judgment becomes the dominant theme. God's mighty acts embrace acts of judgment.

Judgment is the activity of the judge in establishing justice, and its ultimate purpose according to the Old Testament is salvation, as the following words from Isaiah 33:22 indicate:

> For the LORD is our judge, the LORD is our ruler,
> the LORD is our king; he will save us.

The judges in Israel's earlier history were primarily deliverers or saviors. To judge the poor meant to deliver them from oppression, but to judge the oppressors meant to punish them (Ps. 72:1–4). The deliverance of the oppressed required the punishment of the wrongdoer. Judgment, then, has two prongs: one to save and the other to condemn. This view of judgment may be diagrammed in the following manner:

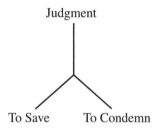

Throughout Israel's history both of these forks of judgment may be seen, the negative being more obvious in the period from the death of Solomon (924 B.C.E.) to the Babylonian exile (587/586 B.C.E.). To speak of "The Judgment of Division" is to say that the splitting of the United Kingdom into two kingdoms (Northern Israel and Southern Judah) was a judgment of God on the sins of Solomon and the sins of Rehoboam, his son and successor.

The time covered in this particular chapter extends from about 924 B.C.E. to about 790 B.C.E. It was a period characterized by revolution, warfare, prophetic counsel, and literary activity. The biblical narrative runs from 1 Kings 12:1 to 2 Kings 14:22. Second Chronicles 10:1–25:28 gives a parallel account of the kings of Judah only. The account in the books of Kings interweaves the history of both kingdoms but gives more details concerning Northern Israel.

## Jeroboam I, Who Made Israel to Sin

### The Division Between North and South

*Read 1 Kings 12:1–24 and seek to determine the causes of schism (or divisions) in Israel.*

The Davidic dynasty was accepted as a fact in Judah. Solomon had succeeded David, and Rehoboam succeeded Solomon there without opposition. But representatives of the northern tribes met Rehoboam at Shechem for the purpose of recognizing his sovereignty over that part of the kingdom.

Jeroboam, the son of Nebat, had served as the taskmaster of the forced labor under Solomon. While he was serving in that capacity, Ahijah, a prophet from Shiloh, tore a garment into twelve pieces and gave ten of them to Jeroboam, indicating that God was going to make him king over ten tribes. Jeroboam fled for protection from Solomon to Shishak, Pharaoh of Egypt (1 Kings 11:26–40). This smoldering antagonism, with its incipient threat of schism, was regarded as a judgment of God on Solomon for his infidelity to the LORD.

On Solomon's death, Jeroboam returned to Israel and led the assembly at Shechem in requesting Rehoboam to lighten the hard service imposed by Solomon. But Rehoboam followed the advice of his younger counselors and promised an even heavier yoke than Solomon had laid on the people. Whereupon they revolted, saying,

> "What share do we have in David?
> We have no inheritance in the son of Jesse.
> To your tents, O Israel!
> Look now to your own house, O David."
> (1 Kings 12:16)

Then, "when King Rehoboam sent Adoram, who was taskmaster over the forced labor, all Israel stoned him to death" (v. 18). Even Rehoboam himself had to flee to Jerusalem. The prophet Shemaiah forbade him to attempt to recover his loss in battle. Solomon's empire had disintegrated under the judgment of God.

## Jeroboam's Policies

*Read 1 Kings 12:25–33.*

At first Jeroboam made Shechem his capital but later chose Tirzah. He realized that the symbolic importance for the people of the Temple in Jerusalem would tend to cause them to turn back to the house of David. Therefore, he set up two shrines within the Northern Kingdom, one at Dan and the other at Bethel. Furthermore, he appointed priests and instituted a feast that corresponded to the Feast of Ingathering in Judah. At each of the two sanctuaries Jeroboam set up a golden bull calf, probably not as a representation of the LORD but as a pedestal on which the invisible LORD was thought to stand.[1] In any case, such figures were definitely conducive to further mixing with Baalism, in which bulls were symbols of fertility.

Ahijah, the prophet who in the first place had helped instigate

Jeroboam's revolution, now pronounced judgment on him and his house on account of his idolatry (see 1 Kings 14:1–20). Jeroboam came to be known as the king who sinned and "made Israel to sin," for later kings and their people followed the precedent set by him. From the point of view of the editor of the books of Kings, to set up any sanctuary in competition with the Temple in Jerusalem was sin, and the bull calves further compounded the sin. Do you think Judah and Israel would have remained divided if there had not also been a division in their religion? Is there a relation to this in the existence of many denominations in the church today? Is this sinful in itself? On what grounds can it be justified? How can we avoid lapsing into idolatry as we make use of symbolism in the church today?

Although Rehoboam erected no rival sanctuaries to the Temple in Jerusalem, he did permit syncretism (the mixing of heathen elements into the religion of Judah). This often involved the practice of fertility rites, including the employment of male and female prostitutes (see 1 Kings 14:21–24).

## The Invasion of Shishak (1 Kings 14:25–28)

You will recall that in the days of the united monarchy Solomon had an effective alliance with Egypt through his marriage to the daughter of Pharaoh. But toward the end of Solomon's reign a new Egyptian dynasty was founded by Shishak, who gave Jeroboam protection from Solomon. Apparently Shishak wanted to reestablish Egyptian control in Mesopotamia, and anything that would cause trouble in Palestine was to his liking. The biblical text records only his attack on Rehoboam of Judah, but archaeological sources, including Shishak's inscription at Karnak, make it clear that he attacked Jeroboam as well.[2] While he did not reestablish Egypt's empire in Palestine or Mesopotamia, he did weaken both of the Israelite kingdoms.

## The End of Jeroboam

Jeroboam died and was succeeded by Nadab, his son, who reigned only two years. The house of Jeroboam was extinguished by Baasha. Rehoboam and his son Abijam had already died, and Asa was king over Judah. From this point on until the fall of Jerusalem in 587/586 B.C.E. the accompanying list of the kings of Israel and Judah will help you keep events in their correct order.

CHRONOLOGY OF THE RULERS OF THE DIVIDED KINGDOM[3]

| ISRAEL | JUDAH |
|---|---|
| Jeroboam I (924–903) | Rehoboam (924–907) |
| | Abijam (907–906) |
| | Asa (905–874) |
| Nadab (903–902) | |
| Baasha (902–886) | |
| Elah (886) | |
| Zimiri (885) | |
| Omri (885–873) | |
| | Jehoshaphat (874–850) |
| Ahab (873–851) | |
| Ahaziah (851–849) | |
| Jehoram (849–843) | Jehoram (850–843) |
| | Ahaziah (843) |
| Jehu (843–816) | Athaliah (843–837) |
| Jehoahaz (816–800) | Jehoash (Joash) (837-?) |
| | Amaziah (?–?) |
| Joash (800–785) | Azariah/Uzziah (?–?) |
| Jeroboam II (785–745) | Jotham (?–742) |
| Zechariah (745) | |
| Shallum (745) | |
| Menahem (745–736) | Ahaz (742–727) |
| Pekahiah (736–735) | |
| Pekah (735–732) | |
| Hoshea (732–723) | Hezekiah (727–698) |
| *Fall of Israel (Samaria: 722)* | |
| | Manasseh (697–642) |
| | Amon (642–640) |
| | Josiah (639–609) |
| | Jehoahaz (609) |
| | Jehoiakim (608–598) |
| | Jehoiachin (597) |
| | *Babylonian Conquest of Jerusalem (597)* |
| | Zedekiah (597–586) |
| | *Destruction of Jerusalem (586)* |

## The House of Omri

After a time of anarchy and civil war in Northern Israel, Omri came out victorious and established a dynasty that was to last for about thirty-four years.

## Omri

Omri was a contemporary of the Judean kings Asa and Jehoshaphat. But the Bible has little to say about him (see 1 Kings 16:21–28). He moved his capital from Tirzah to Samaria, which could be well fortified. He continued the syncretism inaugurated by Jeroboam. Moreover, by his alliance with Phoenicia he laid the foundation for the threat of Phoenician Baalism to the religion of Israel. His power is indicated in certain records of other nations of that age. For example, from the Moabite Stone (a stone inscribed by King Mesha of Moab) we learn that Omri forced Moab to pay tribute to Israel (compare 2 Kings 3:4–27). Furthermore, for more than a century after Omri, the kings of Assyria continued to refer to Israel as "the land of the house of Omri."

## Ahab and Elijah (1 Kings 16:29–21:29)

*As you read these very crucial chapters, draw a line down the middle of a sheet of your notebook paper like this:*

*AHAB AND/OR JEZEBEL*   |   *ELIJAH*

*On the left make an outline of the actions of Ahab and Jezebel, and on the right, an outline of the actions of Elijah. Where actions on both sides of the line are interdependent, make the points of the outlines parallel.*

*When you have finished this procedure, jot down in your notebook what God was doing throughout the whole interchange between king and queen and prophet. Did you run into any problems that you want to take to your class for discussion?*

Ahab succeeded his father Omri as king of Israel. In addition to walking "in the sins of Jeroboam son of Nebat," he married the Phoenician princess Jezebel, thereby sealing the alliance between Phoenicia and the house of Omri. Beyond this, Ahab participated in the worship of the Phoenician Baal, erecting an altar to Baal and Asherah in the capital city. This does not mean that he entirely forsook the worship of the LORD, but he tried to serve both the God of Israel and the gods of Phoenicia. Apparently he was willing to compromise for the sake of political expediency. Phoenician Baalism was a special brand of the Canaanite Baalism already encountered by the Israelites in the days of the judges. The religion of Phoenicia was a real threat to the religion of Israel. In fact, Jezebel was a militant missionary for her faith, even going to the extreme of putting many of the prophets of the LORD to death. Apparently she wanted to make her religion the official cult in Israel.

But God had prepared a man for the hour, Elijah the Tishbite. For centuries this fierce warrior for God was to be regarded as a prototype of the prophets. Much of 1 Kings is devoted to the story of his battle with King Ahab and Queen Jezebel for the soul of his nation. We must look at this dramatic story in detail.

Elijah's first recorded act was the announcement of a severe drought as a punishment for Ahab's sins. After more than three years of drought, Elijah was sent by God to Ahab again. Through Ahab he challenged the 450 prophets of Baal and the 400 prophets of Asherah to a contest on Mount Carmel. The purpose of this contest was to show who was the real Sovereign of rain and fertility. The people of Israel were of a divided mind. Therefore, Elijah put the question to them after they had gathered on Carmel: "How long will you go limping with two different opinions? If the LORD is God, follow him; but if Baal, then follow him." These words call to mind the earlier challenge of Joshua at Shechem (Josh. 24:14–15) and the later precept of Jesus: "You cannot serve God and wealth" (Matt. 6:24).

It was agreed that the prophets of Baal would offer sacrifice to Baal and that Elijah would offer sacrifice to the LORD. It was also agreed that the deity who answered by fire was truly God. After the prophets of Baal failed in their frenzied effort to receive an answer, Elijah prayed to the LORD, the God of Israel, who answered by fire, consuming the burnt offering and all that was around it. Many attempts have been made to explain what happened on this occasion or to explain it away. Perhaps lightning struck the spot on which the sacrifice was made, and the people in faith accepted it as the fire of God. Whatever may be said, it cannot be explained away. But the coincidence of the occasion, the lightning, and the prayer and faith of Elijah was no mere coincidence. For the people of faith, it was miracle, a mighty act of God indeed.

From our vantage point Elijah's slaughter of the prophets of Baal looks cruel, for we do not put people to death because they adhere to a faith different from our own. But in Elijah's day such action was quite differently conceived. The prophets of Baal were understood as God's enemies and a mortal threat to the faith of God's people. The prophets of Baal were placed in a category similar to the ban in holy war. In other words, as Samuel had hewed Agag to pieces (1 Sam. 15:33), so Elijah commanded the prophets of Baal to be killed.

The rain was on its way, and, in the excitement of victory, Elijah ran before Ahab's chariot to the entrance of Jezreel.

After "Ahab told Jezebel all that Elijah had done, and how he had killed all the prophets with the sword," Jezebel sent Elijah a message to the effect that he would join the prophets of Baal in death the next day. When Elijah received this message, he began his cross-country run. He was so depressed that he prayed to die. At that moment death would have been an easy way out of his misery. Sometimes the desire to die may become stronger than the desire to live. Moreover, it sometimes takes more courage to live than it does to die.

We may well ask the reasons for such a change in this great prophet. How are we to account for the fact that the man who had just faced several hundred of Baal's prophets fled in fear from one person? Of course Jezebel was no ordinary person, but her unusual characteristics cannot really account for Elijah's behavior. You may want to make additions to the following reasons for Elijah's sudden despair: (1) He had been through a strenuous ordeal on Mount Carmel and was physically and emotionally exhausted. (2) The very fact that he was for the time being without a constructive task made it easier for him to lose hope and become pessimistic. (3) A strong emotional depression followed his great elation. The time of descending from the mount of great religious rapture is often an occasion of severe testing. (4) Elijah's reaction resulted in a feeling of loneliness. He felt that everyone besides himself had forsaken the covenant. "I alone am left," he said. (5) Finally, Elijah despaired because he believed that the triumph at Carmel was not so great a triumph after all. Jezebel looked triumphant to him, and God seemed less real.

What medicine did God provide for the despondent prophet? (1) Elijah was fed. His physical needs were met. (2) God rebuked him with the question, "What are you doing here, Elijah?" It was no accident that Elijah fled to Horeb (Sinai), the mountain of God's revelation to Moses. Apparently he felt the need to recapture, in some measure, the experience of the former great leader of Israel. But God said in effect, "Elijah, this is not the place for you. Geographical location cannot produce spiritual renewal." At that moment Elijah poured out his heart to God. (3) Then came the wind, the earthquake, and the fire, but God was not in them. They were not the revelation, but the forerunners of the revelation (see Exod. 19). The storm prepared the way for the "sound of sheer silence." (4) Finally, God said to Elijah, "Go." That is, God put him to work again with a threefold commission: to anoint Hazael king of Syria, Jehu king of Israel, and Elisha prophet in his own place. Elijah's mantle was cast on Elisha. Elisha was later responsible for sending a prophet to anoint Jehu (2 Kings 9:1–10), probably at Elijah's command. Elisha was also to plant the seed that was to make Hazael king of Syria (2 Kings 8:7–15). God assured Elijah that things were not as bad as they looked. There were seven thousand, a significant remnant, who had not bowed the knee to Baal.

*How does this part of the story have current meaning for us?*

*Under what circumstances may rebuke be a means of comfort?*

Ahab had not seen the last of Elijah. A man by the name of Naboth owned a piece of land adjacent to the royal palace. Ahab sought to buy this land with money or in exchange for other land. But Naboth refused to sell, because according to ancient custom the land belonged not to himself alone but to his family in perpetuity. Therefore, by means of deception and bribery Jezebel had Naboth put to death in order that Ahab might have his property. But Elijah found Ahab and pronounced the judgment of God on him, his house, and Jezebel. He championed the cause of the commoner against the injustice of the king himself. Ahab had to learn what David had learned earlier, that so far as justice is concerned, God is not partial, even toward the person of the king.

*What does the account of Naboth's vineyard say about the social injustices of our own society?*

## Ahab and Micaiah (1 Kings 22:1–40)

Ahab had his problems with more than one prophet. The last one with whom he had dealings was Micaiah ben Imlah.

*Read 1 Kings 22:40 as you ponder the question: How were Elijah and Micaiah alike, and how were they different?*

Ahab secured the help of Jehoshaphat of Judah in his attempt to take Ramoth-gilead from the Syrians. Before engaging in battle Jehoshaphat said to Ahab, "Inquire first for the word of the LORD." Then Ahab called together about four hundred prophets and asked their counsel concerning his proposed undertaking. And they replied unanimously, "Go up; for the LORD will give it into the hand of the king." Nevertheless, Jehoshaphat was not altogether satisfied and asked for another prophet. Therefore, Ahab sent for Micaiah, whom he hated.

At first Micaiah pretended to get on the popular bandwagon with the other prophets. Ahab knew, however, that Micaiah was mocking him and called on him to tell the truth. Whereupon Micaiah prophesied the death of Ahab in battle with the Syrians and took the consequences of his prophecy—imprisonment. Ahab disguised himself as a common soldier, "but a certain man drew his bow and unknowingly struck the king of Israel between the scale armor and the breastplate. . . ." And Ahab died in the evening. Judgment on the house of Omri had been set in motion.

In Micaiah we find a man who was willing to stand alone against a multitude of other prophets and against the king, because he stood with God. The majority is not always right. There are times when a person may be called to stand alone—yet not alone. How does a person know that he or she is standing with God?

## The Dynasty of Jehu

### The Ministry of Elisha (1 Kings 22:41–2 Kings 8:29)

The political plot by which Jehu seized the throne was encouraged, perhaps even instigated, by Elisha, the prophet. Therefore the rise of the dynasty of Jehu must be seen in the context of this ministry of the successor of the prophet Elijah.

Ahaziah, the son of Ahab, reigned over Israel for only two years and was succeeded by Jehoram (849–843 B.C.E.), another son of Ahab. Elisha's ministry began about the time of Jehoram's accession to the throne and extended into the early part of the eighth century. In other words, it covered the end of the house of Omri and a large part of the dynasty of Jehu.

Elisha was successor to Elijah (2 Kings 2:1–18), and the prophetic mantle was used as the symbol of this succession (1 Kings 19:19–20; 2 Kings 2:13). His request to inherit "a double share" of Elijah's spirit was not a request to be twice as great as his master but to receive the portion as of the firstborn son. In this case it meant the succession to the authority of Elijah as head of "the sons of the prophets" (2 Kings 2:9).[4]

In early Israel Moses and Samuel had been prophets. Nathan and Gad had been advisers to David. In fact, prophecy of a sort was not unknown outside Israel. Balaam, for example, delivered God's message in spite of himself (Num. 22–24). What are known as "ecstatic" prophets were present in Israel as early as the time of Samuel (1 Sam. 10:5, 10; compare 19:20). Such persons formed themselves into bands or schools and made use of musical instruments in reaching the state of rapture sometimes necessary for prophesying. When in such a state, it could be said that the prophet was "turned into a different person" (1 Sam. 10:6). Such prophets were loyal to the LORD and sometimes delivered a message while they were in a trance. Guilds of ecstatic prophets known as "the sons of the prophets" were associated with Elijah and Elisha (see, for example, 2 Kings 2:3–15; 3:15). Prophecy as we know it in Amos, Hosea, Isaiah, and others had its antecedents in the ministry of such persons as Moses, Samuel, and the Ecstatics.

For the most part Elisha's ministry was one of generous compassion and helpfulness. For example, he purified a spring at Jericho (2 Kings 2:19–22), helped a poor woman get out of debt (2 Kings 4:1–7), restored the son of the Shunammite woman (2 Kings 4:8–37), and healed Naaman the Syrian of his leprosy (2 Kings 5:1–27). What similarities do you see between the ministry of Elisha and the ministry of Jesus?

As God's prophet, Elisha also performed a ministry in the political sphere. Moab had been a vassal state of Israel. But when Ahab died, Moab revolted. Jehoram, the king of Israel, called on his vassal, Jehoshaphat of Judah, to help him in his campaign against Moab. In turn Jehoshaphat called on his vassal, the king of Edom, to join them in their attack on Moab. In the process of their march they found no water for their army and animals. Therefore, they called on Elisha for counsel. In response, Elisha assured them that God would provide water that would form pools in the dry river bed. He also encouraged the three allies in their undertaking. All went well for them against the Moabites until Mesha, king of Moab, sacrificed his eldest son in the sight of Israel. Psychologically this action brought courage to the Moabites and resulted in the withdrawal of the three kings and their forces.

On various occasions Elisha protected his king and people from the Syrians (2 Kings 6:8–7:20). Yet, in accord with the command laid on Elijah at Horeb, he spoke the word that helped spark the rebellion that placed Hazael on the throne of Syria (2 Kings 8:7–15).

## The Revolution of Jehu (2 Kings 9:1–10:36)

Elisha sent one of the sons of the prophets to Ramoth-gilead to anoint Jehu king of Israel. Thus the third assignment given to Elijah at Horeb was carried out. Jehu was immediately proclaimed king by his followers and proceeded to one of the most bloody purges in all the history of Israel. He not only killed Jehoram (Joram), king of Israel; Jezebel, the widow of Ahab; and the other heirs of Ahab; he also murdered King Ahaziah of Judah and his kinsmen who were visiting in Israel and slaughtered the worshipers of Baal after tricking them into the house of Baal.

About a hundred years later Hosea pronounced the judgment of God on the dynasty of Jehu for the blood he shed in Jezreel (Hos. 1:4). As the judgment of God had come upon the house of Omri, so in due time it would come upon the house of Jehu as well. With all his purging, however, Jehu did not remove the golden calves from the sanctuaries at Dan and Bethel.

## The Death of Athaliah (2 Kings 8:16–19; 11:1–21)

Jehoshaphat, king of Judah, was succeeded by his son Jehoram (Joram), who married Athaliah, the daughter of Ahab and Jezebel. Ahaziah, Jehoram's successor, was killed by Jehu after a very short reign, as we noted above, whereupon Athaliah seized the government of Judah and put to death the royal family. However, a daughter of Jehoram took the infant Joash, son of Ahaziah, and hid him in the Temple until he was seven years old. Then in a revolt led by Jehoiada the priest, Joash was made king, and Athaliah was put to death. Thus the house of David was reestablished on the throne of Judah.

## Summary

In spite of the witness of such prophets as Elijah and Elisha, Israel's history had become a dismal story. Israel had been called to be "a kingdom of priests and a holy nation" but instead had become two nations like other nations. This was God's judgment on the rebellious people. The people of God were split apart by civil war and weakened by a succession of revolutions. Still the line of David continued on the throne of the Southern Kingdom. The line of Jehu was to continue in the north until 745 B.C.E. But that story will be told in our next chapter.

# Judgment on Northern Israel

*G*od's judgment on the Northern Kingdom reached its climax in the fall of that kingdom to Assyria in 722/721 B.C.E. In this chapter we shall trace the events that led to this judgment. Roughly the period with which we are dealing extends from the early part of the eighth century to the beginning of the seventh. For the Northern Kingdom this means from the accession of Jeroboam II in 785 B.C.E. to the fall of Samaria in 722/721 B.C.E. For the Southern Kingdom of Judah it means from the accession of Uzziah (Azariah) ca. 783 B.C.E. to the death of Hezekiah in 698 B.C.E. This was a time of power politics, entangling alliances, and puppet governments. It was also a time of injustice in human relations and unfaithfulness to God. In order to keep rulers and dates in their correct order, it is suggested that you make use of the chart found in the preceding chapter.

The history of the two kingdoms in the eighth century is recorded in 2 Kings 14:23–20:21. The history of Judah is also recorded in 2 Chronicles 26:1–32:33. Moreover, Isaiah 36–39 is almost identical to 2 Kings 18:13–20:19. The biblical sources are occasionally supplemented by archaeological materials.

## Northern Israel
## in the Eighth Century B.C.E.

The dynasty of Jehu, with which we were concerned at the end of chapter 8, was carried on by Jeroboam II and his son Zechariah. In certain respects Jeroboam was a strong ruler: he so extended the borders of his land that his kingdom and that of Uzziah of Judah together were as great as the united kingdom under Solomon. But even in the relatively prosperous days of Jeroboam, Amos and Hosea saw the moral and spiritual rot of the nation and pronounced the coming judgment of God.

After a reign of only six months, Zechariah was slain by Shallum. With the death of Zechariah the dynasty of Jehu ceased to be, and Israel's history from that point on was one of anarchy and disintegration. Shallum reigned for one month and was murdered by Menahem. When Tiglath-pileser III of Assyria, called Pul in the Bible (2 Kings 15:17–22), came against Menahem, he was bought off by tribute, which Menahem raised by taxing the wealthy.

Menahem was succeeded by his son Pekahiah, who was slain very soon by one of his officers, Pekah. Pekah was anti-Assyrian in his policies. In fact, he, Rezin of Damascus (Syria), and others formed an anti-Assyrian alliance. When these rulers attacked Ahaz of Judah, Ahaz appealed to Tiglath-pileser III for help. The Assyrian king was more than happy to oblige. He seized cities and citizens in Israel, attacked Philistia, and captured Damascus, the capital of Syria, taking many of its inhabitants to other parts of his empire.

Hoshea slew Pekah and reigned over Israel as a puppet king of Assyria. But in the days of Shalmaneser V of Assyria, he appealed to Egypt for help to overthrow the Assyrian yoke. Shalmaneser attacked Samaria in 724 B.C.E., but the city was actually taken by his successor Sargon II in 722/721 B.C.E. Sargon transported over 27,000 Israelites to other parts of the Assyrian empire and brought other captive peoples to the cities of Israel. The people whom we know as the Samaritans were later believed to be the descendants of native Israelites left in Samaria by Sargon, who intermarried with the people brought from other parts of the Assyrian empire to Samaria. Judgment had first come on God's people through the division of the united kingdom. That judgment had now been followed by the destruction of Israel.

## Amos—Prophet of God's Righteousness

The great prophets of the eighth century, the period of Israel's fall (Amos, Hosea, Isaiah, and Micah) performed their ministries against the background of the Assyrian threat. Amos and Hosea prophesied primarily to Israel; Isaiah and Micah, to Judah.

The first of these prophets was Amos. When Amos was first called to speak God's word, Jeroboam II was king of Israel, and Uzziah was king of Judah. Jeroboam was already well established and victorious in battle. One reason for his prosperous reign was the fact that the Assyrians had weakened the kingdom of Syria. Jeroboam controlled lucrative caravan routes. A class of wealthy traders emerged, many of whom were unscrupulous in their business practices. There was a great gap between the rich and the poor, and the poor were at the mercy of the rich. It was a time of flagrant idolatry, greedy luxury, idleness, immorality, and lawlessness. It was a time not unlike the twenty-first century C.E. To the superficial eye everything looked good. But Amos looked more deeply into the heart of the nation, for he was informed by the word of God.

> In order to get a firsthand account of Amos's call, read Amos 7:10–15.

Amaziah was priest at the Bethel shrine, which had been established by Jeroboam I as a rival to the Temple in Jerusalem. At least some of Amos's preaching was delivered at Bethel. Amaziah sent Jeroboam a message in which he accused Amos of treason. Unfortunately, Amaziah, like so many false patriots, was careless with the truth. He quoted Amos as saying, " 'Jeroboam shall die by the sword, and Israel must go into exile away from his land.' " But Amos had not said Jeroboam would die by the sword. Rather did he say, in quoting God's word to him, "I will rise against the house of Jeroboam with the sword" (Amos 7:9). Amos had pronounced exile for Israel but in connection with his message of judgment on sin and a call to repentance.

In his threat to Amos, Amaziah said in effect, "You visionary fanatic, go home to Judah as fast as you can. Ply your trade there. But don't you ever prophesy in Bethel again, for it is the royal sanctuary and therefore above criticism." This statement is very much like saying to a minister today, "Don't mention the sins of the nation, and above all don't criticize the government in Washington, D.C., because it is the capital of the country."

In his reply to Amaziah, Amos made it plain that he was no professional prophet or member of a prophetic band. "But I am a herdsman," he said, "and a dresser of sycamore trees, and the LORD took me from following the flock, and the LORD said to me, 'Go, prophesy to my people Israel' " (Amos 7:14–15; compare Amos 3:3–8). The only credentials Amos had were the call of God and the word of God.

Amos was a layman from Tekoa (a town about six miles south of Bethlehem) whose message revolved around the righteousness of God. He was not the first to know God's righteousness, for he had such predecessors as Abraham, Moses, Samuel, Nathan, and Elijah. In the book that bears Amos's name the word "righteousness" occurs only three times and "righteous" twice. Nonetheless, the righteousness of God is the basis of all that Amos said.

It was the revealed character and activity of God that determined for Amos what is right and what is wrong. A person's relation to others is to be in harmony with the character and work of God. In a sense the text of the entire book of Amos is found in 5:24:

> But let justice roll down like waters,
> and righteousness like an ever-flowing stream.

Righteousness expresses itself in everyday honesty and fair dealing. To be righteous is not to be like a stream that flows today and is dried up tomorrow, but like one that flows constantly. Sin is being out of harmony with God's righteousness and is expressed in many different ways.

## Righteousness in Judgment on the Nations

One expression of God's righteousness, according to Amos, was divine judgment on Israel's neighbors. These neighbors included Damascus (Syria), Philistia, Tyre, Edom, Ammon, Moab, and Judah.

*Read Amos 1:1–2:5, noting the repeated formula used in each oracle (a quotation from God) and listing in your notebook the transgressions enumerated against each nation.*

*Note also the psychological buildup that Amos makes before he begins his oracle against Israel.*

Two things stand out in the study of this passage. One is the fact that these nations were judged both in relation to the character of God and in relation to the knowledge they had. Only the chosen people were judged according to the covenant made at Sinai. The second is the fact that the LORD was regarded as sovereign over all nations. God's sovereignty was by no means confined to the people of Judah and Israel. In fact, a little later Amos made it crystal clear that God had a purpose for other nations too (Amos 9:7).

*What do you feel the message of Amos concerning the nations has to say to us in the international situation today?*

## Righteousness in Judgment on Israel

Amos was not primarily concerned with the nations; he was primarily concerned with Israel.

*To get his basic indictment of the Northern Kingdom, read the oracle in 2:6–16.*

Righteousness and judgment in relation to Israel must be seen against the background of the covenant. It is a breach of God's covenant for those with power to sell other Israelites into slavery and to trample the poor into the dust. It is a breach of the covenant to commit adultery and to carouse in the name of religion, especially in clothes and with drink taken from the helpless. Israel's religion had become so contaminated with Baalism that it was partly responsible for the process of moral disintegration.

These and other transgressions, says Amos, are evidences of base ingratitude to God, who gave Israel the land of the Amorites (Canaan), brought the people out of Egypt, and raised up prophets and Nazirites for their benefit. Amos is the first to include God's gift of the prophets and the Nazirites (see p. 97) in a list of the mighty acts of God on behalf of God's people. We have no difficulty in recognizing the prophets as a gracious gift of God to the people, but what is our reaction to the gift of the austere Nazirites? How do you account for this reaction? "These dedicated ones were a living protest against the paganizing of Israelite life."[1] The Israelites sought to make Nazirites break their vows and prophets cease speaking the word of God. How are we treating our "Nazirites" and our "prophets"?

Amos made it clear to his audience that God's judgment was inescapable. Israel was loaded down with transgressions as a cart with sheaves and was going to collapse.[2] The swift of foot, the bowman, the horseman, and the stout of heart would all prove inadequate in the day of God's judgment.

Most of the rest of the book reiterates the theme of judgment on Israel in first one way and then another. A few illustrations will have to suffice. One is found in a single verse (3:2):

> You only have I known
>    of all the families of the earth;
> therefore I will punish you
>    for all your iniquities.

The word "to know" in Hebrew sometimes means "to choose." And such is its meaning here. God elected Israel to be the covenant people, but this election to privilege was an election to corresponding responsibility. When this responsibility was ignored, election placed Israel under judgment. We are reminded of the words of Jesus: "From everyone to whom much has been given, much will be required" (Luke 12:48).

*How would you apply this principle to the church, the Christian, and the nation?*

The "cows of Bashan" (wealthy women of Samaria) encouraged their husbands in the oppression of the poor (4:1–3). Worship had become a ritual of magic, without ethical involvement (4:4–5; 5:21–27 ). "Those who are at ease in Zion" and live in sin-provided luxury "are not grieved over the ruin of Joseph" (6:1–7). God's judgment is inevitable. In the popular mind the Day of the LORD was anticipated as a time when God would overcome Israel's enemies, establish sovereignty over other nations, and send divine blessings on Israel in abundance. But Amos insisted that this conception was erroneous. The Day of the LORD would be the dark night of judgment for rebellious Israel (5:18–20). The coming exile would be a result of "that day."

## Righteousness in Mercy

Amos is not usually thought of in relation to mercy. In fact, only rarely does he use a word from the vocabulary of love in his entire book. But a word study that is made apart from other considerations can be misleading. For example, no word for sin is used in Genesis 3; yet the whole chapter revolves around the subject.

First of all, Amos's concern for the poor and oppressed was a merciful concern, which was rooted in his understanding of the righteousness of God. God's righteousness is merciful, and a righteousness that has no mercy in it is not the righteousness of God.

In the second place, God's merciful righteousness is seen in Amos's call to repentance. In most of what Amos says such a call is implicit. However, it is sometimes explicit. God had earlier called the people to repentance through famine, drought, blight and mildew, locust, pestilence, war, and destruction of cities; but they did not heed the call. Now God offers them the last opportunity to repent through the preaching of the prophet (4:6–13). "Prepare to meet your God" is a call "for readiness to face God for repentance or for destruction, depending on the response to his offer."[3]

The appeal to repent is even clearer in 5:4–17. Listen to Amos's words: "Seek me and live"; "Seek the LORD and live"; "Seek good, and not evil, that you may live"; and

> Hate evil, and love good,
>     and establish justice in the gate;
> it may be that the LORD, the God of hosts,
>     will be gracious to the remnant of Joseph.

The time for averting all aspects of judgment had passed, but there was still hope for a remnant.

## Hosea—Prophet of God's Love

In the historic events that led to the fall of Israel Amos saw the judgment of God. In national tragedy and personal tragedy another great prophet, Hosea, saw also a message of suffering and love. What God said to and through him in these sad days forms another book of the Bible.

Hosea was a contemporary of Amos and therefore the historical situation was much the same. While Amos was a southerner who went north, Hosea was a northerner who addressed his own people. In fact, he is the only "writing" prophet whose home was in the Northern Kingdom. We do not know his original occupation. And his call to be a prophet cannot be separated from his domestic tragedy.

Like Amos he pronounced the judgment of God time and again on his sinful people. He too anticipated their exile. Amos stressed the social dimension of sin; Hosea its religious dimension, though neither ignored the emphasis of the other. Sin is a breach of the covenant in both cases. In Hosea it is a lack of the knowledge of God and unfaithfulness to the covenant (4:1–3; compare Isa.1:2–4), and such sinfulness expresses itself in specific sins: "[false] swearing, lying, killing, stealing, and committing adultery."

The golden text of Hosea is found in 6:6:

> For I desire steadfast love and not sacrifice,
>   the knowledge of God, rather than burnt offerings.

In various ways Hosea calls attention to that love which motivated God to choose Israel as the covenant people in the first place. He also calls attention to God's steadfast or covenant love, which remains faithful in spite of the unfaithfulness of the people. Just as Amos called Israel to a response to God in righteous actions, so Hosea called for steadfast love in covenant relations. Steadfast love on Israel's part meant devotion and faithfulness to God and to one another. As the parallelism in the passage just quoted indicates, it is synonymous with the knowledge of God. This is not primarily knowledge about God but a personal relationship with God. God has already committed in love to the people. When they respond in love, that relationship is the source of their joy and obedience.

## Love Expressed in the Bond of Marriage

Love is set forth in Hosea most distinctively under the figure of marriage. The covenant of God with Israel is depicted in this daring way. In the Canaanite cult with which Hosea had to contend, there was the so-called marriage of Baal and Anath, through which many thought fertility was made possible. But the marriage of the LORD to Israel, according to Hosea, was not to be associated with fertility rites but with the historical covenant made in the wilderness at Sinai. The very use of the figure of marriage in this way was a challenge to Baalism.

> *Read Hosea 1:1–3:5 carefully, recording in your notebook the name of Hosea's wife, the names of his children, and your understanding of the sequence of events in these chapters. The details of the story are not easy to interpret. Is the story to be taken literally or allegorically?*
>
> *Was Gomer a harlot before Hosea married her?*
>
> *Who is the woman mentioned in chapter 3, Gomer or another?*

There are two major interpretations of Hosea's marriage. The standard reading for the past century or so was that Gomer was not literally a harlot before her marriage to Hosea. But as Hosea looked at his life in retrospect, he realized that from the beginning she was a potential harlot and that God was calling him to the prophetic ministry through the total process and relationship of his marriage. On the basis of more recent research, the second interpretation takes seriously the "symbolic action" announced in the report. The text says that God told Hosea to go and marry a prostitute. Gomer may have been a common streetwalker, but more likely she was a sacred prostitute in the local shrine. By marrying a woman publicly known to be a harlot, the prophet dramatically announced the depth of God's grace and love for Israel. Gomer as Israel was unworthy, but God entered into relationship anyway.

The names of his three children became symbolic of Israel's condition. Jezreel, "He sows," was already the name of a town and a valley where Jehu had wrought vengeance on the house of Omri. It had therefore become a symbol of God's judgment. Just as God's judgment had fallen on the house of Omri, it would also fall on the house of Jehu, which was still in power. "Not pitied" symbolized the coming judgment on the unresponsive nation. And "Not my people" indicated the repudiation of the covenant by the people.

Hosea loved his wife, but she forsook him for other lovers. This infidelity broke Hosea's heart. But his broken heart became a channel of God's special revelation to him. Have you found that suffering has been a channel of God's revelation to you and to others? Can you illustrate? God said something like this to Hosea: "Hosea, I know what you are going through. I was wed to Israel years ago in the wilderness, but she has been unfaithful and gone after other lovers. She will suffer for her sins. Yet, I still love her and will one day win her back in true love and devotion. She will then call me 'My husband' rather than 'My Baal,' because the word 'Baal' is reminiscent of her pagan associates." (The word "Baal" sometimes means "husband.")

Hosea learned his lesson concerning the love of God well, for he bought back his wayward wife, perhaps from slavery, and reinstated her as wife and mother in his home. This is real love, the kind that is begotten of God. Indeed this is the kind of love God has for us. We do not deserve it, and we can never earn it. Through "the cross of Hosea" God's love for Israel was revealed. Through the cross of Christ God's love for all is revealed.

## Love Expressed in Parental Care

Hosea was a versatile prophet. He not only presented God's love as that of a husband for an undeserving wife but also presented it as that of a parent for an undeserving son. Chapter 11 has been traditionally read with the assumption that God is as a father to Israel, but all the things that this parent does are the things done by the mother in Israel's time. So perhaps it is best to think of God as mothering Israel in this passage.

*As you read Hosea 11:1–11, in one column write down the similarities and in another the differences between this passage and Hosea 1:1–3:5. It is interesting that this prophet who had suffered so deeply in his home life should use two family relationships to describe God's relation to Israel.*

The theme of the chapter is found at the very outset (vv. 1–2): God loved Israel, but Israel was disobedient. So much theology is wrapped up in the very first verse:

> When Israel was a child, I loved him,
> and out of Egypt I called my son.

That is, from the very beginning of the people's life, God loved them as a child. The word used for "love" here is often referred to as God's "election–love."[4] It was that quality in God that prompted the choice of Israel as the covenant people in the first place. This choice was revealed to Israel in the historical fact of the exodus from Egypt. Like Amos and so many others, Hosea laid emphasis on the exodus as a mighty act of God. Israel was God's child by adoption; that is, God chose Israel for a special relationship and purpose. But regardless of God's choice and call of the people, they disobeyed by contaminating themselves with Baalism.

Verses 3–4 describe God's early care of the infant people. As Mother, God took Ephraim (another name here for Israel) by the hand and taught him to walk. As the child grew tired of walking, God picked him up and carried him. As Mother, God healed the child and sometimes prevented him from getting sick (see Exod. 15:26). God's guidance was characterized by the same love that had brought the people into being. Indeed, as a kind and gentle teamster eases the yoke on the oxen that they may eat, so God ministered to the people and met their needs—God fed them.

But because the people turned from God and refused to repent, they must suffer the consequences of their rebellion. For love does not cancel all punishment. Chastisement is the necessary consequence of genuine love. Israel must again learn the lessons of slavery, this time not in the original Egypt but in Assyria, the new Egypt.

Nevertheless, in spite of all the sin of the wayward people, God still loves them (vv. 8–11). God will not destroy them completely as with Admah and Zeboiim, cities in the area of Sodom and Gomorrah (see Gen. 14:2, 8; Deut. 29:23). A person in a position of authority might well destroy such disobedient people, but God is not a mortal. God will execute judgment with mercy. Exiles from various places will one day be permitted to return home. Hosea helps to prepare us for the words from the cross: "Father, forgive them; for they do not know what they are doing" (Luke 23:34).

## The Southern Kingdom
### in the Eighth Century B.C.E.

Uzziah or Azariah (ca. 783–742) of Judah was a contemporary of Jeroboam II of Israel. On the whole he was an able ruler, who made advances in building, agriculture, and national defense. In the early part of the eighth century both Israel and Judah were rather wealthy and strong. Toward the latter part of his reign Uzziah was stricken with leprosy, and his son Jotham acted as regent. Isaiah was called to the prophetic ministry "in the year that King Uzziah died" (Isa. 6:1), and this ministry lasted to the end of the century. Micah was his younger contemporary, whose ministry was carried out during the reigns of Jotham, Ahaz, and Hezekiah. Jotham followed the policies set by his father before him.

Ahaz was one of Judah's worst syncretists in worship, even going so far as to burn one of his sons as a sacrifice (2 Kings 16:3; 2 Chron. 28:3), an evidence of his reversion to crude paganism. In the threat from Rezin of Damascus and Pekah of Israel, he refused the counsel of Isaiah to trust in God; instead he put his trust in Assyria, whose aid he purchased with treasures from palace and Temple.

Hezekiah was one of Judah's best and most illustrious kings. He carried out a more thorough religious reform than all that had preceded him. At one time he was very sick and expected to die, but by God's word, delivered through the prophet Isaiah, his life was spared. Among his various undertakings, he constructed the Siloam Tunnel, an underground conduit (still in existence today) to convey water from the Spring of Gihon to the Pool of Siloam. By this means he provided Jerusalem with a supply of water even in time of siege. It was during Hezekiah's reign that Jerusalem was miraculously delivered from Sennacherib the Assyrian (2 Kings 18:13–19:37), and God's people never forgot this mighty act of judgment and salvation.

## Isaiah—Prophet of God's Holiness

During Isaiah's ministry the moral and spiritual disintegration of the Northern Kingdom advanced more rapidly than that of Southern Judah. But Judah was not far behind her unfaithful sister. There, however, in 742 B.C.E., God was to raise up a prophet whose word helped save the southern nation for another century and a half. Perhaps no other Old Testament prophet so influenced the history of Israel in his day as did Isaiah the son of Amoz. Isaiah included a strong message of judgment on Jerusalem and Judah and made some of the same emphases already made by Amos and Hosea. However, he laid a distinctive emphasis on the holiness of God. To Isaiah, God was supremely "the Holy One of Israel" (for example, see 1:4; 5:19, 24; 10:20). At this point we confine ourselves to highlights found in Isaiah 1–39, the first major division of the book.

## The Call of Isaiah

*The sixth chapter of the book of Isaiah is crucial for understanding the prophet and his message. It is the most thoroughgoing account of a call to the prophetic ministry to be found in scripture. Isaiah probably wrote it down sometime after he had entered his ministry. As you read the chapter, try to answer the following questions:*

*1. What makes a prophet a prophet?*

*2. What elements in Isaiah's experience of call should be present in a Christian service of worship?*

*3. Are there valid elements in a Christian worship service that were absent from Isaiah's experience in the Temple?*

### Isaiah's Vision of God (vv. 1–4)

In the year that King Uzziah died a leper, Isaiah had a vision of the heavenly King. As he was worshiping in the Temple of Solomon, he saw the exalted Lord of the universe. The occasion may have been the New Year Festival, when the Kingship of God was celebrated in a special way. Isaiah may have been standing so as to be able to look into the Holy Place, where the smoke was rising from the altar of incense, and in the direction of the Holy of Holies where God was thought to be invisibly enthroned. The total setting seems to have played a part in Isaiah's vision of the heavenly scene.

The seraphim were regarded as some kind of celestial servants, who ministered to the heavenly King. Their antiphonal singing may have been suggested by the singing of the Temple choirs. But it is the content of their song, not its mode of rendition, that is so important:

> "Holy, holy, holy is the LORD of hosts;
> the whole earth is full of his glory."

This song may be regarded as the golden text of Isaiah. He never forgot that God is holy. The word "holy" seems to have come from a root meaning "to be separate." God is separate and distinct from all the creation; God alone is in the category of deity. Holiness is, therefore, "godness." Persons and things can be said to be holy only in a secondary sense, as God sets them apart. In the final analysis, holiness embraces all the attributes of God. For example, God's holiness includes divine righteousness (Isa. 5:16).

The expression "the LORD of hosts" also has a long history. It is drawn from military language. Here it means that God is in command of all the heavenly forces that exist.

"Glory" is the manifestation of God's reign over all creation. "The heavens are telling the glory of God," says the psalmist (Ps. 19:1). God's glory was a medium of God's presence. At Sinai God's glory descended in the midst of fire and smoke. The shaking of the Temple's foundations and the smoke recall God's appearances at Sinai. Real worship is reverently God-centered, and hymns in the strict sense of the word are, like the Song of the Seraphim, songs of praise and adoration.

### Isaiah's Confession of Sin (v. 5)

Isaiah's vision of the Holy One of Israel prepared the way for the confession of his own sin and the sin of his people: "Woe is me! I am lost, for I am a man of unclean lips, and I live among a people of unclean lips; yet my eyes have seen the King, the LORD of hosts!" Amos and Hosea denounced the sins of their people, but we have no record that they confessed their own sinfulness. But in the presence of the Holy King, Isaiah was made aware of his own lostness. It was very appropriate for him to speak of himself as "a man of unclean lips" because he was in the process of being called to use his lips in speaking as a prophet of God.

At the same time Isaiah had a keen sense of responsibility for his people. He was living in a sin-infested society. As you turn here and there in the book of Isaiah, you will discover the prophet spelling out some of the details of that sinfulness: ignorance of God (1:2–4); rebellion (1:5); insincere worship (1:10–17); infidelity, injustice, murder, dishonesty, bribery, oppression (1:21–23); idolatry and pride (2:6–22); greediness of rulers (3:13–15); irresponsible luxury (3:16–4:1; 5:8–9); drunkenness and carousing (5:11–12, 22; 28:1–4); confusion of evil with good (5:18–23); rejection of God's law (5:24–25); lack of faith (7:1–17); and others. That which made it possible for Isaiah to confess his own sin and that of his people was his firsthand confrontation by "the King, the LORD of hosts."

> *Is this true also in our confession of sin? What responsibility do we have for the sin of other people?*

### The Gift of Pardon (vv. 6–7)

In Isaiah's vision, one of the seraphim placed a heated stone on the prophet's mouth, saying: "Now that this has touched your lips, your guilt has departed and your sin is blotted out." Isaiah's sin was burned out by the consuming fire of God's grace. With the word of pardon the burden of guilt was lifted. The word translated "blotted out" is more literally "atoned for." Isaiah preached the gospel of forgiveness that he had experienced on the condition of repentance (1:18–20). For forgiveness is not mechanically and magically applied. It is given and accepted in an interpersonal relationship.

*Commitment and Commission (vv. 8–13)*

After his cleansing and pardon, Isaiah no longer heard the voice of God's servants; he heard the voice of God, saying, "Whom shall I send, and who will go for us?" The word "send" is the missionary word—God does the sending. The word "go" is the word calling for human action in response to the divine initiative. The word "us" refers to the heavenly council, which we encountered in Genesis 1:26. As we worship, we not only hear the voices of the choir and the minister, but above, through, and sometimes perhaps in spite of them, we hear the voice of God. When Isaiah heard that voice, he replied, "Here am I; send me." And God said, "Go." Isaiah accepted a call to be a home missionary to the people of Judah and Jerusalem.

But the commission that he received from God was foreboding. For the sake of emphasis, second causes are passed over, and the consequences of human sin are expressed as the purpose of God. Imperatives are used to underscore the certainty of God's judgment. The very hearing of the God-given message will be the occasion of spiritual blindness and deafness, for "people loved darkness rather than light because their deeds were evil" (John 3:19). Isaiah was distressed by his anticipation of God's judgment on his people and asked, "How long, O Lord?" The answer foretold devastating judgment. And, in his preaching, Isaiah warned the people of judgment in various ways. Like Amos, he announced the coming of the Day of the LORD. And like both Amos and Hosea, Isaiah regarded the Assyrians as an instrument of divine judgment, describing them as "the rod of my [God's] anger," and "the club in their hands is my [God's] fury" (10:5). One of his most interesting presentations of God's judgment is found in his parable of the Vineyard (5:1–7).

The Hebrew text of Isaiah 6:13 is quite unclear. It may well be a gloss from a later hand and not a part of the original account of Isaiah's call at all. It has been interpreted by some, however, in support of a doctrine of the remnant as "the holy seed" or "stump." Regardless of how this particular textual problem is solved, Isaiah's understanding of judgment and hope included a stress on a remnant who will survive. This teaching cuts in two ways at the same time, the way of punishment and the way of salvation. Isaiah named one of his sons Shear-jashub (7:3), which means "a remnant shall return." This can also mean "only a remnant shall return" or "beyond a shadow of a doubt a remnant shall return." The remnant is associated with punishment and destruction in such passages as Amos 3:12 and 5:3. It is associated with salvation in such passages as Hosea 11:8–11 and Isaiah 11:11, 16. Both the positive and the negative aspects of the remnant are expanded in Isaiah 10:20–23.

## Faith as Trust in God

Obviously all the prophets of Israel were people of faith. But Isaiah stands out as prophet of faith par excellence. Apparently he did not have the ups and downs of faith so characteristic of Jeremiah a century later—his faith was always steady and assured.

*To illustrate faith as trust in God we turn to Isaiah 7:1–17. Read these verses and seek to determine for yourself what they actually meant in their original setting.*

### Isaiah's First Encounter with Ahaz (vv. 1–9)

The first nine verses give an account of Isaiah's first visit to see King Ahaz. The occasion was the crisis of 734 B.C.E., when Rezin of Syria and Pekah of Israel tried to dethrone Ahaz as king of Judah because he would not participate with them in their anti-Assyrian alliance. Therefore, God sent Isaiah to Ahaz with a message of assurance: "Take heed, be quiet, do not fear, and do not let your heart be faint because of these two smoldering stumps of firebrands." This call to faith in God was reiterated in these words: "If you do not stand firm in faith, you shall not stand at all."

### The Sign of Immanuel (vv. 10–17)

Shortly after Isaiah's first visit to Ahaz, God sent Ahaz another message through the prophet regarding the same political problem. Ahaz was told to ask for a sign from God, no matter how difficult, that he might have his faith strengthened. But he refused with false piety, saying, "I will not ask, and I will not put the LORD to the test." (It is one thing to attempt *to require* a sign from God; it is quite another *to accept* one that God offers.) Ahaz was being wearisome, and Isaiah announced a sign to Ahaz: "Look, the young woman is with child and shall bear a son, and shall name him Immanuel."

There has been much unfortunate debate concerning the translation of this verse. Some say the second word of the Hebrew text should be rendered "a virgin," while others say it should be rendered "a young woman." So far as the Hebrew word is concerned, it means "a young woman of marriageable age." The word as such does not indicate virginity or lack of virginity. There is another Hebrew word that ordinarily means "virgin," but Isaiah did not use it in this passage. However, the early Greek translation of the Old Testament known as the Septuagint translated the Hebrew word in Isaiah 7:14 with a word that usually means "virgin." It was this translation that was quoted by the author of Matthew in 1:23 in relation to Mary, the mother of Jesus. When we read Matthew 1:18 and 1:20, we know that the writer of the Gospel meant "virgin."

The passage in Isaiah 7:10–17 clearly states that the sign was given to Ahaz. A fulfillment over seven hundred years later could not be a sign to Ahaz in the eighth century B.C.E. The original young woman may have been a virgin when Isaiah's prophecy was made; but she also may have been the wife of Ahaz, or the wife of the prophet, or the wife of someone else. In any case the child would be called Immanuel, which means "God with us." At the age of discriminating choice the child's food would be curds and honey, the diet of nomads. Before the discriminating capacity of the child has developed, Syria and Israel will be deserted.

Isaiah's second son was named Maher-shalal-hash-baz, which means "the spoil speeds, the prey hastens." This name provided an additional sign that "the wealth of Damascus and the spoil of Samaria will be carried away by the king of Assyria." But while this was good news for Ahaz, there is also a word of judgment on him and the house of David. He would pay dearly for deciding to put his trust in Assyrian aid rather than in God.

Yet God in overarching providence was not only concerned with the child to be born in the eighth century B.C.E. In the fullness of time God sent Jesus Christ, Immanuel, "God with us" in the most profound way. One fulfillment does not cancel the other.[5] To ignore the meaning of Isaiah 7:14 in its original setting in the eighth century B.C.E. is to contribute to the undermining of the distinctiveness of biblical faith as historical revelation. To recognize how the Christian community reinterpreted the text in light of the wonder of Jesus Christ as the Incarnate Lord is to contribute to the strengthening of a genuine biblical theology.

## The Coming Davidic King

Isaiah was steeped in the theology of God's covenant with David (2 Sam. 7). And beyond the dark night of judgment he saw a glorious day, when the Ideal Son of David would reign in peace. We shall examine two passages briefly: Isaiah 9:2–7 and 11:1–9. The word "Messiah" means "anointed one." The kings of Israel and Judah were anointed to their office with oil. In time the word "Messiah" came to be applied not only to David and other reigning kings but to the ideal David who was yet to come.

Though Isaiah did not use the word in these passages, they are "messianic" in content.

*As you read each of them, list the characteristics of the anticipated King. At what points do the two passages complement each other?*

### For to Us a Child Is Born (9:2–7)

The prophet speaks with assurance of a new day in terms that were meaningful to the people of his own time. The nation is joyous, for the rod of the oppressor has been broken and peace has come. But the chief source of rejoicing is the birth of the child. As ruler he will be a marvelous guide and counselor, a channel of the divine power, a persevering father, and a prince of peace. The promise of God to the house of David will be kept. While we do not know all that Isaiah had in mind, as Christians we believe that this vision received a deepening and energizing in Jesus Christ, and we recognize the appropriateness of its use especially at the Christmas season.

### A Shoot from the Stump of Jesse (11:1–9)

This picture of the ideal David is very similar to the preceding one. The Spirit of the LORD will rest on him in a special way, and his reign will be characterized by wise counsel, reverence, righteous judgment, and faithfulness. The age that he inaugurates will be characterized by peace in its fullest extent. In fact, this age is pictured as a new Eden (vv. 6–9).

"Peace" in Hebrew means far more than the absence of war. It means complete well-being in every sense of the word. It embraces the wholeness and soundness of both personal and corporate life. This is stressed in Isaiah 9:6 by the epithet "Prince of Peace." It is expressed in 11:6–9 in terms of harmony between humankind and nature. It is presented in 2:2–4 as reconciliation among the nations. Of course, this last passage is also found in Micah 4:1–3, and we do not know whether it originated with Isaiah, or Micah, or some other prophet. Nations are pictured as coming to God's house in Jerusalem to learn God's Law. When they find their true unity in God, they will convert their instruments of war into instruments of peace. How is Isaiah's hope of a new David and a new age related to the Christian gospel and to the world in our time?

## Micah—Prophet of God's Requirement

> He has told you, O mortal, what is good;
>     and what does the LORD require of you
>     but to do justice, and to love kindness,
>     and to walk humbly with your God?

(Micah 6:8)

These words are typical of the last of the great prophets of the eighth century B.C.E. They are a kind of summary of God's word to us through Micah.

Micah's home was in Moresheth, a town about thirty miles southwest of Jerusalem. He was a country boy with an uncommon sensitivity to the suffering of the poor at the hands of powerful and wealthy oppressors. Indeed, God seems to have called him to be a prophet through this sensitivity to the needs of others. Though his ministry was performed primarily in behalf of Judah and Jerusalem, he also spoke to the needs of Samaria (1:1, 5–6).

Look at his familiar statement quoted above. This statement is set in the context of what constitutes the proper worship of God. Many were abusing the sacrificial system by making the worship of the LORD appear as a magical show of sacrifices. That is, they acted as if they satisfied God by going through a prescribed ritual, without regard to the condition of their hearts. Some had gone so far as to revert to the pagan practice of child sacrifice (Ahaz, for example). But in his classic statement Micah set the record straight. He also gave a perfect summary of eighth-century prophecy including his own.

## To Do Justice

This phrase plus much more in Micah reminds us of Amos (see especially Amos 5:24). Justice is the outworking of righteousness. Like Amos, Micah called down the judgment of God on his people for their injustices (see chaps. 1 and 2). But Micah's most notable declaration of judgment on injustice is found in chapter 3. In this passage he indicts the leaders of his people.

> *As you read the chapter, list each distinct group of leaders and record the specific wrongs committed by each group.*

> *On the basis of Micah's standards, how do you think our local, state, and national leaders measure up?*

> *What about our church leaders?*

## To Love Kindness

The word translated "kindness" is the word that is ordinarily rendered "steadfast love" in the New Revised Standard Version. It is the covenant love so stressed by Hosea, and it does include kindness in human relationships. Yet it means far more than kindness. It means faithfulness and dependability in all relationships between human beings (such as the relationships involved in marriage and in the home, business, and politics) and in one's relationship to God. Though it includes living up to legal stipulations, it goes far beyond the fulfillment of the letter of the Law.

## To Walk Humbly with Your God

The humble walk with God is the equivalent of Isaiah's emphasis on faith. The humble person trusts God's guidance; Ahaz refused it when it was offered through God's prophet. Actually the humble walk with God is the source of doing justice and loving kindness, for God is the ultimate standard of what is just and what is kind.

Isaiah's faith in God included his faith in God's promise to David. Micah 5:2–4 is also an expression of faith in a new David. Scholars are not at all agreed on the date of this announcement. Some place it earlier than the time of Micah, others attribute it to Micah, and many insist that it is later than Micah. In the light of Isaiah's vision of an ideal David, there is no compelling reason for denying the word to Micah himself. But whether it came from him or from another prophet, it expresses faith in God's covenant with David. Bethlehem was the adopted home of Ruth and later the home of David. A future ruler is to come forth from the Davidic dynasty, which had its ancient origins in this humble place. After separation and suffering, God's people will be reunited. And the Davidic heir, like David himself, will rule as a shepherd king over his flock. Jesus is identified as this heir in Matthew 2:6 and John 7:42.

As a result of the bold "forthtelling" of the four great prophets of the eighth century B.C.E., the conscience of God's people has never been at ease in the presence of injustice, unfaithfulness, and disbelief. Their task was to claim the hearing and repentance of the people of their own time. Nonetheless, their deep understanding of God and their clear articulation of God's way continue to challenge all who will listen.

# Judgment on Southern Judah

*I*n 587/586 B.C.E. Jerusalem was destroyed by the Babylonians—the climax of God's judgment on Judah. The period with which we are now concerned is one hundred and ten years, as it begins with the accession of Manasseh to the throne of Judah in 697 B.C.E. The history of this period is recorded in 2 Kings 21–25 and 2 Chronicles 33–36. Additional light comes from the seventh-century prophets and from archaeological discoveries. We shall take a brief look at the historical background and then examine the book of Deuteronomy and the seventh-century prophets. See the chronological chart in Chapter 8 for the sequence of rulers.

## Judah in the Seventh Century B.C.E.

### The Reigns of Manasseh and Amon

When Manasseh came to the throne in 697, Assyria was still the dominant power in the Near East. He reversed the policy of his father Hezekiah and became an enthusiastic puppet of the Assyrian king. He rebuilt the high places, or local shrines, as well as the altars of Baal. He worshiped the astral deities of the Assyrians and built pagan altars in the Temple area. Like Ahaz, he sacrificed his own son as an offering and supported various cults of divination and fortune-telling. He shed much innocent blood and seduced his people to commit evils in which even the Amorites (Canaanites) had not engaged. Amon, his son and successor, followed in the footsteps of his father but was murdered after a very short reign. His murderers were slain in turn, and his son Josiah was made king.

### The Reign of Good King Josiah

In spite of apparent strength Assyria was already on the wane when Josiah became king of Judah. The empire was too vast to keep it intact by sheer military compulsion. Various peoples were challenging for supremacy: Medes, Babylonians, Cimmerians, Scythians, and others. Nabopolassar of Babylon defeated the Assyrians in the year Jeremiah began his prophetic work (626 B.C.E.). The Medes and the Babylonians were in the process of finishing off Assyria when Egypt offered aid. Nonetheless, Asshur fell to the Medes in 614 and Nineveh to the Medes and the Babylonians in 612. Soon thereafter Assyria was only a bad memory.

This was a time of great prophets. Zephaniah seems to have brought his message of the Day of the LORD prior to Josiah's reformation. Moreover, Jeremiah's ministry was already in process before the reformation and continued until after the fall of Jerusalem. Nahum exulted in the overthrow of Nineveh very close to the time of its fall to the Medes and the Babylonians. Habakkuk's work was done after the death of Josiah and shortly before the destruction of Jerusalem. We shall consider these prophets later in the chapter.

King Josiah reversed the policies of his father Amon and his grandfather Manasseh. He was, in a sense, a new Hezekiah. Like Hezekiah, he made a bid for the reunion of what was once Israel with Judah under the Davidic dynasty. Because Assyrian power was declining, he actually brought some northern territory under his rule. His reformation began before the discovery of "the book of the law" in the Temple. In fact, the work on the Temple was itself an aspect of the reformation. But tremendous impetus and guidance were given to the reformation by the Book of the Law.

While the Temple was being repaired in 622 B.C.E., Hilkiah the high priest found the Book of the Law, whereupon he reported the find to Shaphan, the king's secretary, who in turn read the book to Josiah. After Josiah had heard the book, he tore his clothes in anguish, for he realized that its curses must rest on the kingdom for its unfaithfulness. Immediately he sent to Huldah the prophetess to inquire about the validity of the book. She assured the king that it was an authentic message from God. Therefore, he read the book in the hearing of the elders and people of Judah, after which king and people renewed their covenant with God. This is reminiscent of the formation of the covenant at Sinai and its renewal under Joshua at Shechem (Josh. 24).

For centuries this book has been identified by many with Deuteronomy or a part thereof on the basis of the correspondence between the requirements of the Deuteronomic law and the reforms of Josiah as set forth in 2 Kings 22–23. The official recognition of this body of writing as a divinely authoritative guide is usually regarded as the first step in the formation of the Old Testament canon. Josiah's reform included the removal of idols and the idolatrous priests from the Temple, the destruction of the houses of religious prostitutes, the centralization of worship in Jerusalem, the repudiation of child sacrifice, the abolition of the shrine and altar at Bethel, the execution of the syncretic priests who served at the high places, and a celebration of Passover.

Pharaoh Neco II of Egypt feared the rising power of Babylon. Therefore, he set out to aid the Assyrians in their attempt to take Haran from the Babylonians.[1] Josiah, whose reformation was anti-Assyrian religiously and politically, did not want to be at the mercy of an Egyptian-Assyrian coalition. Therefore, he attempted to intercept the Egyptians at Megiddo, where he was killed. The good king was dead, and the land was in mourning and in jeopardy.

The question of the permanent value of Josiah's reform has often been discussed. Certainly there were those who opposed it from the start. It is undoubtedly true, as the biblical record makes plain, that the reform was largely a matter of externals. Probably the knowledge that the law had been obeyed according to the letter gave many a sense of false security. In spite of this, however, we must not sell Josiah short. His motivation was genuine: he wanted to do the will of God. Moreover, the official position of a government does affect the thought patterns of its people. Finally, Josiah's life was brought to an abrupt end only thirteen years after the discovery of the Book of the Law in the Temple, and those who succeeded him as kings of Judah were ineffective. Much of what Josiah did was needed, but the external obedience to law does not regenerate evil hearts. Jeremiah was to make that plain. What should be the relation of the law of the state to the religious life of the people?

## The Last Days of Judah

The last days of Judah were filled with one tragic event after another. Josiah was succeeded by his pro-Babylonian son Jehoahaz, who reigned only three months. Pharaoh Neco replaced him with his pro-Egyptian brother Eliakim, whose name was changed by the Pharaoh to Jehoiakim. As a vassal of Egypt Jehoiakim was forced to pay heavy tribute. But at the battle of Carchemish in 605 B.C.E., Nebuchadnezzar of Babylon defeated the Egyptians. Consequently Jehoiakim became the vassal of Babylon—though unwillingly. After Nebuchadnezzar and Neco fought again in 601, Jehoiakim thought it was an auspicious occasion to rebel against Babylon. Evidently Nebuchadnezzar sent bands of Chaldeans, Syrians, Moabites, and Ammonites against Judah. According to 2 Kings 24:1–2 this was

God's doing. In a short time Nebuchadnezzar himself marched against Judah.

Jehoiakim died, and his son Jehoiachin became king in his stead. Jerusalem surrendered to the Babylonians in 597 B.C.E., and Nebuchadnezzar took Jehoiachin and his family, the ablest leaders and craftsmen, and the treasure of the Temple and palace to Babylon; and he made Zedekiah (Mattaniah), Jehoiachin's uncle, king in his place. The country was left in poor hands.

The timid Zedekiah was caught in the middle between his nobles on the one hand and the Babylonian king on the other. The false prophets said that Jehoiachin and the other exiles would soon be sent home and all would be well. But Jeremiah maintained that this message was not the word of God. At first Zedekiah was submissive to the Babylonian yoke, but he later rebelled. This was the occasion for the second invasion by Nebuchadnezzar in 587/586 B.C.E. Zedekiah fled from Jerusalem but was overtaken. His sons were put to death before him, his own eyes were put out, and he was taken as a prisoner to Babylon.

Nebuchadnezzar's troops burned the Temple, broke down the walls of Jerusalem, left only the poorest people in the land, carried with them all things of value found in the Temple, and executed all potential leaders of further revolt. Gedaliah was made provincial governor of the land but was soon murdered by a group of patriots under Ishmael, a member of the royal family. Fearing retaliation from Babylon, many who had not been deported fled to Egypt, forcing Jeremiah to go with them. The dynasty of David had fallen, the Temple of Solomon was in ashes, and the kingdom of Judah was no more.

## Zephaniah—Prophet of the Day of the Lord

> The great day of the Lord is near,
> near and hastening fast . . .
> That day will be a day of wrath,
> a day of distress and anguish,
> a day of ruin and devastation,
> a day of darkness and gloom,
> a day of clouds and thick darkness,
> a day of trumpet blast and battle cry
> against the fortified cities
> and against the lofty battlements.
> I will bring such distress upon people. . . .
> (Zeph. 1:14–17)

This was the kind of message God spoke in those grim days through another prophet whose words form a book of our Bible. Zephaniah was a descendant of King Hezekiah (Zeph. 1:1); his pronouncements seem to indicate that he was a native of Jerusalem. Assyria was on the decline, and Babylonia was on the rise. It is thought that Zephaniah prophesied before the beginning of Josiah's reformation, because Josiah abolished some of the evils mentioned by him.

Zephaniah's entire message centers around the Day of the LORD. We first encountered this in Amos 5:18–20. The idea seems to have been derived from the combination of two factors in the life of God's people. One factor was the victory of the LORD in the events of Israel's history. For example, the occasion of the deliverance of Israel from the Egyptians at the exodus was the day of the LORD's victory, and this victory gave a foreshadowing of final victory (compare Judg. 4: 23). The other factor was the celebration of God's sovereignty at the Feast of Ingathering, or New Year's Day, when God's bringing order out of chaos at creation (Gen. 1:1) was associated with victory over historical enemies. That which had happened in the past and that which was celebrated in worship were also anticipated for the future. Many in the time of Amos thought of the Day of the LORD as a time when their enemies would be overthrown and they themselves would be blessed. But Amos gave the idea a new twist and insisted that it would include judgment on God's own sinful people as well (compare Isa. 2:6–3:26).

Of all the prophets Zephaniah developed Amos's understanding and placed the strongest emphasis upon the Day of the LORD as a day of wrath upon Judah and Jerusalem, and yet upon all others as well (1:1–3:8). He denounced the proud, the idolatrous, the practical atheists, and the people's leaders: officials, judges, prophets, and priests. The practical atheists said, "The LORD will not do good, nor will he do harm" (1:12). They did not deny the existence of God; they simply considered God irrelevant to the issues of life.

*Can you give illustrations of practical atheism today?*

But the Day of the LORD is not associated with punishment alone, for it will issue in the reign of God ( Zeph. 3: 9–20; compare Hos. 2:16–23; Isa. 2:1–5; 24:21–23; Micah 4:1–4; Mal. 4; Joel 1–3; Zech. 14; Ps. 98:9). In the New Testament the Day of the LORD becomes the Day of Christ (2 Cor. 1:14; Phil. 1:6, 10), which will be a day of judgment and wrath (Matt. 10:15; Rom. 2:5, 16; Jude 6) as a prelude to the consummation of the kingdom.

*Read the book of Zephaniah, which consists of only three chapters, and seek to answer this question: What similarities do you find between the warnings and calls to repentance in our time and the message of Zephaniah?*

## Deuteronomy—A Book of Sermons on the Covenant

The Book of the Law (Deuteronomy or a part of it) was much needed in Judah. Hosea had pleaded with Northern Israel to return to the Mosaic faith. And Jeremiah had been speaking to his fellow Judeans about their unfaithfulness and ingratitude to God (2:1–4:4). The discovery of the Book of the Law in the Temple was a providentially ordained find. Evidently many Judeans had accepted the Davidic covenant as an unconditional promise of God's favor and had forgotten the covenant made at Sinai with its demands of obedience upon the people.

Deuteronomy is a book of three sermons on the covenant (1:1–4:43; 4:44–28:68; 29:1–30:20) plus several appendices (31:1–34:12). It is a dynamic re-presentation of the Mosaic faith with a view to contemporary relevance. It is a masterful combination of preaching the good news of God's mighty acts in behalf of God's people and a teaching of what a grateful response should mean. The book was the medicine the seventh-century Judeans needed.

### The First Sermon: The Mighty Acts of God (1:1–4:43)

The first sermon is a rehearsal of the mighty acts of God in behalf of the people. The gift of the Promised Land is viewed in anticipation. Then there is a flashback, which includes the journey through the wilderness and the occupation of Transjordan. The people are to respond in grateful obedience to the law. Then the flashback continues, as the covenant at Horeb (Sinai) and the exodus from Egypt are recalled. The people are warned against idolatry and disobedience: "For the LORD your God is a devouring fire, a jealous God" (4:24). God will tolerate no rivals.

### The Second Sermon: The Law of the Covenant (4:44–28:68)

This second sermon is the heart of the book and includes what is known as the Deuteronomic Code (chs.12–26). After a brief introductory section (4:44–49), the covenant faith is presented 5:1–11:32. At the very outset it is made plain that the Sinai-Horeb covenant was by no means confined to the ancestors (who are now dead): "The LORD our God made a covenant with us in Horeb. Not with our ancestors did the LORD make this covenant, but with us, who are all of us here alive today" (5:2–3). In other words, past revelation is so re-presented that it becomes contemporaneous through proclamation and response. This is still what takes place today when the word of God is truly proclaimed and people respond in faith and obedience. The Ten Commandments are found here (5:1–21) as well as in Exodus 20, with some differences, especially in relation to the Sabbath. The purpose of the divine instruction is the obedience of the people, their reverence for God, their prolongation of life in the Promised Land, and their biological multiplication (6:1–3).

One of the best-known passages in Deuteronomy is chapter 6, verses 4–9. This is the first part of the Jewish Shema, which has been used from ancient times by the Jewish people in daily worship (compare also Deut. 11:13–21 and Num. 15:37–41). It is called the "Shema" because this is the Hebrew word for "hear," with which the passage begins.

> Read these verses over several times as you meditate on their meaning.

You will note in the margin of the New Revised Standard Version that verse 4 may be translated in any one of several ways. But regardless of how it is translated, it calls for an undivided loyalty to the LORD (YHWH). Verse 5 shows that this loyalty is to be expressed in a wholehearted devotion to God: "You shall love the LORD your God with all your heart, and with all your soul, and with all your might." In Hebrew thought, the words "heart," "soul," and "might" are not to be viewed analytically but together. They are an emphatic way of expressing the devotion of the whole person to God.

That which has done most to make this verse well-known among Christians is Jesus' designation of it as the Great and First Commandment (see Matt. 22:37; Mark 12:29–30). In Mark 12:30 the word "mind" has been included in the Greek. This does not add anything to the original, because both "heart" and "soul" include in Hebrew what is meant by "mind" in Greek. The extra word, therefore, was included for the sake of clarity to the Greek reader.

Deuteronomy 6:10–15 makes it clear (and so does the book as a whole) that the love of God's people for God is a response to God's prior love for them. That is, they are to love because God first loved them (compare 1 John 4:19). Jesus coupled love of neighbor (Lev. 19:18) with love of God. Though this is not done in Deuteronomy in so many words, it is done in substance, for at various points great concern is shown for the neighbor.

We return to our original passage, Deuteronomy 6:4–9. "These words" in verse 6 refer to the commands in verses 4 and 5, which are to be taught to the children of God's people. Instructions are given for keeping these commands before the people perpetually (vv. 7–9). In relation to the responsibility of parents for the religious nurture of their children, mentioned in verse 7, we examine verses 20–25. When a child asks questions about the meaning of God's laws, parents are provided with a creedal response. This response does not deal in abstractions but recites the mighty acts of God in behalf of Israel. Here, as in the case of the Ten Commandments that we studied earlier, law is based on grace.

The conquest of Canaan is viewed in the perspective of holy war (7:1–5), which we explored in our study of "The Promised Land." This is tied up with the fact that Israel is an elected or holy people.

*Read 7:6–16 and jot down in your notebook what election involves in this passage.*

As God's people face the tests ahead, they are to remember what God has already done for them (7:17–26). The time will come when they will be tempted to say, "My power and the might of my own hand have gotten me this wealth" (8:17), but they are warned: "Remember the LORD your God, for it is he who gives you power to get wealth" (8:18). Moreover, the gift of the land is not based on Israel's righteousness, for Israel is a stubborn and rebellious people (9:1–29). And God's requirements run in opposition to such stubbornness and rebellion.

*Analyze 10:12–22 and record in your notebook the specific requirements included therein. How do they correspond to those found in Micah 6:8?*

*How is Israel's response to these requirements related to the continuing possession of the Land of Promise (11:1–32)?*

The Code of Deuteronomy (chaps. 12–26) covers many different aspects of life: worship, political and religious leaders, crime, war, property, the family, and others. One of the most celebrated of these laws is the centralization of worship (12:1–31). In earlier times Shiloh was the central sanctuary, and the principle of centralization seems to be applied to Jerusalem here. At least Josiah so understood the law. This was intimately connected with his attempt to abolish idolatrous practices at local shrines.

*You will want to read chapter 12 and compare it with Exodus 20:24.*

*Deuteronomy 26:1–11 contains one of Israel's earliest confessions of faith. It is the Mosaic faith in a nutshell. List the mighty acts of God found in it.*

Deuteronomy is also remembered for its curses and blessings (27:11–28:68). The curses found in 27:11–26 were used in a liturgical ceremony in which the people participated. The blessings found in 28:1–14 and the curses found in 28:15–68 are in the preaching style characteristic of the book as a whole. Obedience to God issues in blessing; disobedience in curse.

## The Third Sermon: The Nature of the Covenant (29:1–30:20)

Here we have another call to obey the requirements of the covenant. The people are reminded that the covenant not only includes those present but also generations yet to come (29:15). Children born into families of the Reformed tradition are likewise regarded as children of the covenant, who are to be brought up to become what they already are. The people are warned to repent when they have sinned that they may be open to receive the grace of God in forgiveness. The word and will of God are immediately available to the people (30:11–14). The choice between the LORD and idols is a life-and-death matter (30:15–20; compare Josh. 24): "I have set before you life and death, blessings and curses. Choose life so that you and your descendants may live" (30:19).

*"Life" is a qualitative word and stands for all the blessings of God. "Death" is also a qualitative word and stands for all the punishments of God. God's sovereignty never obliterates the responsibility of human decision. The fundamental choice is still a choice between God and idols. How may we best communicate the necessity and urgency of accepting God's priority in our decisions?*

## Nahum—Prophet of the Destruction of Nineveh

Nahum's message does not seem to have a close connection with that of Deuteronomy or that of the other prophets of the seventh century. While it does share the element of judgment in common with the others, it does not concentrate, as they do, on the judgment of the chosen people. Rather, the emphasis is on the destruction of Nineveh, the last capital of the cruel Assyrian empire. The fall of Nineveh is regarded by Nahum as an evidence of the justice of God. It should be readily admitted that the spirit of Nahum is more closely akin to Deuteronomy 19:21 than it is to Matthew 5:38–42.

## Habakkuk—A Prophet Who Was Called to Faith

The setting of Habakkuk's message was shortly before the fall of Jerusalem, perhaps about 605 B.C.E. The Deuteronomic reform had taken place, and Josiah was dead. Deuteronomy had promised blessing for the righteous and curse for the wicked. In spite of the reform many Judeans were engaging in their old bad habits again. But Deuteronomy had stressed heartfelt motivation in terms of love, faith, and obedience. External reformation was not enough.

Habakkuk was confused by the popular oversimplification of the Deuteronomic principle of reward and punishment. Reward was not coming in exact proportion to righteous conduct, and punishment was not coming in exact proportion to wicked conduct. Perhaps it was harder to exercise faith in Habakkuk's day than it had been in the time of Isaiah. Be that as it may, Habakkuk found himself with questions concerning the righteousness of God. In effect he said, "O LORD, why do you permit great wrongs in Judah to go unpunished, for 'the wicked surround the righteous—therefore judgment comes forth perverted'?" (Read 1:1–4.) God answered in effect, "I am rousing the Chaldeans (Babylonians) as instruments of my judgment." (Read 1:5–11.) But this answer only deepened Habakkuk's problem: "The Chaldeans are more wicked than the wicked among my own people. How can you as the righteous God allow the wicked to swallow up the more righteous?" (Read 1:12–17.) God answered, "I will judge the Chaldeans, Habakkuk, in my own time and way, 'but the righteous live by their faith.'" (Read 2:1–4.)

The word translated "faith" in 2:4 includes both faith and faithfulness simultaneously. The word "righteous" designates the person who has been set in the covenant relation by God and who seeks to live in that relation. God called Habakkuk to trust, even though he could not fully understand God's providence, and to be faithful regardless of circumstance. In other words, this was a call to a wholehearted commitment. Paul took Habakkuk 2:4b as his text in setting forth the doctrine of justification by faith in Galatians 3:11 and Romans 1:17.[2]

*What does Habakkuk teach us about honest questions to God?*

*To what group of people was Habakkuk 2:4b applied originally?*
*To what group was it applied by Paul? How may it be applied to*
*us who are Christians today?*

## Jeremiah—Prophet of the New Covenant

### A Man of Strife and Contention

The great prophet of the last days of Judah was Jeremiah, a man of heartbreak and hope. It is no accident that in later times he should be regarded as a figure like that of Jesus.

Jeremiah was born of a priestly family in Anathoth of Benjamin about the middle of the seventh century B.C.E. His prophetic activity began about 626 B.C.E., during the reign of Josiah, and continued until sometime after the fall of Jerusalem in 587/586 B.C.E. His entire ministry was characterized by conflict, internal and external. He was by nature a timid and quiet soul who was called by God to act with courage and boldness. The deep hurt of his people was felt as his own:

> O that my head were a spring of water,
> and my eyes a fountain of tears,
> so that I might weep day and night
> for the slain of my poor people!
>
> (9:1)

Yet Jeremiah could call down the vengeance of God upon enemies who had conspired against him, regarding them as the enemies of God (see 11:20; 20:12). Against those who had made plots against him he could pray, "Do not forgive their iniquity, do not blot out their sin from your sight" (18:23). This is more in the spirit of the imprecatory psalms (for example, 69 and 137) than in that of the One who said, "Father, forgive them; for they do not know what they are doing" (Luke 23:34). In other words, Jeremiah was a man of his own time as well as a prophet of God.

Jeremiah has been called the most human of the prophets. At one of his moments of utter loneliness he addressed God in language bordering on blasphemy yet was called on by God to repent (see 15:15–21). On another occasion he accused God of deceiving him and making him a laughingstock, and even cursed the day of his birth (20:7–18; compare Job 3:3–13). But his strong faith in God always brought him through these periods of despair.

While Jeremiah held King Josiah in high esteem (22:15–16; compare 2 Chron. 35:24–25), he knew that Judah needed more than external reformation. His message included, among other things, doom for Judah, Jerusalem, the Temple, and the Davidic dynasty. And this brought him into conflict with both leaders and people. He not only spoke the word of God but also depicted it in symbolic action, which was itself a prophetic word. He was a prophet of "heart religion" whose message culminated in the teaching of the new covenant of forgiveness.

Jeremiah's Temple sermon brought him to trial for his life (chaps. 7; 26). In response to his symbolic message of the destruction of Jerusalem (chap. 19), Pashhur the priest beat him and put him in the stocks overnight (20:1–6). At the LORD's direction Jeremiah dictated to Baruch, his secretary, all his pronouncements from the time of Josiah to the fourth year of King Jehoiakim (chap. 36). The scroll was eventually read to Jehoiakim, who cut it up and burned it as it was being read. Jeremiah and Baruch had already gone into hiding. Again at the LORD's command, Jeremiah dictated another scroll that contained the words of the original scroll and additional material as well. This scroll was a major source of our present book of Jeremiah.

In the early part of Zedekiah's reign Jeremiah dramatized the coming of the yoke of Babylon on Judah and her neighbors by making thongs and yoke-bars and wearing them around his neck (chap. 27). But the prophet Hananiah insisted that God would break the Babylonian yoke and in two years return King Jeconiah (Jehoiachin) and the exiles of the 597 B.C.E. invasion (chap. 28). To dramatize this he broke the yoke-bars that Jeremiah was wearing. Soon thereafter Jeremiah replaced the wooden bars with bars made of iron, repeated his announcement of doom, and predicted Hananiah's death within a year. Furthermore, Jeremiah wrote a letter to these early exiles counseling them to settle down in Babylon, for any restoration would be delayed at least seventy years (chap. 29).

In the beginning of Nebuchadnezzar's final siege of Jerusalem, Zedekiah asked Jeremiah for God's word (chap. 21; compare chap. 34). Zedekiah had made a covenant with Nebuchadnezzar to be his vassal, which, as far as Jeremiah was concerned, was an obligation before God to be kept. But Zedekiah did not keep his word. Therefore, Jeremiah, speaking for God, said, "I myself will fight against you." Perhaps Zedekiah was hoping for a deliverance such as that which came in the reign of Hezekiah at the word of Isaiah. But the time for that kind of deliverance was past.

As the Babylonian army was coming closer, Zedekiah ordered those who had Jewish slaves to free them. According to Deuteronomy 15:12–15, no Hebrew could be held by another Hebrew for more than six years. But this law had been transgressed (Jer. 34:14). Just why Zedekiah and his more well-to-do people freed their slaves is uncertain. But as soon as there was a lull in the fighting, the former owners broke their solemn covenant and took back their slaves. And Jeremiah spoke the terrifying word of judgment: "I am going to command, says the LORD, and will bring them [the Chaldeans] back to this city; and they will fight against it, and take it, and burn it with fire" (34:22).

Again the siege of Jerusalem was interrupted, this time by the Egyptian army. Jeremiah set out to go to his home in Benjamin but was intercepted and accused of deserting to the Chaldeans. Whereupon the princes of Judah beat him and imprisoned him in the house of Jonathan, the secretary. Zedekiah removed him to the court of the guard (see chap. 37). After the resumption of the siege, Jeremiah even counseled surrender to the Chaldeans (38:1–6), not for any lack of patriotism but because he believed that the will of God had been revealed to him. He knew there was no hope for Judah in battle and wanted to save his people from unnecessary tragedy. The princes put him in a cistern to die, but an Ethiopian eunuch pulled him out and placed him in the court of the guard at the king's command.

Right to the end Jeremiah continued to try to persuade Zedekiah to surrender and prevent the burning of the city by the Chaldeans. "And Jeremiah remained in the court of the guard until the day that Jerusalem was taken" (see chap. 38). The fall of Jerusalem, the murder of Gedaliah, and the flight of a remnant to Egypt have already been mentioned earlier (see Jer. 39:1–44:30). According to tradition, Jeremiah was stoned to death by his fellow countrymen who had forced him to go to Egypt with them.

## The Call of Jeremiah

As in the case of Isaiah, the call of Jeremiah is the key to understanding his message.

*The account of the latter's call is found in Jeremiah 1:4–10 and should be studied in connection with the two visions that follow in verses 11–19.*

*Make your own analysis of Jeremiah's call before reading any further in this volume. How was Jeremiah's call like the call of Isaiah? How was it different?*

"Now the word of the LORD came." This and similar expressions occur time and again throughout the book of Jeremiah. The "word" was God's message concerning particular situations and particular persons. It was by the word of God that Jeremiah was called, and it was at God's command that he preached.

Jeremiah was led to see his call as a matter of God's sovereign providence. The initial part of that call may be translated:

> Before I formed you in the womb I knew you,
> and before you were born I consecrated you;
> I appointed you a prophet to the nations.

Note the verbs "knew,""consecrated," and "appointed" are parallels, designating God's electing activity even before conception and birth. Note also that Jeremiah was ordained a prophet not only to Judah but to the nations. His was an international ministry. Moreover, it was not confined to some compartment of life labeled "religious," for everything was of concern to him. Politics and social problems could not be ruled out of preaching in the house of God.

But Jeremiah, like Moses, was not as certain of his prophetic qualifications as God was and sought to be excused on the basis of his youthfulness. God reassured him by promising to be with him: "Do not be afraid of them, for I am with you to deliver you." Moreover, God promised to be the source of his message.

Jeremiah was called to proclaim a word whose purpose was both negative and positive:

> See, today I appoint you over nations
>     and over kingdoms,
> to pluck up and to pull down,
> to destroy and to overthrow,
> to build and to plant.

The vision of the almond rod (1:11–12) and that of the boiling pot (1:13–19) were closely related to Jeremiah's call. In his first vision Jeremiah saw an "almond" (Hebrew *shaqed*) tree and was assured that the LORD was "watching over" (Hebrew *shoqed*) the divine word to do it. The vision of the boiling pot indicated the certainty of judgment that would come upon Jerusalem from the north. Although Jeremiah does not here identify the northern enemy more specifically, it was probably the Babylonians rather than the Scythians, even at this early date. Just as Jerusalem would be attacked by outsiders, Jeremiah himself would be attacked by the leaders of his own people—but God would be with him.

Jeremiah's visit to the potter's house (18:1–12) is very closely connected in thought with his call. The verb "formed" in 1:5 is from the same root as "potter" in 18:1ff. and "am shaping" in 18:11. In fact, this is the distinctive creation word in Genesis 2. As God was the sovereign Creator and Controller of Jeremiah himself, God is also the sovereign Creator and Controller of the covenant people—indeed of all nations. God has the power to re-create a spoiled vessel. Jeremiah was called "to destroy" and "to build" (1:10), but in the ultimate analysis it was God who did the destroying and the building (18:5–11). What Jeremiah did was to announce what God was going to destroy or to build. The responsiveness of the clay to the Potter's touch had a part in determining whether there would be another chance. The nation that repents will be reworked into a beautiful vessel. The nation that does not repent will be destroyed. We now turn to a consideration of illustrations from Jeremiah of the negative and positive aspects of the outworking of his call. As we do this, however, it will be well to keep in mind that tearing down, as well as building up, was a part of the saving activity of God.

## To Destroy and to Overthrow

### The Broken Covenant

Throughout his ministry Jeremiah was very conscious of the covenant made at Sinai. He seems familiar with the messages of Hosea and Deuteronomy. By using Hosea's figure of marriage for the covenant relation, Jeremiah early in his ministry accused his people of infidelity and ingratitude (2:1–4:4). They had forsaken the Fountain of Living Waters. And he pleaded with them to repent by circumcising their hearts.

In fact, everything that Jeremiah said about the chosen people must be seen against the background of the broken covenant, a theme central to Deuteronomy. Consider, for example, Jeremiah 11:1–12:17. The similarity between 11:1–13 and parts of Deuteronomy is easily detected, but how to account for the similarity is not so easily determined. Perhaps Jeremiah was deliberately supporting the Deuteronomic reform under Josiah. Perhaps he was simply recalling the people to the covenant made at Sinai. In any case, his people had broken the covenant by the worship of Baal.

On account of his proclamation of the covenant, there were people in his own hometown of Anathoth who sought his life (11:18–23). Though Jeremiah was satisfied that God would attend to his enemies in the long run, he had difficulty facing the prosperity of the wicked at the present moment and cried out to God in words similar to those of a lament in the Psalter (12:1–4; see Ps. 37). In substance God's answer was, "Cheer up, the worst is yet to come" (12:5–6).[3] If Jeremiah found the going hard among his own people, he found it even more difficult among his enemies in Jerusalem ("the jungle of the Jordan"). But God enabled Jeremiah to see that because his people had broken the covenant, they would be the prey of their neighbors (12:7–13). Still, in the final analysis if Judah's neighbors should repent and turn to the LORD, they too would be numbered among God's covenant family (12:14–17). The various parts of 11:1–12:17 may have come from different occasions, but they all bear on the central theme, the covenant. Jeremiah himself was called to substitute courage for complaint.

### The Foe from the North

The North as the place of origin from which Judah's enemy would come was mentioned in the inaugural vision of the boiling pot (1:13–19). But this is a recurring theme in the book of Jeremiah (see, for example, 4:6; 6:1, 22; 13:20). Furthermore, it is the theme of 4:5–6:26. The real reason, according to Jeremiah, for the coming of this enemy was not political expediency, but the rebellion of Judah against God. We remember that God used Assyria as the rod of divine anger in the eighth century. God was to use Babylonia in the same way at a later date. The Judeans were practicing injustice, they had broken the covenant, they refused to repent, their leaders were leading them astray, and their sacrifices were unacceptable. The foe from the North would come. The destiny of nations is in God's hands.

### The Temple Sermon

This is one of the most famous sermons ever preached. It is called "the Temple sermon" because it was delivered in the gate of one of the Temple courts and because it was focused on the destruction of the Temple.

> *Read Jeremiah 7:1–8:3 for the contents of the sermon, and chapter 26 for more details concerning its setting.*

It was preached at the beginning of the reign of Jehoiakim in the presence of priests, prophets, and people.

It began with a call to all who worshiped God in the Temple to amend their ways and doings—that is, to repent. The people had been deceiving themselves by viewing the Temple as a magic charm against all harm, saying superstitiously, "This is the temple of the LORD, the temple of the LORD, the temple of the LORD." Jeremiah became very specific about what must be amended (7:5–7). Justice must be practiced in person-to-person relationships, and hypocrisy in religion must be abolished. Formal worship can never be a substitute for honesty, respect for human life, sexual purity, telling the truth, and fidelity to God. The Temple, God's own house, has become "a den of robbers" (see Mark 11:17). It was to be destroyed as the sanctuary at Shiloh had been destroyed many years earlier.

Jeremiah was forbidden by God to intercede for the sinful people. Their pagan worship and formal sacrifices only compounded their sin. They had even gone so far as to sacrifice their sons and daughters. They had refused to hearken to God's servants, the prophets.

But that which disturbed those who heard Jeremiah was his announcement of the destruction of the Temple and the surrounding city. In response, they said, "You shall die," and they brought him before the princes. Jeremiah then addressed the princes with a call to repentance (26:12–15). The princes in turn spoke to the priests and the prophets: "This man does not deserve the sentence of death, for he has spoken to us in the name of the LORD our God" (26:16). Moreover, certain elders present reminded the group of Micah's prediction of the destruction of Jerusalem and the Temple (Micah 3:12). This precedent helped to save the day for Jeremiah. Do you feel that the church in our time sometimes attempts to put an end to the prophetic word?

The Law of God (the Deuteronomic law?), like the Temple, was being used as a fetish. Through those who misinterpreted it, it was giving the people a sense of false security (8:8–22). It is possible for God's written word to be used in such a way as to become a barrier to the real intent of that word.

## The Impending Doom

Jeremiah's ministry was performed under the threat of impending doom for his people, whom he loved devotedly. At the very outset he saw the threat from the North (1:13–18). The people would not repent, and the country was certain to be invaded by foreign troops (8:14–17). In fact, the word of God came to him very explicitly, "I will make Jerusalem a heap of ruins" (9:11).

To dramatize the rotten condition of the people, Jeremiah hid a linen waistcloth in a rock beside the Euphrates River and later recovered it. But by then it was spoiled and good for nothing (13:1–11; compare 13:12–14). Jeremiah witnessed King Jehoiachin, the queen mother, and many of the people being taken into exile (13:15–27). Unrepentant Judah was doomed (14:1–15:21). Jeremiah was even told by God not to marry as a sign that the families of Judah were standing under impending judgment (16:1–4; compare 16:5–21). After the first exile of Jehoiachin and many of the people, Jeremiah tried to prevent the utter destruction of his beloved Jerusalem by his counsels to Zedekiah. But this proved to be of no avail.

*The False Prophets*

In spite of Jeremiah's message of impending judgment there were other prophets who preached an entirely different message. Early in his ministry Jeremiah numbered the professional prophets among the condemned leaders of his people (2:26). Judgment would come upon the nation regardless of what the other prophets said (5:13). In fact, the chief responsibility for the coming judgment rested on the behavior of the prophets and priests as leaders of the people.

But the people enjoyed such easygoing leadership (5:30–31). The prophets and priests were "greedy for unjust gain" and cried, " 'Peace, peace,' when there [was] no peace." Instead of receiving the burden of the LORD and placing it on the people or nation as directed by God, the leaders themselves were burdens and substituted their own concoctions for God's message. We have already seen a specific example of a false prophet in Hananiah (ch. 28).

> *On the subject of false prophecy read especially Jeremiah 23:9–40.*
>
> *What distinguished Jeremiah as a true prophet of God from the false prophets?*
>
> *What distinguished him from a traitor to his country?*
>
> *How do we recognize the authentic word of God when we hear it today?*

## To Build and to Plant

We have examined at least in part Jeremiah's response to God's call "to destroy and to overthrow." We now examine the way in which he carried out God's command "to build and to plant."

Much of Jeremiah's preaching of judgment was done in relation to a call to repentance, and the possibility of repentance always entails a message of hope. Even after the first deportation of many of his people in 597 B.C.E., he tried to persuade Zedekiah to surrender and save Jerusalem from destruction. In our present study, however, we now concentrate on Jeremiah's message of hope in relation to the remnant, the Messiah, and the new covenant.

*The Remnant*

In the vision of the two baskets of figs (24:1–10) Jeremiah, in a sense, saw two remnants of his people, one that went into the Babylonian exile and the other that remained at home or fled to Egypt. The future lay with the Babylonian remnant. A remnant would be saved and would return to Palestine (see chaps. 30–31). "There is hope for your future, says the LORD" (31:17).

*Read Jeremiah 31:27–28 and compare it with 1:10.*

Jeremiah was so sure that a second exodus would take place after the exile (16:14–15; 29:10–14 ) that he bought a field in Anathoth, his hometown, signifying thereby that "houses and fields and vineyards shall again be bought in this land" (32:1–44).

## The Messiah

On the basis of a quantity of material preserved in the book of Jeremiah, it is fair to assume that Jeremiah more often preached on the Sinaitic covenant than on the covenant with David. He did this because the people and their leaders had neglected the obligations of the earlier covenant. Nevertheless, he did not omit the Davidic covenant from his message of hope. This can best be seen by reading 21:11–23:8 (compare chap. 30), which gives the setting in which Jeremiah's proclamations are to be understood.

The house of David was supposed to be founded on justice and righteousness, but, for the most part, it had failed to demonstrate these qualities in actual practice (21:11–22:9). First, Jeremiah takes notice of the exile of Shallum (Jehoahaz) (22:11–12). Next, he condemns Jehoiakim (22:13–19) for living in greedy luxury while taxing his people heavily to pay tribute to Egypt (see 2 Kings 23:33–35). His father Josiah demonstrated that he knew the LORD by dealing justly with the poor and needy, but Jehoiakim demonstrated by violence and oppression that he did not know God. Thirdly, Jeremiah tells King Coniah (Jehoiachin) that he and his mother will be taken into exile and that his son will never sit on the throne of David (22:24–30). Finally, Jeremiah puts the final touch on his message to the kings of Judah by denouncing Zedekiah surely, though indirectly (23:1–8).

Zedekiah was not the son of Jehoiachin but his uncle, a younger son of Josiah. Jeremiah points out the failure of so many of the kings ("shepherds") of his people. The name Zedekiah means "the righteousness of the LORD" or "the LORD is righteousness." But Zedekiah had certainly not acted in accordance with his name. Jeremiah announces that God will raise up for David another righteous Branch who will execute justice and righteousness, and his name will be "The LORD is our righteousness." That which Zedekiah's name called him to be would only be actualized by some other of David's line.

*Read Jeremiah 21:11–23:8; 30:9, 21; 33:14–26; and review Isaiah 9:2–7 and 11:1–9. How are these pictures of the new David related to Jesus?*

*The New Covenant*

The most distinctive aspect of Jeremiah's message is his word concerning a new covenant. In spite of all his emphasis on doom, Jeremiah had a hope for Judah's future. His hope, however, did not rest on sinful humans but on the faithful God. The people had failed, but God would preserve a remnant through which to carry on the redemptive purpose. The kings had failed, but God would still "raise up for David a righteous Branch." The old covenant had been broken, but God would make a new covenant with the people.

*Study Jeremiah 31:31–34 as you review what was said about the covenant at Sinai in chapter 5. What are the characteristics of the new covenant as set forth by Jeremiah here?*

While Hosea (2:19–20) and Jeremiah himself (4:1–4) had implicitly spoken of a new covenant earlier, its clearest statement in the Old Testament is found in the passage before us (compare Ezek. 16:60–63; Isa. 61:8). From Jeremiah's standpoint the new covenant is yet to come. It will be made with God's ancient people, Israel and Judah. But it will be different from the covenant made at Sinai, which was broken by the people, in spite of the fact that it was intended to be similar to the covenant between husband and wife. In fact, both the old covenant and the new covenant are evidences of God's love (see 31:3–4).

God had been a loving and faithful husband, but Israel had not been a loving and faithful wife. The new covenant will be a covenant of the *heart*. God's law (instruction) will be written on the hearts of the people. Under the old covenant so many thought of the law as being written on two tables of stone and therefore external to themselves. But life is not fundamentally a matter of externals. The real trouble with ancient Israel and with all people is heart trouble, for "the heart is devious above all else; it is perverse" (17:9). A little salve on the skin will not cure angina of the soul. Therefore the new God-people relationship will be intimate and personal. God's people will not live by secondhand religion; they will each know God in mutual commitment and devotion. Such knowledge is an interpersonal relationship, not simply an idea (see 2:8; 4:22; 9:3, 6, 24; 22:16;

compare Hos. 2:20; 4:1–6; 5:4; 6:6; Isa. 1:2–4). People from all strata of society will know God in this way. Because God will forgive the sin of the people, such intimate fellowship with God will be possible. Yet this personal knowledge will operate within the covenant community, not in selfish isolation.

The promise of the new covenant was given new meaning in and through him who said, "This cup is the new covenant in my blood" (1 Cor. 11:25; compare Mark 14:24; Matt. 26:26–29). In his teaching of the new covenant in Christ, the author of the Letter to the Hebrews quotes Jeremiah 31:31–34 in 8:8–12. In the final analysis the names for the two major parts of our Bible (Old Covenant/Testament and New Covenant/ Testament) owe their origin in part to Jeremiah and Paul (2 Cor. 3:6, 14–16). The disciples of Jesus Christ with whom God made the new covenant are like a new Israel and a new Judah.

In the time of Jeremiah the day of grace passed, and the Daughter of Zion was defiled, but there was yet another day of grace. Through the centuries of judgment and smoke of burning cities, the people of God hoped for a new day, a new people, a new David, and a new covenant. Such a hope was beyond human invention; it was the pure gift of God alone.

# PART FOUR

# GOD'S GRACIOUS ACTS OF RENEWAL

11

# Comfort of the Exiles

*T*hough the Babylonian exile was a righteous act of God's judgment on the chosen people, God did not abandon them in the midst of their tragedy. God worked gracious acts of renewal on their behalf. While they were still in exile, God ministered to them through prophets and poets with words of comfort and assurance.

## God's People Away from Home[1]

### Where They Lived

The period of the Babylonian exile extended from the destruction of Jerusalem by Nebuchadnezzar in 587/586 B.C.E. to the edict of Cyrus in 538 B.C.E., permitting the return of the exiles. The exact number of persons taken to Babylonia by Nebuchadnezzar is uncertain. It is clear, however, that he took what has been called "the cream" of the population, so that there could be no effective revolt against Babylon by those who remained behind. Obviously it was no easy matter for these Judahites to leave their country in ruins and to make satisfactory adjustments to a foreign land. Yet they seem to have made this transition remarkably well. Their status was that of involuntary exiles with some local autonomy but without the freedom to go wherever they might desire.

The Judahites were exiled in several places other than Babylonia. No doubt many died in the fighting against the Babylonians, while others perished of hunger and disease. Some probably fled to towns that were left standing in the Babylonian district of Samaria. Others took refuge in Moab, Ammon, and Edom (Jer. 40:11). It will be remembered that a group fled to Egypt, taking Jeremiah with them against his will (Jer. 42–44). Evidently Israelites had been migrating to Egypt long before the destruction of Jerusalem (Jer. 44:1) and continued to do so after that event. A colony at Elephantine (Aswan) seems to have been established in the early part of the sixth century B.C.E. The future of the covenant people, however, lay primarily not with those that remained in Judah or that went down into Egypt, but with those who were taken to Babylonia (see Jer. 24).

## How They Worshiped

The exile in Babylonia was harder for some than for others. Psalms 74 and 137, as well as the book of Lamentations, bear witness to the deep suffering of many. Those who had thought that the Holy City was indestructible and that the Davidic dynasty could never be overthrown were disillusioned. The nation was gone and the Temple was in ashes. Some who were left in the land continued to worship occasionally on the Temple site, but that was poor comfort for the Babylonian exiles. The victory of Nebuchadnezzar and the dazzling brilliance of Babylonian temples and rituals constituted a sore testing of their faith. Could the Babylonian deity, Marduk, be god after all? The exiles' experience was somewhat like that of someone from the country who moves to the big city to live. Though there is much in the big city that is good, on what basis does one distinguish between the glitter and the "gold"?

It was the quality of the faith of those who preserved the traditions that enabled the covenant people to survive. This faith had been born in crisis, and God's people had lived from crisis to crisis. Their history was a tale of slavery, wanderings in the wilderness, conflicts, the temptations of Baalism, famine, pestilence, division, the fall of the Northern Kingdom, and the climax: the fall of Jerusalem, God's Holy City. Yet through it all there was the faith that the LORD was performing mighty and wonderful acts of judgment and mercy. And this faith was no fair-weather affair. In the exile, prayer and informal worship took the place of sacrifice and Temple ritual. The people operated as a religious community, not as a political state. They learned that they could still be the people of God without the Temple and without a nation of their own.

The priestly writers and editors probably began their work in this period, though the so-called P document was brought to final form in the post-exilic period. The Deuteronomistic history was completed. There were exiles who were studying the Law (the Pentateuch or Torah) and the Prophets that were available in written form, and they were finding help therein to meet the challenges of their predicament. The forerunner of what later became known as the synagogue, an institution of prayer and study, arose in this period.

Moreover, Jeremiah had interpreted the exile in advance as the judgment of God and had promised restoration. He had advised the exiles (by letter) to settle down in Babylonia and live normal lives until the time of restoration came (Jer. 29:1–14). Ezekiel, whom we are to study next, gave essentially the same interpretation of the situation.

## Ezekiel—Prophet of God's Glory[2]

To say the least, Ezekiel was an unusual personality. His visions were extraordinary in their imagery and their quality of transporting the prophet from one place to another. He was fond of parables and allegories, and even outdid Jeremiah in the use of symbolic acts (see 3:25–26; 4:1–15; 5:1–4; 12:1–7; 24:15–18; 37:15–17).

Ezekiel was a priest who was carried into exile in Nebuchadnezzar's 597 B.C.E. deportation, along with King Jehoiachin. He received his call to be a prophet five years later. At the time of his call he had a vision of God's majestic glory and forever after was keenly conscious of the glory of the LORD. As an exile he lived in Tel-abib (3:15) by the Canal Chebar (1:1). For the most part his ministry was carried on among his fellow exiles, but he kept in close touch also with Jerusalem and sent messages to the people there. The two parts of his congregation were widely separated. From the time of his call in 592 until the fall of Jerusalem in 587/586, he was primarily a preacher of judgment and repentance. But from 587 to 570 he was a counselor and reformer.

### The Call of Ezekiel

We have already seen that an understanding of the call of certain prophets is crucial for understanding their ministry and message. This is also true in the case of Ezekiel. As you read the account of Ezekiel's call

(1:4–3:27), keep in mind the fact that some of his language is symbolic. We may think of his call as being divided into three parts: the vision of the mobile throne (1:4–28), the initial call (2:1–3:3), and the commission (3:4–27).

### The Vision of the Mobile Throne (1:4–28)

This vision was seen in the context of a thunderstorm. God's throne symbolized divine sovereignty. It was supported by four living creatures, indicating that the whole of creation is subservient to its King. The wheels make it clear that the throne is in the form of a chariot, and the wheel within each wheel shows that the chariot can move in any direction instantly. That is, one wheel is thought of as running in a north-south direction, while its companion runs in an east-west direction. The eyes in the rims of the wheels symbolize the all-seeing power of God. The "likeness" on the throne represents God. The mobility of the throne means that God is not confined to the Temple in Jerusalem but is sovereign everywhere. This the sorely tempted exiles needed to know. The vision impressed Ezekiel with the glory of the LORD. Such glory is the combination of what we mean by splendor, honor, dignity, and excellence, which call forth reverence, humility, praise, and obedience. Ezekiel's spontaneous response was to fall on his face.

### The Initial Call (2:1–3:3)

God addresses Ezekiel as "mortal" not only here but throughout the book. And God tells him to stand on his feet. He is sent as a prophet to the rebellious house of Israel. "Whether they hear or refuse to hear . . . they shall know that there has been a prophet among them." Success is not promised. It is not for the prophet to determine the outcome of his efforts; this is God's business. The prophet's task is to proclaim the word of God, whether people accept or reject it. Just as God had commanded Jeremiah to be unafraid (Jer. 1:8), so God commands Ezekiel. A scroll of lamentation, mourning, and woe is given to Ezekiel, and he is commanded to eat it. This means that God's message of judgment is to become a part of the very fiber of the prophet's being that he may be intimately involved in the message he proclaims.

### The Commission (3:4–27)

Again Ezekiel is warned not to fear the rebellious house of Israel. He goes to speak to the exiles at Tel-abib and sits overwhelmed for seven days. Then his mission is clarified. As prophet, he is commissioned to be "a sentinel for the house of Israel." In this capacity he is to warn both the wicked and the righteous among his people. If the prophet fails to give the warning, God will hold him guilty. But if he gives the warning and his people do not respond, he has discharged his God-given responsibility. The first message that Ezekiel is given is delivered by symbolic act (3:22–27). He is bound like a prisoner in order to declare thereby that the people of Jerusalem will be brought as exiles to Babylonia.

## The Glory of the LORD Departs

Inasmuch as Ezekiel made extensive use of symbolism, it is necessary that we interpret his message. The departure of God's glory from the Temple was symbolic of the judgment Ezekiel announced was coming, and the return of that glory was symbolic of his message of comfort and hope. In our examination of Ezekiel's inaugural vision, we identified the glory of the LORD as the key to unlocking his thought (1:28; 3:12, 23). While this vision shows that God's glory cannot be confined to any one place, this glory, nonetheless, had a special association with the Temple in Jerusalem.

When Ezekiel was taken in vision to Jerusalem, he saw the glory of God in the Temple (8:4). But he saw the pagan abominations there as well (read ch. 8). And God said to the prophet, "Mortal, do you see what they are doing, the great abominations that the house of Israel are committing here, to drive me far from my sanctuary?" (8:6). This means that idolatrous practices are intolerable to God. Shortly thereafter we read, "Now the glory of the God of Israel had gone up from the cherub on which it rested to the threshold of the house" (9:3). God's glory was thought to rest invisibly on the cherubim in the Holy of Holies. But here God's glory has moved to the threshold of the house, which is about to be destroyed on account of idolatry, violence, and injustice (chap. 9; compare 10:4). Next God's glory moves from the threshold of the Temple to the east gate of the Temple enclosure (10:18–19), thereby signifying that God's presence is in process of departing. The climax of this departure is reached when the glory of the LORD goes up not only from the Temple, but also from the city and stands on the mountain on the east side of the city to watch the destruction of city and Temple (11: 22–23).

Of course Ezekiel made many of the same emphases as his predecessors in announcing the judgment of God upon his own people. But he put his own stamp on his message, as a few illustrations will show.

*First, read with imagination the dramatic portrayal of the siege of Jerusalem in 4:1–17.*

The prophet is instructed to make a map of Jerusalem on a mud brick and, acting as if the map were the city, to simulate the siege of the city. After this he is to lie bound on one side to symbolize the captivity of the Northern Kingdom and then on the other side to symbolize the captivity of the Southern Kingdom.

Another subject on which Ezekiel placed his own stamp is that of individual responsibility. Of course there had always been a recognition of individual responsibility. But in earlier days considerable stress had been laid on corporate guilt. The exiles were repeating the proverb, "The parents have eaten sour grapes, and the children's teeth are set on edge" (see chap. 18). They were thereby claiming that their captivity was the result of their parents' sin and was consequently undeserved. But, like Jeremiah (31:27–30) and Deuteronomy (24:16), Ezekiel insisted on individual responsibility. While Ezekiel never denied the reality of the covenant community, he emphasized God's judgment of the individual. He also made it clear that God has no pleasure in the death of the wicked. If there is to be a new community, it must originate in personal repentance and a new heart.

*In our time there seems to be a preoccupation with laying the blame for a person's misbehavior on parents, heredity, and environment. If this preoccupation is carried to its logical conclusion, a person is no longer to be regarded as a person but as a highly complex animal. How are we properly to relate individual responsibility to the life of the group (family, church, and state, for example)?*

We take a final illustration of Ezekiel's expression of the judgment of God, namely, the death of his wife (24:15–27). She was the delight of his eyes. But God commanded him not to weep and not to do any of the things customary at the time of death. His action was to be a sign to the people. Their suffering at the desolation of beloved Jerusalem was to be a kind of bewilderment without relief in tears, a pining away. The destruction of Jerusalem, like so many of God's actions mentioned by Ezekiel, would provide the opportunity for people to "know that I am the Lord GOD" (24:24; compare 6:7, 14; 7:4; 12:16; 13:23; 15:7; 20:38). The glory of the LORD did depart and the city and the Temple were destroyed.

## The Glory of the LORD Returns

After the fall of Jerusalem Ezekiel became a prophet of consolation and hope. His message of hope is best symbolized in his vision of the return of God's glory to the Temple (43:1–5; compare 44:4). It returned by the east gate, from which it had gone, and filled the whole Temple.

## The Shepherd and His Sheep (34:1–31)

> As you read this glorious promise, jot down in your notebook other passages and images that you can remember from previous Bible study or can find as you study now.

The term "shepherd" in the ancient Near East was the primary metaphor for "king." David, the shepherd lad, had become the shepherd king of Israel. All his successors were called to be trustworthy shepherds of God's flock, but most of them preyed on the sheep instead. Poor leadership was largely responsible for the scattering of the flock (compare Jer. 23:1–4). But, according to Ezekiel, God will rescue the sheep from the various countries where they have been dispersed and will bring them home: "I will seek the lost, and I will bring back the strayed, and I will bind up the injured, and I will strengthen the weak"(34:16). Although there will be a restoration of the flock as a group, God will give attention to individual sheep and judge between them. Individual responsibility, of which we spoke earlier, involves individual judgment. God will also exercise pastoral care through the new David (compare Jer. 23:5–6). This Shepherd-sheep relationship will be "a covenant of peace," and God will visit the people with "showers of blessing." "They shall know that I, the LORD their God, am with them, and that they, the house of Israel, are my people, says the Lord GOD"(34:30). The shepherd concept of authority has great transforming potentiality.

## The Valley of Dry Bones (37:1–28)

Ezekiel's vision of the valley of dry bones has been popularized in a spiritual entitled "Dry Bones." The dry bones are the house of Israel. Ezekiel is commanded by God to speak the divine word that will bring the dead to new life. The bones take on sinews, flesh, and skin; then they are given breath that they may live. God's people will be brought home from the graves of exile. North and south will be reunited under the new David.

## The New Temple in the New City (40–48)

The priestly prophet envisioned the new age in terms of a new Temple and a new Jerusalem. His vision embraces many minute details. One of the grandest pictures in the vision is that of the stream of water flowing from the Temple south and bringing life even to the Dead Sea (47:1–12;

compare Rev. 22:1–2). The new name of the city will be "The LORD is There" (48:35). In other words, the glory of the LORD will have returned. Ezekiel's Temple was never literally built.

*Do you think he ever expected that it would be?*

## Lamentations—Poems on the Fall of Jerusalem

The book of Lamentations is a series of five poems expressing sorrow over the destruction of Jerusalem. These poems have similarities to laments in the Psalter (for example, Pss. 44, 74, 137). The fall of the Holy City had raised questions for many concerning the love and power of God. These poems were composed for use at public fasts commemorating Jerusalem's tragedy and served as a channel of cleansing and release, for God honors the honest complaint of people and uses it as a means of healing. These poems in whole or in part continue to be used today liturgically in Judaism, as well as in Roman Catholicism and in some parts of Protestantism. Their authorship is attributed to Jeremiah in the Septuagint (Greek translation), but no such attribution is made in the Hebrew Bible. Therefore, we are in no position to make an absolute statement about authorship.

*If you have time to read only one chapter, read chapter 2.*

As we meditate on this little book, we must remember that it records the honest sobs of broken hearts. God is as truly concerned with broken hearts as with lofty thoughts. Perhaps the truth or falsity of any system of faith becomes most evident when that faith is tested in the furnace of affliction. For the most part, the contemporaries of Jeremiah and Ezekiel refused to hearken to their preaching of God's word of judgment. But in the furnace of affliction they learned that these men were true prophets and that such prophets as Hananiah were false. Don't sell the little book of Lamentations "short"; you can learn much from those who are honest enough to cry.

## Obadiah—Prophet of Retribution on Edom

The book of Obadiah is the shortest book in the Old Testament, consisting of only twenty-one verses. Theories concerning its date of composition range all the way from 845 B.C.E. to 312 B.C.E. It seems that at least verses 1–14 reflect a time shortly after the fall of Jerusalem in 587/586 B.C.E. and that the book as a whole comes from the sixth century. It was basically intended as a comfort to the discouraged people of God.

The theme is clearly punishment of Edom as a necessary consequence of the righteousness of God. Obadiah was not alone in his condemnation of the "rock fortress" (see Amos 1:11–12; Isa. 34:5–17; Jer. 49:7–22; Ezek. 35:1–15; Mal. 1:2–5), but his is the only book that centers around this theme. The certainty of retribution is set forth in verses 1–9. The reasons for it are found in verses 10–14 (compare Lam. 4:21–22; Ps. 137:7).

Although there had been a history of hostility between the descendants of Jacob and the descendants of Esau, Obadiah's reasons for Edom's punishment center on the period of the destruction of Jerusalem by Nebuchadnezzar. The Edomites stood aloof from the suffering of their "cousins" and behaved as strangers. They gloated over the misfortunes of the Judeans, looted their goods, and delivered up survivors to the enemy.

The last section of the book (vv. 15–21) presents the Day of the LORD as a time of retribution on Edom and a time of reversal of fortune for the covenant people. Obadiah's message ends with the great assurance of faith: "And the kingdom shall be the LORD's."

## Isaiah 40–66—Prophets of the Exile and Return

Like the Pentateuch, the book of Isaiah confronts us with problems that must be explored. Until the twelfth century C.E. it was universally assumed that Isaiah, son of Amoz, wrote the entire book that had been given his name. From that time this assumption began to be questioned in various ways. Today chapters 1–39 are usually referred to as First Isaiah, chapters 40–55 as Second Isaiah, and chapters 56–66 as Third Isaiah. There are many who think that the prophecies of the eighth-century Isaiah are contained in chapters 1–39 but that these chapters also contain some material from later times. Most consider chapters 40–66 to have been written during and/or shortly after the Babylonian exile in the sixth century B.C.E. Some assign chapters 40–55 to one particular prophet. Others include 56–66 along with 40–55. Obviously this is a very complex subject and cannot be developed here in detail. We shall limit our study to an outline of the arguments employed to support the traditional position of one author of all sixty-six chapters of the book and an outline of the arguments used to deny that the same person also wrote chapters 40–66.

## Arguments for One Isaiah

1. Through the centuries Jewish tradition has held that Isaiah, the son of Amoz, wrote the entire book. This tradition appeared as early as the apocryphal book that is known as Ecclesiasticus (second century B.C.E.).

2. The title found in 1:1 leaves the impression that it applies to the whole book.

3. There is no manuscript evidence of the separate existence of any portion of the book. This includes evidence from the Dead Sea Scrolls.

4. The author shows an acquaintance with Palestine, not with Babylon, where "the prophet of the exile" is supposed to have lived.

5. Prediction is an aspect of prophecy, and the predictive element implicit in the traditional position ought not to be denied to Isaiah.

6. God is known in both major parts of the book as "the Holy One of Israel."

7. It would be strange for the names of lesser people to be remembered and that of one of the greatest prophets to be forgotten.

8. The New Testament writers refer to various parts of the book as Isaiah's (for example, see Matt. 3:3 and Isa. 40:3; Matt. 4:14–16 and Isa. 9:1–2; John 12:38–41 and Isa. 53:1; 6:10; Rom. 10:16, 20, 21 and Isa. 53:1; 65:1; 65:2). This is regarded as the strongest argument by those who hold the traditional position.

## Arguments for at Least Two Authors

1. Chapters 1–39 deal largely with judgment, while chapters 40–66 deal primarily with consolation.

2. Chapters 1–39 have Jerusalem as their background and Assyria as the threat, while chapters 40–66 have their setting in the period of the Babylonian exile and Persian restoration.

3. In chapters 1–39 Isaiah is mentioned by name over and over again, but in chapters 40–66 he is never mentioned at all.

4. Chapters 1–39 contain a variety of literary types (poetry and prose, oracles, parables, biography, autobiography, history, and others), but chapters 40–66 are composed almost exclusively of poetry in an exalted vein.

5. In chapters 1–39 we find the Messiah of the house of David, but in chapters 40–66 we find the Servant of the LORD. While these two titles were united in Jesus Christ, they are not identified with each other in the book of Isaiah.

6. In chapters 1–39 Jerusalem is indestructible, but in chapters 40–66 the destruction of Jerusalem has already taken place.

7. The prophet was among the exiles in Babylon (see 42:24).

8. The career of Cyrus the Persian is not "predicted" in chapters 40ff.; he is already on the scene (41:2, 25; 44:28; 45:1).

9. We do not know exactly how this book was put together. It is possible that the work of Isaiah's disciples was associated with that of their master and properly kept together. Our modern concept of copyright authorship was unknown in the ancient world. The New Testament writers did not deal with human authorship as a critical issue; they used traditional names and titles. It is unfair to remake them in our image.

You are invited to make up your own mind concerning the authorship and composition of the book of Isaiah. Most contemporary scholars consider the second of the two positions described above as closer to the truth. However, the human authorship of a particular book or passage is not a life-and-death matter. The entire book of Isaiah is a part of the Bible and is to be read in that context. The position one takes about the authorship and date of Isaiah, of course, will affect the interpretation of the book as a whole and of its parts.[3]

## The Prophet of the Servant of God (Isa. 40–55)

*The Prologue (40:1–11)*

> *These eleven verses are an introduction to much that follows and set the atmosphere for further study. As you read them, try to place yourself imaginatively among the Judean exiles in Babylonia and determine what these verses meant to many of them. Then ask yourself, What do these verses mean to the church in our time?*

In the heavenly council, to which the prophet has access, God gives the command to comfort the people, who are symbolized as Jerusalem (vv. 1–2). The duration of their sentence to exile is ended, and they are forgiven. The expression "double for all her sins" does not mean that God has punished Jerusalem unjustly. It is a vigorous figure of speech to indicate that her time of punishment is completed.

The prophet hears a voice calling for the preparation of a way in the desert for the LORD (v. 3). Verses 3–5 picture God as the returning Victorious King. This coming of the LORD will have relevance for "all people." God has spoken the redemptive word, and it cannot fail to achieve its purpose (v. 8; see 55:10–11). Jerusalem (Zion), as God's herald, is to get up on a high mountain, in order to be seen and heard far and wide, and announce the gospel of the coming of the LORD in victory.

### The One Incomparable God

Although the prophet of the exile by no means originated Israelite monotheism, the doctrine is given its clearest expression here. Repeatedly we find statements similar to the following:

> I am the first and I am the last;
>     besides me there is no god.
>     (44:6; compare 45:5, 21–22; 46:9)

As the only God to be worshiped, the LORD is also the only Savior (43:10–13).

These strong expressions of monotheism were addressed particularly to the exiles who were confronted by the temptations of Babylonian idolatry. "Gods" crafted by humans are not comparable to the Holy One of Israel (40:18–31; compare 46:1–11). Such so-called gods cannot move, see, hear, etc. The nations are called before the divine court and judged for their idolatrous practices (41:1–17; compare 42:17; 45:24–25). Idols cannot announce their plans and carry them out (41:21–29). Idols, idol makers, and idol worshipers deserve to be ridiculed (44:9–20).

But the LORD, the God of Israel, is the One True God, "the Creator of the ends of the earth" (40:28). In comparison with the LORD "the nations are like a drop from a bucket" (40:15). It is God who gives strength to the people (40:27–31). God's creative activity continues in the control of nature and history (41:17–20). God's election of Israel as servant people was a creative act (43:1, 15; 44:21–22). God did not create the earth as a chaos, but formed it to be inhabited (45:18). Nevertheless, God is responsible for darkness as well as light, for woe as for weal (45:7). This does not mean that God is the author of sin, but that God's judgments are realized in history. As Creator of all there is, the LORD is in control of history (compare Ps. 124:8).

The One Incomparable God is not only Creator but is also Redeemer. As such, God will bring the people home from Babylon in a new exodus (43:14–21; 51:9–11; 52:11–12; 55:12). Cyrus, king of Persia, has been raised up by God to be the instrument of this deliverance (44:28–45:8). God will bring back the people from other places where they have been scattered as well (see 60:8–9). But redemption not only has to do with a return to Palestine, it also includes the forgiveness of sins. The prophet began on this note (40:1–2) and elaborates on this theme (43:25–28; 53:4–12). Then in unforgettable language, the prophet calls the people to repent (read 55:6–9).

### The Servant of the LORD

The Servant of the LORD is the heart of the prophet's message. In the Old Testament as a whole various individuals are known as servants of the LORD: Abraham, Moses, David, the prophets, and others. In Isaiah 40–55 Israel is sometimes called the servant of the LORD (41:8–10; 43:8–13; 44:1–5, 21–23; 45:4), and is commissioned to bear a missionary witness to the nations (43:8–13; 44:8; compare 56:7). In some passages known as the Servant Songs (42:1–4; 49:1–6; 50:4–11; 52:13–53:12) the servant is personalized in the singular and depicted as an individual (except in 49:3), but still may be understood as a reference to Israel as well. The prophet was concerned for the deliverance of the people and the nations from their bondage to sin and evil. The instrument of the latter deliverance is the Servant of the LORD.

> *Read each of the Servant Songs listed previously and make an outline in your notebook of what the servant is to be and to do.*

We review *the anticipation of the servant* as presented in Isaiah 52:13–53:12. The servant's ultimate exaltation will follow great humiliation. The servant will not only amaze many people but will also purify them. The word sometimes translated "startle" in 52:15 is better translated "sprinkle," and such sprinkling refers to cleansing. In humiliation the servant is "a root out of dry ground," lacking in beauty, despised and rejected, "a man of suffering, and acquainted with infirmity." The servant is hard to look at, marred of appearance. The word "suffering" is literally "pains," and the word "infirmity" is literally "sickness" (see v. 4 also). Both the language of the Hebrew text and that of the Greek translation (Septuagint) suggest the picture of a disfigured sufferer. This does not mean, however, that the person who fulfilled this prophecy had to be literally sick but was to be a sin-bearing servant. The servant is righteous and as such bears the sins and the sufferings of the righteous (compare Matt. 8:17). Under oppression unto death, the servant is humble, patient, and meek, "like a lamb that is led to the slaughter" (see John 1:29, 36) and like a ewe that remains silent as she is sheared. The servant is stricken for the rebellion of the people.

But the servant's humiliation issues in exaltation (53:10–12). Suffering and death are not a matter of tragedy alone. God's redemptive purpose is accomplished thereby. The mention of "offspring" and prolongation of days gives assurance of divine vindication of the servant no matter what. The servant will find satisfaction in the accomplishment of God's will. By the power of God the servant will be the source of justification of many and will be highly exalted.

In this song we have one of the most profound statements of the "how" of forgiveness to be found in the Old Testament. Certainly basic to the passage is the priestly approach of substitutionary sacrifice, which rests in part on the meaning of the Temple ritual. This principle of atonement means that life comes only through death. Ritually the lifeblood of a sacrificial animal is shed in place of human blood and serves to purify and restore one who is separated from God because of sin. The prophet declares that we have "eternal" life only through the death of the Servant of the LORD. Further, since "all we like sheep have gone astray" (compare 55:6–7), the atoning work of the servant is the means by which "many" will be justified (53:11). Finally, the servant is noted for prayerful intercession (53:12; see Gen. 18:22–32; Exod. 32:9–14; Amos 7:1–6; 2 Chron. 30:18–19; Heb. 7:25).[4]

We now turn to *the revelation of the servant*. As the Ethiopian eunuch read Isaiah 53:7–8, he asked Philip, " 'About whom, may I ask you, does the prophet say this, about himself or about someone else?' Then Philip began to speak, and starting with this scripture he proclaimed to him the good news about Jesus" (see Acts 8:26–40). This is precisely what Christians have done ever since. As we read Isaiah 53, and in light of our experience of Jesus Christ, we rightly think on the Lamb of God. Jesus carried out his ministry as the Servant of the LORD.

In Philippians 2:5–11, we have one of the most glorious affirmations of Jesus as the Servant. It is thought that verses 6–11 are an early Christian hymn that was quoted by Paul to encourage the Philippians to practice unity and humility. Verses 5–8 present Christ as the Servant in his humiliation. The pre-incarnate Christ who had been with God before all creation did not count equality with God something to be grasped. This was quite unlike Adam, who in his grasping wanted to be like God—that is, to obey his own desires. But the eternal Christ emptied himself (see Isa. 53:12) by taking the form of a servant and by being born in human likeness. The incarnation was a humiliating experience (see Isa. 53:7), involving obedience to death on a cross (see Isa. 53:12).

Following the example of Paul and others, through the eyes of faith we look further at the humiliation of Christ. Jesus was certainly a root out of dry ground. In spite of all the good he received from his Jewish heritage, he cannot be accounted for simply in terms of that heritage. He was born in a stable, not in the palace of a king. He was despised and rejected by many. "He came to what was his own, and his own people did not accept him" (John 1:11). He was indeed "a man of suffering [pains], and acquainted with infirmity [sickness]." There is no record in the Gospels that he himself was ever sick, but he ministered to those who were sick. Jesus was hard to look at in the agony of the cross. Though not literally sick, he fulfilled the symbolism of sickness. That is, he bore the sin of others and identified himself with their needs. Indeed he was made to be sin for us (2 Cor. 5:21). He was oppressed and killed by his enemies; yet under oppression he was patient. We behold him as "the Lamb of God, who takes away the sin of the world" (John 1:29).

Paul also presents the exaltation of Christ as the Servant of the LORD in Philippians 2:9–11. When this passage is understood in the light of Paul's thought, the exaltation of Christ includes his resurrection from the dead. It also includes the bestowal of the name LORD, by which God is known in the Old Testament. The Son of Mary already had the name Jesus, but he will receive the "name that is above every name" (2:9). Moreover, it is anticipated that one day every knee shall bow and every tongue "confess that Jesus Christ is Lord, to the glory of God the Father" (2:11).

We also recognize that Christ's exaltation as the Servant of the LORD includes his accomplishment of God's will, his justification of many, his ascension, and his coming in glory.

What are some of the things which this study says to us? First, it says that God carries out the divine purpose of redemption. It is not that the prophet in Isaiah 52:13–53:12 "predicts" Jesus Christ and every detail of Jesus' life. But according to the New Testament, the early Christians rightly recognized the realization of God's promise in Jesus Christ. God stood at the beginning and at the end and all the way between.

Second, this study teaches us that true greatness is to be measured in terms of humility, obedience (to God's will), and service. By those standards many of the so-called great were not great at all. Some have called Alexander of Macedon great, others have called Napoleon Bonaparte great, and still others have called Hitler or Stalin great. Why? Because they flexed their military muscles and by pushing people around they forced obedience to themselves. But such greatness is a false greatness.

History has known but one fully great person throughout the ages. He is the Babe of Bethlehem, for whom there was no room in the inn; the Carpenter of Nazareth, who had calluses in his hands; the Good Shepherd, who laid down his life for the sheep; the Servant of the LORD, who died that we may live. The relative greatness of anyone is to be measured by the true greatness of Jesus Christ: "Whoever wishes to become great among you must be your servant, and whoever wishes to be first among you must be slave of all. For the Son of Man came not to be served but to serve, and to give his life a ransom for many" (Mark 10:43–45).

Third, our study makes clear that life comes through death. We have already stressed this in relation to the Servant's death on our behalf. We must also see this truth in relation to our response. For he said, "If any want to become my followers, let them deny themselves and take up their cross and follow me" (Mark 8:34). Taking up one's cross does not mean doing without chewing gum during Lent. In our present-day situation Jesus is saying, "If any person would be a Christian, that one must say, 'No,' to selfish motivations and crucify self-centeredness and follow me." The reception of the life that comes through Jesus' death involves our death also. For we are the servant people of the Servant Lord. As such, what kind of service are we to render?

Finally, we must remember that all we have just said is our reading into the text a meaning that is rooted in our experience of Jesus Christ centuries after the exilic prophet wrote. For the Judeans then, and for many Jews today, the proper understanding of the "servant" in the literary and social context in which these texts are found is corporate. Israel, or some subset of Israel, is the servant of the LORD. By the dedication and suffering of a people are the nations to see the light. As Christians, we may well rejoice in our own experience of God's love in the person of Jesus, the Servant of God. But we should not denigrate or devalue the reading of the text in another way by others who have known the love of God in a different way just as well.

## The Prophets of the Return (Isa. 56–66)

Some refer to Isaiah 56–66 as Third Isaiah. However, unlike Isaiah 40–55 (Second Isaiah), which was probably written by one author, Isaiah 56–66 shows evidence of several hands. What links the material is a shared postexilic social setting. Isaiah 56–66 seems to have been written after some of the exiles were allowed to return to Jerusalem in 538 B.C.E.

There were several "problems" that faced the returned community. One centered on who properly constituted God's people. Was it only those who had undergone the trauma of exile in Babylon or did it include those who had been left behind? Isaiah 56:1–8 makes clear that all who live by God's way are the new community. A great ingathering will take place that will include even "foreigners" (see Isa. 60:1–18; 62:1–12).

A second issue for the returned community entailed a proper understanding of worship and ethics. Idolatry was denounced as a continuing temptation (see Isa. 57:1–13). Empty ritual fasting in place of proper care of neighbor was blasted (see Isa. 58:1–14). Justice was recognized (see Isa. 59:1–15), for Israel and for all people (see Isa. 65:1–16). All of this is connected with the announcement of the year of the Lord's favor (see Isa. 61:1–11), a part of which Jesus was remembered as using to initiate his ministry (see Luke 4:16–19).

One final concern of critical importance in Third Isaiah is the teaching of God's new creation. Second Isaiah had repeatedly spoken of the Holy God as Creator and Redeemer (see Isa. 40:28; 42:5; 43:1, 14–15; etc.). God's work of creation will not be completed until a new earth and new heaven is fashioned, one where pain and distress and untimely death are no more (see Isa. 65:17–24). Wolf and lamb will feed together in peaceful harmony (see Isa. 65:25 and Isa. 11:6–9). Amid the uncertainties of the restoration, the prophet assured the renewed, struggling community that God would be with them as surely as a mother (Isa. 66:12–13) until the new age God would bring to pass (Isa. 66:18–24; compare Rev. 21:1–22:5).

# Restoration of the Remnant

$A$lthough the Judeans were scattered in various places, we are now primarily concerned with those displaced persons who returned from the Babylonian exile to Palestine. The prophets had promised that such a remnant would be preserved. God fulfilled these promises and brought them home. This period of restoration and settling down is known as the postexilic era (538–333 B.C.E.) and is almost identical with the age of the Persian empire. The Persian empire began with the union of Persia and Media by Cyrus in 549 B.C.E. and lasted until the conquest of Persia by Alexander the Great about 333 B.C.E. This was the era of some of the great thinkers and leaders of Greece—Herodotus, Pericles, Socrates, Plato, and Aristotle.

The returnees found this both a time of revival and a time of disappointment. It is probable that many had associated the coming of God's kingdom with the return from exile, but it soon became evident that the kingdom was yet to be consummated. In a sense, the little community "lived more in the past and the future than in the present."[1] They could think back to the time when there was a king of David's line on the throne of Judah. They could remember also the period of the divided monarchy, and before that the united kingdom of David and Solomon. In fact, they could go on back to the days of Moses and Joshua and other great leaders. They also looked to the future with a hope and expectation that would not give up. The chief biblical sources for the history of the times are the books of Ezra and Nehemiah and the work of Haggai and Zechariah.

## The Early Phases of the Restoration

### The First Homecoming

Jeremiah had promised his people, in the name of the LORD, that there would be a return to Palestine. The prophet of the exile (Isa.

40–55) had designated Cyrus as the instrument of that return. Cyrus conquered Babylon in 539 B.C.E. and gave his decree permitting the Judeans to go home in 538. This decree is found in Hebrew in Ezra 1:2–4 and in Aramaic in Ezra 6:3–5. The latter record is a bit more complete. A famous clay document known as the Cyrus Cylinder makes it clear that such consideration of captives was typical of this enlightened monarch. A group of exiles did return under Sheshbazzar, a descendant of David, who carried with him the vessels that Nebuchadnezzar had taken from Solomon's Temple in Jerusalem, and this group began to lay the foundation of the Temple (see Ezra 1:5–11; 5:14–16).

Zerubbabel, also a descendant of David, apparently succeeded Sheshbazzar as leader of the returnees. He and Jeshua (Joshua) the high priest built an altar on the Temple site, celebrated the Feast of Tabernacles, and finished laying the foundation of the Temple. Samaritans and other adversaries sought to hinder the rebuilding of the Temple. The Samaritans were the inhabitants of the province of Samaria. They were believed to have descended from intermarriage between Israelites and captives from other places settled by the Assyrians in that territory. Their religion was a mixture of Israelite religion with pagan elements (see 2 Kings 17:29–34). They offered their help in building the Temple, but it was rejected. Syncretism (a mixing of religions) at this juncture in Jewish life would have been especially tragic. (In the fourth century the Samaritans erected their own temple on Mount Gerizim.) The work of reconstruction undertaken by Sheshbazzar and Zerubbabel was interrupted until 520 B.C.E.

## The Second Temple

The preaching of Haggai (1–2) and Zechariah (1–8) encouraged the people and their leaders to complete the building of the Temple. Though preexilic (before the exile) prophets had condemned the abuses associated with worship at Solomon's Temple, the postexilic (after the exile) community needed such a center for its life.

Haggai did his preaching in 520 B.C.E., the second year of Darius I (522–486 ). He shamed the people for being willing to dwell in their paneled houses while God's house lay in ruins. Such self-centeredness, he maintained, accounted for many of their hardships as a people. Zerubbabel, Joshua (Jeshua), and the people responded positively to Haggai's message, and God promised to be with them. In the early stages of its building, the older members of the community felt that the Second Temple would not be as glorious as its predecessor. The prophet assured them that its future would be splendid. The concluding verse of Haggai's prophecy concerning Zerubbabel seems to have messianic overtones: "On that day, says the LORD of hosts, I will take you, O Zerubbabel my servant, the son of Shealtiel, says the LORD, and make you like a signet ring; for I have chosen you, says the LORD of hosts."

Zechariah began his ministry of preaching in 520 B.C.E. and continued it for two years. The main thrust of his message is assurance that God cares for the people, will protect them, and will dwell in their midst.[2] Zerubbabel the Davidic prince and Joshua the high priest are "the two anointed ones who stand by the Lord of the whole earth" (4:14). The word "Branch" used of Zerubbabel in 3:8 is the same word used in Jeremiah 23:5 and 33:15 for the Davidic Messiah. Most interpreters also maintain that the name Zerubbabel was the original name in Zechariah 6:11 rather than Joshua. For Zerubbabel had the primary responsibility for building the Temple, and the priest (Joshua) was to stand by his throne. Apparently there were plans to crown Zerubbabel as a new David, but after the building of the Temple (520–515 B.C.E.) Zerubbabel is never heard of again.

## The Hymnbook of the Second Temple

The book of Psalms has often been called "the hymnbook of the Second Temple." This does not mean that all the Psalms were composed in the period after the Babylonian exile, but that many were used in the worship of the Second Temple. The composition of the Psalter extends from pre-Davidic times to the fourth century B.C.E. There are good reasons for thinking that David wrote some of the Psalms but by no means all of them. In the development of Jewish tradition, however, his name became almost a synonym for the Psalter.

Some psalms originated in connection with public worship; others in private devotion. Yet those that originated in public worship could be used in private devotion and vice versa. The Psalms come from many periods of Israel's history, and our present Psalter is the final collection of several earlier collections. The Psalms are, in fact, *the faith of the Old Testament set to music*.

Since the Psalter is composed of 150 psalms, we cannot begin to sample every kind of treasure found there in a book on the whole Bible. We ought to keep in mind, however, that we find there hymns of praise (Pss. 8, 100), royal or messianic psalms (Pss. 2, 110), prayers in time of trouble (Pss. 51, 88), affirmations of faith (Pss. 23, 121), songs of thanksgiving (Pss. 66, 118), and wisdom poems (Pss. 73, 139). Several of the hymns of praise bear witness in a special way to the mighty acts of God in Israel's history (Pss. 68, 78, 105, 106, 111, 114, 149) and are comparable in content to the Old Testament confessions of faith that have been mentioned from time to time (for example, Deut. 26:5–11; Josh. 24).[3]

Because our study as a whole centers around the mighty acts of God, it is appropriate for us to examine one of these hymns in some detail. The one selected is Psalm 114, which may be entitled "From Egypt to Canaan." This poetic gem bears witness to Israel's faith in the God of the exodus, the wilderness wanderings, the covenant at Sinai, and the entrance into Canaan—all of which events were mighty acts of God. It is a part of the Egyptian Hallel, or Hymn of Praise (Pss. 113–118), sung at the celebration of the Jewish Passover. At Passover, Psalms 113–114 are sung before the meal, and Psalms 115–118 after it. The hymn sung by Jesus and his apostles after the Last Supper (Matt. 26:30; Mark 14:26) was probably Psalms 115–118. It is also possible that Psalms 113–114 were sung before the Supper. Psalm 114 may have been written for the celebration of Passover, the festival commemorating the exodus events.

*Psalm 114 is composed of four parts, and you will want to read each part along with the comments on it.*

The theme of part one is *the birth of a nation* (vv. 1–2). Although the patriarchs and matriarchs were forerunners of the nation of Israel, they were not a nation. It was the exodus from Egypt that made the nation possible. The Egyptian language was strange to the Israelites and therefore a barrier between them and the Egyptians. The two chief divisions of the chosen people were to be Israel and Judah.

The theme of part two is *miracles along the way* (vv. 3–4). These miracles are presented in a very imaginative manner. At the very outset of the journey from Egypt the waters of the sea were parted (Exod. 14:21–22), and at the end the Jordan "turned back" (Josh. 3:9–17). The giving of the Law at Sinai was accompanied by an earthquake (Exod. 19:18; Judg. 5:5).

Part three is the *psalmist's challenge to the forces of nature* (vv. 5–6). The sea, the Jordan, and the mountains are asked to explain their unusual behavior.

Part four presents the *Author of Israel's redemption* (vv. 7–8), and thereby answers the questions of part three. Israel's God is the Author of the unusual events at Israel's beginnings. All the earth is called on to tremble at God's presence, before the Lord of all history and creation. It was God who provided water for the people in the wilderness (Exod. 17:6–7;

Num. 20:8–13; Deut. 8:15). As Lord of all, God causes even nature to serve the divine historical purposes.[4]

The royal or messianic psalms (Pss. 2, 18, 20, 21, 45, 61, 63, 72, 89, 101, 110, 132, 144 ) are also closely related to the one story of the Bible. The word "messiah" means "anointed one." All the kings of Israel were messiahs because they were anointed. Yet, as one after another of the kings failed to fulfill the royal ideal, the term "messiah" came to be applied to a future king of David's line who would. These psalms can best be understood in relation to God's covenant with David (see 2 Sam. 7; compare Pss. 89 and 132) and their use in the New Testament. The covenant with David involved a series of kings, but *the* Messiah, according to Christians, is Jesus Christ.

The position of the king in Israel was of far greater religious significance than most people today realize. He was God's adopted son (2 Sam. 7:14; Ps. 2:7) and the representative of all Israel before God. The royal psalms celebrate the king's coronation and marriage and express petition for his guidance and protection. The two royal psalms that are most quoted in the New Testament are Psalms 2 and 110. Careful study indicates that each of them was probably written to celebrate the enthronement of some ancient descendant of David. But no ancient king ever really fulfilled the royal image as set forth therein. This meant that the image increasingly pointed beyond the actual king of the moment.

In God's own time and purpose, Christians believe, this kingly expectation was fulfilled in Jesus Christ. By faith we see God's original intention more clearly in the light of the New Testament revelation. This hindsight, however, does not give us the license to ignore the setting of the messianic psalms in the concrete historic experience of God's ancient people. The unity of biblical revelation is, in the final analysis, God's doing, not that of humans. We can imagine what these psalms must have meant to the little restored community in Jerusalem who had virtually no real autonomy and certainly no Davidic king to rule over them.

*Read Psalm 2 and Psalm 110 and try to imagine what they meant to an ancient king of David's line on the occasion of his enthronement.*

*Then read the references made to these psalms in the New Testament, as found in the footnotes of the New Revised Standard Version.*

*How did Jesus redefine these psalms?*

# The Work of Nehemiah and Ezra

## The Prophecies of Malachi and Joel

Two prophets of the period when God restored Israel were Malachi and Joel, who picture a community that is facing hard problems, but not without hope. Their ministries cannot be dated with precision, but there is some reason for placing them in the middle of the fifth century B.C.E. If this dating is correct, they help us to understand the situation to which Nehemiah and Ezra addressed themselves.

Malachi reflects the fact that the Temple is standing, and his reference to "governor" (1:8) indicates that Palestine is under a Persian official. His theme is loyalty to God. In pursuing it he reminds the people of God's love for them and of their disloyalty to God, and calls them to repentance. The disloyalty of the people is spelled out in terms of unacceptable sacrifices, the divorcing of Judean wives and the taking of heathen wives, sorcery, adultery, false swearing, oppression (of the poor, the widow, the orphan, and the sojourner), and robbing God of tithes and offerings. They are called to repentance against the background of the coming Day of the LORD, when God in judgment will distinguish between the righteous and the wicked. At the end of the book, which is also the end of the second division of the Hebrew Bible (the Prophets), Elijah is promised as the forerunner of the Day of the LORD (compare Matt. 17:11; Mark 9:12; Luke 1:17).

The dating of Joel is even less certain than the dating of Malachi. He reflects the works of earlier prophets (see footnotes in the NRSV), and demonstrates the priestly concern of a postexilic prophet. He preaches on the themes of judgment and redemption. The plague of locusts (1:2–2:11) is a sign of the coming of the Day of the LORD and the occasion for a call to repentance. Although Joel is concerned with ritual, he is also concerned with righteousness. In his call to repentance are these famous words: "Rend your hearts and not your clothing" (2:13). Beyond judgment there is renewal and restoration for God's people. Joel's promise of the outpouring of God's Spirit (2:28–32) was used by Peter in his great sermon at Pentecost (Acts 2:17–21).

## Nehemiah and Ezra: Which Came First?

The exact chronological relationship between Nehemiah and Ezra is one of the most difficult problems in the history of the covenant people. This is not the place for a complete discussion of the subject, but it is necessary to take note of the three chief explanations.[5] The first theory is that Ezra came to Jerusalem in 458 B.C.E. This theory is based primarily on Ezra 7:1–7, according to which Ezra and others went up to Jerusalem in the seventh year of Artaxerxes the king (of Persia). If this reference is to Artaxerxes I (465–424), the date is 458. According to Nehemiah 2:1, Nehemiah received permission in the twentieth year of Artaxerxes to go to Jerusalem and rebuild its walls. Everyone agrees that Nehemiah returned to Jerusalem about 445 B.C.E.

But there is considerable evidence that Ezra followed Nehemiah and that the materials in the books of Ezra and Nehemiah are not arranged altogether chronologically. For example, if Ezra went up to Jerusalem in 458, why did he wait thirteen years to read the Law, that is, until Nehemiah arrived (Neh. 8:1–8)? The second theory, thus, is that Ezra came to Jerusalem in the seventh year of Artaxerxes II (404–358), which would be 398 B.C.E. As the text of Ezra 7:7 does not specify which Artaxerxes, the date 398 is regarded as preferable. This would mean, of course, that Nehemiah's arrival in Jerusalem preceded that of Ezra by a generation.

But the biblical text presents the two men as contemporaries (Neh. 8: 9), and there is no adequate reason for treating this presentation lightly. Thus, the third theory is that Ezra came to Jerusalem in 428 B.C.E. This date is arrived at by reading "the thirty-seventh year" instead of "the seventh year" in Ezra 7:7. The thirty-seventh year of Artaxerxes I would be 428. This reading is easily accounted for on the basis of the possibilities of the Hebrew text. Yet there is no manuscript evidence for it. Although no theory of the date of Ezra has been proved, this last one seems to permit the most consistent interpretation of the Ezra-Nehemiah narrative.

## Nehemiah—The Layman

Nehemiah was neither a priest nor a prophet, but a dedicated layman, who led his people in rebuilding the walls of Jerusalem and in organizing their life in a respectable pattern. The fascinating account of his life and work is recorded in the book of Nehemiah, chapters 1–7 and 11–13. After receiving word of the trouble and shame of the people who had returned to Palestine, he requested the permission of Artaxerxes, to whom he was cupbearer, to go to Jerusalem and make the needed repairs on its walls. The leaders of the people agreed to cooperate, and the rebuilding of the walls and gates of the city was undertaken.

But Nehemiah ran into opposition of various groups under the leadership of Sanballat, a Samaritan; Tobiah, a Jewish-Ammonite; and Geshem, an Arab. Apparently these men saw this undertaking as a threat to the authority that they had been exercising as provincial governors under Persia. Their opposition took the form of ridicule, a plan to kill Nehemiah, accusation of rebellion against Persia, threat, and fifth-column activity.

The people were disheartened, but Nehemiah devised a plan whereby those who worked on the wall were guarded by others. Moreover, each worker was armed. This plan was executed with such zeal and efficiency that the workers did not undress at night.

In addition to opposition from the outside, Nehemiah encountered administrative difficulties within. The poor were being forced to sell their children into slavery to pay high interest on their debts to those who were more fortunate. This practice was stopped, and full restitution was made. Nehemiah did not burden the people by requiring them to provide for him as they customarily provided for a Persian governor. The wall was completed in spite of all difficulties.

Then Nehemiah gave his attention to related matters. Jerusalem was poorly inhabited, for its ruins had been uninviting. Lots were cast, and one out of every ten men moved into Jerusalem. Some did this voluntarily. The wall was dedicated with appropriate ceremony, emphasis being placed on thanksgiving, singing, sacrificing, and rejoicing. Nehemiah and his people realized that their accomplishment had been made only with the help of God (Neh. 6:16). Finally, Nehemiah set the wheels in motion to support the Temple more adequately.

Sometime after this, Nehemiah returned to Persia. He also made a second visit to Jerusalem. When he reached Jerusalem this time, he learned that Tobiah, of all people, was living in a room of the Temple. Tobiah was moved out, and the chambers of the Temple cleansed because he was an Ammonite. Furthermore, Nehemiah made arrangements for the support of the Levites, reinstituted Sabbath observance, and prohibited mixed marriages.

*From your study of Nehemiah 1–7, 11–13 and this summary, what are the chief lessons we learn from Nehemiah's character and activity?*

## Ezra—The Priest and Scribe

Unlike Nehemiah, Ezra was a priest by ancestry and a scribe by choice. As a scribe, he was a student and interpreter of the Law of Moses. Though Nehemiah was a lay administrator and Ezra an ecclesiastical reformer, their efforts overlapped. The account of Ezra's life and work is found in the book of Ezra, chapters 7–10, and the book of Nehemiah, chapters 8–10.

Ezra and other Jewish leaders in Babylonia were given permission to go to Jerusalem and were financially undergirded in their program by Artaxerxes. At the River Ahava, Ezra held a fast for his group of returning exiles and asked God's blessing and protection on their venture. On arriving in Jerusalem he learned of many mixed marriages. Under Ezra's leadership most of the men divorced their foreign wives and sent away their children. This was radical surgery and by modern standards perhaps uncalled for, but Ezra's basic motivation was religious purity rather than purity of race as such. The Jews were never a race in the biological sense. Religious syncretism seemed to threaten the very life of the community, and thus Ezra chose the course he took.

Ezra brought the book of the Law of Moses with him from exile and read it or a considerable part thereof to the people in Jerusalem. Probably this was what we know as the Pentateuch: Genesis, Exodus, Leviticus, Numbers, and Deuteronomy. As he read in Hebrew, the Levites interpreted for the people in Aramaic, since the exiles understood Aramaic better than they did Hebrew. The Jewish festival of thanksgiving known as the Feast of Tabernacles was celebrated. And the people entered into a solemn covenant to be true to the Law of Moses.

Ezra has been called "the father of Judaism" because under him the people of God became the people of the Law (Torah). In a practical sense, it seems that the Pentateuch was canonized under his leadership. While some have suggested that the forces set in motion by him were in part responsible for the development of legalism, Ezra's work should not be minimized. The Law that he read to the people is itself set in the context of grace. The renewal of the covenant under Ezra is set in the context of one of the most thorough recitals of God's mighty acts to be found anywhere in scripture (Neh. 9–10; compare Joshua 24).

> *Read these two chapters and list in your notebook all the mighty acts found in chapter 9.*

Implicitly the motivation to obey the Law is gratitude, as in the covenant at Sinai. In fact, Ezra was a kind of new Moses, who led the people from bondage, through the wilderness, to the Promised Land. Moreover, he gave them the Law and renewed the covenant with them.

## Three Short Stories

Three short stories are appropriately studied in the context of this chapter. They are the story of Ruth, the Moabitess; Jonah, the reluctant missionary; and Esther, Jewish patriot.

## Ruth—The Moabitess

The book of Ruth records one of history's most beautiful stories.

*Read it again and let it speak its own message.*

It has its literary setting in the time of the judges. There are good reasons for believing it is a short story based on solid fact and told around many a campfire through the centuries of Israel's history. It is highly improbable that anyone would have invented a Moabite ancestress for King David. Nonetheless, there are good reasons for thinking that it was edited in its final form in the postexilic era.

On account of a famine in the land, Elimelech of Bethlehem moved to Moab with his wife Naomi and his two sons Mahlon and Chilion. After Elimelech's death Mahlon married Ruth and Chilion married Orpah. Both Ruth and Orpah were Moabites. In approximately ten years both Mahlon and Chilion died, and the bereaved Naomi returned to Bethlehem accompanied by Ruth. It was in Bethlehem that Ruth met Boaz, a relative of Elimelech, as she gleaned in his field. Naomi sent her to his threshing floor at night for the purpose of seeking his protection in marriage according to the custom of the next of kin; that is, the next of kin to her husband. When a nearer kinsman forfeited the right to marry Ruth and redeem the land of Elimelech, Boaz became Ruth's kinsman-redeemer, and to this union was born Obed, the grandfather of David.

No one has ever been able to determine with certainty the original author's purpose in telling the story. But it contains one of the richest expressions of filial devotion ever penned. Although Orpah had turned back to her people, Ruth insisted on accompanying her mother-in-law to Bethlehem, saying,

> "Do not press me to leave you
>     or to turn back from following you!
> Where you go, I will go;
>     where you lodge, I will lodge;
> your people shall be my people,
>     and your God my God.
> Where you die, I will die—
>     there will I be buried.
> May the LORD do thus and so to me,
>     and more as well,
> if even death parts me from you!"
>                                         (Ruth 1:16–17)

According to Deuteronomy 25:5–10, if a man's brother dies without leaving a son, this man shall marry his brother's widow and raise up an heir to his brother, that his name may not be blotted out in Israel. But Boaz was not a brother-in-law to Ruth. The principle involved in the marriage of Boaz and Ruth seems to have been a forerunner of the law stated in Deuteronomy, though it may have been an extension of the Deuteronomic law to more distant relatives.

The use of the book in the postexilic community may have helped to set the exclusiveness of Ezra and Nehemiah in a broader perspective. Interfaith marriages are loaded with danger in any age. We have nothing to gain by denying this. But at the time of her marriage to Boaz, Ruth was a convert to the Israelite faith (1:16; 2:12). However, she was a Moabite. How do you feel this fact should be related to Deuteronomy 23:3 (see Neh. 13:1–3) and the marriage reforms of Nehemiah and Ezra?

## Jonah—The Reluctant Missionary

The book of Jonah is regarded as one of the greatest little books ever written. An eminent German scholar once gave this testimony: "I have read the Book of Jonah at least a hundred times, and I will publicly avow . . . that I cannot even now take up this marvelous book, nay, nor even speak of it, without the tears rising to my eyes, and my heart beating higher."[6] As one reads this story, one cannot escape God's loving concern for all humankind. Unfortunately, the book has often been made a battleground instead of a sanctuary, and in light of the history of its interpretation we cannot escape the battle.

Jonah is the chief human character in the book, whose author is unnamed. Since he is called "the son of Amittai," he is apparently to be identified with the prophet mentioned only briefly in 2 Kings 14:25: "He [Jeroboam II] restored the border of Israel from Lebo-hamath as far as the Sea of the Arabah, according to the word of the LORD, the God of Israel, which he spoke by his servant Jonah son of Amittai, the prophet, who was from Gath-hepher."

Through the years there have been those who have maintained that the book is to be regarded as literal history written by Jonah in the eighth century B.C.E. (1) because it is told in straight narrative form, (2) because it would be a questionable procedure to smear the name of a historical person by misrepresenting him, and (3) because Jesus referred to the story of Jonah as one would refer to a historical account (see Matt. 12:38–42; 16:4; Luke 11:29–32).

Today, however, most persons who have given their lives to the study of the Old Testament regard the story of Jonah as a parable or allegory. According to this interpretation, Jonah's experience represents the experience of Israel (that is, Judah especially). As Jonah was swallowed by the great fish on account of his disobedience, so the Jews were swallowed up in the exile for their disobedience. As Jonah was released by the great fish to bear witness to the heathen, so the Jews were released from captivity to bear witness to the nations.[7]

The second proposal is accepted here for a variety of reasons. First, the arguments of those who accept the book as literal history are unconvincing. Literal historical narrative is by no means the only literary vehicle used in the Bible for communicating God's truth. For example, recall Jotham's fable (Judg. 9:7–15), Nathan's allegory (2 Sam. 12:1–6), and Jesus' many parables and his allegories. For the most part, such stories are told in straight narrative form. Moreover, among the acknowledged parables of Jesus there are those that are not designated as such by the use of the word "parable." They are told in straight narrative fashion. For example, this is true in the case of the parable of the Good Samaritan (Luke 10:25–37) and in that of the Prodigal Son (Luke 15:11–32), two of Jesus' most famous stories. The truth of these stories is in no way dependent on regarding them as literal history.

It is to be doubted that the figurative use of the name of the prophet Jonah would have been interpreted as a smear in the postexilic community. It is so easy for us to modernize God's ancient people and remake them in our own image. Moreover, there may well have been a historical tradition about the Jonah of the eighth century that indicated he was a man of narrow horizons, and this "fact" may have played a part in his selection by the author of the book of Jonah.

Jesus in his use of the story of Jonah was not playing the role of the present-day interpreter nor seeking to pass critical judgment on the issue of historicity. He was communicating a message in answer to a request for a sign and in the process made reference to the story of Jonah as it had been told through the centuries. Just as we make references to various parts of our literary and religious heritage without stopping on every occasion to say whether the book or passage to which we are referring is literal history or not, so did Jesus. We often allude to literary characters as if they were historical persons without any attempt whatsoever to deceive.

The book of Jonah is best understood as an attempt to recall the people of the postexilic community to their task as God's servant as set forth by the great prophets of the exile. According to those prophets, God said to the people, "You are my witnesses" (Isa. 43:10). And, in Isaiah 56:7 we read, "My house shall be called a house of prayer for all peoples." While

Nehemiah and Ezra performed a needed ministry in the renewal of the struggling community, their emphasis on exclusiveness seems to have "snowballed." The people became narrow and were failing to carry out their mission as a servant of the LORD. They needed the message of the story of Jonah, reminding them of God's concern even for their enemies. This emphasis comes close to Jesus' "Love your enemies" (Matt. 5:44).

Both preexilic Israel and postexilic Israel knew that Nineveh had not, as a matter of historical fact, repented. In the eighth century B.C.E., when the son of Amittai lived, Assyria was already a powerful and violent nation (compare Jonah 3:5) and continued to be so. The Northern Kingdom of Israel was put out of existence by Assyria in the latter part of the eighth century. Nineveh was not made the capital of the Assyrian empire until late in the eighth century. The quality of repentance presented in the book of Jonah would have involved some kind of turning to Israel's God. But Nineveh continued to be polytheistic and bloodthirsty. She was destroyed in 612 B.C.E. because she did not repent (see Nahum). The Jews who read the story of Jonah knew these things, and they also knew that the story was told for their benefit, not as a footnote on the history of Assyria.

> *Read the book of Jonah for yourself. Make up your own mind about the literary category to which it belongs. But most of all, seek God's guidance in applying its message to your own sense of vocation. Note especially 1:16; 3:6–10; and 4:1–11.*
>
> *Regardless of what critical position one may hold about the book of Jonah, through this masterpiece one can hear God speak of divine love for all people and all nations.*

## Esther—The Jewish Patriot

When you turn from the reading of Ruth and Jonah to the reading of Esther, you are instantly aware that the climate has changed. In the former there is a spirit of missionary breadth; in the latter, a spirit of patriotic retaliation. Esther, a Jewish maiden, becomes the queen of Persia. In her position as queen she is able to thwart a plot against her people by causing it to boomerang against their enemies. This victory is celebrated in the Jewish Feast of Purim.

It seems best to regard the book of Esther as a short story based on a core of historical data and told for the purpose of recommending the Feast of Purim to other Jews. Evidently this feast originated in the Persian Diaspora, for it is nowhere mentioned in the Pentateuch. Like the people it depicts, the book of Esther has not had an easy life. It is the only book in the Old Testament that has not yet been found in whole or in part among the Dead Sea Scrolls. At the Council of Jamnia in 90 C.E., Jewish scholars debated its right to be included in the scriptures. Martin Luther had a very negative view of Esther. On the other hand, "Maimonides, by contrast, placed it just after the Torah in importance."[8]

Certainly it exhibits a spirit of nationalism and vengeance. But we cannot agree with Luther. Some things in the Bible have not been preserved for our imitation, but for our instruction. The book of Esther is an honest portrayal of how many Jews have felt under godless persecution. This does not justify a Christian in attempting to reject the ethics of the Sermon on the Mount. The reading of the book, however, may help one to understand better the whole history of the persecution of the Jews. Moreover, it reveals the fact that anti-Jewishness did not arise first in the Christian church though it has for far too long been allowed to fester there.

In spite of the fact that the name of God never occurs in the book of Esther, the story communicates a sense of the boundless providence of God. Moreover, when we study it in relation to Isaiah 40–66, Ruth, Jonah, and the New Testament, we are confronted with one of the most vital issues of our time: How are we to relate our loyalty to our own nation to our loyalty to the kingdom of God? This is a question that bears pondering.

## A TIME LINE OF THE PERSIAN PERIOD
### 549–333 B.C.E.

| WORLD HISTORY | | | BIBLICAL EVENTS |
|---|---|---|---|
| Union of Persia & Media by Cyrus | 549 | | |
| Cyrus's Conquest of Babylon | 539 | | |
| The Edict of Cyrus | 538 | 538 | Return under Sheshbazzar |
| Reign of Darius I | 522 | | |
| | | 520 | Haggai & Zechariah |
| | | 520 | Temple Rebuilt under |
| | | | Zerubbabel |
| | | 515 | |
| | 486 | | |
| Reign of Artaxerxes I | 465 | | |
| | | 458? | Ezra's Return |
| | | 450? | Malachi and Joel |
| | | 445 | Nehemiah's Return |
| | | 428? | Ezra's Return |
| | 424 | | |
| Reign of Artaxerxes II | 404 | | |
| | 358 | 398? | Ezra's Return |
| Conquest of Persia by Alexander the Great | 333 | | |

# Words of Wisdom

*T*he "wisdom approach to life" includes a prudential handling of the affairs of everyday life and a meditative reflection on life's hard problems. It is to be found in all cultures, both ancient and modern. Christian missionaries have often placed a copy of the book of Proverbs in the hands of the people to whom they have been sent in order to establish contact, since many of the biblical proverbs resemble the wise sayings in the traditions of these people. The wisdom approach tends to be individualistic and therefore concerned with people as people.

## The Wisdom Movement

### Wisdom in the Ancient Near East

The biblical writers themselves were aware of the international character of wisdom. Egypt had a reputation for wisdom (1 Kings 4:30), and the wise served as advisers to the pharaoh (Gen. 41:8; Exod. 7:11; Isa. 19:11). The wise of Babylon (Jer. 50:35; 51:57; Isa. 44:25) and Edom (Jer. 49:7; Obad. 8) were not left unnoticed. The book of Job is set in the land of Uz (1:1), which was probably a part of the land of Edom. Eliphaz, one of Job's friends, is called a Temanite (2:11), and Teman was located in Edom. Undoubtedly some wise teachers were government officials, who not only gave counsel to the king but also prepared the young for places of political leadership. Archaeological discoveries and research have made available a large body of Egyptian and Babylonian wisdom literature.[1]

### Wisdom in the Bible

The chief examples of wisdom literature in the Old Testament are Proverbs, Job, Ecclesiastes, and several of the Psalms. Somewhat related to wisdom is the Song of Solomon. Further, there are scattered bits of wisdom here and there in other parts of the Old Testament. For example, there are Jotham's fable (Judg. 9:7–15), Samson's riddle (Judg. 14:14), and wisdom passages in the Prophets (Amos 3:3–6; Isa. 5:1–7; 10:15). The wise were recognized along with priests and prophets as religious teachers in Israel (Jer. 18:18). Apparently Ahithophel and Hushai were wise men who served as advisers to the royal house (2 Sam. 15:32–37; 16:23; 17:5–16). In addition to wise men, there were also wise women who served as counselors (Judg. 5:28–30; 2 Sam. 14:14).

No doubt there were many students of wisdom in Israel's history, but Solomon's reputation for wisdom surpassed all others. According to 2 Chronicles 1:10–12 (compare 1 Kings 3:4–15), God gave Solomon wisdom in answer to prayer (compare 1 Kings 5:7, 12). But the most revealing statement concerning Solomon's relation to wisdom literature is found in 1 Kings 4:29–34.

> *Read these verses carefully and compare them with 1 Kings 10:1–10.*

This passage tells us that Solomon was an author, a scholar, and a patron of wisdom literature.

One of the best ways to grasp the thrust of the wisdom movement is to see it in relation to the Law (the Pentateuch) and the Prophets. Both the Law and the Prophets center in covenant history; that is, in the mighty acts of God in relation to the covenant people, those things on which we have thus far been concentrating in this book. In contrast, the canonical wisdom books have little to say about these things. In the Law, "you shall" or "you shall not" is usually addressed to the covenant people. In the Prophets, "Thus says the LORD" is also usually addressed to them. But the wisdom teacher ordinarily addresses the student differently: "Go to the ant, you lazybones; consider its ways, and be wise" (Prov. 6:6). Yet the wisdom literature of the Old Testament was clearly understood by Israel in relation to the covenant. Occasionally this is reflected in the use of the name YHWH (the LORD). Further, these works give evidence of a genuine acquaintance with Israel's heritage. The wisdom psalms include those that deal with the Law (1, 19, 119), and Israel's Law is definitely covenant law. In fact, in the apocryphal book known as Ecclesiasticus, wisdom is identified with the Law.

## Proverbs—A Collection of Wise Sayings

The Hebrew word for "proverb" has in it the basic idea of "likeness" or "comparison," and this basic idea is present in many proverbs. For example, we read in Proverbs 10:26:

> Like vinegar to the teeth, and smoke to the eyes,
> so are the lazy to their employers.

There are not only poetic couplets involving a comparison or contrast but also clusters of proverbs and poems on a wisdom theme. It seems that the single couplet is the forerunner of the more extended wisdom poem.

While much in this book is universal in application, the concern for keeping the teachings of the wise in the framework of the covenant is demonstrated at various points. At the very outset (Prov. 1:7), the attitude with which one is to study the book is stated:

> The fear of the LORD is the beginning of knowledge;
> fools despise wisdom and instruction.

This means that the student of wisdom must approach the task as one who reveres and obeys the God of Israel, for such an undertaking is no secular enterprise (compare 9:10; 15:33). The reference to the Law in 28:4, 7, 9 is probably to the Mosaic Law. It appears that the Law and the Prophets are mentioned in 29:18.

The book of Proverbs contains both preexilic and postexilic materials. There is good reason to think that Solomon was the author of some of these materials, but the book itself provides clear testimony to a multiple authorship by the headings given to its seven divisions. Like the Psalter, the book of Proverbs is a collection of collections.

1. *The Proverbs of Solomon, Son of David, King of Israel (1:1–9:18).* This editorial title marks the first division of the book. It consists of proverb clusters and wisdom poems rather than of independent couplets.

*Read as much of this section and of the whole book as possible, and mark with a pencil those parts on which you wish to meditate more at length. If you cannot read the entire section, the following are minimum suggestions: 1:1–33; 2:6; 3:6; 4:23; 5:23; 6:16–19; 7:1–27; 8:1–9:6.*

Wisdom is of surpassing value. It is the gift of God. The true student of wisdom avoids scoffing, laziness, lying, pride, violence, discord, and above all the "strange woman." The wise of old knew that one of the young's most powerful temptations is to misuse the gift of sex. But, there is probably an even more severe concern associated with the "strange women." The Hebrew term basically means "foreign women." The problem may have been related more to the possible negative influence of "foreigners" than simply the question of sex. Solomon was led into idolatry by his "foreign wives" (1 Kings 11:1–3). The wise may have hoped to preserve their students from that disaster.

The treatment of wisdom as a person is probably the most distinctive element in these chapters. The writers of the Old Testament liked to speak of various things in personal terms, as we saw in our study of Psalm 114. In Proverbs, the wise teacher goes beyond this. Wisdom is treated as a woman, who calls people to be her disciples and to follow her instruction (1:20–3:35). This personal presentation of wisdom reaches its climax in 8:1–9:6. Wisdom is better than riches; she is that by which kings reign; indeed, she was with God at the creation of the world (compare 3:19). This conception of wisdom was carried over into the apocryphal Ecclesiasticus and the Wisdom of Solomon. In the New Testament, Christ is identified by Paul as the Wisdom of God (1 Cor. 1:24, 30), and wisdom is probably associated by John (1:1–18) with the Eternal Word.

2. *The Proverbs of Solomon (10:1–22:16)*. These chapters are composed of simple couplets and constitute the heart of the book. In them the wise and the foolish are contrasted. The wise are the righteous, and the foolish are the wicked. Here are a few samplings:

> There is a way that seems right to a person,
>> but its end is the way to death. (14:12)
> Those who oppress the poor insult their Maker,
>> but those who are kind to the needy honor him. (14:31)
> A cheerful heart is a good medicine,
>> but a downcast spirit dries up the bones. (17:22)
> Wine is a mocker, strong drink a brawler;
>> and whoever is led astray by it is not wise. (20:1)

3. *The Words of the Wise (22:17–24:34)*. Similarities have been found to a part of this division (22:22–23:14) in the Egyptian book known as The Teaching of Amenemope. However, one of the most interesting emphases of the section occurs outside this part, namely one's attitude towards enemy and neighbor. These words sound very much like the teaching of Jesus:

> Do not rejoice when your enemies fall,
>> and do not let your heart be glad when they stumble. (24:17)
> Do not be a witness against your neighbor without cause,
>> and do not deceive with your lips.

> Do not say, "I will do to others as they have done to me;
>   I will pay them back for what they have done." (24:28–29)

4. *Proverbs of Solomon Which the Men of Hezekiah King of Judah Copied (25:1–29:27).* This heading indicates that literary activity was going on in Judah during the eighth century B.C.E. under the sponsorship of the king. Hezekiah's scholars edited this particular collection. Concern is also shown here for one's enemy. In fact, Paul quotes 25:21–22 in Romans 12:20. Choice samplings of this collection include the following:

> Like a city breached, without walls,
>   is one who lacks self-control. (25:28)
> Well meant are the wounds a friend inflicts,
>   but profuse are the kisses of an enemy. (27:6)
> No one who conceals transgressions will prosper,
>   but one who confesses and forsakes them will obtain mercy.
>                     (28:13; compare Ps. 32; 1 John 1:9)

5. *The Words of Agar (30:1–33).* We cannot identify Agar. In his collection of wise sayings there is demonstrated a fondness for numbers.

*Read the most famous of his sayings in 30:18–19.*

6. *The Words of Lemuel (31:1–9).* Lemuel is simply identified as a king who reproduces what his mother taught him. The word "Massa" may refer to a place, or it may mean "oracle." Lemuel's mother warns him against lust and strong drink, and advises him to "defend the rights of the poor and needy."

7. *A Good Wife (31:10–31).* Warnings are given against the "strange woman" in the book as a whole, but here is a poem in praise of a worthy woman. She is faithful, industrious, generous, and wise.

*How would you sum up the value of the book of Proverbs for twenty-first century Christians?*

## Job—Wisdom's Greatest Masterpiece

The book of Job is recognized as one of the greatest literary masterpieces of all time. In it great art and great theology are united. Yet it cannot be classified according to any single recognized literary type. It has been called a drama; it is dramatic, but it is not a drama. It has also been called *The Epic of the Inner Life,* [2] but such a definition contradicts the usual meaning of the word "epic." It is sometimes referred to as a lyrical poem with characters. This definition contains truth, but it is not the whole truth. We must acknowledge the book's uniqueness.

It is widely held that the unnamed author made use of an early story about Job and that this story is especially reflected in the Prologue and Epilogue of the book. Most of the dialogue is attributed to the author, though many feel that the wisdom poem in chapter 28, the Elihu speeches (chaps. 32–37), and the second divine speech (40:6–41:34) were additions to the original book. But these are not issues of great importance in this study. The date of the book is uncertain. It may be sometime during the exile or shortly before or after the exile. Its purpose is to wrestle realistically with three questions:

1. Does one suffer in exact proportion to one's sinning? In other words, this is the question of reward and punishment.
2. "Does Job fear God for nothing?" (1:9) In the language of many in our society, is true religion a slot-machine affair? (You put a nickel in and expect to get a dollar out. If the dollar is not forthcoming, you give up your religion.)
3. "Why did I not die at birth?" (3:11) This is Job's personal question. With the whole dialogue in mind, it may be stated like this: "Why do you, the righteous and all-powerful God, cause me, a righteous man, to suffer the loss of all things, including my health?"

The book of Job is the voice of each crying out in the anguish of personal existence: "Why?" But it is also the voice of God answering not the "why" but the person. In our attempt to grasp the powerful impact of this book, we shall consider Job's suffering, friends, experience, and comfort.

*If at all possible, read the work in its entirety. Jot down in your notebook questions and comments that you would like to see discussed in class.*

*If you cannot read the whole book, by all means read the following passages: the Prologue (1:1–2:13), the first of the three cycles of the debate (3:1–14:22), the speeches of the LORD (38:1–41:34), and Job's repentance (42:1–6) plus the passages cited in the comments below.*

## Job's Suffering

Job was a wealthy and respected man in the land of Uz (a part of Edom). He had a family of ideal size for that day, seven sons and three daughters.

Without Job's knowledge, the heavenly council meets. Among those present is "Satan." In Hebrew the word "Satan" has the definite article with it and means literally "the adversary," for Satan is pictured here as one who tests human allegiance. God calls the upright Job to Satan's attention. It is at this point that one of the book's major questions is raised by Satan: "Does Job fear God for nothing?" "Fear" has the connotation of worship and service. Satan maintains that Job is a prosperous man and that his goodness reflects a fair-weather religion. God permits Satan to destroy Job's property and children. Yet Job does not sin or charge God with wrong. Later God permits Satan to plague Job with loathsome sores, so that he goes to the city dump, sits among the ashes, and scratches himself with a potsherd. His wife counsels him to curse God and die, a demonstration of the attitude that makes of suffering a hell. Yet, in all this Job does not sin with his lips.

As we go beyond the Prologue, we find that Job's suffering is not limited to his loss of health, family, and property. It is involved in his relation to God, to his friends, and to the interpretation of his suffering by his friends. His suffering is so great that he wavers between the desire to live and the desire to die.

## Job's Friends

Job's three friends Eliphaz, Bildad, and Zophar come to comfort him. Their first response to Job's predicament is one of dismay and silence. After Job breaks the silence by cursing the day of his birth (3:1–26; compare Jer. 20:14–18), the debate between Job and his friends begins. These men maintain that Job's suffering is God's judgment on him for sin. That is, they hold the retribution dogma in a very mechanical and literalistic manner. Nevertheless, they also acknowledge that suffering serves a disciplinary purpose. It is this aspect of suffering that the young Elihu emphasizes when he enters the story rather abruptly (ch. 32 ). The friends' accusations become increasingly hostile, and they charge Job with secret sin and arrogance. Job does not claim that he is sinless, but that he has not sinned in such a way as to deserve the suffering that he is undergoing. And from this position he does not turn aside.

The position of the friends must be seen in its larger setting. Obviously there are elements of truth in it. God does punish individuals and nations for sin, and suffering often serves the purpose of discipline. But this is not the whole truth. When generalities are applied to Job mechanically, they are an inadequate appraisal of the situation.

The Law, the Prophets, and the Writings all teach that God blesses the righteous and punishes the wicked. But they do not stop there. All three champion the cause of the poor and afflicted. The poor and the afflicted are often the righteous in the Psalms. There is in human experience a tension between retribution and grace. The Bible does not dodge this tension. It affirms it. We must therefore live by faith, not by complete knowledge. Job's friends, who were representative of many, had emphasized one aspect of suffering and thereby were setting up false standards of judgment. A lopsided theology issues in a lopsided witness.

## Job's Experience

Job complains, but he does not renounce his faith in God. He maintains his innocence but not his perfection. He does not know why he suffers. At times he longs for death, yet he raises the question, "If mortals die, will they live again?" (14:14.) In his loneliness he yearns for true friends, and this loneliness drives him to the God he dreads, for there is no one else to whom he can go. Yet there is a sense in which he appeals to God against God. He appeals to the True God against the caricature of God represented by his friends. He longs for an umpire who might place one hand on him and the other on God and thereby reconcile them (9:33). He expresses faith in a heavenly witness (16:19–21), who may be identified with the umpire.

Then Job comes through with his most famous exclamation of faith in his Redeemer (read 19:23–39). At first Job expresses the desire that he may leave a permanent record of his testimony that, in the future, there may be those who will recognize his innocence. But in the ultimate analysis this would be inadequate. Therefore, he turns to the heavenly Kinsman-Redeemer, who will vindicate him after death. Though the Hebrew of these verses is capable of more than one interpretation, Job seems to express faith in life after death. The Redeemer may be identified with the umpire and the heavenly witness mentioned earlier.

But Job's faith does not remain at this high peak throughout the dialogue. Eventually God addresses him from the whirlwind and challenges him to take an honest look at the power and wisdom manifest in the works of creation: the ocean flood, the light, the hail, the snow, the stars, the seasons, and the living creatures. A mere mortal is not God's size. It is given to humans to live by faith.

In the divine-human encounter Job confesses his faith in God's sovereignty. He also confesses himself a sinner who has talked arrogantly to God. Job's personal question is not answered on the intellectual level; Job himself is answered. The mystery of evil remains, but in the encounter Job is found by God and finds himself:

I had heard of you by the hearing of the ear,
    but now my eye sees you;
therefore I despise myself,
    and repent in dust and ashes.

(42:5–6)

Job had been living on a secondhand religion. He was not suffering from God's judgment on his sin; nevertheless, in his meeting with God he did recognize himself to be a sinner and turned from his pride to the arms of God. When God comes to us and we turn to God, we may still have unanswered questions but we ourselves have been answered at the deepest level of communication. Job found himself small yet cared for personally by God.

## Job's Comfort

Job was comforted in various ways. (1) He had a sense of moral integrity. He had not lived deceitfully, adulterously, oppressingly, covetously, or covertly. (2) He recognized that there is no complete intellectual answer to all human problems. In the final analysis, his remonstrance was with his friends' caricature of God, not with the True God. The friends had made God in their own image, and this left little room for faith in the living God. (3) Job hoped for a meaningful life after death. God's care and the inequalities of this life point in that direction. (4) Job was justified on the basis of faith in God's grace. He was a sinner standing in the need of forgiveness and reconciliation. (5) Job learned that his chief end was to glorify and to enjoy God forever. This involved an attitude of worship, reverence, and humility. One sees one's true significance only as one sees one's insignificance. Happiness is the by-product of glorifying God. (6) Job came to know God in a person-to-person relationship.

## Conclusion

Do people suffer in exact proportion to their sinning? The book of Job says an emphatic "No!" And so does Jesus (John 9:1–3). You cannot necessarily measure a person's sin by the suffering endured.

Will a human serve God for nought? Yes, Job served God for nought but God, and this means it is possible for others to do likewise. Fellowship with God transcends and transforms suffering.

Why do relatively innocent people suffer? We do not know, nor do we have to know. God's grace is sufficient for our needs.

Job spoke better than he knew in his longing for an umpire, a witness, and a redeemer. In the fullness of time one came who had his hand on

God, for he was Very God of Very God; and at the same time had his hand on humankind, for he was truly human. In him we hear the voice of Job reechoed, "Why?" and the voice of God, saying, "I am the Alpha and the Omega, the first and the last, the beginning and the end."

## Ecclesiastes—The Challenge of Skepticism

A free rendering of the word "Ecclesiastes" is "convener," but the traditional reading came from Martin Luther, who translated the term "preacher." The New Revised Standard Version's "teacher" is a good compromise. The writer's skepticism is not the doubt of God's reality or sovereignty. Rather it grows from frustration in understanding the seeming senselessness of nature and human experience. And in this attempt he arrives at a sense of futility:

> Vanity of vanities, says the Teacher,
> vanity of vanities! All is vanity.
> (1:2)

This is the theme of much of the book and of many in our own time as well. The indirect reference to Solomon in 1:1 does not mean that he wrote the book but that he is the ideal representative of wisdom literature. The book was probably written between 400 and 200 B.C.E.

The repetitions of nature suggest the wearisome sameness of human experience (1:2–11). The pursuit of wisdom (1:12–18; 9:17–10:15), pleasure (2:1–11), toil (2:18–23), wealth (5:10–20), and women (7:23–29) has left Ecclesiastes with a sense of futility. He is depressed by injustice (3:16–22), oppression (4:1–3; 5:8–9), occupational hazards (10:8–11), the sinfulness of human beings (7:20, 29), and death (3:19–21; 9:1–6, 9–10; 12:7). He maintains that it is better never to have been born than to have to undergo some types of oppression: "God made human beings straightforward, but they have devised many schemes" (7:29). Though God has put eternity in the human heart, the fate of humans and that of the beasts appears to be the same (3:10–22). Moreover, the same fate comes to the righteous and the wicked in Sheol.

Yet, in spite of all the humdrum and tragic experiences of human existence, this wisdom writer votes for God and life, not death by committing suicide. The writer urges all to find enjoyment in eating, drinking, and working, for these are God's gifts to humankind (2:24–26; 3:13, 22; 5:18–20; 8:15). A husband is to enjoy life with the wife whom he loves (9:9). One is to revere God (3:14; 5:1) and remember the divine as Judge and Creator in the days of his youth (11:9; 12:1). It is usually held that 12:9–14 is an editorial addition to the book. Even so, its contents are not out of harmony with the book as a whole.

In our study of Ecclesiastes we should remember that in the providence of God there is a place for at least one skeptic in the canon. The writer challenges us to face life's questions with integrity and to give a reason for the faith that is in us. Honest doubt is more acceptable to God than dishonest piety. It is often the occasion when God leads one to a deeper faith.

*What role has skepticism played in your own life?*

## The Song of Solomon—A Celebration of Love and Marriage

This song is the most difficult book in the Bible to interpret and has received more different kinds of interpretation than any other. It is not really a wisdom book, but, because it deals with the reality of human love, we will study it as part of wisdom.

According to an early Jewish interpretation, the Bridegroom is God and the bride is Israel. Some early Christians identified Christ as the Bridegroom and the church as his bride. Both of these interpretations are allegorical. Although the prophets sometimes used the husband-wife metaphor to characterize the covenant relation between God and Israel (for example, Hos. 1–3; Jer. 2–3 ) and Paul used it to express Christ's relation to the church (Eph. 1:23; 5:21–22; Col. 1:18; compare Rev. 21:2), there is nothing in the Song of Solomon to indicate that its author had any such idea in mind. Therefore, today, the allegorical interpretation has been largely abandoned. The book was probably attributed to Solomon by an editor (1:1) because he is mentioned several times therein (1:5; 3:9,11). It is generally thought, however, to come from the late postexilic age.

It seems best to take the book at face value, as a collection of dramatic songs celebrating love between bride and bridegroom. The language, of course, is that of the ancient Near East, and there may well be allusions to ancient liturgical ceremonies as well as to ancient weddings. Since God created humankind male and female, why should this fact of creation not be celebrated in the canon of Holy Writ? "For love is strong as death" (8:6). The Song of Solomon reminds us that God's blessing is on the wedding trip as well as on the wedding ceremony. The book, along with the rest of wisdom literature, teaches us that all sorts of human concerns, including sexual love, are of concern to our Creator.

# The Encouragement of Hope

At the end of Old Testament times the Jews were confident that God was at work in all the events of their lives, even in the midst of tragedy and disappointment. They anticipated God's mighty act of salvation in the future.

## The Hellenistic Period (333–63 B.C.E.)[1]

### Alexander the Great

The Persians had ruled the Near East for over two hundred years and had jeopardized the independence of Greece. Review the time line of the Persian Period in chapter 12. The Greeks had successfully defended themselves against the Persians. Philip of Macedon then extended his control over all Greece in 338 B.C.E. Philip's son Alexander took the battle to Persian soil and conquered the Persian empire about 333 B.C.E. This was the beginning of the Hellenistic (Greek) Period. After Alexander's death, his empire was divided into three principal parts: Macedonia, Egypt, and Syria. Palestine was a political ball, first under the control of the Ptolemies of Egypt. Later, however, the Seleucids of Syria contested this arrangement, and in 198 B.C.E. Antiochus III defeated Egypt and annexed Palestine to Syria.

### Antiochus Epiphanes

At first the relationship between Syria and the Jews was a happy one. Antiochus III was generous and kind in his rule over them. He was succeeded by Seleucus IV (187–175). At the death of Seleucus, Antiochus IV (Epiphanes) usurped the throne. According to 1 Maccabees 1:10 Antiochus was "a sinful root," for he came to persecute the Jews without mercy. This persecution was related to problems within his own kingdom, threats from neighboring kingdoms, and conflicts among the Jews themselves.

The people of the Seleucid empire were a mixed group with little to hold them together. Therefore, Antiochus was determined to unify them. But the threats from without were as dangerous as the problems from within. Rome was becoming increasingly dominant in the affairs of the Near East and was in a position to dictate to other powers. Recently Egypt had lost Palestine to Syria, but Rome was friendly to Egypt, and this fact posed a threat to Antiochus. The eastern part of the Syrian empire was menaced by the Parthians. To meet military expenses Antiochus robbed temples within the sphere of his rule, including the Temple in Jerusalem.

He, like Alexander the Great, championed the spread of Greek culture as a means of achieving unity within his dominion. He also promoted Greek religion, including the worship of Greek deities and even the worship of himself.

Some Jews were caught up in this modern trend, while others opposed it vigorously. Sharp struggles centered around the office of the high priest in Jerusalem. These weaknesses within the Jewish community encouraged Antiochus in his interference in Jewish affairs. Humiliated by Rome in his campaign against Egypt in 168 B.C.E. and frustrated by mounting Jewish opposition to his program of Hellenization, Antiochus had Jerusalem ravaged. Afterward he set up a stronghold called "the Acra" in Jerusalem, composed of a Seleucid garrison, other non-Jews, and Hellenized Jews. Finally, in response to Jewish resistance he forbade key practices of the Jewish religion (such as circumcision, sacrifice, and Sabbath observance), set up pagan shrines throughout Palestine, and required Jews to eat swine's flesh. To disobey was to incur the death penalty. Antiochus brought his persecutions to a climax in December, 167 B.C.E., by erecting an altar and image to Olympian Zeus in the Temple. This construction is called in Daniel the "abomination that desolates" (see 9:27; 12:11; compare 11:31; and 1 Macc. 1:54).

## The Maccabean Rebellion

Jewish opposition to Antiochus's persecution was centered in a group of pious loyalists known as the "Hasidim" and simultaneously assumed two major forms: one military and the other literary. The military opposition was the Maccabean rebellion, and the literary opposition was the book of Daniel.

Shortly after the profanation of the Temple, the Maccabean rebellion was sparked by an episode in the village of Modein. Here lived a devout Jew, Mattathias, and his five stalwart sons: John, Simon, Judas, Eleazar, and Jonathan. A representative of Antiochus commanded Mattathias to offer a sacrifice to a pagan deity, and he refused. When another Jew came forward to offer the sacrifice, Mattathias killed both the Jew and the king's officer. He and his sons fled to the hills and were joined there by other loyalists.

After the death of the aged Mattathias in 166 B.C.E., the leadership of the resistance movement fell to his son Judas, known as Maccabeus ("the hammer"). Under Judas the resistance was marked by success, and the Temple was rededicated in December, 164 B.C.E. Jews still celebrate this event by the Feast of Hanukkah (Dedication) each year close to Christmas Day. After the death of Judas in 160 B.C.E., the fight against Syria continued under the leadership of Jonathan and Simon, brothers of Judas.

## Daniel—The Apocalypse of the Old Testament[2]

The book of Daniel was addressed to the Jews who were suffering under the persecutions of Antiochus Epiphanes. Though some of the sources of the book antedate the second century B.C.E., the writer lived in that century and sought to bring God's message of hope to the distressed people.

Daniel is the only major apocalypse in the Old Testament, though there are apocalyptic elements in Ezekiel 1–37, Joel, Isaiah 24–27, and Zechariah 12–14. There are many extrabiblical apocalypses, the most important being 1 Enoch. The book of Revelation is the major apocalypse of the New Testament and is dependent at points on the book of Daniel.

The word "apocalypse" means an "uncovering" or "revelation." In a literary sense it refers to a special revelation or series of revelations written in highly symbolic and visionary language for the purpose of encouraging God's people in time of great trouble by pointing them to the power of God. Apocalypses are usually written under a pen name, include references to angels and demons, and stress the coming catastrophic intervention of God on behalf of the suffering people.

The book of Daniel is divided into two major parts. Chapters 1–6 are composed of narratives concerning Daniel and his three friends. Chapters 7–12 are composed of Daniel's visions of the kingdoms of the world and the kingdom of God. Nowhere does the book itself claim to have been written by Daniel. In part one, Daniel is spoken of in the third person. In part two, there is variation between the first person and the third person, with an emphasis on the first person. However, in 7:1, where the two major divisions of the book are joined, Daniel is introduced in the third person before he begins to speak in the first person. This same type of procedure occurs also in 10:1, where the last section of the book begins. In other words, the book as a whole is placed in the framework of telling a story about Daniel.

Some have felt that Jesus settled the issue of authorship by his mention of Daniel in Matthew 24:15. But there is no reason to suppose that Jesus was making a pronouncement of biblical criticism in a noncritical age. For the position that holds that the book was written in the sixth century by Daniel himself see the note reference.[3]

The author's purpose in writing Daniel was not to produce a modern history but to give an interpretation of history and to inspire faith in, and loyalty to, the sovereign Lord of history. Historical events clearly play a part in both narratives and visions, but the writer was an apocalyptist, not a historian as such. At the time of writing, it was a capital offense to possess a scroll of the Torah (Law). Therefore, the author had to be indirect and mysterious rather than direct and explicit. Daniel, who lived at an earlier time than the writer, was used by the writer to depict the way a loyal Jew should behave under the fiery ordeal of persecution.

## Narratives Concerning Daniel and His Friends (Chaps. 1–6)

In the stories of chapters 1–6, the seer presents Daniel as the faithful Israelite to encourage the covenant community to faithfulness and to a responsible life even in adversity. The time in which we live is filled with adversity and danger. God also calls us to do responsibly the job to which we have been commissioned.

> *Read each of these six stories carefully. After the reading of the story, write down in your notebook what you think the story meant to those who suffered under Antiochus. Keep in mind the fact that God's people were suffering on account of their faith.*
>
> *Next, imagine yourself living as a Christian in some place today where Christians are persecuted because of their faith. What would the story mean to you in such a situation?*
>
> *Are there circumstances in our own society in which persons are sometimes ridiculed on account of their Christian faith? What message does the story have for such persons?*

## Visions of the Kingdoms and the Kingdom (Chaps. 7–12)

In the visions of chapters 7–12, the seer presents the triumph of the kingdom of God over human kingdoms to encourage the people to trust God even when the cause seems lost.

*Read these chapters from the Bible and try to think through what they mean.*

We concentrate in our comments on chapter 7, which deals with the four beasts and the "One like a human being."

The four beasts come from "the great sea." Ordinarily this phrase is used to designate the Mediterranean (for example, see Josh. 1:4), but here it is probably the mysterious Sea of Chaos that is used as a symbol of evil powers. The turbulence of the Mediterranean or any other large body of water suggests confusion and chaos. When the seer in Revelation 21:1 says, "And the sea was no more," the reference is to the end of evil.

The four beasts symbolize four world kingdoms. When the author says these beasts "came up out of the sea," their theological location (evil) is given; when later the author says they "shall arise out of the earth" (v. 17), their geographical and political location are indicated. The fact that this geographical and political location has not been spelled out in explicit detail has given rise to many theories concerning the identifications of the four kingdoms symbolized by the four beasts: a winged lion, a bear, a winged leopard, and a nameless monster. Three principal series of identifications have been made: (1) Babylonian, Medo-Persian, Greek, and Roman; (2) Babylonian, Medo-Persian, the Greek empire of Alexander, and Alexander's successors; (3) Babylonian, Median, Persian, and Greek (Alexander and his successors). No view of this problem is without its difficulties, but the third seems to have the most probability.

The writer gives special attention to the fourth beast, which symbolizes the Greek empire of Alexander the Great and his successors. He is so terrible that he cannot be described in terms of animals and combinations of animals, but corresponds to the kingdom represented by iron in chapter 2. It was Alexander and his successors who deliberately supplanted established Jewish customs with forms of Greek culture. The author of Daniel was most conscious of the kind, and method, of Hellenization adopted by the Seleucids of Syria. The "ten horns" of the monster probably represent ten Seleucid kings. The little horn is Antiochus Epiphanes, who usurped the throne by uprooting three claimants. Antiochus is also referred to in 8:9–14, 24–25; and 11:31–33, and is again called "a little horn" in 8:9.

By way of contrast the scene now shifts from the beasts of the sea to the convening of the court in heaven (vv. 9–10). It is customary for a king to pronounce judgment from his throne. Presumably the thrones in Daniel's vision are arranged for use by the Ancient One (God) and the heavenly assistants. The title "an Ancient One" is a way of saying that God is the Judge of all the generations of humankind. "White snow" and "pure wool" symbolize the Judge's spotless purity and unimpeachable integrity. Much of the Old Testament furnishes a background for associating the appearance of the divine Judge with fire, and the wheels of blazing fire may have their background in the wheels of Ezekiel's visions (chaps. 1, 10; compare 2 Kings 2:10–12). The "thousands" are attendants, members of the heavenly hosts (see Deut. 33:2; 1 Kings 22:19; Rev. 5:11). The "ten thousand times ten thousand" may refer to the same group or to those about to be judged. The court is convened, and the books recording human deeds are opened to reveal the evidence on the basis of which judgment is to be rendered. Here it is primarily the deeds of the four beasts that are to be investigated.

The sentence is executed on the four beasts (vv. 11–12). The fourth beast (the Greek empire) receives the death penalty on account of the blasphemous arrogance of the little horn (Antiochus Epiphanes), in whom its transgressions have reached their full measure (8:23). "Given over to be burned with fire" means that the empire is devoted to complete destruction. "The rest of the beasts" or empires have lost their status as empires, but their existence as self-conscious peoples will continue so long as God decrees.

In contrast to the figures like the beasts from the Sea of Chaos, who have been judged and sentenced, the "one like a human being" who comes "with the clouds of heaven" is presented before the Ancient One in a manner appropriate to the Royal Court, and is given the indestructible kingdom of God. The "clouds" seem to indicate a heavenly being. "One like a human being" means one who has the appearance of an individual human being. The identification of this humanlike figure in this passage is one of the most debated issues in biblical interpretation. There are four principal classifications under which the various theories of identification may be grouped: the messianic, the collective, the literary, and the combined.

It is obvious to us that Jesus was both Messiah and a human being, but the question is, What precisely did the author of Daniel mean by the expression "one like a human being"? The author of Daniel does not use the word "Messiah" or "King" to refer to the Humanlike One. In an extrabiblical work known as *The Similitudes of Enoch,* the same term that

Daniel uses is translated "the Son of Man" and seems to refer to a super-natural individual but is not identified there with the Davidic Messiah. In the New Testament, Jesus is at one and the same time the fulfiller of the messianic promise and the "Son-of-Man" promise (for example, Matt. 25:31; Mark 10:45). In late Jewish documents the "Messiah" and "Son of Man" are identified.

Those who hold the collective theory consider the expression to be a symbolic representation of "the saints of the Most High." The chief argument is that in the vision itself the "one like a human being" is given the eternal kingdom (vv. 13–14) and in the interpretation of the vision (vv. 15–27) by the celestial attendant (v. 16), "the holy ones of the Most High" (God's true people) receive the kingdom (vv. 18, 22, 27). This, it is claimed, corresponds to the fact that each of the four beasts represents a human kingdom.

Many emphasize the fact that the figure of the Humanlike One (Son of Man) is closely related to Near Eastern literature. But they do not agree as to the exact identification of the figure. A person who holds this opinion may also hold one of the other theories as well.

The combined view regards the figure of verse 13 as including both collective and individual meanings. The Humanlike One represents both the kingdom of the saints and its leader or king who inaugurates the kingdom. The four beasts represent kingdoms, and in Daniel king and kingdom interchange (7:17; 2:36–45; 8:21), for the king stands for the kingdom. The combined view best takes all the evidence into consideration and is in harmony with the Hebrew way of thinking of a group and the individual who represents it at the same time.

The four beasts suggest to us who live in the twenty-first century C.E. that just as there are depths of evil in the human heart, so there are evils in political structures. No human government, even the best, can rightly identify itself as the kingdom of God. Of course this does not mean that one form of government is as good as another. This is simply not true. But it is true that all human-made structures, in a sense, come from the sea and stand under the judgment of the Ancient of Days, who is Lord not only of individuals but of all peoples, nations, and tongues. God has a purpose for each nation and for the whole historical process.

## The Jewish Hope

The whole story of the Old Testament is a story of hope. God's promise to Abraham inspired hope in the patriarch and his people. The promise of deliverance announced by Moses gave hope to the slaves in Egypt. The covenant with David was the foundation of the messianic hope. Though God judged the people, the prophets assured them of hope for the future. As we conclude our pilgrimage through the Old Testament let us review three important forms this hope took.

## The Day of the LORD

This combination of judgment and hope is associated with the Day of the LORD in a special way. In Chapter 10 we examined this teaching in relation to Zephaniah and other prophets. Early in Israel's history this day was popularly thought of as a day of blessing on Israel and a day of judgment on other nations. But Amos and other preexilic prophets described it as a time of judgment on the chosen people as well as on others.

In the exile and after, the positive note was again struck. Judgment would pave the way for the coming of the kingdom of God in glory. According to the book of Daniel the kingdom will be given to the "one like a human being," who represents both the people of God and their heaven-sent Leader. While the later doctrine of Jewish hope was complex and varied, it tended to emphasize God's coming in judgment and salvation. In some Jewish circles there was an intense expectation of the coming of the kingdom of God in the first century B.C.E.

## The Deliverer

One of the most important aspects of the Jewish hope was the expectation of a deliverer, which assumed different forms in the Old Testament. One of those forms is that of *the Messiah of the line of David.* The hope of a future king is seen against the background of the covenant made with David. Isaiah looked for the Prince of Peace and the age of peace. According to Jeremiah 23:5–6 God would "raise up for David a righteous Branch."

In Judaism later than the Old Testament period, messianic conceptions varied. For example, the Dead Sea Scrolls community seems to have expected three messianic persons: a prophet, a priest, and a king. The prophet (see Deut. 18:15–18; Acts 3:22) was a messianic forerunner; the priest, the teacher of the scripture; and the Davidic king, the military leader, in the final conflict between the people of light and the people of darkness. We cannot avoid observing that Jesus is presented in the New Testament as prophet, priest, and king, though he was no military leader.

*The individual redeemer of the Servant Songs* of Isaiah 40–55 (pp.

179–82) seems to have been overlooked or bypassed in the time just prior to the birth of Jesus. Though this figure of the deliverer cannot with certainty be identified with the Davidic Messiah in pre-Christian times, Jesus united the two figures in his own Person and work.

In some Jewish circles the deliverer was primarily thought of as *the Son of Man* ("one like a human being"). We concluded, in our study of Daniel, that "the one like a human being" is the leader and the kingdom of the saints simultaneously. This figure came later to be called simply "the Son of Man" and was regarded as the heavenly one and was sometimes identified with the Davidic Messiah.

The ancient Davidic king had a people. Though Jesus did not accept the political and military aspects of this kingship, he was and is the messianic king who has a people of whom he is the acknowledged Lord. The Servant of the LORD was both the community and its future prophet-redeemer. Jesus was the individual Servant in his ministry and death, who thereby released life, and the church is his body, called to an identification with him in his ministry, suffering, death, and resurrection. The Humanlike One (Son of Man) was both Israel and the heavenly One. Jesus Christ is the human/heavenly One through whom the kingdom comes, and the church as the new Israel is his people. "Messiah," "Servant of the LORD," and "one like a human" all converge in him. Jesus has broken the molds in which these titles were fashioned and given them a distinctive incarnation.

## Life After Death

The belief in a meaningful life after death was not made known to Israel suddenly. At first, death was regarded as weakness, which one might begin to experience this side of the grave. It was the occasion of being gathered to one's ancestors in Sheol, a place under the earth where people were thought to exist in a shadowlike state (Gen. 37:35; Job 30:23; Isa. 14:9). Sheol was generally thought to make communion with God impossible (Pss. 6:5; 30:9; 88:6–13; 115:17; Isa. 38:18); yet one psalmist at least believed in God's presence in Sheol (Ps. 139:8; compare 22:29). Death was associated with sin (Gen. 3; Ezek. 18; Ps. 41) and regarded as an evil (Deut. 30:15, 19). Through one's posterity one's name was kept alive (Gen. 15:2–6; Deut. 25:5–10; 2 Sam. 18:18).

Faith in the resurrection of the dead, however, is not absent from the Old Testament. Ezekiel likens the restoration of his people from the Babylonian exile to the resurrection of the dead (chap. 37). Certain of the psalmists appear to have believed in victory over death for at least some persons (Pss. 16, 49, 73). Job implies his own resurrection in 19:25–27. The clearest reference to the resurrection of the dead in the Old Testament, however, is found in Daniel 12:2. Some are raised to eternal life and others to eternal shame and contempt.

At the dawn of New Testament times various views of the afterlife were held. The Sadducees held the view of Sheol already described above. Some Jews believed in the resurrection of the righteous only. Others associated the resurrection with the judgment of both the righteous and the wicked. The Greek idea of the immortality of the soul is sometimes found in nonbiblical Jewish works. The dominant faith of both Jews and early Christians was the resurrection of the body.

Like the other elements in the Jewish hope, the resurrection of the dead is confirmed in Jesus Christ, who was himself raised from the dead.

## The Canon of the Old Testament

From time to time we have made reference to particular books as belonging to some particular division of the Old Testament canon. In this last chapter on the study of the Old Testament, it is appropriate that we take a brief look at the formation of the Old Testament as an authoritative standard for faith and practice. "Canon" is simply the word used to designate the books of the Old Testament (and the New as well) as authoritative. Religious and theological literature of various kinds had been produced by members of the covenant community from very early times. Some of this literature, in God's providence, was accepted as authoritative by the people. The informal process of acceptance preceded the more formal process, and many factors played a part in the selection.

### The Stages in Canon Formation

The stages in the formation of the Hebrew (or Jewish) canon are broadly outlined as follows:

*The Deuteronomic Law (622 B.C.E.)*

It is generally agreed that Deuteronomy or a part thereof was the Book of the Law found in the Temple in the time of Josiah and that it was accepted by Josiah and others as the basis of at least some of his reforms.

*The Law (ca. 400 B.C.E.)*

The Law (Torah) includes Genesis, Exodus, Leviticus, Numbers, and Deuteronomy. It is widely held that Ezra read the Law or a large part of it to the people, and it was accepted by them as authoritative. The Samaritans, with whom Ezra and Nehemiah clashed, have as their Bible only the Law. Presumably the rest of the Old Testament had not been accepted as canonical by any group at the time of the division between the Jews and the Samaritans.

### The Prophets (ca. 200 B.C.E.)

Of course the Torah (Law) continued as canonical, and the Prophets were added to the list of authoritative books. This adding occurred in an informal way not later than 200 B.C.E. The Prophets are divided into the Former Prophets (Joshua, Judges, Samuel, and Kings) and the Latter Prophets (Isaiah, Jeremiah, Ezekiel, and the Book of the Twelve). The Book of the Twelve is composed of the twelve shorter prophetic books, from Hosea to Malachi.

### The Writings (ca. 100 B.C.E.)

All books of the Hebrew Bible not included in the Law and the Prophets are included in the Writings. The Writings are subdivided into three groups: (1) the three largest books: Psalms, Proverbs, and Job; (2) the five festal scrolls: Song of Songs, Ruth, Lamentations, Ecclesiastes, and Esther; and (3) the others: Daniel, Ezra, Nehemiah, and Chronicles.

Jewish scholars discussed the Old Testament canon at the Council of Jamnia, which began ca. 90 C.E. and lasted at least twenty years. Several books were debated, but the list that had been accepted informally by Palestinian Jews was confirmed by this council.

## The Septuagint and the Apocrypha

The Jews living in Egypt in time began to speak Greek. This meant that they needed a translation of their sacred scriptures into Greek. The translation was begun in the third century B.C.E. but was not completed until the first century B.C.E. It came to be known as the Septuagint (from the Greek word for seventy) after the seventy scribes who were reputed to have done the work of translating. The Septuagint was often used by the writers of the New Testament when they quoted from the Bible (our Old Testament).

In the manuscripts of the Septuagint, books and parts of books are present that are not a part of the Hebrew Bible. Furthermore, the order of books is different from that found in the Hebrew Bible. The Vulgate (Latin Bible of the Roman Catholic Church) was influenced by the Septuagint in its canon and in the order of its books. There are a few differences in the

Greek canon and the Roman canon, however. These additional materials are called "the Apocrypha" by Protestants. The word "apocrypha" literally means "hidden." It came to mean "spurious." In other words, the books of the Apocrypha do not have canonical status among Protestants, though Protestants use them as any ordinary books. They throw considerable light on the period between the Old and New Testaments, and their status among Protestants seems slowly to be rising.

Protestants accepted the books found in the Hebrew canon but arranged them in the order of the Roman Catholic canon. Hence, our present-day Protestant English Bibles are arranged according to the following pattern: (1) the Pentateuch: same as the Jewish Law (Torah); (2) the historical books: Joshua, Judges, Ruth, 1 Samuel, 2 Samuel, 1 Kings, 2 Kings, 1 Chronicles, 2 Chronicles, Ezra, Nehemiah, and Esther; (3) the poetical books: Job, Psalms, Proverbs, Ecclesiastes, and Song of Solomon; and (4) the Prophets: Isaiah, Jeremiah, Lamentations, Ezekiel, Daniel, Hosea, Joel, Amos, Obadiah, Jonah, Micah, Nahum, Habakkuk, Zephaniah, Haggai, Zechariah, and Malachi. Compare this list with that of the Hebrew canon already given and note the differences between the two.

Jews obviously follow the order of the Hebrew canon. They call it the "Bible" or the "Hebrew Bible" or more accurately *Tanach,* an acronym from *T*orah (Law, Instruction, Pentateuch), *N*ebi'im (Prophets), and *K*(h)etubim (Writings). The term "Hebrew Bible" is widely used now in academic circles in preference to "Old Testament" because of the inter-faith character of much contemporary biblical study.

## Extrabiblical Literature

From Protestant and Jewish perspectives the Apocrypha, of which we have just spoken, are extrabiblical; that is, not a part of the canon. But there are also a large number of Jewish religious writings, coming for the most part from the period between the Testaments, which form no part of any present-day canon. These documents are known as the Pseude-pigrapha and are about seventeen in number. The word "pseudepigrapha" technically means "written under false [pen] names," but the term now is used more widely to indicate any writing not included in the canon.

## The Dead Sea Scrolls

The Dead Sea Scrolls should be mentioned in connection with the Old Testament canon. These scrolls were found in eleven caves at the north-west corner of the Dead Sea near the Wadi Qumran in 1947 and following. They date between the third century B.C.E. and C.E. 68. It once was widely held that this library belonged to the Jewish sect known as "Essenes," but the identification of the community is currently under debate.

Among the scrolls every Old Testament book has been found in whole or in part except the book of Esther. In fact, some books are represented several times. Apocryphal and pseudepigraphal works also belonged to this ancient "library." The find includes documents that were written by members of the sect, some of which were previously unknown to students of the Bible. On the basis of the evidence now available the limits of the canon accepted by these people cannot be determined with certainty. The fact that Esther has not been found does not necessarily mean that they did not have the book. Furthermore, the presence of apocryphal, pseude-pigraphal, and other works in the library does not mean that these documents were necessarily regarded as canonical.

Thus far the scrolls are proving to be of special value in studying the text of the Old Testament and in shedding light on Palestinian Judaism in the time of Jesus and the apostles. References to them are made from time to time at appropriate places in the book. They will make possible better translations of some passages of the Old Testament and a clearer understanding of others, but there is no reason to think that they will lead to the change of any significant teachings of the church.

## Retrospect and Anticipation

Together we have followed the story of God's mighty acts from creation to the end of the Old Testament period. As we have done this, we have marveled at the power of God's creative word; we have been thrilled by covenant acts of redemption; we have been shaken by righteous acts of judgment; and we have rejoiced in God's gracious acts of renewal. We recognize our humanity and bow before the Lord in reverence, gratitude, and steadfast love.

We realize that with all its treasures, the Old Testament (the Hebrew Bible), in a sense, is a promise to be lived out for both Christians and Jews. God's story continues with both. As Christians we feel that we are standing on the very border of a Promised Land. A new David, a new age, a new covenant, and a new people of God are about to enter the drama of human history. But, in God's inscrutable way, Christians don't displace Jews from the love of God. The New Testament to which we next turn articulates the special way God has opened to us. But the Hebrew Bible, our Old or First Testament, continues as scripture for God's First People. God's grace is sufficient for all. Thanks be to God.

# PART FIVE

# GOD'S MIGHTY ACT IN JESUS CHRIST

15

# The Gospel and the Gospels

*W*hen the cosmic clock struck the hour of destiny, "God sent his Son" (see Gal. 4:4–5). This sending forth of the preexistent Son in human flesh is the incarnation. Indeed, the incarnation, together with all that is involved in it, is the culmination of all the mighty acts of God. That which went before and that which follows find their meaning in Jesus Christ. God's purpose in Jesus Christ is "to redeem those who were under the law, so that we might receive adoption as children." The purpose of the incarnation is redemption from sin and adoption into the redeemed family of God. Jesus came to save us.

## The World of Jesus

Though the people of Jesus' day did not live in the nuclear and missile age, their problems and threats were nonetheless real and painful. They knew political rivalries and intrigue, social inequalities, competing ideologies, and denominational barriers. Poverty, hunger, disease, early death, dishonesty, immorality, and all the evils known to humankind had to be faced.

## The Political World

You will recall from our previous study that the earlier part of the Hellenistic Age (333–63 B.C.E.) was dominated by Alexander the Great and his successors. In response to the persecution of Antiochus Epiphanes of Syria, the Maccabees led the revolt of the Jews and served as their leaders until 134 B.C.E. From this point on, the rulers who descended from the Maccabees are often referred to as the "Hasmoneans," a name derived from Hashmon, an ancestor of the Maccabees. But rivalry within the Hasmonean house and the Jewish people's dissatisfaction with the Hasmonean rule led to the subjection of Palestine to Roman control by Pompey in 63 B.C.E. This was the beginning of the Roman Period (63 B.C.E.–325 C.E.).

Hyrcanus II, a Hasmonean, was appointed ethnarch (governor) and high priest in 63 B.C.E. and ruled in this capacity until 40 B.C.E. However, from 55 to 43 B.C.E. "the power behind the throne" was his ambitious minister Antipater, an Idumean (Edomite). One of Antipater's sons, who came to be known as Herod the Great, was appointed king of Judea and Samaria in 40 B.C.E. Political disorders prevented him from beginning his reign until 37 B.C.E.; he ruled until 4 B.C.E. Herod was an Idumean by birth, a Jew by religion, a Greek in culture, and a Roman in politics. His appointment was confirmed by Augustus Caesar, who brought peace to the Roman Empire and ruled from 27 B.C.E. to 14 C.E.

Herod was a great builder and a champion of Hellenistic (Greek) culture. He built pagan temples, halls, theaters, palaces, and baths. Of course the building project for which he is best known is the renovation of the Jerusalem Temple, which was undertaken to appease the Jews, who hated him. The renovation was begun in 20 B.C.E. but was not completed until about 62 C.E., which was about sixty-six years after his death. The Jews hated Herod not only on account of his Idumean ancestry but also for his promotion of Hellenism and the exaction of high taxes with which to carry on his elaborate building program. It was during his reign that Jesus was born (Matt. 2). Before his death Herod's kingdom included far more than his original Judea and Samaria.

Three of his sons inherited this kingdom. Philip was made tetrarch (subordinate ruler) of Iturea, Trachonitis, Auranitis, Batanea, Gaulanitis, and Panias to the northeast (4 B.C.E.–34 C.E.). On the whole Philip was a good ruler, and his rule lasted thirty years. He named the Caesarea within his territory "Caesarea Philippi" (see Mark 8:27) after himself to distinguish it from other places named Caesarea.

Herod Antipas was made tetrarch of Galilee and Perea (4 B.C.E.–39 C.E.). He built his capital beside the Sea of Galilee and named it Tiberias in honor of the Roman emperor Tiberius (14–37 C.E.). Herod Antipas is the most frequently mentioned Herod in the New Testament. It was he who executed John the Baptist (Mark 6: 14–29 and parallels) and feared that Jesus might be John raised from the dead. During the trial of Jesus, Pilate sent Jesus to Herod (Luke 23:6–17). Herod was eventually banished to Gaul by Emperor Caligula (37–41 C.E.) for suspected conspiracy against Rome. His territory and that of his brother Philip were placed in the hands of Herod Agrippa I (41–44 C.E.).

Archelaus, who is mentioned by name in Matthew 2:22, was made ethnarch of Judea, Samaria, and Idumea (4 B.C.E.–6 C.E.). Because of his incompetent rule, he was deposed and banished to Gaul in 6 C.E. His territory was then placed under a procurator (an administrator of the Roman government). Among the procurators was Pontius Pilate (26–36 C.E.) under whom Jesus was tried, sentenced, and crucified.

*On page 226 you will find a map of Palestine during the time of Jesus. It is designed to help you locate the territories already mentioned and to locate sites of special significance in the ministry of Jesus.*

## The Social and Religious World

In the Greco-Roman world slavery was a recognized institution. There was a great gap between the rich and the poor, and the poor were often oppressed. The combination of Roman and Jewish taxes in Palestine was almost unbearable. Many went to bed at night without knowing whether they would have food on the morrow. "Give us this day our daily bread" meant something to people in that condition. Immorality was widespread among the upper classes of Roman society.

Greek philosophy was on the wane. The greatest philosophers had lived in the Persian Era or shortly thereafter. In the Roman Period, there was a chaos of philosophies and religions, with mystery cults on the rise: "The mystery gods were gods of whom it was told in the myth that they had suffered death and had subsequently risen again. Thus it was intended that man [*sic*] by his initiation into the mystery should participate both in the death and the life of the god, should become 'deified.' The aspiration of many in this age was to assimilate to themselves divine life."[1]

But the most important cultural and religious elements for understanding Jesus and the Gospels are not of Greek and Roman origin. They are

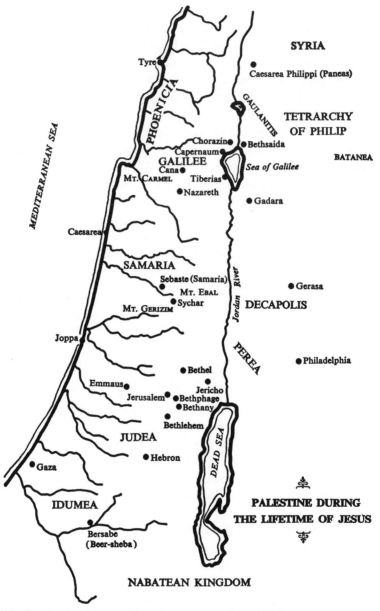

SYRIA

Tyre

Caesarea Philippi (Paneas)

PHOENICIA

GAULANITIS

TETRARCHY
OF PHILIP

Chorazin
Capernaum
Bethsaida

GALILEE
Cana
Mt. Carmel    Tiberias    *Sea of Galilee*

BATANEA

Nazareth

Gadara

MEDITERRANEAN SEA

Caesarea

SAMARIA

Sebaste (Samaria)
Mt. Ebal
Sychar
Mt. Gerizim

Jordan River

Gerasa

DECAPOLIS

PEREA

Joppa

Philadelphia

Bethel

Emmaus
Jerusalem
Jericho
Bethphage
Bethany

Bethlehem

JUDEA

Hebron

DEAD SEA

Gaza

PALESTINE DURING
THE LIFETIME OF JESUS

IDUMEA

Bersabe
(Beer-sheba)

NABATEAN KINGDOM

Jewish. For, humanly speaking, Jesus was a Jew. While he may have been able to speak Greek, he ordinarily spoke Aramaic. Moreover, he read the Sacred Scrolls, which we call the Old Testament, in Hebrew.

Certain institutions played a major role among the Jews of the first century: the Law (Torah), the Temple, the synagogues, and the Sanhedrin. All devout Jews, regardless of denominational affiliation, accepted the supremacy of the Law of Moses. The interpreters of the Law were the scribes. Apparently most of the scribes were Pharisees, and therefore laymen.

Within the Torah itself considerable emphasis is placed on the Temple and its ceremonies. One of the major functions of the priests was to offer sacrifice in the Temple court. Once a year, on the Day of Atonement, the high priest entered the Holy of Holies to make atonement for the unwitting sins of the people. Although a majority of Jews lived outside Palestine, the Temple was a symbol of Jewish unity. It was destroyed in 70 C.E. by Titus.

Synagogues were primarily local assemblies for prayer and the study of the Law. No one knows when the first synagogue arose. Some think it was as early as the Babylonian exile, while others think it was at a later time. Archaeological research has identified several synagogues in Egypt prior to the first century C.E., but the evidence is not so clear in Palestine. By the second century C.E. they are well-attested, making it probable that they developed in the previous century, at least. The numerous references to synagogues in the Gospels, however, may be anachronistic, reflecting the situation after the destruction of Jerusalem in 70 C.E. Nonetheless, particularly in Galilee, synagogues may well have been built in Jesus' day.

The Sanhedrin ("Council" in the NRSV) was the supreme court of the Jewish people and was usually moderated by the high priest. In its early history its membership was wholly or predominantly composed of Sadducees. But in Jesus' day it also included Pharisees. Its powers are not clear, but certainly capital punishment required the sanction and personnel of the Roman governor. The crucifixion of Jesus was accomplished by members of the Sanhedrin and the unscrupulous Roman procurator, Pontius Pilate. Later the Sanhedrin also persecuted the disciples of Jesus—for example, Peter and John (Acts 4:5–22; 5:17–42), Stephen (Acts 6 and 7), and Paul (Acts 22:30–24:27).[2]

The principal denominations or sects among the Jews of the first century were the Sadducees, the Pharisees, the Essenes, and the Zealots. The name Sadducees is probably derived from Zadok, the high priest under Solomon (1 Kings 1:39; 2:35). Annas and Caiaphas were Sadducees. This group was composed of wealthy priestly men, who resisted change and supported the status quo. They were sympathetic to Hellenistic culture and adept at political compromise. They rejected the oral law, which was accepted by the Pharisees, and regarded the written Law alone as canonical. They were concerned with the Temple cultus and supported the

Hasmoneans. On account of their vested interests, Jesus' cleansing of the Temple was a threat to their pocketbooks. They said "that there is no resurrection, or angel, or spirit; but the Pharisees acknowledge all three" (Acts 23:8; compare Mark 12:18). They did not represent the people and therefore gradually became extinct. Judgment was pronounced on both Sadducees and Pharisees by John the Baptist (Matt. 3:7–10) and Jesus (Matt. 16:1–12).

The Pharisees constituted the largest and most influential of the Jewish sects. Their origin goes back to pious loyalists, the Hasidim, of Maccabean times, some of whom were pacifists. Their name means the "separated ones." They stood over against the Sadducees and other religious groups as well as over against "the people of the land." They were more liberal than the Sadducees in accepting all the books that constitute our Old Testament canon and the oral law as well, the resurrection of the dead, the coming of the kingdom of God, the existence of angels and demons, the messianic hope, and the Feasts of Purim and Hanukkah. They did not regard the oral law or tradition as opposing the written Law, but as an adaptation of the latter to changing circumstances.

The Pharisees were laymen. Furthermore, their motivations were more genuinely religious and less political than those of the Sadducees. Yet in the long run they became even more thoroughly Hellenized than the Sadducees. Like the biblical writers, they held the belief in the sovereignty of God and the belief in human free will in a dynamic tension. While the Sadducees were more concerned with the priestly interests of the Temple, the Pharisees were more concerned with the worship and life of the people. In their "book" Ezra the scribe was second only to Moses the lawgiver. The Gospels make it clear that many Pharisees fell into the trap of legalistic self-righteousness. Nonetheless, on the whole they led very upright lives worthy of emulation. In spite of the usual opposition from some of the Pharisees, Jesus was on friendly terms with some of them. However, along with some of the Sadducees, some of the Pharisees had a part in Jesus' death (Mark 3:6; John 11:47–57). The survival of Judaism was largely made possible by the Pharisees. Saul of Tarsus was a Pharisee who became the great Apostle to the Gentiles.

Though the Essenes are not mentioned in the New Testament, they have been known to students of the Bible from extrabiblical sources, such as Josephus and Philo. The people of Khirbet Qumran (the Dead Sea Scroll community) were first identified by scholars as Essenes, but now such an identification is disputed. Nonetheless, our knowledge of this group is now quite extensive. There were some who formed ascetic communities (believers in rigid, enforced denial of pleasure) like that evidenced at Qumran on the northwest side of the Dead Sea. Others lived in towns and were less austere. Most of them did not marry, though some did. They were devoted to the Law of Moses but also had a multitude of other materials they considered authoritative. At Qumran (assuming these were Essenes) they appear to have engaged in manual labor, eaten meals together, and had a common treasury (compare Acts 2:43–47). They thought of themselves as the true people of God, the people of a new covenant.

Long before the discovery of the Dead Sea Scrolls some scholars thought that John the Baptist was perhaps an Essene. This theory now has more to support it, though it cannot be proved absolutely. If the Baptist were at one time an Essene, it seems that he must have broken with the movement, for he called all Israel to repentance and baptism.[3]

While parallels can be found to some of Jesus' teachings among the Essenes and the Pharisees, Jesus was by no means a member of either group. It is not surprising that Jesus would have many things in common with other contemporary Jews. But Jesus' uniqueness shines all the more clearly when the Essene scrolls are studied in relation to the Gospels. The Essenes were ascetic; Jesus was criticized for not being an ascetic. The Essenes were legalistic; Jesus challenged legalism. Jesus attended services in the Temple and in synagogues, but we have no record that he ever visited the Qumran community.

The New Testament church held numerous theological beliefs found among various Jewish groups, including the Essenes. This is to be expected since all Jews had the Old Testament or a part of it in common. For instance, there are some parallels between the terminology of some books of the New Testament (especially the Johannine literature) and the terminology of some of the Dead Sea Scrolls, and between the organization of the church and the organization of the Qumran sect. But the theology of the New Testament and that of the Essenes are seen to be worlds apart when they are examined in detail. Nor are the organizations of the two groups identical. The Essenes were looking for one or two messiahs yet to come; the church proclaimed a messiah who had already come and was coming again. The Essenes were a community in the desert (for the most part); the church was a missionary fellowship. The Essenes had a hierarchy of priests; in the church all persons were priests and the entire church was a priesthood.

The Zealots were extreme nationalists best known for their hostility to Rome. They believed that deliverance from the Roman yoke could be effected by their own military efforts. They fought vigorously in the revolt against Rome, which began in 66 C.E. and ended in the destruction of the Temple in 70 C.E. Because one of Jesus' disciples (Simon) was called a "zealot" (Luke 6:15) and Jesus is compared to Judas the Galilean (Acts 5:37), some have suggested that Jesus was at least sympathetic to the causes of the Zealots. But, if so, Jesus' teaching does not fit with what is known about this group and Mark 12:15 seems to indicate a different path than that of resistance.

In addition to these four groups that have been named, there were those humble folk with whom Jesus had much in common. Some Pharisees, Essenes, and others were looking for the coming of the kingdom of God and for a deliverer, who would be the instrument of God's saving purpose (see Chapter 14). But there was no "orthodox" position. Judaism, as we know it today, had not yet developed. This happened in parallel to Christianity during the two centuries following the destruction of Jerusalem in 70 C.E. Jesus was born into a very diverse theological context.

## The Proclamation of the Good News

The gospel is the good news of what God has done, is doing, and will do for humankind and its salvation through Jesus Christ. It was told before it was written down. Jesus had lived, died, risen, and ascended years before the first written records. The apostles and other early disciples were so busy telling the story at first that they did not bother to write it down. The early preaching of the apostles is reflected in Acts 1–10 and in passages of Paul's Letters. It may be summarized thus: God has (1) kept the prophetic promises, (2) introduced the new age through Jesus of Nazareth, the Messiah and Servant of the Lord, (3) accomplished mighty works through Jesus, who went about doing good, (4) delivered him up to be crucified, (5) raised him from the dead and exalted him as Messiah, the Son of God, and Lord of all. (6) And God will send him back as Judge and Savior to consummate the messianic age. (7) In response to what God has done *in* Christ and what you have done to Christ, "Repent, and be baptized every one of you in the name of Jesus Christ so that your sins may be forgiven; and you will receive the gift of the Holy Spirit" (Acts 2:38).

Of course, the whole gospel scheme was not told on every occasion. On many occasions events from the life of Jesus were told and interpreted in relation to the particular situation at hand. They were used to serve various purposes: worship, evangelism, Christian education, defense of the gospel, and ethical guidance. But the early Christian community did not originate the message. They related Jesus and his message to their situations.

Some of these narratives have been classified according to their forms: pronouncement stories, miracle stories, sayings and parables, the passion narrative, and others.[4] For example, a pronouncement story is a narrative that centers in a saying of Jesus, like Jesus' blessing of the children (Mark 10:13–16). A miracle story is usually composed of a description of the need, the act of healing, and the effect of the miracle, like for example, the healing of Peter's wife's mother (Mark 1:30–31). Others could be given, but this should be sufficient to illustrate the point.

## The Formation of the Gospels

The time soon came when the church needed written records of Jesus' life. There were many Christian communities scattered about in the Roman empire. Eyewitnesses were dying out. It was imperative that the good news be known. Probably there were brief accounts of aspects of Jesus' ministry that are lost to posterity. Luke suggests as much in the opening verses of his Gospel.

Because Matthew, Mark, and Luke have so much material in common (sometimes word for word) and follow the same general outline, they are referred to as the "Synoptic Gospels" and a hypothesis has been developed to "explain" their relationship with one another and with John. (One of the best ways to examine the data is to use a harmony of the Gospels in which parallels are placed in parallel columns. If a harmony is not available, the use of a Bible that has a cross-reference system in the margin or in the footnotes is recommended.)

It is usually held today that Mark is the earliest of the Gospels and that it was written at Rome by John Mark about 60 to 70 C.E. Papias, a second-century Christian, is reported to have said, "Mark became Peter's interpreter and wrote accurately all that he remembered, not, indeed in order, of the things said or done by the Lord."[5] Mark may well have used other oral testimonies also and some that had already been recorded. The chief reason for thinking Mark is the earliest Gospel is the fact that Matthew and Luke have ninety percent of Mark in them. We need to recall that ancient writers did not have our modern concern about copying existing literature. The Gospel writers were only interested in telling the story of Jesus accurately and effectively. They were unconcerned about getting credit for what they had done.

Matthew and Luke have material in common that is not found in Mark at all. This fact has led to the supposition that Matthew and Luke had a source on the teachings of Jesus that Mark did not have. This unknown source is referred to as Q, an abbreviation of the German word *Quelle*, which means "source."

Because Matthew contains material found in no other Gospel, it is thought to have a distinctive source, which is referred to as M. Moreover, Luke is also characterized by distinctive material, and L is posited as its distinctive source. Matthew and Luke may have been composed in the 80s. Some scholars reject this four-document theory, but, like their counterparts, they believe the Gospel writers did use oral and written sources. Those who modify the theory usually posit more sources. In other words, scholars of various schools of interpretation agree that oral and written sources lie behind our Gospels. All believe that the Holy Spirit was active in the whole process. The four-document theory seems to best explain the relationship between the Gospels. It may be made clearer by the following diagram:

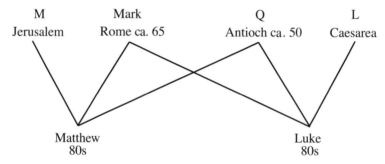

The Gospel of John was not written to duplicate what had already been done. Rather was it written to emphasize the meaning of the gospel in terms of the Person of Jesus.

While the Gospel writers used sources, they were far more than objective reporters. They had a story to tell, a story in which they were deeply involved. Each had a particular emphasis to make. Therefore each selected and presented materials in relation to that purpose. No writer sought to produce a "modern" biography. The aim was bearing witness to Jesus Christ, which is the same thing as preaching the gospel. The Gospels are not ends in themselves; they bear witness to the good news of God's act in Jesus. Some of Paul's Letters were written earlier than the Gospels, but the Gospels remain the principal sources of information concerning Jesus' life and ministry.

## Mark—The Gospel of the Wonder-Working Servant

It has already been noted that the Gospel of Mark is believed to have been written by John Mark at Rome ca. 60–70 C.E. Mark was well qualified to write the earliest Gospel. He was a friend of Peter (see Acts 12:12) and undoubtedly of other eyewitnesses as well. He may be the young man who is mentioned in Mark 14:51–52. He was Barnabas's cousin (Col. 4:10) and accompanied Barnabas and Paul on the first missionary journey as far as Cyprus (Acts 12:25–13:13). Barnabas wanted to take Mark on the second journey, but Paul refused because he felt Mark had failed them; therefore, Paul and Silas went to Syria and Cilicia, and Barnabas and Mark to Cyprus again (Acts 15:36–41). Evidently Mark had changed and Barnabas was right, for at a later time Paul said to Timothy, "Get Mark and bring him with you, for he is useful in my ministry" (2 Tim. 4:11).

Mark's Gospel is very much like an extended sermon. In Peter's words to Cornelius in Acts 10:34–43, Peter summarizes the apostolic preaching, beginning with Jesus' baptism and ending with the resurrection. In a sense, the Gospel of Mark is an expansion of Peter's words. Even so, it is not a long expansion, for it moves rapidly toward its climax in the death and resurrection of Jesus. According to Paul, the earliest preaching of the gospel emphasized Jesus' death and resurrection (1 Cor. 15:3–5). Moreover, the later Gospels (Matthew, Luke, and John) all give major attention to the same theme. This is to say, the death and resurrection of Jesus have been pivotal in the proclamation of the gospel from the earliest days of the Christian church.

Another major emphasis of Mark is the power of God at work in Jesus' miracles of healing. Peter had also emphasized this in his sermon to Cornelius: "how God anointed Jesus of Nazareth with the Holy Spirit and with power; how he went about doing good and healing all who were oppressed by the devil, for God was with him" (Acts 10: 38). People who lived in Rome, the capital of the great empire, were very aware of Roman power. Mark confronts them with the power of God in Jesus Christ. Moreover, many of the situations faced by Christians in Rome were similar to situations faced by Jesus in Palestine. Mark's Gospel is powerful and relevant. Jesus is presented as the Son of God, the Son of Man, the Davidic Messiah, and the Servant of the Lord. Indeed, Mark is the Gospel of the Wonder-Working Servant.

*At this point make an outline of Peter's sermon to Cornelius, which is found in Acts 10:34–43. Then read the Gospel of Mark through at one sitting, if possible, all the while filling out the out-line of Peter's sermon with the content of Mark's Gospel. What impact did Mark make on you?*

## Matthew—The Gospel of the Jewish Messiah

According to an ancient tradition, Matthew the Apostle wrote the Gospel that bears his name. Yet many students have felt that this tradition needs to be modified as one of the Twelve would not likely have needed 606 of Mark's 661 verses.[6] Papias, who was mentioned in relation to Mark, is reported to have written, "Matthew collected the oracles in the Hebrew language, and each interpreted them as best he could."[7] The "oracles" may refer to a collection of passages from the Old Testament that were used by Christians in showing how Jesus fulfilled the Old Testament. More likely, however, the word "oracles" refers to a collection of Jesus' teachings, perhaps the hypothetical collection that scholars call Q. In this case Matthew's collection was one of the Gospel writer's sources. The nature of the Gospel certainly identifies the author as a Jewish Christian. And it is thought that he wrote from Antioch in the 80s C.E.

Certain characteristics distinguish the Gospel of Matthew very clearly.

1. It is the Gospel of the Jewish Messiah. It was written by a Jewish Christian, primarily to Jews and Jewish Christians, about Jesus, who he believed fulfilled the messianic announcements of the Old Testament. The early church was led by the Spirit of God to place Matthew as the first book in the New Testament canon, since its very opening sentence as well as its contents tie the Old and the New Testaments together so clearly: "An account of the genealogy of Jesus the Messiah, the son of David, the son of Abraham." Yet Matthew makes it clear that the gospel is by no means confined to the Jews; it is intended for all (see 2:1; 28:16–20). Furthermore, he uses all the titles for Jesus that we found in Mark. Some feel that Matthew also regarded Jesus as a new Moses, who gave the new Law (teaching ) from a new Sinai.

2. Matthew follows the basic outline of Mark yet with revision and addition. It is at once obvious that Matthew begins with material concerning the ancestry and infancy of Jesus, which is not found in Mark or the sermon by Peter to Cornelius (Acts 10:34–43). While Mark lays heavy stress on Jesus' miracles, Matthew lays heavy stress on his teachings. Yet each includes both miracles and teachings. Some scholars emphasize the relationship of Jesus' teaching and person with materials in the wisdom writings of the Old Testament and intertestamental period.

3. Matthew organizes his material in systematic groupings. For example, there are five discourses in his Gospel: (1) the Sermon on the Mount (chaps. 5–7), (2) the Charge to the Twelve (chap. 10), (3) the Parables of the Kingdom (chap. 13), (4) the Teaching on True Greatness and Forgiveness (chap. 18), and (5) the Teaching on Last Things (chaps. 24–25). Moreover, there are seven parables in chapter 13 and seven woes in chapter 23.

4. Matthew has an ecclesiastical (or churchly) interest. This is the only Gospel in which the word "church" occurs (16:18; 18:17). Though Mark (8:27–9:1) and Luke (9:18–27) both record the messianic confession of Peter, only Matthew includes Jesus' word to Peter about the church (16:18). Furthermore, this is the only Gospel that has the saying on church discipline (18:17).

5. Matthew gives special attention to Jesus' denunciation of his opponents. Of course all the Gospels deal to some extent with this fact of Jesus' experience. But Matthew has thirty-nine continuous verses on this theme (23:1–39) in addition to what is found elsewhere in the Gospel. Matthew gives due attention to Jesus' gentleness, but wants the readers to understand Jesus' judgment on those who are guilty of false piety (6:1–18), rejecting his message (7:26–27), cruelty to others (18:23–35), and hypocrisy (23:1–30).

## Luke—The Gospel of the Savior of All Sorts of People

According to tradition, Luke, an associate of Paul, wrote the Gospel that bears his name, and there is no reason for denying this tradition. The preface to the Gospel of Luke and that to the book of Acts, along with other considerations, indicate that one person wrote the two-volume work Luke-Acts. The "we" passages in which the writer uses the word "we" to tell the story in Acts (16:10–17; 20:5–21:18; 27:1–28:16) also show the close association of the author of the work with Paul. Both Paul and Luke emphasize the world-embracing purpose of the gospel. The exact date and place of Luke's writing are uncertain. Perhaps it was about 80 C.E. though it may have been a little earlier.

Theophilus (1:3) and other Gentiles like him needed a more complete understanding of the things in which they had been instructed concerning Jesus and the church. Therefore, Luke provided them with the needed instruction in his two-volume work (see Luke 1:1–4; Acts 1:1–5). In addition to what many others had already written (1:1), he felt there were certain emphases yet to be made.

Though the Gospel of Luke is one of the Synoptics, it is still very distinctive. Almost half of its contents are not found in the other Gospels. You will recall that Mark has no infancy narratives. Both Matthew and Luke do, but the two sets of infancy narratives are composed of different materials. Much of Luke's independent material is found in the section devoted to Jesus' journey to Jerusalem.

The distinguishing features of Luke's Gospel are easily recognized.

1. The gospel is for all people. Of course Mark and Matthew know this, but Luke emphasizes it strongly. Jesus remains for Luke the Messiah, the Son of God, the Servant of the Lord, and the Son of Man. Yet the distinctive stress rests primarily on Jesus as the Savior of all sorts of people. The birth of Jesus is placed in the context of world history: "In those days a decree went out from Emperor Augustus that all the world should be registered. This was the first registration and was taken while Quirinius was governor of Syria" (2:1–2). While Matthew traces Jesus' ancestry back to Abraham, Luke takes it back to Adam (3:23–38). Among other things the aged Simeon calls the baby Jesus "a light for revelation to the Gentiles" (2:32).

Since the ancient world was thought of as being divided into seventy nations, it is probable that the sending out of the seventy disciples is symbolic of the worldwide scope of the gospel (10:1). In 24:44–49, the risen Christ gives his disciples a mission to the nations. And in the book of Acts, the second volume of Luke's work, we see the steps by which the Christian witness is in process of being taken from Jerusalem to the ends of the earth (Acts 1:8).

2. The Samaritans are objects of Jesus' concern and commendation. The breach between the Jews and Samaritans was of long standing. In Jesus' day, Jews "do not share things in common with Samaritans" (John 4:9), but Jesus did (Luke 9:51–56). The parable of the Good Samaritan (10:25–37) is one of Jesus' most powerful stories. And again, of the ten lepers whom Jesus healed (17:11–19), only the Samaritan among them returned to thank Jesus.

3. Jesus came to save the outcasts of society too. He was the friend of tax collectors and sinners. Of course the tax collectors were among the sinners. For "sinners" included all who were guilty of wrongdoing and those who did not observe the Jewish ceremonial laws. The tax collectors were hated because they collected revenue for the Roman government and many were dishonest. Only Luke records the parable of the Pharisee

and the Tax Collector (18:9–14). He alone tells the story of the conversion of Zacchaeus, a chief tax collector (19:1–10). The story of the Prodigal Son (15:11–32) and the account of Jesus' pardon of one of the robbers who were crucified with him (23:39–43) are found in no other Gospel.

4. Jesus champions the cause of the poor. Though this concern is not confined to Luke, it is especially emphasized by him. At the very outset it is found in Mary's Magnificat (1:53). In Luke's account Jesus pronounces Beatitudes upon the poor and Woes upon the rich (6:20–26). The poor were frequently oppressed by the rich. Only Luke records the parable of the Rich Fool (12:13–21), the parable of the Rich Man and Lazarus (16:19–31), Jesus' counsel to "sell your possessions, and give alms" (12:33), and his advice to "invite the poor, the crippled, the lame, and the blind" to dinner (14:12–14). Both Jesus and Luke recognized the temptations involved in wealth.

5. Women have a prominent place in Luke's Gospel. Special attention is given to Mary, Elizabeth, and Anna in the infancy narratives. Only Luke records the following: Jesus' restoration of the son of the Widow of Nain (7:11–17), the healing of the woman who had been sick for eighteen years (13:10–13), the parable of the woman who searched for the lost coin (15:8–10), the parable of the widow who annoyed the unjust judge until he vindicated her (18:1–8), and the note concerning the weeping of the women as Jesus was being led to the cross (23:27). Although John has more to say about Jesus' relation to Mary and Martha (John 11:1–12:3), Luke has some material not found in John (Luke 10:38–42).

6. Joy is a recurring theme in the Gospel of Luke. The gospel is by definition "good news" and therefore joyous. But Luke keeps the reader aware of this fact constantly. At the very beginning the angel announces the coming birth of John the Baptist with a promise of joy (1:14), and Mary's Magnificat begins on a joyous note (1:46–47). In the angel's announcement of Jesus' birth to the shepherds are these words: "Do not be afraid; for see—I am bringing you good news of great joy for all the people" (2:10). The seventy, whom Jesus sent out, rejoice on their return (10:17–20). Many people rejoice over Jesus' mighty works of healing (13:17) and on the occasion of his triumphal entry into Jerusalem (19:37). The whole fifteenth chapter of Luke is a series of heavenly rejoicings over the sinner who repents. According to the very end of Luke's first volume, the risen Christ parted from his disciples, and they "returned to Jerusalem with great joy; and were continually in the temple blessing God" (24:52–53).

7. Luke gives special recognition to the significance of prayer. Jesus prays at his baptism (3:21), in the wilderness after his cleansing of a leper (5:16), all night before choosing the Twelve (6:12), on the occasion of Peter's great confession (9:18), at the Transfiguration (9:28), for Peter (22:32), and for those who crucified him (23:34). He gives the Lord's Prayer in response to a request to teach his disciples to pray (11:1). Three of Luke's distinctive parables deal with prayer: the Friend at Midnight (11:5–10), the Unjust Judge (18:1–8), and the Pharisee and the Tax Collector (18:9–14). Jesus' last words are a prayer: "Father, into your hands I commend my spirit" (23:46).

8. Luke is the Gospel of the Holy Spirit. Elizabeth is filled with the Holy Spirit when she is greeted by Mary (1:41). Zechariah is filled with the Holy Spirit as he delivers the Benedictus (1:67). The Holy Spirit is active in the devout Simeon (2:25–27). Jesus is full of the Holy Spirit after his baptism (4:1) and begins his Galilean ministry "with the power of the Spirit" (4:14). From Isaiah 61:1–2, Jesus applies to himself the words beginning "The Spirit of the Lord is upon me" (4:18). Jesus rejoices in the Holy Spirit (10:21), and God gives the Holy Spirit to those who ask (11:13). The promise of the risen Christ in 24:49 anticipates the fulfillment of the promise that is recorded in Luke's second volume, sometimes referred to as the Acts of the Holy Spirit.

## John—The Gospel of the Son of God

The Gospel of John, it is widely held, was written by John. But there is disagreement concerning the identification of "John." A tradition of the second century identifies the author as John the son of Zebedee and one of the Twelve. In support of this identification, it is held that certain passages are best understood in relation to this John. The author claims to have been an eyewitness (1:14; 19:35; 1 John 1:1–4), and John the Apostle was an eyewitness. The references to "the one whom Jesus loved" (13:23; 19:26; 20:2; 21:7, 20) point in the same direction. Moreover, the author had firsthand information about Palestinian geography.

Nevertheless, there are those who do not think John the Apostle was the author. John the son of Zebedee was a Galilean fisherman, and much of Jesus' ministry was performed in Galilee. Why would this John treat Galilee lightly and concentrate so much on Jerusalem? Would an author keep referring to himself as "the one whom Jesus loved"? If we assume that the same person wrote the Gospel of John and the three Letters of John, the self-designation of this person in 2 and 3 John becomes very important. In both letters he calls himself "the elder." Papias, to whom reference has already been made, mentions "the Elder John." Whether this elder is to be distinguished from the Apostle is uncertain.

These are not the only theories of authorship. Various dates for the writing have also been proposed, ranging all the way from 40 C.E. to the middle of the second century. Many place it about 90 C.E. In the light of a comparative study of John and the Dead Sea Scrolls, however, there is a tendency among some students of the New Testament to date the Fourth Gospel earlier.

The author's purpose is explicitly and clearly stated in 20:30–31:

> Now Jesus did many other signs in the presence of his disciples, which are not written in this book. But these are written so that you may come to believe that Jesus is the Messiah, the Son of God, and that through believing you may have life in his name.

This sentence is a key to understanding the book. John plainly says that he did not intend to tell everything about Jesus' life. Evidently he knew one or more of the Synoptics, which included many of the details of Jesus' miracles and teachings. It was not John's intention to duplicate what had already been done. He wanted to bring into sharper focus the Person of Christ and the meaning of the gospel. He enables us to see the meaning behind the event. The Synoptics have been likened to the news coverage on the front page of a newspaper, and John to the editorial page.[8] Both types of approach to the good news of the gospel are needed.

Through his approach, John also calls people to faith in Jesus as the Messiah and Son of God. But he stresses the unique relation of Jesus to the Father. To "believe" in John's sense means to have faith in Christ as God's Son (3:16). This kind of faith is the link to eternal life, that quality of life that a person may have in fellowship with God both now and forever. A response to Jesus Christ is the most crucial decision a person is ever called upon to make.

One helpful way to study the Gospel of John is to note the differences between it and the other Gospels.

*If you cannot read the entire Gospel, look up all the references cited.*

(Because this Gospel is also related to the Letters of John, there will be further treatment of this book in Chapter 22.)

1. "Only about eight percent of this Gospel has any parallel in the other Gospels."[9]

2. In John, the highest good is eternal life; in the Synoptics, the kingdom of God.

3. John begins in eternity; the Synoptics begin at various points in time. Mark begins with a quotation from the Prophets, Matthew with the patriarch Abraham, and Luke "in the days of Herod, king of Judea."

4. Instead of the parables and short sayings of Jesus found in the Synoptics, John has allegories (see chaps. 10 and 15), long discourses, and the "I am" statements of Jesus. Jesus says, "I am the bread of life [6:35] . . . the good shepherd [10:11, 14] . . . the resurrection and the life [11:25] . . . the true vine [15:1] . . . the way, and the truth, and the life [14:6]." Events and their interpretation are closely interwoven.

5. In John the chief scene of Jesus' ministry is Jerusalem, while in the Synoptics it is Galilee.

6. John mentions three Passovers (2:13; 6:4; 11:55), and Mark only one (14:1).

7. The attempt to relate John to the Synoptics presents chronological problems. For example, John places the cleansing of the Temple early in Jesus' ministry (2:13–22), but the Synoptics at the end (Mark 11:15–19 and parallels). Which is right? Or were there two cleansings? Another chronological problem concerns the date of the Last Supper. According to John it was celebrated on the evening before Passover (see 13:1; 18:28; 19:14), but according to the Synoptics at the time of the Passover meal itself (Mark 14:2, 16, and parallels). These problems have not yet been solved to the satisfaction of all.

8. In John, Jesus is publicly announced as the Messiah and Son of God at once, but in the Synoptics the confession of Peter is a climactic event.

9. In John, Jesus' miracles are signs of his deity, but in the Synoptics they are works of compassion and signs of the kingdom.

One way to get a quick view of the relation between the Synoptics and John is to compare the two outlines that follow:

## AN OUTLINE OF THE SYNOPTICS

| THEME | MATTHEW | MARK | LUKE |
|---|---|---|---|
| Infancy Narratives | 1:1–2:23 | | 1:1–2:52 |
| Introduction to Jesus' Work | 3:1–4:11 | 1:1–13 | 3:1–4:13 |
| Galilean Ministry | 4:12–18:35 | 1:14–9:50 | 4:14–9:50 |
| From Galilee to Jerusalem | 19:1–20:34 | 10:1–52 | 9:51–19:27 |
| Last Days in Jerusalem | 21:1–27:66 | 11:1–15:47 | 19:28–23:56 |
| Resurrection | 28:1–20 | 16:1–8 | 24:1–53 |

## AN OUTLINE OF JOHN

Prologue: The Incarnate Word (1:1–18)

The Witness to Jesus as the Messiah and Son of God (1:19–51)

Jesus' Self-revelation in Judea, Galilee, and Samaria (2:1–4:54)

Signs and Controversies (5:1–12:50)

Jesus' More Intimate Revelation to His Disciples (13:1–17:26)

Jesus' Suffering and Death (18:1–19:42)

Jesus' Resurrection (20:1–21:25)

Though the differences between John and the Synoptics cannot be bypassed, they should not be exaggerated. For John is also a Gospel (for many, the greatest of the Gospels), which bears witness to the same good news about the person and deeds of Jesus Christ. In spite of the sparse amount of literal parallel between the Fourth Gospel and the other three Gospels, there is an overall kind of parallel. All four Gospels include the following emphases:

1. the ministry of John the Baptist,
2. the baptism of Jesus,
3. a calling of disciples,
4. a ministry of word and deed,
5. opposition from adversaries,
6. the crucifixion and resurrection of Jesus,
7. the unique Messiahship of Jesus.

We thank God for the gospel and the Gospels, but most of all for Jesus Christ, the theme of both and the Lord of all.

A particular word of caution is necessary as we begin a careful review of the Gospels and the rest of the New Testament. These documents were fashioned in the midst of controversy between the Christian community and the Jewish community. While Jesus, his family, and all his disciples were Jewish, there is animosity expressed at times by the writers of the New Testament toward "the Jews." Often this only means "certain of the Jews" or the "Jewish authorities." Clearly not all the Jews were hostile toward Jesus and his followers. It is important, therefore, when we reflect on texts that speak about "the Jews" to keep this in mind. Especially we should not move from "the Jews" of Jesus' time to contemporary Jews, thereby continuing the animosity that for too long has poisoned the relationship and distorted understanding between Christians and Jews.

# The Life of Jesus

$W$hen we come to Jesus and the Gospels, we realize that we are in
the Holy of Holies of God's revelation. We have already accepted
Matthew, Mark, Luke, and John as longer announcements of the
good news about Jesus rather than as modern biographies. Many persons have been the subject of biographies, but only Jesus has been
the subject of Gospels. Because the Gospels are Gospels and not
modern biographies, some feel that a life of Jesus should not be
attempted. But such a conclusion is unwarranted. While the Gospels
contain theological interpretation in the light of Jesus' resurrection,
they also contain history. Events from Jesus' life are recorded and
interpreted. The unit of revelation is the interpreted *event*. No one
claims to know enough from the Gospels to put all the known details
of Jesus' life in a strictly chronological order. The most that can be
expected is a general approximation. It should be remembered that
we cannot deal with every event of Jesus' life nor can we treat completely the main events in the space of this one chapter.

> *Nothing can take the place of reading the Gospels them-
> selves. But if you cannot do this, then read as many of the
> selected references as possible.*

> *It is also suggested that you make your own outline of Jesus'
> life as you read the Gospels in connection with this lesson.*

> *Write down questions that you would like to raise.*

## The Days of Preparation

### The Birth and Childhood of Jesus (Matt. 1–2; Luke 1–2)

The days of preparation extend from the birth of Jesus to his
entrance upon his public ministry. Only Matthew and Luke tell us of

Jesus' birth and early years. Yet John tells us, "And the Word became flesh and lived among us" (1:14).

Matthew's genealogy traces Jesus' ancestry back to Abraham, the first Hebrew; Luke's traces it back to Adam, the first human (3:23–38). Both show that Jesus is a descendant of David. "In the time of King Herod . . . Jesus was born in Bethlehem of Judea . . ." (Matt. 2:1). Bethlehem had been the birthplace of David. The Herod referred to here was Herod the Great. Caesar Augustus was the emperor of the Roman empire at that time (Luke 2:1). The exact date of birth is unknown but was about 6 B.C.E. To speak of Jesus' birth as occurring "before the Common Era" sounds odd. The reason lies in a mistake which was made in a revision of the Christian calendar in the sixth century, C.E.

Both Matthew and Luke tell us that Jesus was conceived by the Holy Spirit and born of the Virgin Mary. The birth of Jesus was the incarnation of God in human life. The revelation to humble shepherds stands over against this world's scale of values. The adoration of the Wise Men bears witness to the worldwide purpose of the gospel. Jesus' circumcision shows that Jesus was a Jew, "born under the law" (Gal. 4:4). Simeon and Anna remind us that there was a godly remnant with hearts open to God's salvation.

Jesus grew up in Nazareth, an inconspicuous town, yet one that was close to some of the main highways of the day. Joseph was a carpenter (Matt. 13:55), and he probably began very early to train Jesus to be a carpenter too (Mark 6:3). Jesus had both sisters and brothers, but only the names of the brothers are recorded: James, Joses, Judas, and Simon (Mark 6:3 ). It was customary for Joseph and Mary to go to Jerusalem each year to attend the Feast of Passover. When Jesus was twelve years of age, he went with them (see Luke 2:41–51). Festal journeys to Jerusalem were ordinarily made in large groups. Therefore, on the journey home, Joseph and Mary did not realize that Jesus was not with them until they had gone the distance of a day's travel. They returned to Jerusalem and found him talking with the teachers at the Temple. Mary spoke to him in mild rebuke, "Child, why have you treated us like this? Look, your father and I have been looking for you in great anxiety." He said to them, "Why were you searching for me? Did you not know that I must be in my Father's house?" In these words Jesus showed an early consciousness of his relationship to God.

At the end of this account of the visit of the boy Jesus to Jerusalem, Luke makes this summary statement: "And Jesus increased in wisdom and in years, and in divine and human favor" (Luke 2:52). This clearly means that Jesus matured in a wholesome way in all respects: intellectually, morally, physically, spiritually, and socially.

### John the Baptist (Matt. 3:1–12; Mark 1:2–8; Luke 3:1–20)

John the Baptist, the son of Zechariah and Elizabeth, was the forerunner of the Messiah. He was a hermitlike prophet from the wilderness, like Elijah (Matt. 11:14). He preached, "Repent, for the kingdom of heaven has come near." This was a call to turn from sin to God, a reorientation of life in view of the nearness of God's kingdom. This kingdom or reign of God would be manifested in final judgment. Repentance was to be accompanied by baptism in the Jordan. This act marked the end of the old life and the readiness for God's coming reign. Many came to John to be baptized, confessing their sins. Among them, in addition to tax collectors and soldiers (Luke 3:10–14), were some Pharisees and Sadducees whom John warned to "bear fruits worthy of repentance." But the most important aspect of his message was the announcement of the Coming One. John said that he himself baptized with water, but the Messiah would baptize with the Holy Spirit and with fire.

After John was imprisoned and heard of Jesus' ministry, he sent two of his disciples to Jesus to ask, "Are you the one who is to come, or are we to wait for another?" Jesus told them, "Go and tell John what you have seen and heard." In the course of Jesus' discourse about John, he made this startling statement: "I tell you, among those born of women no one has arisen greater than John; yet the least in the kingdom of God is greater than he" (see Matt. 11:2–15; Luke 7:18–28). John stood as God's spokesman at the end of the old age. But the new age of the kingdom, inaugurated in Jesus, is so much more wonderful than all that went before, that the least in the kingdom is more privileged than John.[1]

### The Baptism of Jesus (Matt. 3:13–17;<br>Mark 1:9–11; Luke 3:21–22; John 1:31–34; Acts 10:37–38)

The fact of Jesus' baptism is recorded in Peter's sermon to Cornelius and in all four Gospels. He came from Nazareth and was baptized by John in the Jordan. But why was he baptized? John was "proclaiming a baptism of repentance for the forgiveness of sins," but we have no record of any sin or consciousness of sin on Jesus' part at any time. In fact, the writers of the New Testament consistently maintain that he was without sin (2 Cor. 5:21; Heb. 4:15; 7:26; 1 Peter 2:22; 1 John 3:5). Matthew records the purpose "to fulfill all righteousness" (3:15).

But what was involved in fulfilling all righteousness? In the light of the whole story of Jesus, we can make certain suggestions. First, Jesus showed that he accepted John's ministry as ordained of God. Second, he was willing to be numbered among those who in baptism turned from the old age to the kingdom of God at hand. Third, he identified himself with the people he had come to save: "For our sake he made him to be sin who knew no sin, so that in him we might become the righteousness of God" (2 Cor. 5:21). Finally, Jesus' baptism was an act of dedication to the Father's will and an anointing "with the Holy Spirit and with power" (Acts 10:38).

"The heavens were opened." That is, the communication between the Father and the Son was unhindered. The Spirit descended like a dove in preparation for the ministry ahead. The heavenly voice brought well-known words to Jesus. "This is my Son, the Beloved" (Matt. 3:17) are words echoing Psalm 2:7, a royal or messianic psalm. But Jesus understood these words at a deeper level than others who had read them. Most people thought of them in relation to a military and political messiah. Jesus seems to have thought of them as designating his special relation to God. "With whom I am well pleased" is drawn from Isaiah 42:1, a part of one of the passages that deal with the Servant of the LORD. Jesus was called to be the Servant-Messiah. Kings did not ordinarily think of themselves as being servants of the people. No wonder the disciples of Jesus were so slow in coming to an understanding of the true nature of Jesus' messiahship.

*In what respects is Christian baptism like Jesus' baptism by John?*
*In what respects is it different?*

## The Temptations of Jesus
### (Matt. 4:1–11; Mark 1:12–13; Luke 4:1–13)

The temptation of Jesus is recorded very briefly in Mark. Matthew and Luke go into more detail. They both delineate the three forms that the temptations took, but they differ on the sequence of the second and third temptations. We follow the order given in Matthew.

*Read the eleven verses carefully.*

After his baptism, Jesus chose to go apart and think through his messianic vocation, and this involved temptation. Of course temptation was by no means confined to one period in his life. The Gospels make that clear, and the Letter to the Hebrews tells us that he was tempted in every respect as we are (4:15). The temptations recorded in Matthew and Luke are representative of the temptations that came to Jesus as the Son-Servant-Messiah. Jesus was led by the Spirit to this encounter with the evil one because he had come into the world to engage him in battle and overcome him. Some think that the devil (Satan) is only the personification of human sin, but the New Testament writers seem to have a different view. The devil and his demons mean that evil is purposeful, powerful, and cosmic. It is both outside and within humankind, but it is not outside the sovereignty of God. Temptation is not sin but an appeal to disobey God. The temptation of Jesus reminds us that his humanity was real. Jesus was not play-acting to put on a good show. There was no hypocrisy in his humanity.

Unquestionably the evangelists thought of the parallels between the experience of Jesus and that of Moses and Israel. Their mention of the wilderness, the forty days, and the temptation (or testing) calls to mind a number of Old Testament passages (see Exod. 34:28; Deut. 8:2; 9:9). Though the parallels between Jesus' temptation and Israel's testing are not complete, they are real. From God's standpoint a temptation is a testing, for the purpose is positive; from the devil's standpoint a testing is a temptation, for the purpose is negative. The same Hebrew or Greek word means "to test" or "to tempt" according to the perspective in which it is viewed. Israel was tested in the wilderness forty years and found wanting. Jesus, the Israelite, was tested (tempted) in the wilderness forty days and was found acceptable.

The first temptation for Jesus was to be an *economic* messiah: "If you are the Son of God, command these stones to become loaves of bread." Of course a part of this temptation was to use supernatural power for his own benefit, but this is not the main thrust of the tempter. Moses, God's great leader in the past, had been the instrument of providing manna and quails for the people in the wilderness (Exod. 16:4–36; compare John 6:30–31). But more than that, Jesus' own hunger enabled him to be acutely aware of his hungry people, whom he loved and for whom he had compassion. The temptation was real. But Jesus answered with words from Deuteronomy 8:3: "One does not live by bread alone, but by every word that comes from the mouth of the LORD."

In other words, Jesus recognized the necessity of food for the sustenance of life in this world, but he was unwilling to make the feeding of people the center of his message and ministry. He refused to measure the kingdom of God in terms of "things." While Jesus was always sensitive to human physical need and sometimes literally fed the people, he would make no idol of materialism. The things of life are God's gifts and to be held as such, but they are not to become the chief end of human pursuit. Jesus refused to make an economic program the center of his ministry; rather he calls all economic systems to the judgment bar of God. The Bread of Heaven sets the bread of earth in its proper perspective (see John 6:25–71). What does Jesus' first temptation and his answer to it say to us about our own vocations, purposes, and standards and about the rampant materialism of our culture?

The second temptation was to be a *marvelous* messiah. That is, Jesus was tempted to secure a following by working spectacular miracles. Moses had worked miracles in Egypt and in the wilderness. By casting himself dramatically from the pinnacle of the Temple, the center of Jewish life, and being rescued by God, Jesus could begin his ministry with a large group of supporters. By continuing to perform such feats he would accumulate more and more disciples. Moreover, he would demonstrate his trust in God's protection (Matt. 4:6; Ps. 91:11–12).

But Jesus again answered the tempter with words from Deuteronomy (6:16): "Do not put the LORD your God to the test." Over and over again during his ministry, Jesus was requested to amuse and amaze the people by giving signs (for example, see Matt. 12:38; 16:1; Mark 8:11; Luke 11:16; John 2:18). Just as he fed people but would not be an economic messiah, so he performed miracles but would not be a marvelous messiah. Jesus consistently refused to put on a stunt show. He worked miracles out of compassion and in relation to the kingdom's purpose, but not for entertainment and the accumulation of superficial disciples. For example, we read in Matthew 11:20: "Then he began to reproach the cities where most of his deeds of power had been done, because they did not repent." In other words, proper response to Jesus' miracles is repentance. But have we not supported worthy causes by unworthy means, saying, "Oh well, it's a worthy cause"? Jesus insists that the means as well as the end must be right. What, then, do Jesus' second temptation and his response to it say to us about our witness to the gospel?

The third temptation was to be a *political* messiah. David had been a political and military messiah, and it was in relation to him and his house that the messianic promise was given. Jesus felt keenly the heel of Rome upon the neck of his people. Many were oppressed not only by Rome but also by their own people. The temptation to be an exact duplicate of David was the temptation to avoid the way of the Suffering Servant. At his baptism the voice from heaven had come not only in terms of Psalm 2:7 but also in terms of Isaiah 42:1, authority and suffering. To "fall down and worship" Satan meant to fulfill the kingdom's purpose by political compromise and military force and thereby avoid the suffering.

Jesus answered the third temptation with words from Deuteronomy 6:13—"The LORD your God you shall fear; him you shall serve." God's will and God's way would remain the will and the way of Jesus. Later when Jesus interpreted his role as the Suffering Servant to his disciples, Peter renewed the temptation to avoid the Servant role. And Jesus said to Peter, "Get behind me, Satan! You are a stumbling block to me; for you are setting your mind not on divine things but on human things" (see Matt. 16:21–23). By refusing to be a political messiah, Jesus did not say we have no need of politics but implied that our political systems must be judged by the heavenly King, for no earthly kingdom is the kingdom of God. Evil people may, in a measure, be restrained by force, but their transformation cannot be coerced. The kingdom does not come by the power of the sword, but by the power of the Spirit (see 2 Cor. 10:4).

*How, in your opinion, is the political state related to the kingdom of God?*

## A Brief Preparatory Ministry

If we had only the Synoptics, we would assume that, immediately after his temptation, Jesus entered his Galilean ministry. But John seems to say that there was a brief preparatory ministry primarily to individuals, and including some time in Judea. Some students place all the events listed in John 1:19–4:54 in this period.

## The Galilean Ministry

### The Beginning of Work in Galilee (Mark 1:14–45)

We follow the general sequence of events found in Mark. Parallels in Matthew and Luke are noted in the footnotes of the NRSV.

It has been conjectured that Jesus worked in association with John the Baptist for a while. Whether this be true or not, it seems that the arrest of John had something to do with the time at which Jesus began his public ministry in Galilee, for we read:

Now after John was arrested, Jesus came to Galilee, proclaiming the good news of God, and saying, "The time is fulfilled, and the kingdom of God has come near; repent, and believe in the good news." (Mark 1:14–15)

John had sounded the note of judgment and repentance in preparation for the coming of the kingdom. Jesus did not neglect judgment and repentance, but his emphasis was on the gospel, the good news or positive meaning of God's reign, which was dawning. All of Jesus' preaching, teaching, and miracles are to be seen in relation to the kingdom of God, which has come in him but which is also yet to come in its full consummation.

Perhaps it was at this point in Jesus' ministry that he went to his hometown Nazareth, where he read a part of Isaiah 61 in the synagogue and interpreted it to the people (Luke 4:16–30). Some interpreters feel the incident belongs with Matthew 13:53–58 and Mark 6:1–6 at a later time. In either case, all three passages speak of his rejection by the people of Nazareth.

This unpopularity at home probably played a part in Jesus' decision to move his base of operations to Capernaum, on the coast of the Sea of Galilee. As he was passing along the sea one day, he called the fishermen Peter, Andrew, James, and John to be his disciples; and they left their nets to "fish for people" instead (Mark 1:17). At Capernaum, he healed a man with an unclean spirit, Peter's mother-in-law, and others. From Capernaum "he went throughout Galilee, proclaiming the message in their synagogues and casting out demons" (Mark 1:39). At some unspecified place he healed a leper. Thus Jesus began his public ministry in Galilee, and from there his fame began to spread.

## Popularity and Opposition (Mark 2:1–3:12; Luke 5:17–6:11)

In this period many recognized the authority and power of Jesus, but opposition to him was rising from the leaders of the people. At Capernaum Jesus healed the paralytic borne by four and pronounced his sins forgiven. This led to the charge of blasphemy. Jesus called Levi, a tax collector on a highway that ran through Capernaum, to be his disciple. In the house where Jesus stayed at Capernaum tax collectors and other "sinners" were eating and drinking. For associating with such outcasts Jesus was criticized by his enemies.

Jesus made clear the distinction between traditional Judaism and John's message on the one hand, and his gospel on the other, by his words concerning fasting, patching clothes, and putting new wine into new wineskins. His message was joyous and different; it could not be contained in the traditional patterns of his people. Opposition also arose against Jesus on account of his activity and that of his disciples on the Sabbath Day (compare John 5:1–18). The account of this period of popularity and opposition ends with a large crowd from many places following Jesus.

## Jesus and His Disciples
### (Mark 3:13–19a; Matt. 5:1–7:29; Luke 6:12–49)

From among his many followers Jesus chose twelve leaders or apostles. He appointed them to a threefold purpose: "to be with him, and to be sent out to proclaim the message, and to have authority to cast out demons" (Mark 3:14–15). As disciples or learners they needed to be with their Master. As Jesus' apostles they had a mission of word and healing. Mark lists them as follows: Simon Peter, James, John, Andrew, Philip, Bartholomew, Matthew, Thomas, James the son of Alphaeus, Thaddaeus, Simon the Cananaean, and Judas Iscariot (3:16–19a; compare Luke 6:12–19; Matt. 10:1–4; and Acts 1:13). Instead of Thaddaeus, Luke has Judas the son of James. Were they the same person? Or did the personnel of the Twelve change?

The famous Sermon on the Mount is a collection of Jesus' teachings concerning life in the kingdom of God, given in the presence of his disciples and others. There is no record of this "sermon" in Mark and John. It is found in Matthew 5–7 and with some parallels in Luke 6:20b–49, which is frequently called "The Sermon on the Plain" (see Luke 6:17–19).

## Mighty Words and Mighty Deeds

Several events that took place in Galilee are not mentioned by Mark: Jesus' healing of the centurion's servant (Matt. 8:5–13; Luke 7:1–10), the raising of the widow's son at Nain (Luke 7:11–17), Jesus' reply to the question of John the Baptist (Matt. 11:2–30; Luke 7:18–35), the anointing of Jesus' feet by a woman (Luke 7:36–50), and a preaching tour in which certain women participated (Luke 8:1–3).

After Jesus had healed a blind and dumb demoniac, his enemies accused him of being in league with Beelzebul, the prince of demons (see Matt. 12:22–30; Mark 3:19b–27). But Jesus made it clear that Satan does not work against himself. Jesus has already bound Satan and is able to plunder his house by doing works of healing. Indeed, his healings indicated that the kingdom of God had begun to dawn. Apparently Jesus took occasion to give a warning concerning the sin against the Holy Spirit, to speak of the sign of Jonah, and the parable of the empty house (see Matt. 12:31–45; Mark 3:28–30). Jesus' true relatives are those who do the will of God (Matt. 12:46–50; Mark 3:31–35; Luke 8:19–21).

*Many of Jesus' mighty words were given in the form of parables. As you read the passages in the outline that follows, pay special attention to those that are parallel. What do you learn from this examination of parallels?*

| PARABLE | MATTHEW | MARK | LUKE |
|---|---|---|---|
| The Soils | 13:1–9 | 4:1–9 | 8:4–8 |
| Reason for Using Parables | 13:10–17 | 4:10–12 | 8:9–10 |
| Explanation of the Soils | 13:18–23 | 4:13–20 | 8:11–15 |
| How to Hear | | 4:21–25 | 8:16–18 |
| The Tares | 13:24–30 | | |
| The Seed Growing of Itself | | 4:26–29 | |
| The Mustard Seed | 13:31–32 | 4:30–32 | |
| The Leaven | 13:33 | | |
| Jesus' Custom of Using Parables | 13:34–35 | 4:33–34 | |
| Explanation of the Tares | 13:36–43 | | |
| The Hidden Treasure | 13:44 | | |
| The Pearl of Great Price | 13:45–46 | | |
| The Dragnet | 13:47–50 | | |
| Treasures New and Old | 13:51–52 | | |

Jesus' mighty words were accompanied by mighty deeds. The Gospels give the following mighty deeds in sequence:

| MIRACLE | MATTHEW | MARK | LUKE |
|---|---|---|---|
| The Calming of the Storm | 8:18–27 | 4:35–41 | 8:22–25 |
| The Healing of the Gerasene Demoniac | 8:28–34 | 5:1–20 | 8:26–39 |
| The Raising of Jairus' Daughter and Healing of the Woman with a Hemorrhage | 9:18–26 | 5:21–43 | 8:40–56 |
| The Healing of Two Blind Men | 9:21–31 | | |
| The Healing of a Dumb Demoniac | 9:32–34 | | |

But in spite of all that Jesus had done, on returning to Nazareth he was rejected (Matt. 13:54–58; Mark 6:1–6a; Luke 4:16–24).

Early in his ministry Jesus had appointed the Twelve, the nucleus of the new Israel. After they had been with him for a while and thereby learned at least something of his mission, he gave them specific instructions and sent them out by twos in order to preach the kingdom and to heal (Matt. 9:35–11:1; Mark 6:6b-13; Luke 9:1–6).

John the Baptist was put to death by Herod Antipas at the request of Herodias's daughter (Matt. 14:1–12; Mark 6:14–29; Luke 9:7–9). When the Twelve returned from their mission, Jesus took them aside for rest. It is also possible that he did not want to precipitate a conflict with Herod. In any case, he did not succeed in finding rest. The crowds still came, and Jesus "had compassion on them, because they were like sheep without a shepherd." He taught them and then he fed them.

The feeding of the five thousand is the only miracle recorded in all four Gospels (Matt. 14:13–21; Mark 6:30–44; Luke 9:10–17; John 6:1–14). This means that it made a deep impression and was of great significance. Though Jesus had refused to perform a miracle to feed himself or to win a following, he was willing to do so in order to meet the needs of the people. Moreover, this meal had messianic import. The eating of a meal was associated with the coming of God's reign (Matt. 8:11). In a sense, this was a pledge of the messianic banquet. Therefore, it had something in common with the Last Supper, which was yet to be celebrated.

Jesus' walking on the sea (Matt. 14:22–36; Mark 6:45–56; John 6:15–24) and his condemnation of the traditionalism of the elders (Matt. 15:1–20; Mark 7:1–23) bring the continuous ministry in Galilee to a close.

## The Ministry In and Out of Galilee
### (Matt. 15:21–18:35; Mark 7:24–9:50; Luke 9:18–50)

This phase of Jesus' work began with a journey into the region of Tyre and Sidon, where he healed the little daughter of a Syrophoenician woman. On his return to the region of the Sea of Galilee, he healed a deaf mute. After the feeding of the five thousand, Jesus went to the district of Dalmanutha. Some Pharisees and Sadducees asked for a sign, which he refused to give. And he warned his disciples to beware of their leaven. At Bethsaida he healed a blind man.

The disciples had been with Jesus long enough now to have the crucial question put to them: "Who do you say that I am?" In answer Peter made the great messianic confession. But Jesus charged his disciples to tell no one about him. He did not want the title Messiah (Christ) tossed about, because it was understood primarily in political terms. Moreover, when Jesus interpreted his messiahship in relation to his suffering and death, the very same Peter demonstrated that he did not understand the true meaning of his Master's vocation.

The transfiguration of Jesus in the presence of Peter, James, and John is one of those profound mysteries that can neither be fully explained nor explained away. It was a special meeting of heaven and earth. Jesus was prepared for what lay ahead. The confession of Peter was confirmed and clarified. The three disciples were enjoined to listen to Jesus. The presence of Moses and Elijah, representatives of the Law and the Prophets respectively, indicates that both the Law and the Prophets are confirmed in Jesus. When Jesus and the three returned to the other disciples, Jesus healed an epileptic boy, whom the disciples had been unable to heal for lack of faith. Jesus continued to try to prepare his disciples for the events ahead.

## The Journey to Jerusalem

### The Departure from Galilee

Matthew (19:1–2), Mark (10:1), and Luke (9:51–56) all tell us of Jesus' departure from Galilee, and Luke stresses the fact that his face was set to go to Jerusalem. Luke also tells of the inhospitable reception that Jesus received in a Samaritan village. Both Luke and Matthew record Jesus' sharp words to reluctant would-be disciples (Matt. 8:19–22; Luke 9:57–62).

### Jesus' Reasons for Going to Jerusalem

Certainly Jesus wanted to carry his kingdom ministry to Jerusalem. But the Gospels indicate that he was already aware of his coming suffering and death. Even in liberal Galilee he had encountered conflict. How much more would he encounter it in traditional Jerusalem! At his baptism he had accepted the messiahship of the Suffering Servant, though his disciples did not comprehend its meaning. As the Servant of the Lord he was going to Jerusalem to teach, suffer, die, and rise from the dead. The unnamed servant of Isaiah 40–55 was to do all of these things, and Jesus knew it.

### The Independent Lukan Material (Luke 10:1–18:14)

Between Jesus' departure from Galilee and his triumphal entry into Jerusalem, Luke has over eight chapters of material not found in any of the other Gospels. Luke does not give the specific setting for all these materials and seems to mean that they are materials that must be understood in relation to the cross that lies ahead. Jesus shows that his disciples are servants of the kingdom, who are to be characterized by love for neighbor, communion with God, spiritual discernment, genuine religion, courageous witness, freedom from materialism, and constant hope. Membership in the kingdom requires repentance, humility, unselfish generosity, an affirmative acceptance of God's invitation, and wholehearted commitment. The God of the kingdom loves, seeks, and receives the lost. The members of the kingdom are to be aware of the danger of riches, thoughtlessness, egoism, ingratitude, false security, and self-trust.[2]

## The Final Approach to Jerusalem
### (Matt. 19:3–20:34; Mark 10:2–52; Luke 18:15–19:27)

After the long independent section of Luke, parallels among the Synoptics appear again, though there is some material appearing in only one Gospel or in two Gospels. Jesus speaks about marriage, divorce, and adultery, and blesses little children. The rich young ruler is unwilling to respond affirmatively to God's revelation and goes away sorrowful. Matthew records the parable of the Laborers and the Vineyard; and Luke, the parable of the Pounds. Jesus foretells his death and resurrection for the third time.

In spite of Jesus' teaching concerning kingdom living, James and John, encouraged by their mother, request the preferred positions in the kingdom. But they do not know what they are asking. At his baptism Jesus committed himself to the messiahship of the Suffering Servant. Jesus' disciples are also called to be suffering servants. Their greatness is not to be measured in terms of preferred positions but in terms of sacrificial service: "For the Son of Man also came not to be served but to serve, and to give his life a ransom for many" (Mark 10:45).

At Jericho Jesus heals Bartimaeus, a blind beggar, who addresses him as "Son of David." This suggests that Jesus' unusual ministry had aroused popular messianic hopes. Also at Jericho Jesus works the transformation of Zacchaeus, a hated tax collector: "For the Son of Man came to seek out and to save the lost."

## The Last Days in Jerusalem

Jesus' last days in Jerusalem were characterized by controversy with his enemies. The chief priests, scribes, and elders questioned his authority

(Matt. 21:23–27; Mark 11:27–33; Luke 20:1–8), whereupon he countered with another question: "Did the baptism of John come from heaven or was it of human origin?" The parables of the Two Sons (Matt. 21:28–32), the Wicked Tenants (Matt. 21:33–46; Mark 12:1–12; Luke 20:9–19), and the Marriage Feast (Matt. 22:1–14) were all directed toward Israel's unfruitfulness. Some of the Pharisees and Herodians tried to trap him with the question, "Is it lawful to pay taxes to the emperor, or not?" To this question he gave the now famous answer, "Give to the emperor the things that are the emperor's and to God the things that are God's" (see Mark 12:13–17 and parallels). Some of the Sadducees, who did not believe in the resurrection, asked him about the relation of marriage to the resurrected life. Jesus told them that marriage is a category of earth, not of heaven, but that life after death is a reality (see Mark 12:18–27 and parallels). In Jesus' own question about David's son (Mark 12:35–37 and parallels), he implied that the Messiah cannot be accounted for simply in terms of biological ancestry. He pronounced woes on the scribes and Pharisees for their false leadership (Matt. 23:1–39; Mark 12:38–40; Luke 20:45–47).

Jesus' last days in Jerusalem were also characterized by his teaching concerning last things. The destruction of Jerusalem, the end of the age, and the coming of the Son of man are woven together in "the little apocalypse" (Mark 13:1–37 and parallels). The parables of the Ten Maidens and the Talents and the picture of the Last Judgment (Matt. 25:1–46) all point to the last judgment.

## The Triumphal Entry (Matt. 21:1–11; Mark 11:1–11; Luke 19:29–44; John 12:12–19)

Jesus' triumphal entry into Jerusalem is easily misunderstood. The people greeted him with excitement and with words from Psalm 118:25–26. They wanted a political messiah just like David. Jesus' humble, yet royal, entrance on the colt of an ass was an acted parable, such as the prophets used. Jesus sought to reveal the nature of his messiahship as the Prince of Peace rather than as a military commander, who rode on a horse or in a chariot (see Zech. 9:9) He remained true to his vocation.

## The Cleansing of the Temple (Matt. 21:12–17; Mark 11:15–19; Luke 19:45–48; compare John 2:13–25)

The Temple stood for lucrative business to those who sold sacrificial animals and provided the means whereby foreign currency could be exchanged for the half-shekel to pay the Temple tax. Jesus' cleansing of the Temple was a protest against unjust practices that had grown up in connection with this business. This attack was one of the factors that led to the crucifixion. But Jesus was doing more than making a protest. Again he was asserting his true messiahship as Lord of the Temple (see Mal. 3:1–3).

### Judas Iscariot and a Woman of Bethany
### (Matt. 26:1–16; Mark 14:1–11; Luke 22:1–6; compare John 12:1–11)

The leaders of his people were seeking a way to put Jesus to death. Why? They claimed he was guilty of blasphemy. He had challenged their customs and interpretations of the Law. Jesus had bested them in controversy. They were jealous of his popularity with the people. They were afraid of him and the messianic hopes associated with him. He was bringing about a revolution in the thinking of his people. And he had threatened the dishonest practices in the Temple.

The leaders sought a way to dispose of Jesus, and Judas offered his services. What did Judas betray about his Master? It has been suggested that he disclosed the fact that Jesus claimed to be the Messiah, thereby giving the Jewish leaders a ground for Jesus' arrest. But there is no record that Judas gave testimony at the trial. It is far more likely that Judas told the enemies of Jesus the time and the place to apprehend him without stirring up his followers. This Judas agreed to do. But why? Why and how do we betray Jesus today?

The evangelists' interweaving of the plot of Judas to betray Jesus and the anointing of Jesus by a woman of Bethany is not accidental. The humble devotion of this woman stands in glaring contrast to the treachery of one of the Twelve. Her action was more significant than she realized: she anointed Jesus' body for burial.

### The Last Supper (Matt. 26:17–35; Mark 14:12–31;
### Luke 22:7–38; 1 Cor. 11:23–26; compare John 13:1–17:26)

According to the Synoptics, the Last Supper was eaten on the day of the Jewish Passover. According to John, it seems to have been eaten on the day before the Passover (John 13:1; 18:28). Though this problem in chronology has not been resolved, the meal that Jesus ate with the disciples, while probably not the actual Passover meal, came to be interpreted with Passover symbolism. Passover is the Jewish "sacrament" of redemption from bondage to Egypt. The Lord's Supper is the sacrament of redemption from the bondage to sin. As Paul put it, "For our paschal lamb, Christ, has been sacrificed" (1 Cor. 5:7).

Jesus sent two disciples to make the necessary preparations for the supper in a large upper room in Jerusalem. At the table Jesus announced that one of the Twelve would betray him. It is interesting that no one of the group pointed the finger at the other but said instead, "Is it I?"

The broken bread and the poured-out cup were tokens of Jesus' death. The new covenant promised by Jeremiah (31:31–34) was in process of being enacted. The old covenant had been sealed by blood (Exod. 24:8), and Jesus was to pour out his life for many (see Isa. 53). Repeatedly Jesus had shown that he was conscious of being the Suffering Servant, through whose atoning death others might have life. Life in such a covenant involved fellowship between Jesus and his disciples. Moreover, this meal, like the one in Galilee (the feeding of the five thousand), pointed to the messianic banquet with the Messiah in his kingdom, for Jesus said, "I will never again drink of this fruit of the vine until that day when I drink it new with you in my Father's kingdom" (Matt. 26:29; compare 1 Cor. 11:26).

After the supper Jesus and his disciples sang a hymn, probably Psalms 115–118, customarily sung after the Passover meal. They went out to the Mount of Olives, and Jesus announced Peter's impending denial and the falling away of the other disciples.

The Lord's Supper carries many meanings for Christians today, for it is the whole gospel in dramatic form. Indeed it is the visible gospel—the gospel that can be seen and tasted, that can be responded to with the whole self. Through it God renews the offer of life, and in faith we receive God's gift and renew our covenant vows.

## Gethsemane (Matt. 26:36–56; Mark 14:32–52; Luke 22:39–53; John 18:1–12)

The Garden of Gethsemane is located on the slope of the Mount of Olives. Leaving most of the disciples behind, Jesus took Peter, James, and John with him into the garden. He began to be greatly distressed and troubled and said to the three, "I am deeply grieved, even to death; remain here, and stay awake with me." Then he went a little farther and prayed: "My Father, if it is possible, let this cup pass from me; yet not what I want, but what you want." Thus he prayed three times. And Luke tells us that "his sweat became like great drops of blood falling down on the ground."

How are we to account for the agony in Gethsemane? Of course the Master was facing suffering and death. But others had faced suffering and death calmly. He was experiencing the hostility and rejection of the leaders of his people. Yet others had faced rejection too. He saw how weak and fearful his disciples were. Still all of these things together do not account fully for the agony of Jesus. Though we cannot pretend to comprehend the mystery of Jesus' experience, perhaps he was here battling to the last ditch the temptation to be a messiah without a cross. And his cross was not just another cross. He was dying as the sin-bearing Savior. What this meant in the Father-Son relationship is too deep for our human minds to exhaust. Jesus rose from his prayer fully committed to God's will. Indeed, he was the embodiment of the reign of God.[3]

As Jesus was leaving the garden, Judas betrayed him by addressing him as "Rabbi" and by kissing him. Jesus was arrested, and the disciples fled.

## The Trials (Matt. 26:57–27:31; Mark 14:53–15:15; Luke 22:54–23:25; John 18:13–19:16)

### Before the Sanhedrin

It appears that Jesus was informally examined at night and officially tried in the morning. At his trial before the Sanhedrin, he was falsely accused. A statement he had made concerning the Temple was garbled by the witnesses. The high priest asked, "Are you the Messiah, the Son of the Blessed One?" According to Mark, Jesus answered, "I am; and 'you will see the Son of Man seated at the right hand of the Power,' and 'coming with the clouds of heaven' " (14:62). According to Matthew, he said, "You have said so . . ." (26:64). According to Luke, "You say that I am" (22:70). In some manuscripts of Mark, the beginning of Jesus' reply reads, "You said that I am."[4] In any case, Jesus did not deny that he was the Son of God and the Messiah. But he was not a political messiah.

Apparently it was his statement about the Son of man, as the Jewish authorities understood it, that gave them something on which to make the charge of blasphemy. Jesus was condemned and mocked.

> *Peter, who had boasted about his loyalty to Jesus, denied him three times. Why?*
>
> *In what ways do we deny Jesus? Why?*

### Before Pilate

After the trial by the Sanhedrin, Jesus was taken for further trial before Pilate, the Roman governor. Pilate was not concerned with strictly religious accusations. What concerned him was the political accusation: "We found this man perverting our nation, forbidding us to pay taxes to the emperor, and saying that he himself is the Messiah, a king" (Luke 23:2). Pilate, therefore, asked Jesus, "Are you the king of the Jews?" And Jesus answered, "You say so." The word "king" indicates that Jesus was being accused of treason against Rome. There were also other charges. But Jesus remained silent, and his silence disturbed Pilate. Yet Pilate could find no crime in Jesus and desired to release him.

According to Matthew 27:3–10 (compare Acts 1:18–19), when Judas saw that Jesus was going to be condemned, he was so filled with remorse that he went out and hanged himself. According to Luke 23:6–12, Pilate sent Jesus to Herod. After Herod had mocked Jesus, he sent him back to Pilate.

Then the trial was resumed by Pilate. It was customary for the governor to release a prisoner at the Feast of Passover, and the people gathered to make their customary request. Pilate offered them a choice between Jesus and the notorious Barabbas. The people chose Barabbas and demanded that Jesus be crucified. Why did the people do this? They were stirred up by certain leaders. Moreover, they were probably disappointed in Jesus' refusal to be a political Messiah. In any case, Pilate passed sentence on one he knew to be innocent, thereby committing judicial murder. Jesus was mocked by the soldiers and led away to be crucified.

## The Crucifixion and Burial (Matt. 27:32–66; Mark 15:21–47; Luke 23:26–56; John 19:17–42)

It was customary for the condemned to carry the crossbeam of the cross to the place of crucifixion. Jesus began his walk along the *Via Dolorosa* with his crossbeam across his shoulder. But soon Simon of Cyrene was required to bear it for him. It is probable that this was made necessary by Jesus' lack of sleep, scourgings, mockings, and "heart suffering." Women lamented along the way, and Jesus' reply to them indicates that he was still thinking of the judgment that was to come to his beloved Jerusalem. The way led to Golgotha, the place of a skull. There they offered him the usual sedative, wine mingled with myrrh, but he refused it.

Then they crucified Jesus at nine o'clock on the morning of either the fourteenth or fifteenth of Nisan (March–April) ca. 30 C.E. The soldiers divided his garments among them by casting lots. It was customary to place the accusation over the head of the one condemned to die on a cross. The charge against Jesus read "The King of the Jews." That is, so far as Rome was concerned, Jesus died for treason, but the very governor who ordered the inscription to be placed there knew it was not true. In a far deeper sense, however, the statement of the charge was true. Jesus was and is the King not only of the Jews but of all.

Two nameless robbers were crucified with Jesus. One of them, along with others in the crowd, mocked Jesus. But the other asked Jesus to remember him when he came into his kingdom.

The traditional sequence of the seven last words is as follows: (1) "Father, forgive them; for they do not know what they are doing" (Luke 23:34); (2) "Truly, I tell you, today you will be with me in Paradise" (Luke 23:43); (3) "Woman, here is your son. . . . Here is your mother" (John 19:26–27); (4) "My God, my God, why have you forsaken me?" (Matt. 27:46; Mark 15:34); (5) "I am thirsty" (John 19:28); (6) "It is finished" (John 19:30); and (7) "Father, into your hands I commend my spirit" (Luke 23:46). In what way is each of these statements related to us?

The splitting of the Temple curtain signifies that through the death of Jesus the way into the Holy of Holies (to the presence of God) has been opened. The Roman centurion recognized something of the greatness and innocence of this man at whose crucifixion he had presided. Some of the women who were devoted to Jesus witnessed what was taking place. Joseph of Arimathea with some assistance from Nicodemus buried the body of Jesus. Jesus was "crucified, dead, and buried." Who really crucified Jesus?

## The Resurrection

### The Witness of the Gospels (Matt. 28:1–20; Mark 16:1–8; Luke 24:1–53; John 20:1–21:25)

After the crucifixion, the disciples of Jesus were despondent. Their cause seemed to be lost. This mood is expressed by the two on the road to Emmaus: "We had hoped that he was the one to redeem Israel" (Luke 24:21). But each evangelist in a distinctive way tells the story of the resurrection. Though a part of the ending of Mark's Gospel is lost, that which remains tells of the empty tomb and the announcement of the resurrection. The other Gospels also tell of various appearances of the risen Lord.

> *Outline the story as reported by each writer. Note the parallels and the differences. The differences are marks of authenticity, for each writer gives the account in a memorable way.*

The evangelists were not making up a tale. Some students try to play down the evidence of the empty tomb. But if the enemies could have produced a corpse, they would certainly have done so, and it would have had a negative effect on the proclamation of the gospel. While Paul, whose letters were written before the Gospels, does not specifically mention the empty tomb, his language implies it. For example, he says, "that he was buried, and that he was raised on the third day in accordance with the scriptures" (1 Cor. 15:4; compare Acts 2:31; 13:29–30).

## Witness of Other New Testament Passages

*The earliest written witness to Jesus' resurrection is found in 1 Corinthians 15:3–8. Paul received this information from those who had preached the gospel before his own conversion. Make an outline of the passage in your notebook. What is the importance of each element in the outline?*

The apostolic preaching as recorded in Acts is full of announcements of Jesus' resurrection (see, for example, 2:24, 32; 3:15; 4:10; 5:30; 10:40). In fact, the crucifixion and resurrection constitute the interpreting center of the entire New Testament. The apostles were witnesses of the resurrected Lord.

## Other Types of Witness

The despondent apostles were transformed by their meeting with the risen Christ. He was the Jesus of Nazareth, whom they had known, raised from the dead. This encounter laid the foundation for the great empowering on Pentecost.

The very fact of the Christian church in history is a witness to the resurrection of Jesus. The attempt to account for the church on some other basis simply does not ring true. Furthermore, the existence of the New Testament is a witness to the same event. Nobody would have preached the good news found in the New Testament about a good dead man. The dead heroes of other religions have not produced gospels.

The early Christians recognized the Jewish Sabbath and the Lord's Day in a special way. But in time the Lord's Day took the place of the Jewish Sabbath as the primary day of public worship. With the resurrection of Jesus a distinctive newness was brought into this world. To Christians the resurrection of Jesus is more central than the creation of the world (Exod. 20:8–11) or the exodus from Egypt (Deut. 5:12–15). Every Sunday is a little Easter.

Finally, throughout the centuries the lives of millions have been transformed through the power of Jesus' resurrection (see Phil. 3:10). We are raised from the death of sin to walk in newness of life.

## The Significance of the Resurrection

Throughout the New Testament Jesus' resurrection is treated as an event, not as an idea. To be sure, it is interpreted at various points, but it remains basically an event. This is in keeping with the rest of biblical revelation. Although the risen Christ appeared only to those "who were chosen by God as witnesses" (Acts 10:41), his resurrection is a datable historical event. Anything short of this leads to many kinds of imaginary inventions. We can neither explain the resurrection nor explain it away. It explains the Christian church.

By the resurrection our faith is strengthened. We live in Christ, and he lives in us. We are enabled to take the long view of life and see death in a new perspective. We too shall be raised from the dead. We can offer our loved ones to God at the time of their death in an act of worship, whereby we thank God for their life with us and commit them to God's faithful keeping.

Someone has said, "The resurrection is God's 'Amen' to Jesus' 'It is finished.' " For in Jesus' resurrection all that for which he lived and died is confirmed. By his resurrection Jesus was designated Son of God in power (Rom. 1:4). That is, faith in Jesus as the Son of God was validated by God's raising him from the dead. Good is not at the mercy of evil; it will triumph. The last word is not with the powers of evil, it is with God. We have, therefore, an ultimate gospel, and we can say with Paul, "In all . . . things we are more than conquerors through him who loved us" (Rom. 8:37). "Thanks be to God, who gives us the victory through our Lord Jesus Christ" (1 Cor. 15:57).

*Try to imagine what life would be like if Jesus had not been raised from the dead. What difference has his resurrection made in your own life?*

# The Ministry of Jesus

*J*esus performed a ministry of the spoken word, a ministry of the mighty deed, and a ministry of the given life.

### Jesus' Ministry of the Spoken Word

The tendency of many people today is to play down the importance of the spoken word. Yet we do as much talking as any people who ever lived. The biblical writers take the spoken word very seriously. This fact is bound up with the nature of revelation itself. God speaks to people, and people speak to God. Moreover, people speak to one another for God. There is a sense in which speaking is a deed (compare Matt. 12:37). A person's speech reveals the inner being. Jesus spent much time speaking, but his speaking was intertwined with the other aspects of his ministry.

### Jesus' Proclamation

The chief text concerning Jesus' preaching is Mark 1:14–15 (compare Matt. 4:17; Luke 4:43):

> Now after John was arrested, Jesus came into Galilee, proclaiming the good news of God, and saying, "The time is fulfilled, and the kingdom of God has come near; repent, and believe in the good news."

Apparently the arrest of John the Baptist was a sign to Jesus that he was to enter his own public ministry in Galilee. There are several words used to denote "proclaiming" in the New Testament. The one that occurs in this passage means to announce the message of the king as a herald. Teaching is more the interpreting of the message. But so far as Jesus' proclaiming and teaching are concerned, this distinction cannot be drawn at all times. From the standpoint of origin, the word "gospel" means "good news." In this particular passage, it refers to the message that Jesus preached. Some manuscripts of Mark's Gospel read "the gospel of God." This reading suggests that God is the source of the good news. Other manuscripts read "the gospel of the kingdom of God." This reading indicates that the message concerns God's kingdom. Regardless of which reading is original, each of them states a truth.

Obviously Mark does not give us an entire sermon. Rather Mark gives us those words of Jesus that summarize Jesus' whole message. And this message is divided into three parts: (1) "The time is fulfilled"; (2) "and the kingdom of God has come near"; and (3) "repent, and believe in the good news." "The time is fulfilled." What time? The time announced by God's ancient heralds, the prophets of Israel; the time of judgment and salvation; the time long anticipated by many of God's people.

"The kingdom of God has come near." "Kingdom" here does not mean "territory." Jesus did not say, "God's territory has come near." The word "kingdom" means kingship, sovereignty, reign, and rule. Of course God has always been King. But the reference in the Gospels is to that special manifestation of God's kingly rule that would mean the completion of the old age in the new age. The nearness of the kingdom had been preached by John the Baptist, who associated the Messiah with its coming. Indeed, the dawning of the kingdom could be recognized in the work of the Baptist as the new Elijah, but primarily in Jesus' presence and ministry. Most of Jesus' contemporaries, however, failed to recognize this.

"Repent, and believe in the good news." "Repent" literally means "change your mind," but it involves the change of one's behavior as well. That is, it is a turning from sin and a turning to God, a reorientation of life. In this context, it envisions a turning from the past to the coming reign of God. "Believe" is the verb "have faith in" and involves the commitment of the inner being to the good news. Sometimes people argue whether repentance or faith comes first. It would be the part of wisdom to acknowledge that true repentance is impossible apart from faith and true faith is impossible apart from repentance. Repentance and faith constitute the response that Jesus placed on those who heard his message. Is the response that Jesus expects from us in any way different from that of the first disciples?

## Jesus' Teaching

Teaching was a part of Jesus' ministry of the spoken word. Some of his teachings have already been encountered in our study of the four Gospels and of his life.

*Jesus as a Teacher*

In some respects Jesus was like other teachers; otherwise no one would ever have thought of calling him a teacher or a rabbi. He had disciples. Sometimes he quoted and commented on passages of scripture. He said many of the things that other teachers had said.

At the same time, Jesus was quite different from other teachers. He sifted the important from the trivial. Jesus is the only teacher who ever practiced perfectly what he taught. He embodied the will of God in his own life. Moreover, Jesus said some things that others had never said. For example, he gave love a new dimension. He taught that his disciples were to love their enemies (Matt. 5:44–47; Luke 6:27–28). Many people in his day agreed that the two great commandments are to love God with all one's being and one's neighbor as oneself, but few, if any, would have defined "neighbor" as Jesus did in the parable of the Good Samaritan (Luke 10:29–37). But even when Jesus used the same language as others, he gave it a new meaning because of his view of the kingdom of God, and of himself as the Messiah of that kingdom.

People recognized the distinctiveness of Jesus as a teacher especially in relation to his authority. For example, we read, "He taught them as one having authority, and not as the scribes" (Mark 1:22; compare Matt. 7:29). The scribes quoted authorities; Jesus spoke with authority. The ancient prophet had said, "Thus says the LORD"; but Jesus said, "I say to you." In fact, Jesus indicated that his authority was superior to the authority of the revered Law of Moses (see Matt. 5:38–42; Exod. 21:24; Lev. 24:20; Deut. 19:21).

But it was not only in relation to the scribes and the Law that people were made aware of Jesus' authority. He spoke directly to people and called for spontaneous decision: "Repent, and believe in the gospel." Jesus left no time, in his demand, for postponement, rationalization, and evasion (Luke 9:57–62). One writer says, "There is nothing in contemporary Judaism that corresponds to the immediacy with which he teaches."[1] His relation to God was so intimate that people felt themselves in the very presence of God as they stood in his presence. To accept Jesus' teaching requires the acceptance of the Teacher. He pulls away the blinds behind which we hide and addresses us at the point of our real need.

As a teacher Jesus used many different methods informally. It mattered not where it was: synagogue, home, hillside, by the sea, or in a boat. He spoke to multitudes and carried on conversations with individuals and small groups. Much of his teaching was analogical. That is, Jesus talked about everyday affairs in such a way that the hearer was invited to use what Jesus said as a window through which to see some aspect of the kingdom. Of course Jesus' most obvious use of analogy is found in the parable. The word "parable" means "something thrown alongside." As it was used by Jesus, a parable is a picture story thrown alongside the kingdom of God in such a way as to illuminate some aspect of the kingdom for those who are willing to see and hear. A parable is an extended simile and usually has one main point of comparison. An allegory (John 15:1–11) is an extended metaphor and the comparison is present throughout.

*Select a parable from Matthew 13 and interpret it on the basis of the definition given above.*

One of the most difficult problems in the whole of biblical interpretation concerns Jesus' purpose in using parables. This problem is occasioned by the statement found in Mark 4:10–12 (compare Matt. 13:10–15; Luke 8:9–10):

When he was alone, those who were around him along with the twelve asked him about the parables. And he said to them, "To you has been given the secret of the kingdom of God, but for those outside, everything comes in parables; in order that 'they may indeed look but not perceive, and may indeed listen, but not understand; so that they may not turn again, and be forgiven.'"

On the surface this statement sounds as if Jesus taught the multitudes in parables to keep them from understanding his message and to prevent their forgiveness. But our knowledge of Jesus from many passages in the Gospels tells us instantly that this cannot be the purpose of Jesus' parables. At least four different interpretations of the passage have been made.[2] A version of the one that seems most likely follows, but remember, it is but one of several possibilities.

The statement in question is, in part, a quotation from Isaiah 6:9–10. It is typical of Hebraic writers to express result in terms of purpose (see Ps. 51:4). Isaiah's preaching was to result in many deaf ears and blind eyes, and somehow this result was to be related to the sovereign providence of God. Isaiah tried to get through to his people with God's message, but many did not respond in faith and obedience. They saw but they did not perceive and turn in commitment to God's will.

Jesus had much the same experience as Isaiah. He came to seek and to save the lost, but few responded to his message in depth. The support of the crowds was based in part on their misunderstanding of his mission. By teaching in parables he challenged people to think through to the ultimate meaning of the parable and make a genuine heart response. Those who stopped with the surface meaning did not have ears to hear with understanding. Jesus was not interested in winning a popularity contest; he was interested in changing people. When people refused to see the truth of his parables, their hearts became increasingly hardened against his message. What was preeminently true of the parables was also true of all Jesus' teaching.

In addition to the spoken parable, Jesus made use of the acted parable (Mark 9:36–37; 11:4–8; 11:15–19), wisdom sayings (Luke 12:15; Matt. 16:26), paradox (Mark 10:31), counterquestion (Mark 11:30), hyperbole (Luke 14:26), and other literary forms. He was the Master Teacher.

*The Kingdom of God*

The kingdom of God was the chief theme of Jesus' teaching as well as of his preaching. God had long been acknowledged as the eternal King. The issue was how the fullness of God's reign as King was to be realized. There is a school of thought that says that God has already brought in the kingdom in the Person and work of Jesus. Another school looks for the coming of the kingdom entirely in the future. There is truth in both viewpoints, as we shall see, but neither by itself contains the whole truth.

The kingdom was *present* in the Person and work of Jesus. At his baptism Jesus understood his vocation to be the Servant-Messiah of God's kingdom. His temptations were related specifically to this vocation. Because most people did not recognize the nature of God's kingdom and Jesus' own messiahship, the kingdom in a sense was hidden. Peter's confession in the vicinity of Caesarea Philippi was a recognition of the presence of the kingdom in Jesus, albeit a confession that was only partially understood by Peter and the other disciples at that time. Jesus' interpretation of his miracles shows clearly that they were an evidence of the presence of the kingdom: "If it is by the finger of God that I cast out the demons, then the kingdom of God has come to you" (Luke 11:20; see also 10:9; Matt. 12:28; 10:7). Moreover, Jesus could speak of a person's entering the kingdom (Luke 16:16). He said to the Pharisees, "The kingdom of God is not coming with things that can be observed; nor will they say, 'Look, here it is!' or 'There it is!' For, in fact, the kingdom of God is among you" (Luke 17:20–21). In other words, the kingdom is not a political state to which one can point and say, "Here it is." But it was already in the midst of the Pharisees in the Person and ministry of Jesus.

In Old Testament times, the kingdom of God was manifested in God's people, but the people themselves were not the kingdom (kingship, rule).

In the days of Jesus' flesh, the kingdom was apparent in his disciples, but his disciples were not the kingdom. In our time, the kingdom is apparent in the life of the church, but the church is not the kingdom. Ultimately the kingdom is revealed in the interpersonal relationship between God and the believer.

The kingdom is also *future*. We shall note a few of Jesus' statements on this theme. We begin with Mark 9:1, a much debated passage. At least one writer has interpreted this verse primarily in relation to the cross:

> Truly, I tell you [thus asserting his divine authority], there are some standing here [his eyes were on his disciples] who will not taste death until they see that the kingdom of God has come with power [they will be executed by human hands but not before they have experienced the judging and redeeming power of God]. (9:1; compare Acts 1:54–56)

In short, Mark believed that just as the Messiah would enter into his power through dying (v. 31), so his disciples would see his kingdom coming with power through their own dying.[3]

Another interpreter lays stress on the resurrection as the fulfillment of this announcement:

> The saying contrasts a Kingdom already come with one to come "with power," or "with a miracle." The clue to its interpretation is in Rom. i. 3f., where Paul says that by the Resurrection God "appointed" Jesus as the Son of God "with power." When therefore Jesus says that the Reign of God will, at some not far distant date, come "with power," He is referring to His triumph in the Resurrection and what followed it.[4]

Other interpretations have been given: the coming of the Holy Spirit at Pentecost, the fall of Jerusalem in 70 C.E., the spread of the Christian faith throughout the Roman empire, and the second coming of Christ. In spite of their great variation, all these interpretations indicate that their authors view the fulfillment of Mark 9:1 as future in relation to the time it was spoken. However, from our present-day perspective only one could be future. Regardless of what coming of the kingdom Jesus had in mind in this statement, his crucifixion and resurrection, the coming of the Holy Spirit on his people, the spread of the Christian faith, and the final coming of the Lord are all vitally related to the kingdom of God.

Jesus taught his disciples to pray, "Your kingdom come" (Matt. 6:10; Luke 11:2). This petition involves, as indicated in Matthew's version of the prayer, the doing of God's will on earth as it is done in heaven. It means that the kingdom keeps on coming wherever the will of God is done. It also anticipates the final victory over all God's enemies.

At the Last Supper Jesus said, "Truly, I tell you, I will never again drink of the fruit of the vine until that day when I drink it new in the kingdom of God" (Mark 14:25; compare Matt. 8:11; Luke 13:28–30; 22:29–30). Here Jesus was speaking of the messianic banquet in the kingdom of the future. We read in Mark 13:32, "But about that day or hour no one knows, neither the angels in heaven, nor the Son, but only the Father." Apparently "that day" refers to the final coming of the Lord and the consummation of the kingdom.

Certain parables tend to form a bridge between the kingdom as a present reality and the kingdom as future event. The parable of the Seed Growing Secretly (Mark 4:26–29) involves a planting and a harvest. The emphasis is on God who by mysterious power causes the produce. The parable of the Mustard Seed (Matt. 13:31–32; Mark 4:30–32; Luke 13:18–19) gives assurance of the extension of the kingdom. And the parable of the Leaven (Matt. 13:33; Luke 13:20–21) speaks of the permeation of life by God's rule and the conquering of evil by God's hidden power.

The fact is the kingdom of God is past, present, and future. God has always been sovereign. In a unique sense God's sovereignty was present in the Person and work of Jesus and is present today in God's people as the Holy Spirit. Wherever people accept the Lordship of Christ and do the will of God, the kingdom has come. But all evil is not subjected. The kingdom in its fullness is yet to come. God's people live in the necessary tension between the kingdom that is present and the kingdom as it is yet to come.

Because the kingdom of God was such a central idea in the teaching of Jesus, and because it is so often not understood, let us look in greater detail at this particular aspect of Jesus' ministry of the spoken word.

## The Kingdom Life

### *The Parenthood of the King*

The nature of the kingdom life is rooted in the nature of the King. The King is not a tyrant but a parent. In ancient Israel God was described as both Father and Mother, and Israel as a whole was regarded as God's child (Exod. 4:22). It was implied that God was also the Parent of each individual Israelite (Ps. 103:13). God was known as Parent among the Jews. God was not considered Father or Mother in terms of procreation but in terms of care and authority.

Jesus placed great emphasis on the parenthood of God. He not only taught this by word of mouth, as the unique child of God but also mediated it to his disciples. God's authority is that of a loving parent.

A child's relation to parents is essentially one of interpersonal communication. On the child's part this means trust, obedience, love, dependence, petition, gratitude, and the like. Jesus manifested all of these qualities in his relation to his parents and to God. The heart of this communication is comparable to prayer. He lived a life of prayer. Luke tells us that he was praying at the time of his baptism (3:21) and that his last words on the cross were a prayer (23:46). Moreover, all the Gospels picture Jesus as a man of prayer. He taught his disciples to pray, "Our Father in heaven" (Matt. 6:9; compare Luke 11:2). It is as Father, Parent, that God gives the kingdom to the people (Luke 12:32). The Parent's children are siblings.

### Entering the Kingdom

Jesus placed a high value on every person and wanted everyone to enter the kingdom. To him people were more valuable than birds (Matt. 6:25–33), property (Matt. 12:12), and institutions, even the Sabbath (Mark 2:27; Matt. 12:9–14). He cared for all people and made a special effort to show his love for those who were cast out by others.

To Jesus people were in need of redemption as well as compassion. Sin is primarily a matter of the heart and the motivations of life (Mark 7:20–23). It is self-centeredness (Mark 8:34–37). It places one so heavily in debt that one can never pay out and is therefore thrown, in an absolute sense, on the mercy of God (Matt. 18:23–35; Luke 7:41–43; compare Matt. 6:12). In other words, humans are lost (Luke 15), but Jesus "came to seek out and to save the lost" (Luke 19:10) and call sinners to repentance. No one can earn a right to be in the kingdom (Matt. 20:1–16). One must put aside all pretense and enter like a child (Mark 10:15). Biological ancestry (Matt. 21:43; John 8:21–59) and social position (Matt. 21:31) have nothing to do with it, though riches may well be a barrier (Mark 10:23–31). While God makes it possible for a person to enter the kingdom, such entrance involves decision on the part of that person. Therefore Jesus said, "Repent, and believe in the gospel." This is precisely what happened in the case of Zacchaeus (Luke 19:1–10).

### Living in the Kingdom

Living in the kingdom means living a distinctive kind of life. Jesus said, "Be perfect, therefore, as your heavenly Father is perfect" (Matt. 5:48;

compare Luke 6:36). The heavenly Father, not some sinner like ourselves, is the standard of our life. The Messiah of the kingdom could set nothing less than God's perfection as that by which our lives are to be examined. But we say, Who can bear such teaching? Even when we do our best, our motives are not unmixed. We live in tension between what we are and what we ought to be. The peace of God that passes all understanding was not designed to remove that tension. It is in that tension that we throw ourselves anew on God's grace and mature in the direction of the Father's love. The disciple remains a sinner (Simon Peter, for example), but a sinner who is aiming at the will of God.

All of this means that the reign of God has first place on the disciple's priority list. Jesus expressed this in various ways: "Strive first for the kingdom of God and his righteousness, and all these things will be given to you as well" (Matt. 6:33). This means getting rid of anything that interferes with doing the will of God (Mark 9:42–48). It means sacrificing everything required by one's commitment to the kingdom (Matt. 13:44–46). Commitment to the kingdom is the same thing as commitment to God or to Jesus. This does not mean that other loyalties are nonexistent or unimportant, but that they can only be rightly honored when they are subjected to the highest allegiance. For example, citizens have a responsibility to their government, but their responsibility to God must govern the lesser allegiance (Mark 12:17 and parallels): "God alone is Lord of the conscience." Moreover, a disciple's commitment to Jesus must take precedence over commitment to family (Luke 14:26). "None of you can become my disciple if you do not give up all your possessions" (Luke 14:33).

The ethic of Jesus is the ethic of God's love. God's will is expressed in love for us. Our response is to love God with all our being and our neighbor as ourselves (Mark 12:28–34 and parallels). Even to attempt to live by such a standard means that transformation has already begun to take place in us. Our actions are to be governed by wholehearted devotion to God, an outgoing commitment to our neighbor, and a genuine respect for ourselves as children of the heavenly King.

Jesus still says, "Unless your righteousness exceeds that of the scribes and Pharisees, you will never enter the kingdom of heaven [God]" (Matt. 5:20). The scribes and Pharisees of whom Jesus spoke led exemplary lives. Jesus' disciples are called to live even more righteously as an expression of their new relation to God. The motivations of life are internal. Jesus calls people to live out the ultimate intention of the Law, not its letter. This is clear in his teaching concerning the Sabbath (Mark 2:13–3:6), murder (Matt. 5:21–26), adultery (Matt. 5:27–30), marriage (Matt.

5:31–32; Mark 10:11–12; Luke 16:18), vows (Matt. 5:33–37), retaliation (Matt. 5:38–42), love (Matt. 5:43–48), and piety (Matt. 6:1–18). Kingdom living is deeply happy living (Matt. 5:1–12). It is based on God's forgiveness of us (Luke 15:11–32; 18:9–14). And it requires our repeated forgiveness of others (Matt. 6:12; Luke 17:3–4). We are to be good stewards of God's gifts (Matt. 25:14–30), but we are to remember that "one's life does not consist in the abundance of possessions" (Luke 12:15). We are to be characterized by humility and service (Mark 10:43–44; Luke 14:7–11).

*The Sermon on the Mount (Matt. 5–7; compare Luke 6:20–49; 12:22–31; 11:9–13)*

This so-called "sermon" is actually teaching, according to Matthew (5:2). It deals with life in the kingdom of God. Some have made it into a series of rules and thereby defeated its purpose. Others have found it irrelevant. But it is not a set of new laws, and it is vitally relevant. It is not to be dissolved into general principles. Rather it is to be read and applied by each of us, as the Spirit leads, to our particular situations. Who is the enemy that I am to love? On whom have I been passing judgment? Where is my treasure? On what occasions do I practice piety to be seen of others?

*Read the Sermon on the Mount and the parallels in Luke (see above) with the aid of the outline that follows. Fill in the outline and change it as you see fit.*

*Ask the Spirit to help you apply Jesus' words specifically to your own life. The Spirit will help us but never makes puppets of us. We are accountable for the decisions we reach.*

## THE CHARTER OF THE KINGDOM

Introduction (Matt. 5:1–2)
The Disciple of the Kingdom (Matt. 5:3–16)
    Characteristics (the Beatitudes)
    Purpose: To Be Salt and Light
Kingdom Living and the Law ( Matt. 5:17–48)

| The General Relationship | Truthfulness |
|---|---|
| Murder | Revenge |
| Adultery | Love of Enemy |
| Divorce | |

Acts of Devotion in Kingdom Life (Matt. 6:1–18)
Almsgiving
Prayer
Fasting
Kingdom Proverbs (Matt. 6:19–7:12)

| | |
|---|---|
| Treasure in Heaven | The Measure of Judgment |
| The Lamp of the Body | Pearls Before Swine |
| God and Mammon | Asking God |
| Faith and Anxiety | The Golden "Rule" |

Tests of Kingdom Living (Matt. 7:13–27)

| | |
|---|---|
| Entering the Narrow Gate | Doing the Father's Will |
| Bearing Good Fruit | Building upon the Rock |

Conclusion (Matt. 7:28–29)

## Jesus' Ministry of the Mighty Deed

If there are those who underestimate the ministry of the spoken word, there are even more who underestimate Jesus' ministry of the mighty deed. This is a serious mistake. The evidence for his miracles is as solid as that for his preaching, teaching, death, and resurrection. Miracles are recorded in all four Gospels. The overall count is usually given at thirty-seven. Of these, eighteen are found in only one Gospel, six in two Gospels, twelve in three Gospels, and one in four Gospels. The order of the Gospels according to the number of miracles included is as follows: Luke, twenty-two; Matthew, twenty-one; Mark, nineteen; and John, eight. Almost a third of Mark deals with miracle, directly or indirectly.[5] In fact there are five references to miracles in the first chapter alone of Mark.

There is further evidence of the important place of miracle in Jesus' ministry. The following summary of his ministry from Matthew 4:23 is typical:

> Jesus went throughout Galilee, *teaching* in their synagogues and *proclaiming* the good news of the kingdom and *curing* every disease and every sickness among the people (compare Matt. 9:35; Mark 1:39; Luke 6:17–18).

"He healed" is a recurring expression of the Gospels. Moreover, the Twelve were entrusted by Jesus with a ministry similar to his own (Matt. 10:1, 7–8; Mark 6:13; Luke 9:1, 6; 10:9). At the synagogue in Nazareth Jesus interpreted his mission in relation to Isaiah 61:1–2, and he saw in this passage a combined ministry of the spoken word and the mighty deed. The Spirit of the Lord anointed him to this task. When John the Baptist was in prison, he sent disciples to inquire of Jesus, "Are you the one who is to come, or are we to wait for another?" Jesus replied, "Go and tell John what you hear and see: the blind receive their sight, the lame walk, the lepers are cleansed, the deaf hear, the dead are raised, and the poor have good news brought to them" (Matt. 11:2–6). His miracles were evidence of his compassion for people (Mark 1:41; Luke 7:13) and a sign that the kingdom of God was present in his ministry and Person (Luke 11:20).

## Categories of Miracles

### Miracles of Healing, Including Exorcisms

Exorcism refers to the casting out of evil spirits or demons. Most of the miracles fall into the category of healing. A few examples are the two blind men (Matt. 9:27–31), the demoniac in the synagogue at Capernaum (Mark 1:21–28; Luke 4:31–37), and Peter's mother-in-law (Matt. 8:14–17; Mark 1:29–34; Luke 4:38–41).

> *Read the account(s) of at least one of these miracles and seek to answer these questions about it: What did this miracle mean to Jesus and to those who witnessed it? What did it mean in the life of the early church? What does it mean now?*

### Miracles of Restoration

These are restorations to life in the flesh in this present world and therefore to be distinguished from Jesus' own resurrection and the resurrection of the dead as that is ordinarily understood. In other words, a restored person still has to die again. A resurrected person does not die again. Only three of Jesus' miracles may be placed in this category: the raising of the widow's son at Nain (Luke 7:11–13), the raising of Lazarus (John 11:43), and the raising of Jairus' daughter (Mark 5:21–43 and parallels).

> *Study one or all of these miracles as you did those in the preceding category.*

### Nature Miracles

Examples of the nature miracles are stilling the storm (Mark 4:35 and parallels), walking on the water (Mark 6:45–52 and parallels), and feeding the five thousand (Mark 6:30–44 and parallels).

*Examine one or more of these miracles as you did those in the two preceding classifications.*

Because miracle is a difficult subject for many people, we shall now attempt to look at the miracles of Jesus in the larger setting of miracle in general.

## Toward an Understanding of Miracle

Many think of miracle as "a suspension or violation of a law of nature," but this was not the approach of the biblical writers. There are three primary concepts of miracle in both Testaments: mighty act, wonder, and sign. A *mighty act* is a special manifestation of the power of God to which God's people are to respond in faith, praise, gratitude, and witness. A *wonder* is that which produces amazement in those who experience it. It corresponds to the basic meaning of our word "miracle," which is derived from the Latin *miraculum*, "wonder." A *sign* is that which points out or distinguishes by pointing beyond itself to its Author. In actual usage these three meanings overlap and sometimes refer to the same events. Objective occurrence and personal appropriation in faith are present in these biblical concepts. God's goodness, power, personal activity, special revelation, and redemption are usually present in miracle.

## Miracles Philosophically Considered

Philosophy, by and large, is not a common undertaking. Biblical people generally were not given to this kind of exercise, but it is an inevitable undertaking in our kind of world. Some philosophers are hostile to miracle. Pantheists say the universe is God; deists think God leaves the universe to tick itself down like a watch; and some naturalists say there is no personal God.

But miracle is philosophically defensible. The reason and purpose observable in the universe imply a personal God. Belief in mere Chance, spelled with a capital "C," is to attribute purpose to purposelessness, a form of magic. The biblical writers were not concerned with the laws of nature in our precise terms. Yet they recognized a dependability in God's activity. For example, we read in Genesis 8:22 that "as long as the earth endures, seedtime and harvest, cold and heat, summer and winter, day and night, shall not cease." Laws, as we conceive them, are human descriptions of regularities in the universe. The Cause lies behind the law. Harry Emerson Fosdick is reported to have said, "Man works on nature and produces invention; God works on nature and produces miracle."

An airplane does not break the law of gravity but is able to fly by using many laws of nature. Nature is not a closed system to the God who made it, and God does not have to work against divine law to produce miracle. But humans, as well as nature, are the objects of miracle. The gospel tells of a God who can break the "determinisms" of life. If this were not true, regeneration would be impossible, and there would be no gospel at all. God is not a glorified supercomputer. God is our heavenly Parent. But to believe in a God who can produce "spiritual" miracles of human transformation and to deny God's direct healing of the physical body is an inconsistency amounting to philosophical schizophrenia. A person is a body-spirit unity, and God is the Lord of the whole person.

*Read the account of the paralytic borne of four in Mark 2:1–12. Jesus forgave the man's sin and healed his afflicted body. He was interested in saving the whole man, and still is.*

## Miracles Historically Considered

In the Old Testament, miracles affirm God's personal direction of history. They are usually prominent at the times of great crisis. We have already noted the unanimous testimony of the Gospels to Jesus' working of miracles. Many miracles are also recorded in the book of Acts. Miracle as such cannot be denied on the basis of historical evidence. Those who deny miracle to Jesus and others in biblical days do so on the basis of presuppositions hostile to the presuppositions of the biblical faith itself. This does not mean that all miracle stories in the Bible are to be understood in exactly the same way. Each requires that it be studied carefully in its own setting to discover precisely what constitutes the miracle and what its meaning is. In other words, we should always ask, What is the purpose of this miracle?

## Miracles Theologically Considered

Miracles stand at the very center of the biblical message, not on the circumference. The mighty acts of God are miracles. The Bible is a lengthened confession of faith in the mighty acts of God. In a sense, the Old Testament is an elongation of the short confessions of Israel's faith to which we have frequently referred. In a sense, the New Testament is an elongation of the confession expressed in the apostolic preaching. This preaching was an announcement of the mighty acts of God in Jesus Christ. At Pentecost Jews who had gathered from various parts of the world said of those who witnessed to Jesus, "In our own languages we hear them speaking about God's deeds of power" (Acts 2:11). Some of these miracles are then enumerated by Peter in his sermon to them: the fulfillment of prophecy, the "deeds of power, wonders and signs that God did through him [Jesus] among you," the crucifixion of Jesus, the resurrection and exaltation of Jesus, and the outpouring of the Holy Spirit (read Acts 2:1–47). In other words, Peter preached miracles from beginning to end. The death of Jesus is included among the miracles, not because murder is miraculous, but because God revealed and let loose divine redemptive power through that death. To make a murder into an instrument of the salvation of humankind is miracle indeed.

The miracles that Jesus performed in the days of his flesh were associated with compassion, the reign of God, and the repentance of people. He was not concerned to attract notoriety to himself, but he expected people to repent when they were confronted by his mighty works: "Then he began to reproach the cities in which most of his deeds of power had been done, because they did not repent" (Matt. 11:20; compare Luke 10:13). He still calls people to repentance by his mighty works.

In the final analysis, Jesus is the supreme Miracle himself. If he had not been a miracle, he would not have been Jesus.

## Miracles Religiously Considered

Perhaps we should have begun our study of miracles at the point of religious experience, for in this dimension we recognize ourselves in face-to-face contact with God. Miracle is in the sphere of revelation and is to be appropriated in faith. The Bible speaks from faith to faith. H. H. Farmer, a great British theologian, has helped a great deal in appreciating miracle in the religious dimension.[6] He tells of a mother who was informed by the physicians that so far as they could judge her child could not get well. Whereupon she called another Christian to join her in prayer to God that God restore her child. The two friends prayed, "and within a few hours the child was on the way to a recovery which confounded all the experience of the doctors, as they were frank to admit, even including one whose whole philosophy of life tended to profound scorn of 'all that sort of thing.' " These two friends did not say, "This is providential," but "This is a miracle."

Farmer has outlined the elements in such an experience of miracle. First, there is the recognition of serious need and human inadequacy. Second, there is a turning to God for help. Third, there is the redemptive answer to the prayer. And fourth, there is the response of joyous wonder and gratitude. Many of us have had such experiences, and no amount of rationalization will ever convince us that this was something other than miracle. This is not to say that God does not work through medical science. God most assuredly does. But God also works through faith, prayer, love, and hope. Through the particular and special God lets us know that God is constantly working in all the affairs of life. God is personal in dealing with us. God is our heavenly Parent.

But miracle may also take place when God does not grant the request but answers in another way. For example, Paul once described a problem of his as a thorn in the flesh. He turned to God in prayer for deliverance. He was not delivered from the thorn, but God answered him redemptively, "My grace is sufficient for you, for power is made perfect in weakness." The miracle is that this grace enabled Paul to boast of Christ's power (2 Cor. 12:1–10).

Do you believe in a personal God who is your Creator, Sustainer, and Savior? Do you believe that Jesus lived the only life wholly committed to the will of God? Do you believe that he died for you and that he was raised from the dead? Do you believe in the transformation of life by the Spirit of God? Do you believe in direct revelatory answer to prayer? If you do, you believe in miracle. But more than that, if you are a new creation in Christ, you *are* a miracle. Biblical faith is miraculous faith. The Bible, the church, and the Christian life cannot be accounted for apart from the mighty acts of God that center in Jesus Christ.

## Jesus' Ministry of the Given Life

### Jesus' Interpretation of His Death

Jesus' whole life was a ministry dedicated to God's will and the service of those around him. But this dedication involved the ministry of suffering and death. At his baptism, he accepted the ministry of the Servant-Messiah. And he knew that the servant referred to in Isaiah 42:1 (see Mark 1:11) was the same as the servant in Isaiah 53. He was tempted to dodge the ministry of the Suffering Servant. But from the outset it was his meat to do the will of the One who sent him and accomplish God's work (John 3:34).

Early in his ministry Jesus indicated that he (the Bridegroom) would be taken away from his disciples (Mark 2:18–20). After Peter's confession near Caesarea Philippi, he made it clear that there was a divine necessity laid on him as the Son of Man to suffer and die (Mark 8:31–33; compare 9:30–32; 10:33–34). The baptism of the cross referred to in Mark 10:38 was to be the fulfillment of the commitment made at the baptism in the Jordan. Undoubtedly Isaiah 53 played a large part in Jesus' thinking about his ministry through death. For he combined the vocation of the heavenly Son of Man with that of the Suffering Servant when he said, "The Son of Man came not to be served but to serve, and to give his life a ransom for many" (Mark 10:45). His life of service was to issue in a death of service.

In our study of the life of Jesus, we noted the connection of the Last Supper with redemption, the new covenant, and atonement. The "cup" at the Last Supper and the "cup" of Gethsemane recall the fact that "cup" usually refers to God's wrath against sin. When this fact is coupled with the cry of desolation (Mark 15:34) and the call to be the Servant of the Lord, it is clear that Jesus thought of himself as pouring out his life in atonement for the sins of others (compare Luke 22:42). Thereby he would be accomplishing the objective of the kingdom for which he came into the world.

## The New Testament Doctrine of Atonement

Throughout the New Testament Jesus' death is interpreted as making atonement for sin. But this does not mean that his death in this regard stands apart from his incarnation, life, and resurrection. The mighty acts of God in him are all parts of one mighty act of salvation. Atonement is the means by which right relations with God are effected. The following presuppositions underlie this doctrine: (1) God and humankind should be at one; (2) God is holy love; (3) humankind acts as a rebel against God; and (4) God judges the rebel. This judgment is both negative and positive, but its ultimate purpose is redemptive. For God does for humankind through Jesus what humankind cannot do for itself. God bears the ultimate consequences of sin, assuming them directly. By faith we may know that Christ has died for us according to the scriptures. In the light of what has been said, our definition of atonement may now be enlarged: atonement is God's work through Christ whereby God brings to bear love and justice through judgment on the sinner and the sin that the sinner may be at one with God. "That is, in Christ God was reconciling the world to himself" (2 Cor. 5:19).

1. Through his death and resurrection Jesus dealt the crucial blow to Satan and the demonic forces (see Luke 22:53; John 12:31). Jesus battled with Satan in the wilderness, in his ministry, and in Gethsemane and

bound "the strong man." But through his death and resurrection he dealt him the mortal wound. That is, Jesus' death has cosmic significance.

2. Jesus died in behalf of others. Therefore, we speak of his atonement as vicarious.

*Meditate on each of the following statements in this connection.*

"This is my blood of the covenant, which is poured out for many" (Mark 14:24). There are allusions here to Exodus 24:8; Jeremiah 31:31–34; and Isaiah 53:12.

"Christ died for our sins in accordance with the scriptures" (1 Cor. 15:3). To what scriptures is Paul referring?

"He who did not withhold his own Son, but gave him up for all of us, will he not with him also give us everything else?" (Rom. 8:32). What elements do you find in this quotation not present in the two preceding ones?

"We do see Jesus, who for a little while was made lower than the angels, now crowned with glory and honor because of the suffering of death, so that by the grace of God he might taste death for everyone" (Heb. 2:9). What factors are associated with Jesus' death in this verse? In what sense did Jesus "taste death for everyone"?

"I lay down my life for the sheep" (John 10:15). How does the metaphor of the Shepherd and his sheep add enrichment to what has already been said on the subject of atonement?

3. Jesus died in the place of others. This is known as substitutionary atonement. Obviously such atonement is also vicarious.

*Reflect on the statements that follow as you did on those in the preceding section:*

"The Son of Man came not to be served but to serve, and to give his life a ransom for [instead of] many" (Mark 10:45). The word "ransom" means "price of release." The word "for" literally means "instead of or in place of."

"For our sake he made him to be sin who knew no sin, so that in him we might become the righteousness of God" (2 Cor. 5:21). Christ so thoroughly identified himself with us in our need that we may become identified with him in his victory.

"You know that you were ransomed from the futile ways inherited from your ancestors, not with perishable things like silver or gold, but with the precious blood of Christ, like that of a lamb without defect or blemish" (1 Peter 1:18–19; compare 2:24). What are the "futile ways" of the ancestors? The idea of substitution is here clearly associated with sacrifice. That

Jesus' death was sacrificial is evident in the concept of the Servant, in the accounts of the Last Supper, and in various places in the New Testament. Jesus is "our paschal lamb" (1 Cor. 5:7), "a sacrifice of atonement [or mercy seat] by his blood" (Rom. 3:25), "a fragrant offering and sacrifice to God" (Eph. 5:2), high priest and offering (Hebrews), and "the Lamb of God, who takes away the sin of the world" (John 1: 29).

4. Jesus died as the representative of others. "For the love of Christ urges us on, because we are convinced that one has died for all; therefore all have died. And he died for all, so that those who live might live no longer for themselves, but for him who died and was raised for them" (2 Cor. 5:14–15). "As one man's trespass led to condemnation for all, so one man's act of righteousness leads to justification and life for all. For just as by the one man's disobedience the many were made sinners, so by the one man's obedience the many will be made righteous" (Rom. 5:18–19). In the context of Paul's thought this means that, as Adam represents all humankind in its sin and condemnation, so Christ (the last Adam) represents the new humanity in its obedience and justification.

5. The cross was the necessary issue of Jesus' way of life, for it is only as "a grain of wheat falls into the earth and dies" that "it bears much fruit" (John 12:24 ). What does this say about the issue of our way of life?

6. The revelation of God's love in the "lifted up" Jesus has tremendous power to draw people to him (John 12:32). Another way to say this is found in the Synoptics: "The curtain of the temple was torn in two, from top to bottom" (Matt. 27:51; Mark 15:38; Luke 23:45). "Here was the decisive revelatory event: man's [sic] age-long fumbling quest was at an end."[7] The poured-out life of Christ, offered through Eternal Spirit, purifies the conscience "from dead works to worship the living God" (Heb. 9:14 ).

## Response to the Atonement

The atonement is what God has done for us in Christ, but it anticipates our response. How are we to respond?

1. By faith we identify ourselves with Christ who has identified himself with us. In this identification he does for us what we cannot do for ourselves. Mark put this matter this way: "If any want to become my followers, let them deny themselves and take up their cross and follow me. For those who want to save their life will lose it, and those who lose their life for my sake, and the sake of the gospel, will save it" (Mark 8:34–35). Jesus has a cross, and Jesus' disciple also has a cross. The disciple's cross

does not make atonement but means death to self-centeredness and surrender to Christ. Indeed, it may mean literal death. Jesus taught his disciples to pray, "Thy will be done." He prayed the same prayer in Gethsemane, and he enacted it on Calvary. The die-to-live principle applies to the disciple also. It is only as we die that we rise and bear fruit. It is only as we die to self-centeredness that we live in true freedom. Following Jesus means a daily living according to the cross.

2. We also respond to the atonement by confessing our sin and accepting God's forgiveness. All need God's forgiveness, for all are sinners. But many in our contemporary society refuse to admit this and try to make their morality a substitute for forgiveness. Humans, however, are unable to live the life they know they ought to live and have "moral-failure complexes," similar to inferiority complexes. This attitude creates a horrible condition within. But when one confesses one's sin to God and accepts forgiveness, one begins to live. Of course the person who does this sees the need for making right the wrongs done against others insofar as that is possible, but this is not what brings forgiveness; it is a consequence of forgiveness. Christ died for us because God's forgiveness is not cheap indulgence but costly love. In Christ God bore the cost of our sin. Christ died once for all and lives to make intercession for us as the heavenly Priest (Heb. 7:25).[8]

> When I survey the wondrous cross
> On which the Prince of glory died,
> My richest gain I count but loss,
> And pour contempt on all my pride.[9]

# The Person of Jesus

*P*eople do not come to know Jesus Christ and receive him as Savior and Lord by hearing his name repeated seventy times in a vacuum. The Old Testament, the New Testament, the church, the world, the Spirit all have a part in helping us to know who he is. And our task of affirming who he is never ceases. The history of God's deliverance is the story of the Savior. Christology (the doctrine of the Person and work of Christ) and theology are, in the final analysis, one. The doctrine of Christ and the doctrine of God are, from the Christian point of view, inseparable.

## The Christ Who Was to Come

By "the Christ who was to come" we mean the one toward whom the faith of Israel pointed and in whom that faith was fulfilled. Our study of the Old Testament has developed this theme in some detail. For a brief review of the subject, reread that part of Chapter 14 entitled "The Jewish Hope."

## The Christ Who Did Come

There are so many names and titles by which Jesus is identified in the New Testament that it is impossible to list all of them here.

*Therefore, we concentrate on some of the most prominent. As you read what is said about each and look up some of the scripture references, write down in your notebook your personal response to each designation of Jesus. For example, what does it mean to you to accent Jesus as the Messiah?*

## Messiah

The Hebrew-Aramaic word *messiah* means "anointed one" and was used in Israel with reference to both kings and priests. The corresponding Greek word is *christos*, from which we get the word "Christ." We have seen that the Jewish hope was expressed in terms of different kinds of messiahs. In the New Testament the Messiah is often thought of as the Son of David.

That Jesus was the Messiah is implicit in the accounts of his baptism and temptation. While he did not deny his messiahship, he did not favor the use of the term in his early ministry because most of his people associated it with a political kingdom and a military deliverer. However, he did not reject the title when it was applied to him by Peter near Caesarea Philippi, and he seems to have acknowledged it at his trial before the high priest. The charge on the basis of which he was sentenced to death by Pilate was that he claimed to be a messiah. The title Messiah (Christ) soon came to be regarded as a part of his name. Therefore we often speak of him as Jesus Christ. All the writers of the New Testament regarded Jesus of Nazareth as the Christ, for his resurrection had clarified for the early Christian community what was meant by his messiahship. This would have been impossible, however, if there had not been messianic teachings and acts that needed clearer recognition.

## Son of God

In ancient times Israel was regarded as God's son (Exod. 4:22–23; Hos. 11:1; compare Deut. 14:1). Moreover, the king of God's people, a very real human king, as their representative, was also considered to be God's son (2 Sam. 7:14; Pss. 2:7; 89:27). While Jesus did not become the Son of God at the resurrection, faith in his Sonship was undergirded by that event (Rom. 1:4). In both the Synoptics and John, Jesus is called the Son of God. Strange as it seems, this title is mainly aimed at affirming Jesus' humanity.

Occasionally the title is closely related to the idea of messiahship (for example, Mark 14:61; Matt. 16:16), but in the case of most of its occurrences in the Gospels and in the other books of the New Testament it refers more specifically to Jesus' unique relationship with God. As a boy in the Temple, Jesus expressed a consciousness of a special filial relationship with God (Luke 2: 49). This consciousness was present on the occasion of his baptism and temptation and was probably present all the time.

In the parable of the Vineyard and the Tenants (Mark 12:1–9), Jesus came to be seen as the son who was killed. One of the clearest statements of the special Parent-Son relationship is found in Matthew 11:27 and Luke 10:22 (compare Matt. 10:32). According to John, Jesus is the "only" Son (1:14, 18; 3:16); that is, the one especially beloved. He and the Father are one (10:30). The Son is in the Father, and the Father in the Son (14:11). Yet the Son obeys the Father (5:30; 6:38) and prays to the Father (14:16; 17:1–26).

## Son of Man

Earlier we saw that the primary background of this title lies in Daniel 7:13 and Jewish interpretations of this passage although Ezekiel's use of the term went in quite a different direction. In the New Testament, "Son of Man" is largely confined to the Gospels, and in them exclusively to the lips of Jesus. This was his favorite title for himself. Before his birth some Jews apparently had identified the Son of man with a heavenly divine figure who would come as deliverer. In any case, the Son of man title was not laden with political and military associations. Rather, its emphasis was on the divine character of the Savior. Jesus related the title to that of Messiah (Mark 14:61–62) and to that of Servant (Mark 10:45). You will recall that the "one like a human being" (literally, "Son of Man") in Daniel represented both leader and people. Jesus as the Son of man had (and has) a people, of whom the Twelve were the original core. The title also looks to the future (Matt. 19:28). The question of Jesus' divinity, not his humanity, is particularly at stake in this title.

## Servant of God

Considerable attention has already been given to this title in our study of the ministry of Jesus. It seems to have played a major role in Jesus' thinking at his baptism, throughout his ministry, and in connection with his death. He united it with the title Son of man (Mark 8:31; 10:45) and connected it with the interpretation of the Last Supper (Matt. 26:28). In his preaching of the gospel, Peter laid emphasis on Jesus as God's Servant (Acts 3:13, 26; compare 4:27, 30). And Paul recognized him as God's Servant in his humiliation and in his exaltation (Phil. 2:5–11; compare Isa. 52:13–53:12).

Closely related to the Servant of God is the Lamb of God. According to Isaiah 53:7 the servant of the LORD is "like a lamb that is led to the slaughter." The Ethiopian eunuch was reading this passage when Philip the evangelist joined him and "proclaimed to him the good news about Jesus" (Acts 8:26–40). As the Servant of God, Jesus is also "the Lamb of God, who takes away the sin of the world" (John 1:29; compare 1:36; 1 Peter 1:19).

## Prophet

Jesus was sometimes called rabbi, teacher, and master, as well as prophet. He was classified by others as a prophet on various occasions (for example, see Mark 6:15; Matt. 21:11). Apparently he thought of himself as a prophet (Luke 13:33), yet more than a prophet. The servant in the Servant Songs of Isaiah is depicted as a prophet (see chap. 11). Some feel that Matthew was thinking of Jesus as the new Moses, God's prophet (Deut. 34:10), giving the new Law on the new Sinai in the Sermon on the Mount (chaps. 5–7). If this is true, the new Law is not law in any literal sense. It is the guide to kingdom living. Whether this approach to the Sermon on the Mount is correct or not, Jesus was considered the new Moses (Acts 3:22; compare 7:37; Deut. 18:15–16; John 6:14; 7:40). Such titles as prophet and teacher tended to pass out of use because they were felt to be inadequate.[1]

## Priest

In the Letter to the Hebrews, Jesus is presented as the High Priest. In this capacity, he was made like us in every respect and was tempted in all points as we are, yet without sinning (2:17–18; 4:14–16). Therefore, he is in a position to sympathize with us and help us in our times of need. "He learned obedience through what he suffered" (5:8); not that he was ever disobedient, but that he came to know on the basis of actual experience what it means to obey. He is not a *theoretical* Savior.

He is a royal priest after the order of Melchizedek (chaps. 5–10; see Ps. 110:4; Gen. 14:17–20). Melchizedek was a priest-king of whose ancestry, birth, and death the Old Testament gives no record. In this sense he was without beginning of days and end of life. There is, then, a certain resemblance between Melchizedek and Christ, since Christ's priesthood is eternal—without beginning or end. The Levitical priests died, but Jesus continues a priest forever. Moreover, they had to offer sacrifices for sins repeatedly, but Jesus offered himself once for all (7:27; 9:28; 10:10). Through him we have access to God.

## Mediator

A mediator, in the sense in which we are using the term, is one who stands between God and humankind either to bring about reconciliation or to establish or maintain a covenant between the two.[2] Moses, the prophets, the priests, and the kings were mediators of the earlier covenant. But Jesus was and is a mediator who in his Person and work transcends all mediators, so that we may say, "There is also one mediator between God and humankind, Christ Jesus himself human, who gave himself a ransom for all" (1 Tim. 2:5–6). Indeed, he is the mediator of the new covenant (Heb. 9:15; 12:24), which transcends the Sinaitic covenant (Heb. 8:6; compare Rom. 8:3). "The efficacy of his mediation . . . rests on the fact that he is the Son of God, able to represent God perfectly, and also partaker of flesh and blood and therefore a merciful and faithful high priest."[3]

In other words, Jesus' mediatorial work as Reconciler to God and as Minister of the new covenant is based on who he is. The titles we have thus far studied and those that are yet to be studied emphasize both his kinship to God and his kinship to us. The conception by the Holy Spirit emphasizes his kinship to God; his birth of the Virgin Mary, his kinship to us. Jesus claimed a unique Sonship (Matt. 11:27; compare Mark 8:38), and the apostles in their preaching acknowledge him as Son of God and Lord.

Although Jesus was and is the Son of God, the Gospels make it clear that he was truly human. This is not only true in the Synoptics, it is also true in the Gospel and Letters of John, where his Sonship to the Father is emphasized so strongly. "The Word became [real] flesh" (John 1:14; compare 1 John 4:2). Perhaps Jesus' most human words from the cross are "I am thirsty," and they are found only in John (19:28). We read in 2 John 7, "Many deceivers have gone out into the world, those who do not confess that Jesus Christ has come in the flesh; any such person is the deceiver and the antichrist!" Jesus was the son of Mary, the son of David, the son of Abraham, and the son of Adam. He "increased in wisdom and in years, and in divine and human favor" (Luke 2:52). His teachings are filled with a knowledge of everyday affairs in first-century Palestine. He hungered, grew weary, and slept. He claimed ignorance of the time of the consummation of the kingdom (Mark 13:32). He was tempted in every respect as we are (Heb. 4:15). He lived as a man of prayer and faith. His suffering and death were real. There was no hypocrisy in his humanity. Yet which of us can convict him of sin? His temptation, unlike ours, did not issue in sinning. Even as we behold the humanity of the Master, we are constrained to cry out, "This man is the Son of God!"

Centuries before Jesus was born, Job cried out to God, "There is no umpire between us, who might lay his hand on us both" (9:33). Job felt the need of a mediator. Though the New Testament contains no quotation of this verse, Jesus Christ answers the need of the human heart expressed in Job's words. Indeed he has his hand on God, for he is "Very God of Very God," and he has his hand on humankind, for he is truly human. There have been, from early times, those who have denied the deity of Christ in their theory or in their practice; and there have been others who have denied his humanity in the same way. But the church has not been willing to settle for half-truth.

We do not have to be able to explain the incarnation in order to accept it. But it is even harder to attempt to explain it away. The incarnation tells us that God cares for us not only enough to send a prophet to speak to us, but enough to become involved directly in our nasty predicament. God in Jesus comes to us and sits where we sit. Jesus gets his hands dirty and his feet wet. He cries over the city and beside the grave. He takes the heavy load of our sin to Calvary. He triumphs over the forces of evil and says, "Don't be afraid. I am with you."

## The Christ Who Is with Us

Jesus Christ is still with his people. The titles that have already been examined carry their meaning beyond the days of Jesus' earthly life. There are additional titles that came into special prominence after his resurrection. As the risen Christ he assured his disciples of his continuing presence: "Remember, I am with you always, to the end of the age" (Matt. 28:20). There is a similar promise in John 14:18, "I will not leave you orphaned; I am coming to you." This coming is by context closely connected with the coming of the Holy Spirit.

### Lord

To appreciate this title, knowledge of its background is an asset. In the Hellenistic world, rulers were often called "Lord." Moreover, some rulers were considered divine. The word was also used in relation to certain so-called deities. But the primary background is found in Judaism itself and in the Greek Old Testament. In the Septuagint the Greek word for "Lord" translates the Hebrew words meaning "sovereign" and also the term "YHWH," the personal name of God.

In the days of his flesh, the word "Lord" was probably applied to Jesus occasionally with the meaning "Master." But in his interpretation of Psalm 110 (Mark 12:35–37), he paved the way for a more exalted understanding of the term in relation to himself. The disciples had an allegiance to the

One who had selected them. They had witnessed his mighty deeds and his teaching with authority.

But it was the resurrection that gave the word "Lord" a new dimension when applied to Jesus. "Jesus is Lord" may have been the earliest baptismal confession of faith. Paul wrote to the Romans (10:9), "If you confess with your lips that Jesus is Lord and believe in your heart that God raised him from the dead, you will be saved." To the Corinthians he wrote, "No one can say 'Jesus is Lord' except by the Holy Spirit" (1 Cor. 12:3). In fact, saints (Christians) were those who called "on the name of our Lord Jesus Christ, both their Lord and ours" (1 Cor. 1:2). Sunday, the day of his resurrection, became known as "the Lord's day" (Rev. 1:10; compare Acts 20:7). Because of Jesus' ministry as the Suffering Servant, God exalted him and gave him the name Lord (Phil. 2:11). Christ is our Lord, and we are his willing slaves. He gives the orders, and we obey. Or do we?

## Head

Very closely related to the idea of Lordship is that of Headship, for it too expresses authority. The most inclusive statement about Christ as Head is Ephesians 1:22–23—"And he has put all things under his feet and has made him the head over all things for the church, which is his body, the fullness of him who fills all in all." In other words, Christ is the Head of the universe and the church (compare Eph. 4:15; 5:23; Col. 1:18; 2:19; 1 Cor. 11:3). He is also the Head of all angelic powers (Col. 2:10; compare 1 Peter 3:22).

## Savior

In the Old Testament God is the Savior. Sometimes God is also called Savior in the New Testament. Though Jesus is occasionally referred to as Savior in some of the earlier books of the New Testament, this title is more frequently applied in certain of the later books. Of course the name Jesus is the same as the Hebrew Joshua, which means "The Lord is salvation." There is a play on this meaning in Matthew 1:21—"She [Mary] will bear a son, and you are to name him Jesus, for he will save his people from their sins." In the message of the angel to the shepherds, Jesus is called Savior (Luke 2:11). God brought Israel a Savior as promised (Acts 11:23; compare 5:31). Christ is not only the Head of the church but also its Savior (Eph. 5:23). In John 4:42 (compare 1 John 4:14) Samaritans confess Jesus as "the Savior of the world." He is also called "our Savior" (Titus 1:3; 3:6), "our Lord and Savior Jesus Christ" (2 Peter 1:11; 2:20; 3:18), "our great God and Savior Jesus Christ" (Titus 2:13), "our God and Savior Jesus Christ" (2 Peter 1:1), and "the Lord and Savior" (2 Peter 3:2). The Bible as a whole tells the story of salvation, which is the story of the Savior.

## The Christ Who Was Preexistent

Through the incarnate and risen Christ, God led Paul and others to see that the One who came into the human family already existed as God. The incarnation was the enfleshment of God. Christ's preexistence is set forth in relation to at least three names or titles.

### Word

The best-known presentation of the pre-incarnate Christ is that found in the Prologue to the Gospel of John (1:1–18). Much speculation has gone into the attempt to identify the antecedents of John's understanding of the Word. Certainly Genesis 1 had a part in John's thinking as evidenced by his phraseology, "in the beginning." Moreover, the word of God in Genesis 1 is powerful and creative. The concept of wisdom in Proverbs 8:22–31 may well have been in John's mind too. Some think John was acquainted with the idea of the Word in Philo and other sources. But regardless of what materials and ideas were grist in John's spiritual mill, he was led by the Spirit to give the church its most distinctive view of the word of God.

The Word was eternal, personal, and divine. The Word was the Agent of creation, the Source of life and light. Yet when the Word came into the world in the incarnation, even Jesus' own people, for the most part, rejected him. Nevertheless, to all who received him he gave the power to become God's children through regeneration. "The Word became flesh"— the incarnation was real. And the Word of God is the Son of God (vv. 14, 18). Throughout one's reading of the Gospel, John intends that one remember the preexistence of the Word who is also the Son (see 8:58; 17:5).

### Son of God

Paul also taught the preexistence of the Son. In Galatians 4:4–5, Paul means that God sent forth into this world the preexistent Son. This same thought lies behind his statement in 2 Corinthians 8:9 and the hymn in Philippians 2:5–11. Read Colossians 1:15–20 for Paul's most emphatic statement of the Son's preexistence. As the image of God the Son became the visible manifestation of God in this world. "Firstborn" has nothing to do with being created. It refers to relationship just as the word "Son" does. As firstborn Son Christ has the divine dignity and sovereignty. He was the Agent of creation, and this creation included angelic beings. Therefore, he is superior to all powers, physical and spiritual, in the universe. Indeed, creation took place for him. He is the one who unifies the universe and keeps it from becoming a chaos. He is not only the Head of the universe but the Head of the church as well. "The three predicates . . . head, beginning, first-born—all have *cosmic* significance; when they are applied to Christ in respect of his relation to the church, they point toward the thought that the church too has cosmic significance as the nucleus of a redeemed universe."[4] All God's fullness was pleased to dwell in Christ, and this incarnation was involved in God's purpose to create a cosmic peace "by the blood of his cross." God's purpose includes humankind, but it is bigger than humankind.

While John explicitly identified the Son with the Word, the author of Hebrews did this implicitly: "Long ago God spoke to our ancestors in many and various ways by the prophets, but in these last days he has spoken to us by a Son, whom he appointed heir of all things, through whom he also created the worlds" (see Heb. 1:1–4).

> *Read the whole of these four verses and compare them with Colossians 1:15–20 by making a tabulation and placing parallels opposite one another:*

| HEBREWS 1:1–4 | COLOSSIANS 1:15–20 |
|---|---|
| 1. *"through whom he also created the worlds"* | 1. *"in him all things in heaven and on earth were created"* |
| 2. _____ | 2. _____ |

### God

John said, "The Word was God" (1:1; compare 20:28). According to the New Revised Standard Version, Jesus Christ is called God in Titus 2:13 and 2 Peter 1:1. Some feel that the same thought is intended in 2 Thessalonians 1:12 and 1 Timothy 3:16. Only in John 1:1 is this name categorically associated with preexistence. Nevertheless, to be God in itself implies existence before creation.

## The Christ Who Is Yet to Come

The kingdom of God was inaugurated in the first coming of Christ, but it was not consummated. Almost every book in the New Testament gives expression to the expectation of what is ordinarily called the second coming of Christ, though the precise phrase is never used there. Perhaps it would be more accurate to speak of the "final coming" of Christ, since the event referred to is the coming of Christ at the end of history as we know it. This coming is associated with the consummation of God's kingdom.

Because this subject will be treated at various points in the chapters that follow, only a few of the relevant biblical passages will be cited here. In Matthew 24:3, the disciples ask Jesus: "What will be the sign of your coming and of the end of the age?" (See vv. 27, 37, 39.) The final coming has an especially prominent place in 1 and 2 Thessalonians. By the time 2 Peter was written, there were some who scoffed at the promise of the final coming of Christ, and the author reminded the readers "that with the Lord one day is like a thousand years, and a thousand years are like one day" (3:8).

Various aspects of this subject are warmly debated. It is not our purpose to enter into this debate at the moment. Rather is it to call attention to the strong New Testament emphasis on the expectation. The second coming means that God will consummate the kingdom through the same Jesus Christ who inaugurated the kingdom in his life, death, and resurrection, and who is already the Lord of all, though yet unacknowledged by most. The Christ who has stood at the center of history is the Christ who was, who is, and who is to come.

# PART SIX

# GOD'S TRANSFORMING ACTS THROUGH THE CHURCH

19

## The Earliest Witness of the Church

*T*he book of Acts is a treasure chest containing the only extended record of the earliest witness of the church.[1] The key that unlocks this chest is found in 1:8—"But you will receive power when the Holy Spirit has come upon you; and you shall be my witnesses in Jerusalem, in all Judea and Samaria, and to the ends of the earth." These words have actually stated the church's program of witness throughout the ages. We move from our own Jerusalem to our Judea and Samaria and to the ends of the earth. Here we will follow Luke's description of the church's expanding witness "in Jerusalem and in all Judea and Samaria" (Acts 1:1–12:25).

*Read the passages from Acts as they are listed and follow the other suggestions for your independent study as they occur.*

### The Preparation for Witness (Acts 1:1–26)

The first chapter of Acts records the preparation for witness. At the very outset Luke reminds us that Acts is the second volume of a two-volume work, Luke-Acts (Acts 1:1–2). In the first volume he "wrote about all that Jesus did and taught," and in the second volume he deals with what the Lord continues to do and teach by the Spirit and through the church. The beginning is continued.

*Be sure to read the first twenty-six verses of Acts.*

In these verses we see that the preparation for witness included the appearances of the risen Lord to his disciples, his charge to them to wait for the baptism of the Holy Spirit, his commission to them to be his witnesses, his ascension, the prayerful and harmonious waiting of the disciples, and the reconstitution of the Twelve. Note that the ascension is the dividing line between the appearances of the risen Lord to eyewitnesses and the coming of the Holy Spirit upon the church.

## The Witness "In Jerusalem" (Acts 2:1–8:3)

### The New Pentecost (Acts 2:1–42)

Among the Jews there were three major festivals: Passover, Weeks, and Tabernacles. The Feast of Weeks was also called Pentecost (fiftieth) because it came fifty days (or seven weeks) after Passover. Many Jewish pilgrims thronged to Jerusalem on this occasion. In Old Testament times Pentecost was an agricultural festival celebrating the harvesting of the firstfruits. In later Judaism it was made also a commemoration of the giving of the Torah at Sinai. But the events recounted in Acts, chapter 2, created a new Pentecost. This new Pentecost is also a harvest festival, celebrating the ingathering of the first three thousand converts to Christ. Instead of the giving of the Law, it commemorates the gift of the Spirit.[2]

The disciples were gathered together in one place and the Holy Spirit, like wind and fire, came upon them (Acts 2:1–4). "The Spirit is like the wind: uncontrollable, mysterious, powerful, seen only in his [*sic*] effects. In Hebrew and in Greek the same word means both 'wind' and 'spirit.' The Spirit is also like the flame: cleansing and consuming, awesome and dangerous."[3] In Old Testament times the Spirit came upon a leader in preparation for a particular task. It was anticipated that the Spirit would rest on the Messiah (Isa. 11:1–3). The Spirit of God was active in the conception of Jesus (Luke 1:35), and Jesus was endowed with the Spirit throughout his ministry. Yet in the Old Testament the Spirit is never said to be given to all the people of God. Joel announced that the day would come when the Spirit would be poured out on all flesh (Joel 2:28–29). At Pentecost this promise was kept, and the Spirit has remained with the church throughout the centuries. The time in which we live is, in a special sense, the Spirit's time.

The speaking with tongues, described in Acts 2:5–13, is beyond our complete comprehension. Various interpretations have been offered, but no one of them has received unanimous endorsement. In any case, what occurred was a marvelous evidence of the power of the Spirit in witnessing to the mighty works of God.

> *Peter's sermon on this occasion is one of the most celebrated of all time. Its chief emphases are recorded in 2:14–40. Many present-day sermons have three points. Peter's had at least five. Identify them and write them down in your notebook.*

The sermon reached its mark. Those present "were cut to the heart" and said in consternation, "Brothers, what shall we do?" And Peter replied with his last point:

Repent, and be baptized every one of you in the name of Jesus Christ so that your sins may be forgiven; and you will receive the gift of the Holy Spirit. For the promise is for you, for your children, and for all who are far away, everyone whom the Lord our God calls to him.

Both John the Baptist and Jesus had preached repentance. Here, however, repentance included the acceptance of the one whom the hearers had crucified. The baptism by the Baptist was associated with repentance and expectation of the coming of the Messiah (Matt. 3:11). Peter associated baptism with repentance, the forgiveness of sins, and the gift of the Holy Spirit. It was to be done in the name of Jesus Christ. Apparently the gift of the Spirit usually followed baptism (compare Acts 19:5–6; 8:12–17), though this was not always the case (Acts 10:44–48). The promise of the Spirit was to those who heard Peter and to their children, and to those who were not present on the occasion of the new Pentecost at all. Indeed the promise extends to us and our children.

The response to Peter's preaching was remarkable (2:41–42). Three thousand received his word and were baptized. Perhaps some of these persons had been touched by the life and ministry of Jesus, and Peter was entering into his Master's labors. Nevertheless the response must be regarded as extraordinary. The new converts "devoted themselves to the apostles' teaching and fellowship, to the breaking of bread and the prayers." As the apostles' preaching was designed to win new converts, so their teaching was designed to build up the believers in the faith.

The new Pentecost raises the question of the origin of the church. Where did the church come from? Key words in the answer of this question are Israel, Jesus, and the Holy Spirit. *Israel* was the people of God under the old covenant, and the promises made to Israel were claimed by the people of the new covenant (for example, see Gal. 3:29; 1 Peter 2:4–10). But the Christian fellowship is more than a simple outgrowth of Jesus' religion. *Jesus* by all that he was and did brought into being a new community, which in time came to be known as the church of Jesus Christ. Finally, the *Holy Spirit* came to stay with the people as never before in guiding, baptizing, empowering, witnessing, and judging. It is through the history of the covenant community of the church that God has been revealed as Trinity: Father, Son, and Holy Spirit.

## The Life of the Community (Acts 2:43–47)

The church was and is the fellowship of those who live under the Lordship of Christ. The early Christians took their fellowship in all seriousness. People in contact with them were impressed by their life of love in action and by the miracles of healing performed by the apostles. The believers' having the Spirit in common led to their having "all things in common." Although the word "communism" is sometimes used to describe this sharing of the early Christians, it was by no means the Communism of the twentieth century. To use this word in relation to the early Jerusalem church is misleading. These people voluntarily shared what they had with one another to meet the needs of the less fortunate.

At this time Christians operated within the overall framework of Jewish tradition, attending services at the Temple, yet separating themselves from other Jews by some of their own practices. For example, the breaking of bread "in their homes" called to mind such experiences as Jesus' feeding of the five thousand and his Last Supper with the Twelve. The disciples were characterized by gladness, generosity, and spontaneous praise. "And day by day the Lord added to their number those who were being saved."

## Opposition from Jewish Authorities (Acts 3:1–4:31)

Like their Master, the apostles faced opposition. The earliest recorded opposition to the ministry of Jesus centered about the healing of the paralytic carried by four people (Mark 2:1–12). The earliest recorded opposition to the ministry of the apostles centers about the healing of a man lame from birth (Acts 3:1–10). Peter and John healed this man at the

Beautiful Gate of the Temple. A crowd gathered quickly about Peter and John, and Peter took the occasion for preaching the gospel (Acts 3:11–26).

Peter and John were arrested by the same leaders who had seen to it that Jesus was put to death (Acts 4:1–4). The leaders were "much annoyed" because Peter and John "were teaching the people and proclaiming that in Jesus there is the resurrection of the dead." The Sadducees, who are named as a part of the opposition, were particularly sensitive on the subject of the resurrection from the dead, since they did not believe in it. Although Peter and John were arrested, many believed their message.

On the next day the two apostles were brought before the Sanhedrin (Acts 4:5–12). The question put to them by the court was this: "By what power or by what name did you do this [That is, heal the lame man]?" Then Peter, "filled with the Holy Spirit" preached a sermon to the Sanhedrin. Peter, who had denied his Master three times, was now ready to speak boldly to the very people who had plotted Jesus' crucifixion. The resurrection of Jesus and the gift of the Holy Spirit had made a new person of Simon. At last he was on the way to becoming Peter the Rock. His answer to the question of the court was to the point and included the heart of his preaching found elsewhere: "This man is standing before you in good health by the name of Jesus Christ of Nazareth, whom you crucified, whom God raised from the dead." Peter ended his sermon with the now famous statement: "There is salvation in no one else, for there is no other name under heaven given among mortals by which we must be saved."

The authorities did not know exactly what to do (Acts 4:13–22) but finally let them go after threatening them again, for the healing of the cripple by the two apostles had evidently made them popular with the people.

Thus far in our study of Acts we have had samples of three apostolic sermons. Here we find a sample of an apostolic prayer (Acts 4:23–31). When Peter and John were released, they reported what had happened to their Christian friends, whereupon the group spontaneously turned to God in prayer.

*Take time to analyze this prayer. How is God addressed?*

*Note that a part of Psalm 2 is quoted and that Isaiah 53 is alluded to.*

*What do you think this prayer teaches about the doctrine of fore-ordination?*

*What did the disciples ask for themselves? How do our prayers in time of crisis measure up to this apostolic standard?*

## Ananias and Sapphira (Acts 4:32–5:11)

The theme of having everything in common enters the narrative again (Acts 4:32–37). We have already indicated that it is misleading to use the word "communism" to designate the sharing of the early Jerusalem Christians. No one was forced to sell property and place the proceeds in the common fund. But this was the usual practice. Barnabas, for example, sold a field and laid the money at the apostles' feet. The teaching and example of Jesus had made the disciples aware of their obligation to those in need, and the kind of sharing described in Acts was the way the obligation was met only for a time. Ananias and Sapphira sold a piece of property and pretended to give all the proceeds to the common fund. They lied to the Holy Spirit and died under the pressure of guilt. Even in the early church, life was not perfect.

## A Second Clash with the Authorities (Acts 5:12–42)

The popularity of the apostles (Acts 5:12–16) was the occasion of jealousy on the part of the high priest and the Sadducees, who arrested them and put them in prison (Acts 5:17–21). But they were released by "an angel of the Lord," and they entered the Temple and taught. They were apprehended again and brought before the Sanhedrin (Acts 5:21–26). Then they were questioned by the high priest, who reminded them of the charge that they were not to teach in Jesus' name (Acts 5:27–32). Peter and the other apostles replied, "We must obey God rather than any human authority" (compare Acts 4:19–20). The early disciples obeyed authorities so long as they did not require them to disobey God in the process. Jesus had said, "Give to the emperor the things that are the emperor's, and to God the things that are God's" (Mark 12:17). But a disciple dare not render to the emperor the things that are God's alone.

Peter again preached a sermon (5:30–32) that so enraged the authorities that they wanted to kill all the apostles, but a Pharisee in the council named Gamaliel prevailed upon the group to spare their lives (Acts 5:33–39). Though they took his advice, they still beat them (compare Luke 22:63) and again warned them not to speak in Jesus' name. "As they [the apostles] left the council, they rejoiced that they were considered worthy to suffer dishonor for the sake of the name." Suffering for Christ's sake was regarded as a joyous privilege. And this is no isolated statement. Reflect on the following words from 1 Peter 4:13—"Rejoice insofar as you are sharing Christ's sufferings, so that you may also be glad and shout for joy when his glory is revealed" (compare Phil. 1:29; Col. 1:24). The apostles did not obey the council, for "in the temple and at home they did not cease to teach and proclaim Jesus as the Messiah." What actually do we know about suffering for Christ's sake?

## The Appointment of the Seven (Acts 6:1–7)

The troubles of the early church did not all originate outside the covenant community itself, as we have already seen in the tragedy of Ananias and Sapphira. A problem arose in connection with the daily distribution of food. "The Hellenists complained against the Hebrews because their widows were neglected in the daily distribution." The identification of the Hellenists and the Hebrews is a debated issue. It seems probable, however, that both groups were Jewish Christians. The Hellenists were more Greek in their culture, and the Hebrews were more Jewish.

To solve the problem the Twelve called a meeting of the body of disciples and said,

> It is not right that we should neglect the word of God in order to wait on tables. Therefore, friends, select from among yourselves seven men of good standing, full of the Spirit and of wisdom, whom we may appoint to this task, while we, for our part, will devote ourselves to prayer and to serving the word.

"The word of God" here is the gospel. Serving tables means attending to all things necessary to the administration of the economic life of the community. Note the characteristics of the seven men selected for this task. The Seven have been variously identified: as the first deacons, as the first elders of the Jerusalem church, and as a special group parallel to the Twelve with particular responsibility for the Hellenists.[4]

The manner in which they were chosen and set apart is clearer. They were elected by the entire congregation and inducted into their office by the apostles through prayer and the laying of their hands on them (compare Acts 13:3). As the word of God was preached, the church grew in numbers, and this growth included the conversion of some Jewish priests.

## Stephen, the First Christian Martyr (Acts 6:8–8:3)

Stephen, one of the Seven, was carrying on a powerful and effective ministry when he was falsely accused in relation to what he had said about the Law and the Temple (Acts 6:8–15). Jesus had already encountered the same kind of antagonism before him (Mark 14:57–59; John 2:19). When

Stephen was brought before the Sanhedrin, he, like the apostles, did not try to defend himself but preached a sermon instead. In his sermon he told much of the story of God's mighty acts with which we have been dealing in this book.

> *As you read what Stephen said, try to put yourself in the place of a member of the Sanhedrin as a defender of the Law and the Temple as traditionally understood and with vested interests in both. In this way look for the subtle meanings in Stephen's words.*

Stephen made it clear that the story of Israel is the story of one rebellion after another against the Holy Spirit. The Law and the Temple were being abused. They were never intended to take the place of the living God.

The crowd was enraged against Stephen (Acts 7:54–8:3). Filled with the Holy Spirit, he said, "Look . . . I see the heavens opened and the Son of Man standing at the right hand of God!" At this point it seems that the orderly court session was turned into mob violence. Stephen was cast out of the city and stoned.

Just as there are parallels between the accusations brought against Jesus and those brought against Stephen, so there are parallels between the death of Jesus and the death of Stephen. Jesus said, "Father, forgive them; for they do not know what they are doing" (Luke 23:34); Stephen said, "Lord, do not hold this sin against them" (Acts 7:60). Jesus said, "Father, into your hands I commend my spirit" (Luke 23:46); Stephen said, "Lord Jesus, receive my spirit" (Acts 7:59).

When Jesus died, all seemed lost, but it was far from lost. When Stephen, the first Christian martyr, died, his life seemed of little significance to many. But he had given a witness that would never die. Saul of Tarsus was one of those consenting to his death. Up to this point in the history of the early church the persecution of Christians had been limited, but on that day a great persecution arose, which resulted in the scattering of the disciples and, with them, the gospel throughout Judea and Samaria. God even makes human evil to serve the divine purpose.

## The Witness "In All Judea and Samaria" (Acts 8:4–12:25)

### Philip the Evangelist (Acts 8:4–40)

"Now those who were scattered went from place to place preaching the word." Among these scattered disciples was Philip. In all probability this

Philip was one of the Seven (Acts 6:5) rather than Philip the Apostle, for we are told in Acts 8:1 that the apostles remained in Jerusalem. Philip went to a city in Samaria, preached the word, and performed miracles of healing. Earlier in our study we dealt with the history of the Samaritans and the racial-religious barrier between the Jews and the Samaritans. The antipathy between them had continued. In other words, Philip was, in a sense, breaking new ground. The mission of the church was entering non-Jewish territory. Yet Jesus had ministered to the Samaritan woman at Jacob's well (John 4), had told the parable of the Good Samaritan (Luke 10:29–37), and had healed a Samaritan leper (Luke 17:11–19).

Among those baptized by Philip was Simon, a magician (Acts 8:9–13). When the apostles at Jerusalem heard of the work in Samaria, they sent Peter and John to Samaria (Acts 8:14–24). Though the Samaritan converts had been baptized, they had not received the Holy Spirit. Of course they would never have been ready for baptism if the Spirit had not already been at work in them. But the reception of the Holy Spirit referred to in the text was evidenced in some special way. It is probable that the reference is to speaking with tongues (see Acts 10:44–48). In any case, they received the Spirit when Peter and John laid their hands on them. "Belief on the 'name' of Jesus, baptism, the laying on of hands, and the reception of the Holy Spirit are all ideas of tremendous importance in Acts, and they are all closely connected. But when we seek to discover the exact connection, we are baffled."[5]

Peter and John not only approved of what was being done in taking the gospel to the hated Samaritans, they also participated in the work. En route back to Jerusalem they preached "the good news to many villages of the Samaritans" (Acts 8:25). The evangelization that took place in Samaria was no insignificant accomplishment. The gospel was on its way.

Philip was divinely led to his encounter with the Ethiopian eunuch (Acts 8:26–40). An "Ethiopian" in Philip's day was a member of a dark-skinned people from below Egypt. This man was probably a God-fearer, that is, one who was attracted to the Jewish faith but who had not become a convert. He was reading from the fifty-third chapter of Isaiah when Philip joined him: "The eunuch asked Philip, 'About whom, may I ask you, does the prophet say this, about himself or about someone else?'" Then Philip used this scripture and told him the good news of Jesus as the Suffering Savior. The eunuch believed and was baptized. This indicates that the gospel was reaching people from far places and other races and cultures.

## Peter's Ministry in Gentile Territory (Acts 9:31–11:18)

Acts 9:31 marks a transition from the account of Saul's conversion to the account of Peter's ministry in Gentile territory. Peter visited Lydda, Joppa, and Caesarea, all of which were in the general range of Philip's ministry. At Lydda, in the name of Jesus, Peter healed a paralytic named Aeneas. At Joppa Peter raised up Dorcas.

In his presentation of Peter's ministry in Gentile territory, Luke emphasizes Peter's visit to Cornelius, a Roman centurion at Caesarea (Acts 10:1–11:18). Cornelius was a God-fearer, one favorably inclined to the Jewish religion, who "gave alms generously to the people and prayed constantly to God." In response to his devotion God gave Cornelius a vision in which he was instructed to send for Simon Peter.

Peter also had a vision, in which he saw a sheet full of all kinds of animals let down from heaven. A voice came to him: "Get up, Peter; kill and eat." But Peter replied, "By no means, Lord; for I have never eaten anything that is profane or unclean." This happened three times, and Peter was perplexed. As a good Jew he had kept the dietary laws concerning clean and unclean animals as set forth in Leviticus, chapter 11.

While Peter was going through inner turmoil on account of his vision, the three men sent by Cornelius stood at Peter's gate. Peter, directed by the Spirit, went to meet them, whereupon they told him about their master's vision. Peter invited them to be his guests for the night.

The next day Peter, Cornelius's delegates, and others (that is, Christians) from Joppa began their journey to Caesarea. On their arrival in Caesarea, they found a sizeable group to greet them, since "Cornelius was expecting them and had called together his relatives and close friends." Cornelius tried to worship Peter, but Peter interrupted him, explaining, "I am only a mortal." The Spirit had led Peter to an understanding of his vision, and Peter immediately informed the assembled company that he should "not call anyone profane or unclean." In other words, Gentiles were not profane or unclean even though they were not Jews. Cornelius then explained how he had sent for Peter in response to his own vision at the time of prayer and gave Peter a door wide open to the gospel.

"Then Peter began to speak to them" and preached (Acts 10:34–43).

*Read this sermon, identify its main points, and compare it with Peter's other sermons (Acts 2:14–42; 3:11–26; 4:8–12; 5:29–32).*

*On the basis of your study, how would you identify the gospel?*

*What is preaching?*

"While Peter was still speaking, the Holy Spirit fell on all those who heard the word" (Acts 10:44–48). The believers who accompanied Peter were amazed at this outpouring of the Spirit on Gentiles. In this case at least and probably in other cases, the "speaking in tongues and extolling God" constituted the immediate evidence of the gift of the Spirit. But here the gift of the Spirit preceded water baptism. It was this gift that made it clear to Peter and his friends that these Gentiles ought to be baptized. After all, who can reject those whom the Lord has received?

But Peter had to give account of his behavior on his return to Jerusalem (Acts 11:1–18). The strict Jewish party criticized him for eating with the uncircumcised. Therefore he told the whole story of his encounter with Cornelius. But his experience was more than an encounter with Cornelius; it was an encounter with God. He concluded, "If then God gave them the same gift that he gave to us when we believed in the Lord Jesus Christ, who was I that I could hinder God?" Can you think of ways in which people do try to hinder God? Peter won his case, the opposition was silenced for a time (see Acts 15:1), and all glorified God, saying, "Then God has given even to the Gentiles the repentance that leads to life." What meaning is there for us today in the story of Peter's visit to Cornelius?

## The Church at Syrian Antioch (Acts 11:19–30)

The persecution that arose in relation to Stephen played a part in a number of significant events: the ministry of Philip, the conversion of Saul, Peter's ministry in Gentile territory, and the establishment of the church in Syrian Antioch.[6] We speak of "Syrian" Antioch to distinguish this place from Pisidian Antioch, which is located farther north and west. It was the third largest city in the Roman empire. Believers from Cyprus and Cyrene first preached the gospel to Greeks in Antioch.

As was its custom when a new work was begun, the church in Jerusalem investigated this work at Antioch. On this occasion Barnabas was the representative. He was pleased with what he found and secured the help of Paul, who worked with him for a year in Antioch. The citizens of Antioch nicknamed the disciples "Christians," which means "followers of Christ." The only other New Testament passages in which the word occurs are Acts 26:28 and 1 Peter 4:16. The more common name for disciples in the early church was "saints," that is, those separated unto God.

Among the prophets who went to Antioch from Jerusalem was one Agabus, who announced a famine. The disciples at Antioch sent relief to the believers who lived in Judea by Barnabas and Saul. This was additional evidence of the effect of the gospel on the economic behavior of the early Christians.

### Persecution Under Herod Agrippa I (Acts 12:1–25)

Herod Agrippa was descended from Idumean (Edomite) and Jewish ancestry. To gain the favor of Jews who hated the followers of Jesus, he executed James the brother of John and arrested Peter shortly thereafter. Peter was being kept in prison until after the days of Unleavened Bread, and the church was praying in his behalf. Peter was miraculously delivered from the prison and made his way to the place of prayer. At first the group could not believe their prayers had been answered so quickly and literally. Herod ordered the execution of his sentries and soon thereafter met sudden death himself. "But the word of God continued to advance and gain adherents."

## The Ministry of the Early Church

In the light of Acts 1–12 we are in a position to say something, by way of summary, about the ministry of the early church. We use the word "ministry" here not to refer to the official leadership of the church as such but to the kind of service rendered by the church. Luke wrote his Gospel to tell what "Jesus did and taught" (Acts 1:1), and in Acts he tells what Jesus continued to do and teach through the church. The mission of the church is the mission of Christ. The church is a witness to what God has done in Christ and an instrument of what God is doing through him. Its mission is witness. Its witness is ministry.

### The Ministry of Word and Sacrament

We have already seen that Jesus carried on a ministry of the spoken word, and proclamation was an aspect of this ministry. His apostles carried on this ministry in light of Jesus' ministry, death, resurrection, and ascension. Jesus preached, saying, "The time is fulfilled, and the kingdom of God has come near; repent, and believe in the good news." We have studied the apostolic sermons in Acts 1–12 and have found that the apostles preached Christ, for the reign of God is embodied in him. The proclamation of Jesus and that of the apostles may be compared as follows:

| JESUS' PROCLAMATION | THE APOSTLES' PROCLAMATION |
|---|---|
| 1. The time is fulfilled. | 1. The promises are fulfilled. |
| 2. The kingdom of God is at hand. | 2. The new age has begun in Jesus Christ (including all that has been said about him). |
| 3. Repent, and believe in the gospel. | 3. Repent, believe, be baptized, and receive the Holy Spirit. |

Proclamation is not to be understood as confined to Sunday morning or to the place of common worship. In the early church it took place in houses, in a part of the Temple area, before the Sanhedrin, and in a chariot. It was essentially an announcement of God's gracious deed in Jesus Christ and a call to respond in repentance and faith. The message was addressed to thousands, to smaller groups of varying sizes, and to individuals. That is, the early Christians employed a variety of methods of evangelism: mass (Acts 2:1–47), household (Acts 16:11–15), and person-to-person (Acts 8:26–40).

The ministry of the spoken word also included teaching. Jesus spent much of his time teaching his disciples and others. The apostles followed his example. In general, proclamation was addressed to nonbelievers, while teaching was addressed to believers. Teaching emphasized the interpretation and application of the good news. However, there was and is overlap between proclamation and teaching. Much of the New Testament falls into the category of teaching. Our teaching must be based on that of Jesus and the apostles. They used the media of communication available to them; it is incumbent on us to use the media available to us.

The Reformed tradition recognizes two sacraments: Baptism and the Lord's Supper. While the word "sacrament" is not found in Acts 1–12 or in any other book of the New Testament, the idea is present. "A sacrament is a holy ordinance instituted by Christ, wherein, by sensible signs, Christ and the benefits of the new covenant are represented, sealed, and applied to believers" (The Shorter Catechism, Q. 92). Through them God acts in grace and humans respond in faith and obedience. The sacraments are the visible gospel.

Water-baptism and Spirit-baptism are not the same, but they are closely connected. To the early church baptism was no mere formality. It was serious business. By it a person was marked as belonging to Christ. It placed the emphasis on the grace of God.

In the earliest church the Lord's Supper was closely associated with the

Last Supper and bound up with common meals. This is the implication of the phrase "the breaking of bread" (Acts 2:42, 46; 20:11).

## The Ministry of the Mighty Deed

The apostles followed Jesus' example in their ministry of the mighty deed. They even preached Jesus' ministry of the mighty deed as a part of the gospel itself (Acts 2:22; 10:38). Of course they could not forgive sin, but they could and did point to the One who could. The spoken word was interpreted by the mighty deed, and the mighty deed was interpreted by the spoken word, so that together they issued in the mighty Word-deed of God.

The church today takes its ministry of spoken word seriously, and in many cases does much good in meeting human needs. But comparatively little attention is given to the ministry of the mighty deed as such. Do we do all that is necessary to fulfill this ministry by operating hospitals on mission fields? Or do we believe that the age of miracles is past? Can you find anything in the scriptures that cancels this aspect of the church's ministry?

## The Ministry of the Given Life

We have seen how Jesus' whole life was one of commitment to God's will—even unto death. Though the apostles and other disciples could not by their suffering and death make atonement for sin, they were committed to Christ and to others through Christ. We have already seen how Stephen and James suffered martyrdom. Many others were soon to follow in their steps. Our study of Acts 1–12 has shown clearly how these early Christians hazarded their lives for the sake of the gospel. They followed the guidance of the Holy Spirit in overcoming prejudices of long-standing. They prayed for one another and demonstrated their genuine concern in tangible and sacrificial sharing.

Our ministry is rooted in Christ's commitment to us (Mark 10:45) and our commitment to him (Mark 8:34–37). Stewardship of time, talent, money, property, and opportunities arises out of this prior commitment. Do we think of ourselves as exercising a ministry of the given life? Or do we think of Christ as exercising his ministry through us? Do you agree that it is largely through the quality of the church's total ministry that the gospel is communicated to its own members and to the world?

## The Nature of the Church

While Acts 1–12 does not contain all aspects of the doctrine of the church to be found in the New Testament as a whole, it does contain some very important teachings and implications.

*On the basis of your study of these chapters, how would you answer the question, What is the church? In seeking the answer, you will find the following passages of special value:*

1. Acts 1:8, 22.
2. Acts 1:16; 2:29, 37; 6:3.
3. Acts 2:42, 43–44; 4:32–37.
4. Acts 5:11; 7:48; 9:31.
5. Acts 5:14; 2:44; 4:4; 11:17.
6. Acts 26:1–2, 7; 9:1, 10, 19, 25–26, 38.
7. Acts 11:26; 26:28.
8. Acts 11:18.
9. Acts 1:26; 6:2.

## In Retrospect and Prospect

Looking back over the account of the emergence of the church as recorded by Acts, we are struck with the difficulty the early Christians had with their Jewish counterparts. Frequently some within the Jewish community either attacked or incited others to deal harshly with the Christians. It is important to remember that "the Jews" is not a phrase that should be understood as all-inclusive nor should we transfer the antagonism of then to now.

We are next to study in some detail the writings and work of Paul and others of the New Testament's authors. In some texts "the Jews" actually is a reference to Judaizers, Christians who wanted to maintain some of the customs of the Jews (e.g., circumcision, Sabbath observance, etc.). The distinction beween "Jews" and "Judaizers" is not always made clear in the text, but we should always ask the question as to the intention of the authors. Much confusion and hostility has been fostered by failing to understand and acknowledge who the "enemies" of the early church really were. Most of the struggle was between Christians who held different views of the Gospel (non-Judaizers versus Judaizers) rather than between Christians and actual Jews.

# Paul's Witness by Life

*P*aul's witness by life is a vital part of the one story of the Bible. The sources of this witness are his letters and Acts 9:1–30; 13:1–28:31. Peter was the chief leader in the first period of the church's life. Then under Paul's leadership the witness was carried into ever expanding territories on its way to the ends of the earth.

## The Years of Preparation

All that transpired in Paul's life before his first missionary journey is here regarded as a part of his preparation to be the great Apostle. Of course Paul could not himself have regarded any years thus until after his conversion. But as we look at these early years in the light of his whole life, we can, through the eyes of faith, see God's hand mightily at work in him and through him in the church and in the world.

### A Hebrew Born of Hebrews

This man who called himself "a Hebrew born of Hebrews" had the Aramaic name Saul and its Latin counterpart Paulus, from which we get Paul. He was a Roman citizen by birth (Acts 22:27–28 ). To a tribune in Jerusalem Paul said, "I am a Jew, from Tarsus in Cilicia, a citizen of an important city" (Acts 21:39). Tarsus was located in the territory known as Cilicia, which was at that time in the province of Syria. It was truly "an important city," for it could boast wide commercial relationships, a university, and a cosmopolitan population. Paul was the heir of a rich Jewish heritage and a broadening Hellenistic culture.

Paul was born only a few years after Jesus himself (10–15 C.E.). Little is known of his family. A sister is mentioned in Acts 23:16. He was "circumcised on the eighth day, a member of the people of Israel, of the tribe of Benjamin, a Hebrew born of Hebrews; as to the law, a Pharisee; as to zeal a persecutor of the church; as to righteousness under the law, blameless" (Phil. 3:5–6; compare 2 Cor. 11:22; Rom. 11:1; and Acts 23:6). He had the name of Israel's first king and was a member of the same tribe. His ancestry was as impeccable as that of any other Jew. His interpretation of the Law of Moses was strictly Pharisaic (see the treatment of the Pharisees in ch. 15). He studied in Jerusalem under the famous teacher Gamaliel (see Acts 5:34; 22:3), who was himself a Pharisee. He was later to call the Law a custodian or schoolmaster "until Christ came" (Gal. 3:23–25).

As a young man Paul was already well known (Acts 26:4). He tells us, "I advanced in Judaism beyond many among my people of the same age, for I was far more zealous for the traditions of my ancestors" (Gal. 1:14). This zeal led him to become a persecutor of the church. Though he was a tentmaker by trade (Acts 18:3), his real devotion was to seeking the righteousness that one attains by keeping the Law. His linguistic equipment (Aramaic, Hebrew, and Greek), his combined Jewish and Greek heritage, his Roman citizenship, his educational attainments, and his zeal for the Law were all to be put to the use of bearing witness to the gospel.

## Conversion and Call

Paul's conversion to Christ and his call to be an apostle are two aspects of one experience. Probably there were factors in Paul's life that paved the way, so to speak, for the vision (Acts 26:19) on the Damascus Road. He knew both the Jewish Law and disciples of Christ, and these two aspects of his experience were in conflict with each other and helped to produce conflict within him. He seems to have been disturbed by Deuteronomy 27:26—"Cursed is everyone who does not observe and obey all the things written in the book of the law" (Gal. 3:10, which is based on the Greek Septuagint's translation of the verse). Said he, "The very commandment that promised life proved to be death to me" (Rom. 7:10).

Surely the stoning of Stephen left an indelible mark on Paul's conscience. Stephen's Christlike prayers and spirit must have shaken the ardent persecutor to the very foundation of his being (see Acts 22:20). But Paul did not become a Christian at once. His sense of guilt and his fear that Stephen might be right after all seem to have driven him to further persecution of the church with intensified fury (Acts 8:3). He could never forget that he had persecuted the church of God (Gal. 1:13, 23; 1 Cor. 15:9; Phil. 3:6; Acts 22:4–5, 20; 26:9–11).

In his letters, Paul refers to his Damascus Road encounter from time to time. His most complete statement is found in Galatians 1:15–16 (compare v. 12): "But when God, who had set me apart before I was born and called me through his grace, was pleased to reveal his Son to me, so that I might proclaim him among the Gentiles, I did not confer with any human being." His awareness of God's foreordination recalls Jeremiah's understanding of his call to be a prophet (Jer. 1:5).

Paul's call was wholly a matter of grace; he deserved it in no way whatsoever. God revealed his Son to him on the road to Damascus. The purpose of this revelation was that Paul might preach the gospel to the Gentiles. In writing to the Corinthians he speaks of his experience as seeing "Jesus our Lord" (1 Cor. 9:1). Later in the same letter, as he gives a list of the appearances of the risen Christ, he says, "Last of all, as to one untimely born, he appeared also to me" (15:8). For this appearance was much later than the ascension, before which the other appearances of the risen Lord had taken place.

The most detailed accounts of Paul's conversion and call are found in Acts 9:1–19; 22:5–16; and 26:12–18. The first of these passages is placed by Luke at the chronologically appropriate point in the narrative of Acts. The second is a part of Paul's defense before the Jewish people in Jerusalem. The third is a part of his defense before King Agrippa II. While the essentials in these three accounts are the same, there are some variations in the narrations.

*Analyze the three passages, listing in your notebook the elements common to all and the elements distinctive of each. To do this most clearly, draw a chart like the following and fill it in:*

## THE CALL AND COMMISSION OF PAUL

| EVENTS | ACTS 9:1–19 | ACTS 22:5–16 | ACTS 26:12–18 |
|--------|-------------|--------------|---------------|
|        |             |              |               |

*While engaging in the thrill of your research, be sure not to overlook the following matters:*

*1. It is not required that all persons who become Christians must have experiences identical with that of Paul. In fact, no other biblical character is recorded to have duplicated Paul's experience. Nevertheless, what elements in Paul's experience are essential to any Christian?*

*2. What we today call "Christianity" is frequently referred to in Acts as "the Way" (9:2; 19:9, 23; 22:4; 24:14, 22). Perhaps this designation of the early Christian movement is to be associated with the use of the word "way" in Isaiah 40:3–5; 42:15–17; 43:19; Mark 1:1–4; and John 14:3–6.[1] The covenanters of the Dead Sea Scrolls called their movement "the way." Some of this group lived in Damascus, to which Paul was going when he was converted. It is certainly possible that some of them became Christians.*

*3. Jesus identified and identifies himself with his people. "Saul, Saul, why do you persecute me?" To mistreat Jesus' disciples is to mistreat Jesus (compare Matt. 25:31–46).*

*4. Ananias, who had heard of the evil done to the saints by Paul, still addressed Paul as "Brother" when the two men first met.*

*5. Apparently Paul received the gift of the Holy Spirit before he was baptized (Acts 9:71).*

*6. Paul was called to be a witness to all people. This is variously expressed in Galatians 1:16; Acts 9:15; 22:15; and 22:16. And Paul was able to say, "I was not disobedient to the heavenly vision" (Acts 26:19).*

## A Time of Reorientation

Paul had done an about-face and needed some time to get his Christian feet on the ground, so to speak. It is a bit difficult to know how to arrange the details of Acts 9:19–30 and Galatians 1:17–18 in chronological sequence. After a brief introduction to the Christians at Damascus, Paul seems to have gone away to Arabia for a while. Apparently Paul needed time to think through his radical transformation and its implications. He returned to Damascus and carried on a witness there. When some of the Jews plotted against him, he escaped over the wall in a basket (see 2 Cor. 11:32–33).

After three years in Arabia and Damascus, he returned to Jerusalem, with the special purpose of seeing Peter. During his visit of fifteen days he became acquainted also with James, the Lord's brother. Hostility arose against him, and with the aid of friends, he returned to his native Cilicia and Tarsus, where he seems to have spent between seven and ten years.

The church in Syrian Antioch had been established by disciples who had been scattered by the persecution following Stephen's death (see Acts 11:19ff.). Some of these disciples preached only to Jews there, but others took the gospel to the Gentiles. This resulted in a congregation composed of both Jews and Gentiles. Perhaps it was because Barnabas thought Paul would be of special help in integrating this church that he secured Paul's assistance for about a year. The two men took an offering from the church in Antioch to the famine-stricken church in Jerusalem. (See Acts 11:27–30. Is this the same visit as that recorded in Gal. 2:1?)

## The First Missionary Journey

*The record of Paul's first missionary journey is found in Acts 13–14. Read these chapters carefully, underlining the key words in such a way that you are able to review the narrative at a glance. A red pencil is especially useful for this purpose.*

*Follow the journey on a map in a Bible atlas (see p. 408).*

Apparently the Apostle planned his general missionary strategy well. He seems to have selected great urban centers in which to establish Christian communities both for their own sake and as places from which the churches could reach out into the surrounding area. Paul was obligated to Greeks and to barbarians, not because they had done anything for him, but because Christ had done everything for him (Rom. 1:14).[2]

### The Commissioning Service (Acts 13:1–3)

In response to the promptings of the Holy Spirit, the prophetic leaders of the church at Antioch in Syria commissioned Barnabas and Paul to their world mission task with the laying on of hands. Paul was already an apostle, and this ceremony in no way repudiated this fact.

### Witness on the Island of Cyprus (Acts 13:4–12)

Witness on the first missionary journey began on the island of Cyprus, the home of Barnabas. Up to this point in Luke's account of the relation between Barnabas and Paul, Barnabas has been preeminent. But at this juncture Paul begins to stand in the forefront of the narrative. Luke first uses his Latin name Paul in Acts 13:9. On this first journey Paul and

Barnabas were accompanied by Barnabas's cousin, John Mark. These men set sail from Seleucia on the Syrian coast and landed at Salamis, on Cyprus. First, they preached the gospel in the synagogues at Salamis and worked their way across the whole island to Paphos, the capital, where Sergius Paulus the Roman proconsul lived. This man wanted to hear the gospel from the two missionaries, but a sorcerer named Bar-Jesus tried to interfere. Whereupon Paul, with special power from the Holy Spirit, struck him blind temporarily. The proconsul believed.

## Witness at Pisidian Antioch (Acts 13:13–52)

Paul and company sailed from Paphos to Perga in the province of Pamphylia, located on the southern coast of Asia Minor. It was at this point that John Mark left his companions and returned to Jerusalem. Paul and Barnabas quickly made their way to Antioch of Pisidia, not to be confused with Antioch in Syria from which the missionaries had set out. They had now entered the province of Galatia.

On the Sabbath Day they attended the service in the synagogue. After the customary reading of the Law and the Prophets was completed, Paul and Barnabas were given the opportunity to speak. Paul rose to the occasion. In his sermon he first recounted the mighty acts of God in Israel's history down to David. Then he rehearsed certain of the events within God's mighty act in Jesus Christ (such as Peter had done in his various sermons). In other words, he combined the mighty acts of God recorded in the Old Testament with God's mighty act in Jesus Christ.

> *In one column list the mighty acts that Paul enumerated from the old covenant, and in a second column those that he enumerated under the new.*

The people asked that the sermon be repeated the next Sabbath. When the next Sabbath arrived, so many people gathered to hear the word that some of the Jews were jealous and argued with Paul and abused him. Therefore, he and Barnabas said, "It was necessary that the word of God should be spoken first to you. Since you reject it, and judge yourselves to be unworthy of eternal life, we are now turning to the Gentiles." Many Gentiles believed, though others did not. The Jewish leaders stirred up opposition to Paul and Barnabas among the Gentile aristocracy, at least some of whom may have been God-fearers. Consequently the two missionaries "shook the dust off their feet in protest against them, and went to Iconium" (compare Luke 9:5; 10:10–11).

## Witness in Iconium (Acts 14:1–7)

At Iconium Paul and Barnabas also spoke in the synagogue. Many Jews and Greeks believed. Though the unbelieving Jews stirred up trouble for them, they continued their ministry at Iconium for some time. This ministry included both spoken word and mighty deed. The whole city was eventually divided on their account, and to avoid being stoned they moved on to Lystra and Derbe.

## Witness at Lystra (Acts 14:8–20)

Lystra, along with Antioch, Iconium, and Derbe, was in the Roman province of Galatia. After Paul had healed a cripple there, the people thought the two men were gods. They identified Barnabas as Zeus, perhaps because he was large, and Paul as Hermes, because he was the chief speaker. Under the leadership of the priest of Zeus, the people were about to offer sacrifice to these two men, but finally they were dissuaded. The missionaries preached to them about the living God, "but Jews came there from Antioch and Iconium and won over the crowds. Then they stoned Paul and dragged him out of the city, supposing that he was dead." Paul never forgot this stoning (see 2 Cor. 11:25). As he was being stoned, the scene of Stephen's death must have flashed across his mind in all its vividness. As he had done to another, it was now being done unto him.

## Witness on the Return Home (Acts 14:21–28)

The two apostles retraced their steps on their return to Antioch in Syria. But they did more than return. They strengthened the disciples and appointed elders in every congregation. On their arrival in Syrian Antioch, they reported to the church that had sent them out. And in their report they stressed the fact that God "had opened a door of faith for the Gentiles."

## The Apostolic Council in Jerusalem

The First Apostolic Council (Acts 15) is one of the most important church councils that ever met. But its precise place in the chronology of Paul's life is very hard to decide. The problem arises in the attempt to relate Acts 15 and Galatians 2. If one assumes that both of them are records of the same meeting, it is difficult to weave them into a consistent whole. If one assumes that they are records of different meetings, the great similarity between them is troubling.

The view taken here is that these two chapters do not record the same meeting. Galatians 2:1–10 is Paul's account of his visit to Jerusalem, which is mentioned in Acts 11:27–30, and Acts 15 is Luke's account of the meeting of the Apostolic Council at a later time.[3] Some of the reasons for this position will emerge in the process of interpretation. Galatians 2 was reserved for treatment here because it deals with the same basic theological issue of Christian freedom as Acts 15.

## A Private Conference with the Pillars of the Church (Gal. 2:1–10)

In these verses of Galatians Paul describes a private conference with the "pillars" of the church: James, Peter, and John—not a public meeting such as that described in Acts 15. He indicates that the visit to Jerusalem recounted in Galatians 2:1–10 was his second. Acts 11:27–30 records his second visit also. Paul says, "I went up in response to a revelation" (Gal. 2:2). But Acts 15:2 (in the account of the meeting of the Apostolic Council ) reads, "Paul and Barnabas and some of the others were appointed to go up to Jerusalem to discuss this question with the apostles and the elders." However, according to Acts 11:27–30, Paul went to Jerusalem on the basis of the revelation concerning the famine there that was given by the prophet Agabus.

While Paul was in Jerusalem, he wanted to get a clean bill of health from the pillars of the church regarding his ministry of Christian liberty. For he did not require converts to the Christian faith to be circumcised and to assume the religious customs of the Jews. The three pillars gave him and Barnabas "the right hand of fellowship, agreeing that we should go to the Gentiles and they to the circumcised. They asked only one thing, that we remember the poor . . ." (vv. 9–10).

This division of labor did not mean that Paul and Barnabas would not preach to Jews and that Peter and the others would not evangelize Gentiles. It was a matter of emphasis in witnessing. It may also have had something to do with geography. Peter and the others worked closer home; Paul and Barnabas moved into wider horizons. The request concerning the poor was welcome to Paul. Had not he and Barnabas just brought relief for them from Antioch? He would continue this concern (see 1 Cor. 16:1–4; 2 Cor. 8; Rom. 15:25–29; Acts 24:17).

## Paul's Rebuke of Peter (Gal. 2:11–21)

The encounter between Paul and Peter recounted in these verses seems to have taken place at some time between the private conference mentioned above and the meeting of the Apostolic Council in Jerusalem. When Peter came to Antioch, he ate with Gentile Christians without any hesitation. But after certain members of the circumcision party also came to Antioch from Jerusalem, Peter withdrew from table fellowship with these Gentile Christians. Moreover, he carried the other Jewish Christians with him, including Paul's devoted friend Barnabas. The circumcision party was composed of Jewish Christians who thought Gentiles should adopt some Jewish customs as part of becoming Christians. Peter may have felt that his whole witness to the Jews would be undermined if he did not give in to this party.

Paul saw that the very nature of the gospel was at stake and therefore opposed Peter publicly. Paul pointed out that by eating with Gentile Christians Peter had already lived like one of them. He had accepted the basic principle of justification for both Jews and Gentiles on the basis of faith. How could he now try to make Gentiles live like Jews? After all, it was the risen Christ who had led Peter to see that justification is by faith and that Gentiles receive the Spirit.

It is possible that Paul wrote Galatians from Syrian Antioch about 49 C.E.

## The Council in Jerusalem (Acts 15)

Those of the circumcision party were determined to win their case. Earlier Peter had to defend his behavior in baptizing Cornelius and other Gentiles with him (Acts 11:1-18). Paul's activity at Antioch and in Galatia disturbed them greatly. What would happen to the Temple and the Law if Paul's doctrine were allowed to prevail? These people wanted the church to remain a Jewish sect. Therefore some of them again went from Jerusalem to Antioch and taught, "Unless you are circumcised according to the custom of Moses, you cannot be saved."

Apparently Paul had won Barnabas back into his camp in connection with his rebuke of Peter. For he joined Paul in the debate against the Judaizers. The church at Antioch appointed Paul and Barnabas and others to take the question to the apostles and elders of Jerusalem. The apostles had a general authority and oversight over all the churches. The elders in this case seem to have been those of the mother church in Jerusalem. Though there was representation only from Jerusalem and Antioch, the council appears to have had churchwide authority.

Luke has given us a brief sketch of the proceedings. The circumcision, or Pharisee, party reiterated their position. Peter was the first to reply.

Evidently Paul's rebuke had found its mark, for Peter rehearsed the experience by which God's Spirit had led him to see that God made no distinction between Gentile and Jew. "We believe that we will be saved through the grace of the Lord Jesus, just as they will."

Next, Barnabas and Paul told their story of God's mighty works among the Gentiles, after which James (who was moderator of the Jerusalem church) gave "the sense of the meeting." It would not be necessary for Gentiles to be circumcised in order to be Christians. But they should abstain from eating meat that had been offered to idols, unchastity, eating the flesh of animals that have been strangled, and eating blood in any form. These abstentions were not a matter of salvation, but they would make for a happier association between Jewish converts and Gentile converts.

*Sometimes this judgment of James is called a "compromise"; do you think this is the correct word?*

Judas Barsabbas and Silas ("Silvanus," 1 Thess. 1:1) were selected to accompany Paul and Barnabas back to Antioch and to bear the letter containing the judgment of the council. The letter was read to the assembled congregation, and Judas and Silas encouraged the believers for a time and departed. Paul and Barnabas continued their ministry there.

*How is Paul's fight for freedom being carried on today?*

## The Second Missionary Journey

### The Beginning of the Journey (Acts 15:36–16:8)

The time soon came when Paul felt the churches that were founded on the first missionary journey should be revisited. It is probable that the Jewish-Gentile controversy at Jerusalem and Antioch had something to do with this decision. Therefore, he suggested a second journey to Barnabas. Barnabas wanted to take John Mark, but Paul did not think it wise because Mark had withdrawn from the first journey. Paul has been sharply criticized for his behavior on this occasion. Could he have known the following statement of Jesus and been influenced in his position by it: "No one who puts a hand to the plow and looks back is fit for the kingdom of God" (Luke 9:62)? At least Paul continued to hold Barnabas in high esteem (1 Cor. 9:6) and came to realize he had been mistaken about the genuineness of Mark's commitment (2 Tim. 4:11).

So far as the second missionary journey is concerned, however, Paul and Barnabas separated. Barnabas took Mark and revisited Cyprus, his homeland, while Paul took Silas and journeyed through Syria and Cilicia to Galatia. Presumably the latter companions spent a bit of time in Tarsus, Paul's original home. Because the trip this time was overland, the sequence of visitation of the churches in Galatia was different.

At Lystra Paul secured the assistance of a young disciple named Timothy. Timothy's mother was a Jewess, but his father was a Greek. This meant that he was technically a Jew. Paul circumcised him to placate the Jewish Christians in the area. Paul has been much criticized for this action on the basis of his own principles of Christian freedom fought out at Jerusalem and Antioch. What do you think? As Paul and his companions made their way from congregation to congregation, among other things they delivered to each one the decisions of the council in Jerusalem (Acts 15).

"They went through the region of Phrygia and Galatia, having been forbidden by the Holy Spirit to speak the word in Asia." Students divide on the interpretation of this verse because "the region of Phrygia and Galatia" is an ambiguous expression. The view followed here is that Paul and Silas visited the territory in the neighborhood of Iconium and Pisidian Antioch, where Paul and Barnabas had gone on the first missionary journey.

"Asia" in Acts 16:6 does not refer to the continent of Asia or to Asia Minor, but to a particular part of Asia Minor known as the province of Asia. Under the guidance of the Spirit of Jesus, Paul and his two companions went down to Troas on the Aegean coastland.

## The Macedonian Call (Acts 16:9–17:15)

The Macedonian call as such is recorded in Acts 16:9-10, but the response to that call follows immediately and should be considered with the call itself. The call came to Paul in a vision, in which he saw a man of Macedonia standing and pleading, "Come over to Macedonia and help us." Paul took the vision as the word of God and sought to obey the command at once. At verse 10 Luke uses "we" for the first time. This may indicate that he joined the missionary party. In fact, it has been conjectured that Luke was the "man of Macedonia." It is supposed that he was in Troas for a time, gave Paul medical treatment, and became a Christian. After his pleading with Paul to go to Macedonia, Paul, it is surmised, had his vision and accepted it as divine confirmation of Luke's plea. This is attractive but uncertain. In any case, the gospel was taken westward into Europe. For this we can thank God, and Paul.

*Philippi (Acts 16:11–15)*

Paul with Silas, Timothy, and Luke sailed the Aegean and landed at Neapolis. From there they made their way quickly to Philippi, a very important city and a Roman colony within the province of Macedonia.

It was Paul's custom to speak first in the synagogue of a city. Apparently there was no synagogue in Philippi, but the missionaries found a group of worshipers by the river on the Sabbath. They spoke to the group. One of their number was Lydia, who was already a God-fearer, one of a group who were attracted to the God of the Jews. She believed, and she and her household (presumably including children and servants) were baptized. Moreover, she offered her house to the missionaries while they sojourned at Philippi. You will recall how Luke in his Gospel gives a prominent place to women. This he also does in Acts.

While Paul and his companions were in Philippi, they were met by a slave girl who had an illness on which her owners capitalized. Paul was the instrument of her healing, and he and Silas were accused before the magistrates. The accusation was vague and based on the appeal to anti-Jewish prejudice. The two men were stripped, beaten, and thrown into prison (compare 1 Thess. 2:2; 2 Cor. 11:25).

When Jesus faced the cross, he chose it and used it to the glory of God. When Paul and Silas were imprisoned with backs sore and bloody, they "were praying and singing hymns to God, and the prisoners were listening to them." Suddenly there was an earthquake that shook the doors of the prison open and the fetters of the prisoners loose. When the jailer saw the doors of the prison open, he realized what that would mean for him. He was about to commit suicide when Paul restrained him, saying, "Do not harm yourself, for we are all here." He fell at once before Paul and Silas and said, "Sirs, what must I do to be saved?" And they said, "Believe on the Lord Jesus, and you will be saved, you and your household." They interpreted the meaning of this statement to him and to all that were in his house. He washed their wounds, which he had not done earlier, and was baptized together with his family. Moreover, he fed Paul and Silas. He was already giving evidence of his transformation.

When morning came, the magistrates ordered the police to release the two prisoners. Why? Had it dawned on them that they had no case against them? Or had Luke and Timothy been at work on their behalf? But Paul insisted that the magistrates themselves come and release them, for they had beaten uncondemned Roman citizens. To treat a Roman citizen thus was serious business. The magistrates came, apologized, released them, and asked them to leave the city. Whereupon they visited Lydia, encouraged the other disciples, and departed. Since the "we" does not occur again until Paul comes back to Philippi, it is inferred that Luke remained there. It is possible that Philippi was his home.

### Thessalonica (Acts 17:1–9)

The three missionaries passed through Amphipolis and Apollonia en route to Thessalonica, where there were enough Jews to have a synagogue. Some Jews and many God-fearers believed. But other Jews stirred up trouble and brought Jason, in whose house the missionaries were staying, and others before the authorities, saying, "These people who have been turning the world upside down have come here also, and Jason has entertained them as guests. They are all acting contrary to the decrees of the emperor, saying that there is another king named Jesus."

> *In what way had Paul and other disciples turned the world upside down? Can you name particular Christians who are turning the world upside down today? Jesus had been crucified on the accusation that he claimed to be a King. If a person really takes the Kingship of Jesus seriously in our times, will there be opposition? Jason and the other brethren were released after they had given bond.*

### Beroea (Acts 17:10–15)

The brethren sent the missionaries out of town by night to Beroea. There they had unusual success in response from the Jews as well as some success among the Gentiles. Note Luke's reference to women at Philippi (Acts 16:13–18, 40), at Thessalonica (17:4), at Beroea (17:12), and at Athens (17:34). Soon Jews from Thessalonica stirred up trouble for Paul at Beroea, and the believers sent him on his way to Athens. For a time Silas and Timothy continued to work in Beroea. Evidently they were not as objectionable to the opposition as Paul. Soon, however, Paul sent for them to join him.

## Athens (Acts 17:16–34)

Evidently Paul had not planned a ministry in Athens. But while he was waiting there for Silas and Timothy, he was stimulated to break his silence by the idols of the city. Apparently he argued with the Jews and the God-fearers on the Sabbath in the synagogue and with others on weekdays in the marketplace. In this way he came into contact with some of the Epicurean and Stoic philosophers. Those who listened could not understand Paul very well. Therefore, he was brought to the Areopagus. This name may refer either to a place, Mars' Hill, situated very close to the acropolis on which the Parthenon stood and still stands, or to the court that met close by.

Paul accepted this opportunity to preach to the people of Athens. Of course Luke has given us only a brief summary of his sermon. It is different from Paul's other sermons of which we have record, yet not wholly different. Note that he took as his point of contact an inscription, "To an unknown god." At Pergamum in 1910, there was found an inscription, "To unknown gods."

> *Analyze Paul's sermon by making a list of its main points in your notebook.*
>
> *What points do you find in this sermon that are not present in any of the other apostolic sermons recorded in Acts?*
>
> *How do you account for the difference in approach at Athens?*

## Corinth (Acts 18:1–17)

Paul left Athens and went to Corinth, the capital of Achaia. There he met two disciples who were to be his devoted friends: Aquila and his wife Priscilla, who had, along with other Jews, been expelled from Rome by the Emperor Claudius. The three of them were by trade tentmakers; therefore they worked together and made their home together. As was his custom elsewhere, Paul witnessed in the synagogue at Corinth each Sabbath.

Silas and Timothy arrived from Macedonia. According to 1 Thessalonians 3:1–2, Paul had sent Timothy back to Thessalonica from Athens.

> The probable course of events was this: (1) Paul went to Athens alone; (2) Timothy and Silas met him there; (3) their report of the persecutions in Macedonia led Paul to send them back; (4) Paul moved on to Corinth; (5) they rejoined him there.[4]

As usual Paul ran into difficulty with some of the Jews. He moved, therefore, to the house of a God-fearer named Titius Justus, who lived next door to the synagogue. Crispus, the ruler of the synagogue, became a Christian. Paul carried on a fruitful ministry in Corinth for a year and a half.

Finally, the Jews brought Paul before Gallio, the new proconsul of Achaia and the brother of the famous Stoic philosopher Seneca. The accusation brought against Paul was clearly religious; hence, Gallio dismissed the case at once. Sosthenes, the ruler of the synagogue, was beaten by the crowd. We do not know why. Nor do we know Sosthenes's relation to Crispus (v. 8) or to the Sosthenes of 1 Corinthians 1:1.

When Timothy arrived in Corinth from Thessalonica, he brought news from the believers there. Problems had arisen, especially one concerning the second coming. Paul addressed himself to these problems in the two Letters to the Thessalonians during his stay in Corinth.

## Route from Corinth to Antioch (Acts 18:18–22)

Paul did not leave Corinth immediately after his accusation before Gallio. Eventually, however, he did set sail with the intention of going home, taking with him his new friends, Priscilla and Aquila. But en route home he stopped at the great city of Ephesus, which was located in the province of Asia. Earlier Paul had wanted to go to Asia, but the Spirit had led him elsewhere; now the time was ripe. Paul stayed there only a short time and left Priscilla and Aquila to continue the work. After landing at Caesarea on the Palestinian coast, he reported to the mother church in Jerusalem and returned home to Antioch in Syria.

## The Third Missionary Journey

### Ephesus (Acts 18:23–20:1)

Paul had promised the Ephesian Christians, "I will return to you, if God wills." He was now returning by way of Galatia and Phrygia, for he wanted to check on the churches there.

Before his arrival in Ephesus, a disciple named Apollos from Alexandria, Egypt, was engaged in a ministry there. But "he knew only the baptism of John." Therefore, Priscilla and Aquila gave him further instruction in the Christian faith. Apollos undertook a ministry in Achaia with the blessing of the believers in Ephesus. Corinth was one of the places of this ministry (Acts 9:1; compare 1 Cor. 1:12; 3:4–6). When Paul arrived in Ephesus, he found some disciples who, like Apollos, knew only the baptism of John. They had never heard of the Holy Spirit. Therefore, they were baptized in the name of the Lord Jesus. Paul placed his hands on them, and they received the Holy Spirit, spoke with tongues, and prophesied.

For three months Paul spoke in the synagogue at Ephesus. After opposition arose, he witnessed daily in the hall of Tyrannus, which was used by various kinds of speakers. This ministry was carried on for two years, so that people from various parts of the province of Asia had opportunity to hear the gospel, for Ephesus was a great commercial and religious center: "From Smyrna, and Pergamum, and Thyatira, and Sardis, and Philadelphia, and Laodicea, and Colossae, and Hierapolis men [*sic*] came to Ephesus, heard Paul, and went back to found the churches of Asia."[5] It was during his stay at Ephesus that Paul carried on some of his correspondence with the church at Corinth. In fact, he made a hurried trip to Corinth in the midst of this correspondence (see 2 Cor. 2:1; 12:14; 13:1–2). While at Ephesus, he also underwent severe persecution (1 Cor. 15:32; 2 Cor. 1:8). Some think that he was imprisoned there and that during the imprisonment he wrote one or more of the prison epistles: Philippians, Colossians, Philemon.

Paul not only carried on a ministry of the spoken word at Ephesus, he also carried on a ministry of the mighty deed. There were magicians who tried to imitate his healings in the name of Jesus. After these magicians were attacked by a demoniac, many Ephesians became believers and burned their books of magic (compare Acts 8:9–24; 13:4–12).

Paul was planning to do some revisiting of churches in Macedonia and Achaia before going back to Jerusalem. His long-range plans included a visit to Rome. Apparently he had already made contact with various churches to be engaged in raising funds for the poor saints in Jerusalem (1 Cor. 16:1–4). Presumably he sent Timothy and Erastus ahead into Macedonia to assist the local congregations in this endeavor.

But before Paul left Ephesus, a great stir was precipitated by a silversmith named Demetrius. The temple of Artemis was located in Ephesus. Demetrius and his fellow craftsmen sold souvenirs associated with the goddess and the temple. But sales had fallen off as a result of Paul's witness. The silversmiths cried out, "Great is Artemis of the Ephesians!" The rioters rushed into the theater and took with them two of Paul's companions. Paul wanted to face the mob himself, but his friends prevented him. One Alexander attempted to make a defense but could not. Finally, the town clerk quieted the people, and, among other things, reminded them that the courts were available for settling disputes in an orderly manner. "After the uproar had ceased, Paul sent for the disciples; and after encouraging them and saying farewell, he left for Macedonia."

### To Macedonia and Corinth (Acts 20:2–3)

At first Paul had planned to go to Corinth directly from Ephesus (2 Cor. 1:16), but on account of dissension in the church there, he sent a letter by Titus (2 Cor. 7:6–8 ). Then he made his way toward Macedonia (Acts 20:1). When he reached Troas en route, he found a door open for the preaching of the gospel, but he was disturbed because Titus had not returned from Corinth (2 Cor. 2:12–13). It was therefore with heavy heart that Paul continued his journey to Macedonia. But Titus met him in Macedonia with good news from the church at Corinth, and he was overcome with joy (2 Cor. 7:5–16). He was in process of gathering the offering for the poor in the Jerusalem community (see especially 2 Cor. 8–9). Undoubtedly he expected this offering to assist in healing the breach between the Jewish and the Gentile factions in the church. He was always deeply concerned about the unity and peace of the whole church.

Eventually he came to Greece and spent three months in Corinth. It was during that time probably that he wrote his greatest work, the Letter to the Romans (Rom. 15:23–33).

### From Corinth to Jerusalem (Acts 20:3–21:16)

Paul was about to sail for Syria. When, however, he learned of a plot against him, he made his way back through Macedonia. Traveling companions went ahead and waited at Troas. Apparently Luke rejoined Paul at Philippi (Acts 20:5), and they sailed together to Troas, where they met their friends. At Troas Paul preached until midnight on Sunday evening when a young man named Eutychus went to sleep and fell out of the window. After he was picked up, the disciples celebrated the Lord's Supper and Paul conversed with them till daybreak.

*Follow the journey in Acts 20:13–16 on a map in a Bible atlas.*

Paul wanted to get to Jerusalem by Pentecost in order to present the collection from the mission churches at that time. He did not trust himself to return to Ephesus, for he would then not be able to get to Jerusalem as he had planned. Hence, he asked the elders of the Ephesian church to meet him at Miletus, some thirty miles away.

His farewell to the elders is a moving and instructive discourse (Acts 20:18–35). It is quite different from the sermons he preached to nonbelievers.

*Identify the themes of this discourse in outline and show how each theme is developed.*

*What do you feel is the permanent value of this message?*

*Note the beatitude in verse 35. What does it mean?*

The actual parting of the great Apostle and these leaders of the church at Ephesus where he had labored so long was a deeply significant occasion. He knelt down and prayed with them; they wept, embraced him, kissed him, and told him good-bye for the last time. Such a parting was not easy for him or for them. The great theologian and preacher was also a pastor of pastors.

*Follow Luke's narrative (Acts 21:1ff.) on a map in a Bible atlas.*

While his ship was unloading at Tyre, Paul stayed with the disciples there for a week. When the time came for him and his companions to leave, the disciples—men, their wives, and their children—all went down to the beach to say farewell. They all knelt on the seashore and prayed together—a glorious sight to behold.

At Ptolemais the missionaries greeted the believers and moved on immediately to Caesarea. There Philip the evangelist, whom we met earlier, was their host. Philip had four unmarried daughters who had the gift of prophecy. The prophet Agabus (compare 11:28) came from Judea, and in the manner of an Old Testament prophet acted out the prediction of Paul's imprisonment that lay ahead. All present tried to persuade Paul not to go to Jerusalem. "I am ready," said he, "not only to be bound but even to die in Jerusalem for the name of the Lord Jesus."

Therefore, Paul and the other missionaries and disciples from Caesarea all made their way to Jerusalem.

## The Journey to Rome—and Beyond?

### Arrested in Jerusalem (Acts 21:17–23:35)

Paul was received by the believers in Jerusalem gladly. James, the head of the mother church, and the elders of the church received Paul's report of his ministry and glorified God. We assume that Paul presented the gift from the younger churches at this time.

But a new problem had arisen. Jewish Christians who were zealous for the Law expected all Jews who became Christians to continue to keep the Law. It had been rumored that Paul taught Jews who became Christians to forsake the Law and not to circumcise their children. Though Paul himself continued to observe at least some Jewish customs, his teachings gave no support to requiring such observance of anyone.

James and the elders proposed a compromise demonstration to Paul. Four Jewish Christians had taken a Nazirite vow. Paul was requested to join them in their ritual of purification and pay their expenses. This would help to clear Paul's reputation among the strict party. Evidently Paul felt he could do this without surrendering any basic principle of the gospel, since he was a Jew and ordinarily followed Jewish law (see 1 Cor. 9:19–23; Acts 18:18). However, his behavior would be understood by many as implying that he believed a Jewish Christian must keep the Law.

> Read Galatians 3:23–29; 4:21–31; 5:4; Romans 3:21–31; 7:4–6. Do you feel Paul was consistent with his own teaching on this occasion?

> What do you think you would have done in Paul's situation?

Jews from Asia (probably Ephesus) stirred up trouble for Paul in Jerusalem, bringing essentially the same charge as that which had been brought against Stephen (Acts 21:28; 6:13). Moreover, they thought he had taken Trophimus, a Gentile, into the Temple with him. A Gentile was forbidden to go beyond the court of the Gentiles on pain of death. Soon a mob had gathered and was about to kill Paul. The tribune intervened and took him to the barracks. He thought Paul was an Egyptian revolutionary, but Paul addressed him in Greek and identified himself. Paul requested that he be permitted to speak to the people. The permission was granted, and he spoke from the steps of the Tower of Antonio. The word "Hebrew" in Acts 21:40 probably means Aramaic, since the latter was much better known at that time. Paul told the story of his life. But the crowd broke out with shouts of destruction. The tribune gave the order to beat him until he confessed his crime. However, he reversed his decision when he learned that Paul was a Roman citizen.

In order to discover the real reason for the accusation against Paul, the tribune called on the Sanhedrin to meet and set Paul before them. Paul recognized the danger of having his case committed to this group. Therefore, he played on the differences between the Pharisees and the Sadducees to set the court at odds with itself by identifying himself as a Pharisee and with the hope of the resurrection of the dead. The Sadducees did not believe in the resurrection. The members of the court were thrown into dissension among themselves, and Paul was brought back into the barracks. The following night Paul had a vision in which he was assured that he would bear witness in Rome.

Forty men made a plot to kill Paul. They took an oath not to eat or drink until the deed was done. But Paul's nephew heard of it and informed Paul.

Paul in turn sent him to the tribune with the message, whereupon the tribune sent Paul under armed guard at night to the governor Felix, whose headquarters were in Caesarea. The tribune, Claudius Lysias, also required Paul's accusers to appear before Felix to make their accusation.

## Imprisoned at Caesarea (Acts 24:1–27)

Paul, therefore, had to appear before Felix. The high priest Ananias along with some elders of the Jews and a spokesman, one Tertullus, brought their charges against Paul.

*What were these charges (Acts 24:2–9)?*

*How did Paul defend himself (Acts 24:10–21)?*

Felix seems to have been a rather indecisive fellow, for he put off making a decision until he could confer with Lysias. He did permit Paul to have visitors, however. Felix and his wife Drucilla came to hear Paul speak on faith in Christ Jesus. Felix was shaken by Paul's message, but he did not become a Christian. He wanted Paul to bribe him with money.

We do not know how long Paul was in prison at Caesarea, because the precise reference of "two years" (v. 27) is uncertain. Does it refer to the length of Paul's imprisonment or to the length of Felix's term of office? In either case Paul was there long enough to have done some writing if he so chose. Some think one or more of the prison epistles may have been written at Caesarea.

## The Appeal to Caesar (Acts 25:1–26:32)

Porcius Festus succeeded Felix. Almost at once he went to Jerusalem, where Paul's enemies presented their case against him. They wanted Paul sent back to Jerusalem. But Festus insisted that they go to Caesarea instead. Again Paul was put on trial. His accusers brought many unsubstantiated charges. Luke has summarized Paul's defense: "I have in no way committed an offense against the law of the Jews, or against the temple, or against the emperor." In order to curry favor with the accusers, Festus suggested holding a trial in Jerusalem. Paul pointed out that he was already standing before Caesar's tribunal where he belonged as a Roman citizen, and that there was no real charge that could justify his appearance before the Jewish court. Said he, "I am appealing to the emperor's tribunal." Paul made this appeal because he knew the danger of being tried in Jerusalem and because he believed this was God's way of sending him to witness in Rome. Paul's appeal was a way out for Festus: "You have appealed to the emperor; to the emperor you will go."

But before Paul was sent on his way to Caesar, he was to appear before King Herod Agrippa II (Acts 25:13–26:32). Agrippa and his sister Bernice came to pay a social call on Festus, the new governor. In the process of conversation Festus laid Paul's case before the king, and Agrippa expressed a desire to hear Paul. Festus needed some help in formulating a statement of charges to the emperor. Consequently Paul made his defense before King Agrippa. Paul never let an evangelistic opportunity slip by. He tried to convert King Agrippa. Those present agreed that Paul had done nothing deserving death or imprisonment. And Agrippa volunteered, "This man could have been set free if he had not appealed to the emperor."

## The Voyage to Rome (Acts 27:1–28:31)

Festus lost no time in sending Paul to Rome.

*Luke's story of this voyage is so marvelously told you cannot afford to miss reading it just as he wrote it. Follow the various places mentioned on a map in a Bible atlas.*

Luke (see the "we" in 27:1) and Aristarchus accompanied Paul on his voyage. Julius, the centurion in charge of prisoners, was kind to Paul. At Myra the prisoners were transferred to another ship. At the harbor of Fair Havens Paul warned the centurion of the danger of further travel until the winter had passed. The "fast" mentioned in 27:9 was the Day of Atonement, which was observed in late September or early October.

Sailing became increasingly dangerous as winter approached. But Paul's advice was not heeded. The attempt was made to reach Phoenix, a harbor of Crete. But a storm came and all hope was abandoned. Paul had a vision, however, in which he was assured that he and his companions would be saved. "So keep up your courage," he said, "for I have faith in God that it will be exactly as I have been told."

For two weeks the men had been unable to eat. Paul encouraged them to eat and be strengthened. "He took bread, and giving thanks to God in the presence of all, he broke it and began to eat." The ship ran onto a shoal, and the stern was broken. The soldiers wanted to kill the prisoners because their own lives would be forfeited if they should escape. But the centurion prevented them for Paul's sake. All persons escaped to land. Paul's faith was vindicated.

The island of escape was Malta. The people there welcomed the escapees generously. Publius, a man of some means, showed special hospitality to at least some of the party. While they wintered on Malta, Paul carried on an extensive ministry of the mighty deed, healing Publius's father and many others.

After three months, the voyage was resumed on a ship that had wintered at Malta. Eventually the ship reached Puteoli on the western coast of Italy. "There we found believers," says Luke, "and were invited to stay with them for seven days." Who took the gospel to Puteoli? We do not know. The book of Acts and the epistles do not give us the whole story of the church, just as the Gospels do not give us the whole story of Jesus. But there were many disciples here and there who bore their witness to Jesus and the resurrection. Though the Christians at Puteoli had never seen Paul, Luke, and Aristarchus before, they welcomed them as members of the one church of Jesus Christ.

Much of the journey from Puteoli to Rome was on the famous Appian Way. Undoubtedly messengers were sent by the believers of Puteoli to the believers in Rome concerning Paul's arrival, for a delegation from Rome met him and escorted him to the imperial city. Paul had reached Rome at last! Although he was a prisoner, he was allowed to stay by himself, except for the soldier who guarded him. Several things may have played a part in the considerate treatment he received: the letter from Festus, the report of the centurion who took him to Rome, and the influence of certain Christians in Rome.

After only three days in Rome, Paul called together the local leaders of the Jews. He thought that the accusation of the leaders in Jerusalem might have been sent to them. Hence, he rehearsed his problem for them, whereupon they indicated that they had received no letters from Judea about him. They wanted to hear more about his views. The day was set, and they came to hear him at his lodging. He talked from morning to evening. Some were convinced; most were not. He again turned to the Gentiles.

For two years Paul lived in Rome at his own expense (see Phil. 4:18) and performed a notable ministry. People came to him, and he preached the kingdom and taught about the Lord Jesus Christ. It was probably during this house imprisonment that he wrote Philemon, Colossians, Ephesians, and Philippians.

What happened to Paul after the two years in Rome? Luke does not tell us. Some have conjectured that he wrote a third volume (or at least planned to), in which he included the answer to our question. There are those who claim that Paul suffered martyrdom under Nero after the two-year ministry about 61 C.E. There are others who maintain that he was released in 61 and carried on a further ministry in Asia, Macedonia, Spain,

Crete, and Greece. Paul had expressed a desire to go to Spain (Rom. 15:24). A statement by Clement of Rome may imply that he saw his desire fulfilled.

Evidence from the pastoral epistles supports the view that he was released from the first imprisonment in Rome (see 2 Tim. 4:16–17). Then, Paul was again imprisoned, the theory goes, when the Roman government changed its attitude toward the Christian movement, and he was put to death under Nero about 68 C.E. Regardless of when that last hour came, we can be grateful for the life of the great Apostle. "At Paul's conversion Christianity was a Jewish sect. At his death it was a world-religion."[6]

# Paul's Witness by Letter

*P*aul's witness by letter is intertwined with his witness by life, for writing letters was a part of his life. You will find it helpful, therefore, to refer to particular sections of Chapter 20 from time to time. Paul was a man who covered a large territory in his ministry. This meant that he was not always able in person to attend to issues that arose in a particular field. On some occasions he sent one of his assistants to take care of the matter. At other times he carried on his pastoral ministry by letter.[1] In general a Greek letter of the first century was composed of four parts: the greeting, the thanksgiving, the body or chief subject matter, and the farewell. Paul had this general pattern in mind but filled it with Christian content and varied it as he saw fit.

## Galatians—The Magna Carta of Christian Liberty

Galatians has rightly been called "the Magna Carta of Christian Liberty." It is the first document ever written on the subject. The declaration it propounds has greatly affected the life of the church from the time it was penned. It made it impossible for Christianity to remain a Jewish sect. This pronouncement was much in the thinking of the Reformers of the sixteenth century. And it is much in the thinking of many believers in our day.

You will recall that Paul wrote Galatians to the congregations at Pisidian Antioch, Lystra, Derbe, and Iconium, which he had established on his first missionary journey; and that this writing took place before the meeting of the Jerusalem Council described in Acts 15.

Paul and Barnabas had not required those who professed faith in Jesus Christ to be circumcised and undertake the observance of the Jewish laws and customs. Soon after they had returned home from Galatia, certain Jewish Christians had told the Galatians that they must observe Jewish customs in order to be real Christians. The Letter to the Galatians was written to counteract this teaching. In it Paul makes three major points: a defense of his own apostleship, a defense of the gospel, and a defense of Christian freedom.

> *The letter is short. Read it in its entirety and supplement the comments offered here with an outline of your own in your notebook.*
>
> *Record questions that you would like the class to discuss.*

## Paul's Defense of His Own Apostleship (Gal. 1:1–2:21)

Paul's opponents brought certain accusations against him. One of them was that he was not a real apostle, since he was not one of the Twelve. Therefore, Paul begins his letter with the affirmation that he is an apostle not by human appointment but by God's. Apparently some in the Galatian congregations were being taken in by the Judaizers. And Paul refers to the gospel of these people as "a different gospel" from the one he had proclaimed to them. He did not receive the gospel from other people but in a special revelation. At this point Paul tells the story of his conversion; his visit to Arabia; two visits to Jerusalem; the approval of his ministry by James, Peter, and John; and his opposition to Peter at Antioch.

> *What do you think is the strongest point in Paul's defense of his apostleship?*

## Paul's Defense of the Gospel (Gal. 3:1–4:31)

The gospel according to Paul is this: Justification (that is, being made right with God) is on the basis of faith, not on the basis of keeping the Law. The Galatians themselves received the Holy Spirit not by works of the Law but "by believing what they heard." Abraham "'believed God, and it was reckoned to him as righteousness.'" People of faith are the children of Abraham who had faith. In fact, the promise had been made to the patriarch that in him *all nations* would be blessed. To rely on the works of the Law for justification is to rest under a curse, because no one can keep the Law perfectly. It is Christ who has redeemed us from that curse by becoming a curse for us.

God's promise to Abraham was made long before the Law was given and is in no way annulled by the Law. The Law was a custodian or "disciplinarian until Christ came," but Christ has made a difference in our relation to the Law. It is through faith, not through the Law, that we become children of God. "As many of you as were baptized into Christ have clothed yourselves with Christ. There is no longer Jew or Greek, there is no longer slave or free, there is no longer male or female; for all of you are one in Christ Jesus."

*What are the implications of this statement for the church in relation to culture, race, social status, and sex?*

Just as a minor does not enjoy the full privilege of inheritance until coming of age, so the Jew was bound to the Law and the Gentile to idolatry until the coming of the gospel. "But when the fullness of time had come, God sent his Son, born of a woman, born under the law, in order to redeem those who were under the law, so that we might receive adoption as children." We become children of God, whether we are Jews or Gentiles, through the Son of God.

## Paul's Defense of Christian Freedom (Gal. 5:1–6:18)

It seems that Paul's opponents brought a third accusation against him, namely, that his gospel would lead to moral degeneration. In speaking to this issue Paul begins, "For freedom Christ has set us free." If one submits to circumcision, one thereby demonstrates that one does not accept Christ as an adequate Savior. Moreover, the person who does this is obligated to keep the whole Law. But "in Christ Jesus neither circumcision nor uncircumcision counts for anything; the only thing that counts is faith working through love."

At this point Paul begins to concentrate on the Christian ethic, which is the ethic of true freedom. The key words in this presentation are "faith," "love," and "spirit." Christian faith is to express itself in Christian love. And Christian freedom is not pagan license. We are not to ridicule the Law; we are to fulfill it by loving our neighbors as ourselves. To enable us to do this God has given us the Spirit. And "the desires of the Spirit are against the flesh." "Flesh" means not our biological system but that which is yet unregenerate in the motivations of our life.

The fact that we are under the Spirit does not mean that we cannot get specific about ethical matters. "Now the works of the flesh are obvious: fornication, impurity, licentiousness, idolatry, sorcery, enmities, strife, jealousy, anger, quarrels, dissensions, factions, envy, drunkenness, carousing, and things like these. I am warning you, as I warned you before: those who do such things will not inherit the kingdom of God." In other words, the person who does such things gives evidence of a lack of Christian faith. On the positive side: "By contrast, the fruit of the Spirit is love, joy, peace, patience, kindness, generosity, faithfulness, gentleness, and self-control. There is no law against such things. And those who belong to Christ Jesus have crucified the flesh with its passions and desires." The Spirit gives new life and ethical guidance.

What really matters is not whether one is a circumcised Jew or an uncircumcised Gentile, but that one is a "new creation" in Christ Jesus. Today Jewish law and customs are not the real stumbling blocks, but rather societal rules on the one hand and disregard for responsible ethical behavior on the other. In justification by Christ we are set free from trying to save ourselves and are promised the Spirit to enable us to set the highest standards in response to God's grace.

## First and Second Thessalonians—The Second Coming of Christ

The second coming of Christ is a major concern in Paul's Letters to the Thessalonians. In 1 Thessalonians he refers to it repeatedly (1:10; 2:19; 3:13; 4:13–18; 5:1–3, 23), and in 2 Thessalonians he seeks to correct a misunderstanding about it.

*Review the account of Paul's founding the church at Thessalonica that is recorded in Acts 17:1–9.*

Thessalonica was a great commercial center, situated on the famous Egnatian Way and boasting an excellent harbor. It was a strategic center also for the proclamation of the gospel. While there were some Jewish Christians in the church there, the majority of the members were Gentiles who had "turned to God from idols" (1 Thess. 1:9). Though Paul had not been able to return to Thessalonica himself, he sent Timothy to visit the church. After Timothy rejoined him, Paul wrote 1 Thessalonians from Corinth about 51 C.E. and 2 Thessalonians shortly thereafter.

### First Thessalonians

First Thessalonians has two main parts. In part one Paul records his personal relations with the church (chaps. 1–3), and in part two he speaks to problems with which the young church is confronted (chaps. 4–5). One of these problems was occasioned by the death of some of the Thessalonian Christians before the coming of the Lord. Evidently the return of Christ was expected at any time. This return or coming was a part of the apostolic preaching (Acts 3:20). The Thessalonians wanted to know the status of those who died before the second coming. Paul gives his answer in what has been called "the Pauline apocalypse" (1 Thess. 4:13–18).

*Read these much discussed words carefully.*

Among these verses are expressions drawn from Jewish apocalyptic literature in an attempt to express that which transcends the capacity of humans fully to comprehend. But we can grasp the heart of Paul's assurance. The resurrection of Jesus from the dead assures Christians of their own resurrection. Those who have died and those who are still alive at the Lord's coming will share alike in his victory. This consummation will take place suddenly.

## Second Thessalonians

In Paul's Second Letter to the Thessalonians, he touches on a number of topics, but the burden of the letter is again the second coming and closely related themes. Some of the Thessalonians had received the wrong idea about the Day of the Lord. They had stopped work either because they thought the day had arrived or was just around the corner. Furthermore, they claimed to have received the idea from a letter of Paul. Yet in 1 Thessalonians Paul had counseled the believers to work with their hands (4:11). Second Thessalonians 2:2 seems to imply that a letter had been forged in Paul's name.

Before the coming of the Lord, Paul expects the coming of some kind of apostasy and "the lawless one" who "takes his seat in the temple of God." But when the Lord comes, the "lawless one" will be destroyed. Various suggestions have been made about the identity of "the lawless one," but nothing certain can be said. The Thessalonians probably understood whom Paul was talking about, but that "inside knowledge" has not been transmitted to us. What we do know certainly is that Paul assures the Thessalonians of Christ's victory and charges them to bring any idle believer into line with Paul's teaching: "Anyone unwilling to work should not eat."

## The Corinthian Correspondence— Ethical Problems in a Young Church

The city of Corinth was noted for its culture, its commerce, and its immorality. It was the capital of the Roman province of Achaia (Greece). Paul's correspondence with the church that he established there was more complicated than his correspondence with any other church. In order to understand this correspondence, we shall attempt to set each part of it in its historical sequence and context insofar as that is possible.

## Paul's First Visit to Corinth (Acts 18:1–18)

Paul made his first visit to Corinth on his second missionary journey about 51 C.E. It was during his eighteen-month stay in Corinth that the church of Corinth was founded.

*Review the last chapter and read Acts 18:1–18 again to get the facts clearly in mind.*

## The Earliest Letter

On the basis of Paul's own word, we know that our "First Corinthians" was not his earliest letter to the church at Corinth (1 Cor. 5:9–13). In verse 9 he says, "I wrote to you in my letter not to associate with sexually immoral persons." This prior letter may be totally lost unless, as some think, parts of it are now included in 1 Corinthians 6:12–20 and 2 Corinthians 6:14–7:1.

A reading of 1 Corinthians 5:9–13 reveals at once that Paul was not telling the Corinthians that they could not have any kind of contact with the non-Christian citizens of Corinth. Such an injunction would keep them from evangelistic effort where it was greatly needed. Rather Paul is saying that worldly living cannot be tolerated in the church. There is such a thing as necessary church discipline. In our Reformed churches today we have the means necessary for exercising church discipline, but it is rarely used in a local congregation. Why do you think such discipline is largely a thing of the past? Should a different approach to discipline be worked out?

## Our First Corinthians

The letter we call "First Corinthians" was written by Paul from Ephesus during the third missionary journey about 56 C.E. to deal with an oral report he had received and with issues raised in a letter sent by the Corinthians to Paul (1 Cor.7:1). Here we outline the letter but, of necessity, comment only briefly on some parts of the outline.

*Dissensions in the Church (chaps. 1–4)*

Those who generate party strife in the church are reminded that Christ is not divided.

*Sex and Marriage (5:1–13; 6:9–7:40)*

The individual Christian's body is a temple of the Holy Spirit and to commit immorality is to dishonor the indwelling Spirit.

*Lawsuits (6:1–8)*

It is better to suffer wrong than to wrong another (compare Matt. 5:39; 1 Peter 2:23).

*Food Offered to Idols (8:1–11:1)*

Christian liberty exercised apart from Christian responsibility becomes the occasion of sin against one's associates and against Christ himself.

*Women in the Church (11:2–16; 14:34–36)*

Certain problems arose in Corinth in relation to services of worship. And Paul deals with these problems in chapters 11–14. The first of them is the role of women in church.

As we try to understand what Paul says on this subject, it is necessary to remember his Hebraic heritage and the environment in which the Corinthian believers had their being. In the first passage (11:2–16), Paul indicates that a woman should not pray or prophesy with her head unveiled. This was an acceptable way to show modesty in his day. How ought a woman or man show modesty in church today? In the world today?

The passage with which we have just dealt is based on the assumption that women are to pray and prophesy in public worship (compare Acts 21:9; Exod. 15:20; Judg. 4:4; 2 Kings 22:14; 2 Chron. 34:22). But the second passage (14:33b–36) states, "As in all the churches of the saints, women should be silent in the churches" (compare 1 Tim. 2:11–12). We assume that Paul and his readers understood how both of these statements could apply, but we can only hazard a guess. Perhaps chapter 11 had reference to the meetings in the homes of church members and chapter 14 to the larger gatherings of the entire congregation.[2]

Obviously Paul was dealing with societal customs by which Christian women were to express modesty in the first century. No Reformed or Presbyterian congregation today follows literally all of Paul's injunctions on this or any other such subject. Indeed, the ordination of women as elders and pastors is well-established practice now.

> *How are we, then, to hear Paul's exhortation and advice from so long ago? Do we deny the authority of scripture when we take a stance different to Paul's? What is the role of the Holy Spirit in the ongoing interpretation of the Bible in the church?*

*The Lord's Supper (11:17–34)*

The Lord's Supper, as it is described by Paul here, was joined with a meal. But there were divisions among those present, perhaps the same divisions mentioned in chapter 1 or divisions based on social status. Some ate like pigs and others got drunk. This was a desecration of the Supper. Paul has given us the best known and the earliest written record of Jesus' celebration of the Last Supper with the Twelve. Here is emphasized the vicariousness of that for which the elements stand, the remembrance of Christ, his sealing of the new covenant in his blood, and a proclamation of his final coming.

In seeking to correct the abuse of the Supper in the Corinthian congregation, Paul warned against participating in the bread and cup in an unworthy manner: "For all who eat and drink without discerning the body, eat and drink judgment against themselves." The "body" to be discerned is both the literally broken body of Christ and the church as his body now in the world. One meaning does not cancel the other. It must be recognized that Christ's body was broken for each one who participates in the Lord's Supper. But one must realize also that one celebrates as a member of the church, which is also Christ's body. Not only does the Supper involve a believer's relation to Christ but also a relation to other believers.[3]

*What constitutes a worthy participation in the Lord's Supper?*

*Spiritual Gifts (chaps. 12–14)*

Evidently the Corinthian Christians had questioned Paul about the relative value of different spiritual gifts.

*List all the gifts treated by Paul in chapter 12.*

*How many of these particular gifts have you witnessed in a present-day congregation?*

*What makes the difference between the early church and the church today?*

In confronting the issue of spiritual gifts, Paul develops the doctrine of the church as the body of Christ. The one Spirit is the Author of all these gifts for the benefit of the one body. The church is like a human body. It is made up of Jews and Greeks, slaves and free; and the various gifts with which its members are endowed contribute to the overall unity. No one organ of the human body can say to another organ, "I have no need of you." The fact is that unity (not uniformity) is possible only through diversity.

Instead of making the diversity of gifts an occasion for argument, let us respond to the gift of God's love in such a way that all gifts are used as God intended. It is in this setting that Paul has given us the famous thirteenth chapter of 1 Corinthians.

*Keeping this in mind, what is the message of this passage to the local congregation and to the church at large?*

Speaking in the ecstasy of tongues was a special problem in the church at Corinth. Therefore, Paul set this gift in the perspective of the church's edification that all things might be done decently and in order.

### The Resurrection of the Body (chap. 15)

This is the climax of Paul's "first" Letter to the Corinthians. No greater statement of the wonder of the resurrection of the dead has ever been penned.

*Read it for yourself.*

The Corinthians had raised certain questions about the resurrection of the dead, and Paul answers them here.

In the gospel that Paul had already preached to the Corinthians the death and resurrection of Christ were "of first importance." Christ's resurrection was witnessed by a large number of disciples, including Paul himself. But the Corinthians had a Greek background of belief in the immortality of the soul rather than in the resurrection of the body. The flesh was thought to be an evil prison in which the soul was confined. Death was considered the occasion for the release of the soul from its evil body. It was, therefore, not easy for the Corinthians to accept the proclamation of the resurrection of the body.

Paul was a Jew, and his scriptures were the Old Testament. Jews viewed the person as a "psychosomatic" unity. To be a person was to be a body. Life after death involved resurrection of the person in full integrity. Moreover, Christ was raised as a body from the dead. The Christian's faith in life after death does not rest on nature but on Christ's own resurrection. Apart from the resurrection of Christ, there is no gospel.

The question is asked, "How are the dead raised? With what kind of body do they come?" There are different kinds of bodies within the world about us. The body adapted to this world will be transformed into a body adapted to the world to come.

> What is sown is perishable,
>     what is raised is imperishable.
> It is sown in dishonor,
>     it is raised in glory.
> It is sown in weakness,
>     it is raised in power.

It is sown a physical body,
   it is raised a spiritual body.
If there is a physical body,
   there is also a spiritual body.
(1 Cor. 15: 42–44)

There is identity between the person-body of this age and the person-body of the age to come, but there is also difference; and this difference is spelled out by Paul in a series of contrasts. The word translated "physical" is an adjective based on the Greek word for "soul." Literally speaking, Paul says the "soulish body" of animal vitality disintegrates. But the "spiritual body," which is a body adapted to the world to come, is imperishable. Just as, in this life, we have a body of identification, communication, and service; so in the life to come we shall have a body of individuality, communication, and service. Such a faith carries with it the assurance that our labor is not in vain in the Lord. "Thanks be to God, who gives us the victory through our Lord Jesus Christ."

## A Painful Visit to Corinth

As wonderful as 1 Corinthians is, it did not bring peace within the church at Corinth. False teachers from the outside were attempting to undermine Paul's influence (2 Cor. 11). Apparently under their guidance a member of the Corinthian church became especially antagonistic to Paul. But when he repented, Paul forgave him and called on the Corinthians to do the same (2 Cor. 2:5–8).

It was while the rebellion against Paul was still in process that he made a painful visit to Corinth (2 Cor. 2:1; 12:14; 13:1–3). But the visit did not achieve its purpose. Paul returned to Ephesus a disappointed apostle.

## A Severe Letter from Ephesus

Paul did not take defeat lying down. He kept on trying. From Ephesus he wrote the severe letter referred to in 2 Corinthians 2:3–4; 7:8. It is possible that at least a part of this letter is to be found in 2 Corinthians 10–13. This suggestion has been made because these chapters are severe and quite different in tone from the preceding nine chapters. These first nine chapters give the impression of having been written after the severe letter.

*It is, therefore, recommended that you read 2 Corinthians 10–13 at this point in your study.*

We summarize these chapters here. Paul was accused of being humble in face-to-face contacts with the Corinthians but bold in his distance from them. This Paul denies. Moreover, he reminds them that the authority he exercises among them comes from the Lord. In 1 Corinthians 4:15, he had already reminded them that he was their father in Christ; and a father has authority (see 2 Cor. 10:14). He was accused of being inferior "to these superlative apostles." It was true that Paul took no remuneration from the Corinthians for his ministry among them, but this was no sign of inferiority. The fact is these troublemongers are "false apostles." But if it is necessary to compare notes, let the Corinthians look at his record of service and suffering.

*Read 11:21–12:13.*

In these famous verses, Paul records what his Christian commitment has cost him and tells his story of the thorn in the flesh. The facts speak for themselves.

## Our Second Corinthians (1–9)

Titus delivered the severe letter and later met Paul in Macedonia with the good news of the church's repentance (2 Cor. 7:5–8). In response to this good news, Paul wrote our 2 Corinthians 1–9—perhaps all of the letter originally.

Recently he had escaped death in Asia. After reviewing his relations with the Corinthians briefly, he moves into a description of the apostolic ministry (2:14–6:10). The true apostolic minister is not a peddler of God's word. Both the "product" and those to whom it is "sold" are of vital concern. Indeed, Paul does not need to commend himself, for the Corinthian Christians are themselves his letter of recommendation.

The apostolic minister is a minister of the new covenant. The old covenant was expressed in a code; the new covenant is expressed in the Spirit. Paul's life as a Pharisee under the old covenant was a kind of death. According to Paul, when a Jew reads the Mosaic Law, a veil lies over the mind. But when one reads it in light of the revelation of Christ, the veil is lifted, for in Christ the Law is truly illuminated. The Spirit brings a freedom to be progressively transformed into Christ's likeness. God "has shone in our hearts to give the light of the knowledge of the glory of God in the face of Jesus Christ."

Paul as apostolic minister has the treasure of the gospel in a vessel made of clay "that it may be made clear that this extraordinary power belongs to God and does not come from us." This means the endurance of all sorts of afflictions, but God keeps on renewing Paul's inner nature as he looks beyond that which is temporal to that which is unseen and eternal.

The apostolic minister performs a ministry of reconciliation (5:11–16:13). The dynamic motivation of this ministry is the love of Christ—Christ's love for the minister and the minister's love for Christ. The touchstone of this love is the in-behalf-of death of Christ.

*Read 5:16–21 again and again.*

Here we have a description of the divine initiative and the human response, of the new creation and the atonement, of the call to be reconciled and the call to be God's ambassadors. Paul's ministry of reconciliation is characterized in 6:1–13. The following question is addressed to those who are planning to be ordained ministers: If you were confronted by the prospect of having a ministry similar to that of Paul, what would your response be?

Paul was not only concerned about the quality of his ministry but also about the quality of the congregation's life (6:14–7:1). "Do not be mismatched with unbelievers" does not mean that the Christian can never speak to a non-Christian but that the Christian should not form ties that create compromising situations.

Chapters 8–9 are Paul's reminder to the Corinthians of their opportunity to fulfill their commitment toward the contribution for the poor saints at Jerusalem. Paul uses the poverty-stricken Macedonian churches as an example of joyous and generous giving. They considered taking part in this contribution a "privilege." But such a tangible response was grounded in the prior heart-dedication of themselves to the Lord. But beyond all human examples of giving is that of our Lord himself, who "though he was rich, yet for your sakes . . . became poor, so that by his poverty you might become rich." Christian giving is not a matter of coercion, "for God loves a cheerful giver." In the final analysis, we must say by word and gift, "Thanks be to God for his indescribable gift!"

## Paul's Last Visit to Corinth

Soon after Paul wrote 2 Corinthians, he made his last recorded visit to Corinth (see p. 326). He spent three months in Achaia (Greece) (Acts 20:1–3), and much if not all of that time was used in a ministry in and around Corinth.

## Romans—The Constitution of Christian Liberty

As Galatians is the Magna Carta of Christian liberty, so Romans is its constitution. According to Luther, Romans is "the clearest gospel of all." Whether one agrees with Luther or not, the four Gospels and Romans are complementary. The Gospels are proclamations of the gospel; Romans is a statement of the Christian faith. Paul wrote Romans about 58 C.E. from Corinth. There is a claim that Peter founded the church in Rome, but this is improbable. Some from Rome heard Peter preach on the occasion of the new Pentecost in Jerusalem (Acts 2:10); they may have started the Roman congregation.

The fact is we do not know who started the church there. Most of Paul's letters were addressed to churches he himself had established, but not so in the case of Romans. The fact that Paul had not visited the Christians in Rome perhaps accounts for the more formal style of this epistle. While it is by no means written in the manner of a modern book on systematic theology, it is the most complete statement of the Christian faith in any one New Testament book.

*Paul's own introduction is found in 1:1–17. Give special attention to the text of the letter in 1:16–17.*

"I am not ashamed of the gospel" is an understatement. The fact is Paul was proud of the gospel. It is God's power or mighty work for salvation to everyone who receives it in faith. It was offered to the Jew first, but it was as truly intended for the Gentile. Its real theme is the righteousness of God, which is revealed through faith for faith: "The one who is righteous will live by faith" (see Hab. 2:4). That is to say, the person who is right with God on the basis of faith is the person who shall have that quality of life that God offers in the gospel.

## The Righteousness of God in Judgment (Rom. 1:18–3:20)

The Old Testament constitutes a chief part of the background for understanding Paul's doctrine of the righteousness of God in judgment. God's wrath, which is introduced in 1:18, is but the other side of God's love. It is love rejected and scorned. It is love with a backbone. Any other kind of love is no good. People sometimes have difficulty with the idea because they are too conscious of the sinful quality of their own wrath.

First, Paul presents God's wrath against the unrighteousness of the Gentiles (1:18–32). For the Gentiles are without excuse, as God through the creation has revealed to all the reality and power of God. Yet they have turned to idolatry. In wrath God gave them up to their own desires and let them sin as they chose. In some cases their sinfulness issued in degrading sex perversion related to idol worship, and in other cases in various kinds of baseness (note the list in 1:28–32).

Next, Paul presents God's wrath against the unrighteousness of the Jew (2:1–3:20). God judges the Jews on the basis of the Mosaic Law and the Gentiles on the basis of the light they have received. Jews have had the advantage of God's special revelation ("oracles"). But both Jews and Gentiles stand together under the power of sin. Sin is a universal human predicament: "There is no one who is righteous; not even one." This means that " 'no human being will be justified in his sight' by deeds prescribed by the law, for through the law comes knowledge of sin."

*Memorize this verse (3:20) as you meditate on its meaning.*

## The Righteousness of God in Justification (Rom. 3:21–4:25)

Because of sinfulness, everyone, whether Jew or Gentile, stands in need of a remedy for this predicament. In other words, each one needs to be justified—made right with God. Such a justification or righteousness has been made manifest that does not depend on a self-justification by keeping the Law but on faith in Jesus Christ (3:21–31). (Of course, no one was ever good enough to be justified on the basis of keeping the Law, but many thought they were so justified.) Justification is the gift of God's grace made possible through Christ's atonement for sin (see chap. 17) to be received by faith.

Abraham, who stands historically at the head of the covenant people, was justified on the basis of faith (4:1–25). Indeed God justified him on the basis of faith before he was ever circumcised. Furthermore, he is the "father" of all people of faith, Jews and Gentiles.

*What makes it so hard for us to accept grace?*

## The Righteousness of God in Salvation (5:1–8:39)

Salvation is the new life into which the believer is initiated by justification. Justification is that saving act of God by which the Christian's pilgrimage is begun. Salvation includes all the freedoms that God graciously bestows.

### Freedom from the Wrath of God (5:1–21)

This freedom is not only deliverance from condemnation but also deliverance to positive blessings. Justification is the gateway to peace with

God. Salvation is future as well as present: "We boast in our hope of sharing the glory of God." We are now reconciled to God, but there is also a future consummation of our salvation. All this is made possible by the love of God revealed through the death and resurrection of Jesus.

*Memorize 5:8.*

*How many expressions are used to describe the meaning of salvation in chapter 5?*

### *Freedom from Sin (6:1–23)*

Christians are not to take the attitude that because they are forgiven by God's abounding grace, they will therefore continue in sin. On the contrary, says Paul, at one's baptism one died to sin and was raised to walk in newness of life. One is not a slave to sin but to righteousness. Paul uses the word "sanctification" twice in this chapter. It comes from a root meaning "to be holy." It is, therefore, a making holy or separating unto God. Sometimes it is regarded as a gift of God in past time, simultaneous with justification (1 Cor. 1:2; 6:11; Heb. 10:29). By justification a person is set free; by sanctification a person is given the status of a saint, bound to the Holy God and his people. Sanctification, however, looks to the future for completion (compare 1 Thess. 4:3; 2 Cor. 7:1). The saint (Christian) is to live out increasingly in practice what has already been established in status and relationship.

*Memorize 6:23.*

### *Freedom from the Law (7:1–25)*

The Law here is what we call the moral Law as it is summarized in the Ten Commandments. Freedom from the Law is a matter of dying to the Law. That is, a Christian's ultimate guide is not a code but the Holy Spirit. This does not mean, however, that the Law is bad. It shows a person to be a sinner deserving of death. In verses 13–25 Paul presents his own inner struggle against evil. The Christian must continue to engage in battle with temptation. Our Lord himself was not exempt from this, and neither are we. But we rejoice with Paul that Jesus Christ helps us in our battles (v. 25).

### *Freedom from Death (8:1–39)*

Though the Christian has battles as described by Paul in Romans 7, there is also assurance: "There is therefore now no condemnation for those who are in Christ Jesus." Christians are those who walk by the Spirit and fulfill the just requirement of the Law. Indeed they enjoy the freedom of being Children of God. As such they are also heirs of a more complete freedom yet to come in the consummation of God's new creation. This consummation is even now greeted in hope. Christians are those who pray with the help of the Spirit. They are those who know that their salvation from beginning (God's purpose) to end (glorification) is the work of God. They are sure that absolutely nothing can separate them "from the love of God in Christ Jesus our Lord." They are truly superconquerors.

*Memorize 8:35–39.*

*How would you sum up Paul's doctrine of salvation as it is found in Romans 5–8?*

*What similar phrases do you find at the end of each of these chapters?*

## The Righteousness of God in History (Rom. 9:1–11:36)[4]

The "history" here referred to is God's dealings with the Jews. Paul was deeply concerned about the Jews, the majority of whom had not accepted the gospel. He begins by saying in effect that he would be willing to be damned himself for the sake of his beloved kin, the Israelites, who are the heirs of the blessings of the old covenant (9:1–5). Even though most Jews have not accepted Christ, God's word has not failed. To be a descendant of Abraham is, in the final analysis, not a matter of biology but of election (9:6–13). And even if God's election were arbitrary, no mortal (a mere lump of clay) is in position to challenge it (9:14–29). But the fact is that God's election is not arbitrary (9:30–10:21). The Jews have rejected God's message and must bear the responsibility for their decision.

This does not mean that God has rejected Israel. There is now a remnant, selected by grace, and Paul is a member of that remnant (11:1–6). Moreover, God has used the trespass of the Jews to serve the divine purpose of salvation for the Gentiles and even, in the final analysis, for the Jewish people themselves. For Paul teaches that one day the Jews as a group will accept Christ and be regrafted onto their own olive tree. In God's own time "all Israel will be saved" (11:25–32). That is, Paul looks forward to the time when the Jews as a group will hold out against the gospel no longer and the old Israel and the new Israel will be one Israel in Christ (11:26). While Paul cannot logically explain this mystery, he knows God is a keeper of promises and, therefore, Jews continue in valid relationship with God.

In chapters 9–11, Paul has been grappling with the problem of God's sovereignty and human freedom. Though human responsibility is by no means the equivalent of God's sovereignty, it is real, since God does not put humans in the category of animals. The biblical writers nowhere attempt to harmonize God's sovereignty and human freedom. The human brain is too inadequate to encompass so great a mystery, and it is the part of humility and wisdom to leave the matter where Paul left it: "O the depth of the riches and wisdom and knowledge of God! How unsearchable are his judgments and how inscrutable his ways!" (See all of 11:33–36.)

The earliest Christians were Jews. Paul was a Christian Jew. There have been Jews who have become Christians throughout the centuries. There have been many others persecuted because they would not.

*How are we to exercise a responsible witness to the Jews today?*

*Is the church in need of repentance for its attitude and actions toward the Jews?*

*What is the proper relation between church and synagogue?*

## The Righteousness of God in Christian Living (Rom. 12:1–15:13)

In the light of all that has been said about God's saving righteousness up to this point, Paul now makes a special appeal for response: "I appeal to you therefore, brothers and sisters, by the mercies of God, to present your bodies as a living sacrifice, holy and acceptable to God, which is your spiritual worship" (see 12:1–2). The appeal here is not for an animal sacrifice, but the commitment of the whole living self ("bodies") so that to live is to worship God in the doing of God's will.

Such commitment is to be expressed in Christian love at work. This love is to operate in the church, which is the body of Christ (12:3–13; compare 1 Cor. 12:12–14; Eph. 4:4, 16). It is also to be expressed toward one's enemies (12:14–21; compare Matt. 5:44; Luke 6:28) and by implication toward the state (13:1–7; compare Titus 3:1; 1 Peter 2:13–14). Of course the Roman government had not yet begun its persecution of the church when Paul wrote Romans.

*In the light of Romans 13:1–7; Acts 4:19; 5:29; and Mark 12:17, how does one go about formulating the ethic of love in relation to a political government?*

"Love is the fulfilling of the law" (see 13:8–10). Christians are to "lay aside the works of darkness" (13:11–14). Indeed, they are to go beyond this. Christians are to be responsibly concerned about their influence on others (14:1–23). One Christian is not to pass judgment on another Christian in areas where differences of opinion necessarily arise. God is Judge. But a Christian should not put a stumbling block in another's way: "It is good not to eat meat or drink wine or do anything that makes your brother or sister stumble."

*Can you think of modern examples for the power of influence for good and for evil?*

## The Prison Epistles—Rising Above Circumstance

The prison epistles are Philemon, Colossians, Ephesians, and Philippians. In all of them Paul rises above his circumstances as a prisoner and bears a marvelous Christian witness. Not all students of Paul agree that all of these letters were written from Rome. Some maintain further that Ephesians was written by a follower of Paul. The position taken here is that Paul wrote all of these letters during the first Roman imprisonment 61–63 C.E.

### Philemon—A Christian Response to a Slave

*This little gem is only twenty-five verses long. You can read it in two minutes.*

Philemon was a Christian leader in the church at Colossae in the province of Asia. Since Paul had not been to Colossae, Philemon was probably led to Christ by Paul during his ministry at Ephesus. The letter is addressed to Philemon and his family.

The burden of the letter is Paul's concern for Onesimus, a slave of Philemon. After stealing from his master, Onesimus had run away from home. He came into contact with Paul, under whose ministry he was converted. Paul sends Onesimus back to his master, and in this letter appeals to Philemon to forgive him and receive him as a beloved brother. In what ways does Paul underscore his appeal? Verse 21 has been interpreted to mean that Paul was confident Philemon would set Onesimus free. In any case, the kind of spirit expressed in this letter, whereby a slave is recognized as a real person and as a member of a Christian community, was in time to have a part in breaking the shackles of human slavery. What does Paul's message of Christian community say to us in our contemporary situation?

## Colossians—Christ the Head of the Universe and the Church

The church at Colossae was confronted with heresy. The threat came from those who combined aspects of philosophy, pagan religion, Judaism, and Christianity. They thought that physical matter was somehow evil and therefore that the incarnate Christ was inferior to angels as pure spirits. They also promoted certain ascetic practices and rules, and the worship of angels.

*Read Colossians in relation to the three major emphases outlined below.*

### The Adequacy of Christ (1:13–2:7)

After his salutation, thanksgiving, and intercessory prayer for the Colossians (1:1–12), Paul presents at once that which is foremost in his thinking in relation to the church at Colossae—the adequacy of Christ. (See that section of Chapter 18 entitled "The Christ Who Was Preexistent" for an interpretation of Colossians 1:15–20.) This Christ is Head of the universe and the church and is superior to all angels. His physical flesh is not something to apologize for. It was through his death in this physical body that the Colossians themselves were reconciled to God. As Christ's minister, Paul also suffers in his flesh. Paul assured the Colossians that they could trust the gospel of Christ as they had received it.

*What religious groups today are akin to the Colossian heretics?*

### An Exposure of the Heretics (2:8–23)

Do not be deceived by any human-centered philosophy that runs counter to the gospel of Christ. For in Christ alone all the divine fullness dwells bodily; he "is the head of every ruler and authority." In Christ you have been raised to newness of life. In Christ God triumphed over all supernatural powers. Do not be led astray by those who want to mix the Christian faith with legalistic and ascetic practices. These things "are of no value in checking self-indulgence."

### The New Life in Christ (3:1–4:6)

When you became Christian, you put off the old nature and put on the new. Therefore, have nothing to do with those expressions of the old nature in which you once walked. Rather practice those things which are in harmony with your new nature.

*In your notebook, make a list of the old characteristics (3:5–11) and then make a list of the new characteristics (3:12–17).*

## Ephesians—Unity in Christ

This is one of the greatest books of all ages. Some feel it even excels Romans. The position accepted here is that Paul wrote it from Rome about 62 C.E. (Eph. 3:1; 4:1; 6:20; Col. 4:10, 18). On the basis of the following evidence, Ephesians was probably a circular letter intended for the churches in the province of Asia of which one was the church at Ephesus: (1) The words "in Ephesus" are not found in the three oldest manuscripts of the letter. (2) The letter does not contain the customary Pauline greetings to friends, even though Paul worked at Ephesus more than two years on his third missionary journey. (3) No local situation is alluded to in the letter. Those who hold that a disciple of Paul wrote Ephesians point to this lack of customary greetings and to a somewhat different literary style and vocabulary. Inasmuch as Ephesus was the largest city and the evangelistic center of the area, the letter or a copy of it would be kept there. Information about the church at Ephesus may be found in Acts 19–20 and Revelation 2:1–7.

Paul's purpose in writing was to set forth the theme of unity in Christ. In all of his letters he assumes the unity of the church. We saw that he was concerned about unity in the congregation at Corinth (1 Cor. 1:12–13; compare Gal. 3:28). His message in Ephesians certainly stresses the church's unity but is not limited to that subject. It is God's purpose to re-create a fragmented creation. Jesus Christ is the embodiment of this creation-wide activity. The church as his body is the fellowship through which God is working out the divine purpose. As instruments of this purpose Christians are to "walk in the Spirit."

### The Fact of Unity in Christ (Eph. 1:1–3:21)

Unity in Christ is not only a goal to be achieved but a present fact to be accepted. To this subject Paul devotes the first half of his letter. After a brief salutation (1:1–2), he moves into the most glorious of all his thanksgivings (1:3–14). Though it is technically not poetry, it still sings. Read it and see for yourself. In most of his letters, Paul included a thanksgiving. But, as someone has said, he wrote this entire epistle "on his knees" (see 1:15–23; 3:14–21; 5:19–20; 6:18). Whenever the theme is Christian unity, it seems that prayer is the appropriate language (see John 17). Perhaps we would make more progress in our acceptance of this unity, which is already a fact, if we did more conscientious praying about it. Note the blessings for which Paul is grateful.

This passage is one of great significance for the later development by the church of the Christian doctrine of the Trinity or Triunity of God.

*What do you learn about the Father, the Son, and the Holy Spirit from 1:3–14?*

The most-used Trinitarian benediction is the last verse of 2 Corinthians.

Paul's thanksgiving is followed by an intercessory prayer for his readers' enlightenment (1:15–23). This is typical. In his correspondence, he prays repeatedly for his readers but never for himself. He prays for himself privately and asks his readers to pray for him. The intercession here includes a petition for "a spirit of wisdom," for knowledge of the Christian hope, and for the greatness of God's power at work in believers.

True life is God's gift in Christ (2:1–10). It is more than biological existence. And spiritual death may characterize a walking corpse. "For by grace you have been saved through faith, and this is not your own doing; it is the gift of God—not the result of works, so that no one may boast" (2:8–9). We are not saved by good works but for good works.

This new life is for both Jew and Gentile; indeed the two are united in Christ (2:11–22). This is a fact. Gentiles, formerly without hope, are now "brought near by the blood of Christ." Christ has broken down "the dividing wall, that is, the hostility between us"—probably a reference to the stone fence in the Temple area, separating the Court of the Gentiles from the inner precincts. Christ is the one through whom the various walls of human hostility have been broken down. In this context Paul states what has been called "the Trinity of experience" in these words: "Through *him* [Christ] both of us have access in one Spirit to the Father." Gentiles are now members of the household of God, indwelt by the Holy Spirit. In God's plan for this union of Jew and Gentile, Paul was given a special commission to the Gentiles (3:1–13). This first half of the letter ends with an intercessory prayer for spiritual power (3:14–21).

*The Call to Unity in Christ (4:1–6:20)*

It may seem strange for Paul to speak of unity in Christ as a fact and then call people to unity in Christ. But this should not seem strange. As Christians are always becoming what they are, so the church is always becoming what it is. Paul's call to unity is really a series of four calls.

The *first* call is to promote the church's unity (4:1–16). The pursuit of this objective requires the exercise of humility, love, and peace. In emphasizing the church's unity Paul uses the word "one" seven times: one body, one Spirit, one hope, one Lord, one faith, one baptism, one God and Father of us all. God has endowed each of us with gifts for the purpose of building up the body of Christ and causing us to reach maturity.

The *second* call is to break with unchristian ways (4:17–5:20). This call is subdivided into the following specifics: (1) Put off the old nature and put on the new nature (4:17–24); (2) put away heathen vices and practice Christian virtues (4:25–5:2)—

> *list the vices in one column and the virtues in another;*

(3) take no part in the unfruitful works of darkness, but walk as Children of Light (5:3–14)—

> *list the works of darkness in one column and the fruit of light in another;*

and (4) do not walk in folly, but commit yourselves to Christian fervor (5:15–20).

The *third* call is to build Christian homes (5:21–6:9). In Paul's society this involved mutual respect and love not only between husbands and wives and parents and children, but also between slaves and masters. Indeed, the dynamic of Christian love and respect was to eat away at the institution of slavery.

The *fourth and final* call is to put on the whole armor of God (6:10–20). Earlier we saw that Paul understood that the Christian life requires battle. Here he points out that, in the ultimate sense, we are contending against "spiritual forces of evil." Therefore, we are to put on the whole armor of God. The presence of his Roman guard may have suggested this figure to Paul.

> *Analyze what he says by listing the various pieces of armor and stating beside it the purpose it is designed to serve.*

## Philippians—A Joyous Thank-you Note

Review Paul's earliest contact with the Philippians (Acts 16:11–40). Of all the churches he founded, the one at Philippi gave Paul the greatest satisfaction. Though this church was not without its problems, it did not have as hard a time growing up as some of the others. Moreover, it had sent Paul gifts when he labored at Thessalonica (4:16). Paul's purpose in writing the letter was multiple, but a major purpose was to thank the Philippian Christians for sending him a recent gift (4:10–20). At the very beginning of our study of the prison epistles, we indicated that Paul rose above circumstance in all of them. This is notably true in this Letter to the Philippians. As a prisoner he said more about joy than most people ever say under any kind of circumstance.

*As you read this thank-you note, underline every occurrence of every word in the vocabulary of joy.*

*When you have finished reading, go back and check the context and thought of each passage in which such a word occurs.*

*What does your study teach about the Christian way of life?*

## The Pastoral Epistles—Matters Ecclesiastical

The pastoral epistles are 1 Timothy, Titus, and 2 Timothy. Timothy and Titus were two of Paul's valued assistants. What is said in these letters is really addressed not only to these assistants but to all pastors and other church leaders.

The authorship of the letters is debated. (1) Some maintain the Apostle Paul wrote them as they now appear. Paul is named as the author in each case, and there are references within the letters that indicate Paul as the author. Tradition names him the author and also states that he was released from the first Roman imprisonment and carried on a further ministry. The pastorals were written between Paul's release and his martyrdom. (2) Others maintain that they were not written by Paul. They do not fit into the account of Paul's life recorded in Acts. Some of the doctrinal emphases are different from those encountered in the other Pauline letters. In the pastorals faith is sometimes understood as orthodox belief, while it is dynamic commitment in the other Pauline letters. The pastorals exhibit great concern for sound teaching. The concern for ecclesiastical leaders is distinctive of these letters. So are the style of writing and a part of their vocabulary. Thus, it is argued that a friend or disciple of Paul wrote in the name of Paul as the writer thought Paul would have written in the later situation. (3) A third group hold that a secretary or friend of Paul put Paul's ideas or shorter letters into their final form either near the end of Paul's life or at a later time. The personal references and the travels are authentic. While not the literal author, Paul speaks in these letters.[5] This theory does justice to all the evidence available and is assumed here.

So many details are treated in the pastorals that it is impossible to list all of them. Nothing can take the place of reading the epistles themselves. Attention is called to certain of the choice statements often memorized from them:

1. *First Timothy* "There is one God; there is also one mediator between God and humankind, Christ Jesus, himself human" (2:5). "We brought nothing into the world, so that we can take nothing out of it" (6:7). "The

love of money is the root of all kinds of evil" (6:10). "Fight the good fight of the faith" (6:12).

2. *Titus* "Teach what is consistent with sound doctrine" (2:1). "When the goodness and loving kindness of God our Savior appeared, he saved us, not because of any works of righteousness that we had done, but according to his mercy, through the water of rebirth and renewal by the Holy Spirit. This Spirit he poured out on us richly through Jesus Christ our Savior, so that, having been justified by his grace, we might become heirs according to the hope of eternal life" (3:4–7).

3. *Second Timothy* "I know the one in whom I have put my trust, and I am sure that he is able to guard until that day what I have entrusted to him" (1:12). "Share in suffering like a good soldier of Christ Jesus" (2:3). "Remember Jesus Christ, raised from the dead, a descendant of David—that is my gospel" (2:8). "The word of God is not chained" (2:9). "Do your best to present yourself to God as one approved by him, a worker who has no need to be ashamed, rightly explaining the word of truth" (2:15). "All scripture is inspired by God and is useful for teaching, for reproof, for correction, and for training in righteousness, so that everyone who belongs to God may be proficient, equipped for every good work" (3:16–17). "I solemnly urge you: proclaim the message; be persistent whether the time is favorable or unfavorable; convince, rebuke, and encourage, with the utmost patience in teaching" (4:1–2). "I have fought the good fight, I have finished the race, I have kept the faith. From now on there is reserved for me the crown of righteousness, which the Lord, the righteous judge, will give me on that day, and not only to me, but also to all who have longed for his appearing" (4:7–8).

## Ecclesiastical Organization and Leadership

The pastoral epistles are primary sources for the ecclesiastical concerns of the church in the latter part of the first century. Though the institutions of the new covenant were influenced by those of the old covenant, the two sets of institutions were not identical. From the very beginning the early Christians considered themselves one people of God under the Lordship of Christ. Christ was the one and only Head of the church. In the earliest days of the apostolic period, spontaneity characterized ecclesiastical organization and rites. Early Christians followed certain elements in the worship of the synagogue: prayer, reading of scripture, interpretation of scripture, and singing of psalms and hymns. At first the Lord's Supper and the fellowship meal were celebrated together (see 1 Cor. 11:17–34). Baptism could be informally administered as in the case of Philip's baptizing the Ethiopian eunuch (Acts 8:36–37).

The twelve apostles were the leaders par excellence from the inception of the church, and they continued to hold this position as long as they lived. Like Moses, Joshua, the judges, Saul, David, and the prophets of Israel, some of the first ministries of the church were charismatic (that is, brought into being directly by the Holy Spirit). These ministries included prophets, teachers, workers of miracles, healers, speakers in tongues, interpreters of tongues, and forms of leadership (1 Cor. 12). The selection of elders and deacons was less charismatic than that of other ministries.

Elders had a part in the government of Old Testament Israel and in later Judaism. In fact, elders had such a role in various ancient societies. In the New Testament church the terms "elder" and "bishop" (that is, "guardian" or "overseer") were interchangeable (Acts 20:17, 28; Titus 1:5, 7). In 44 C.E. elders already existed in the church at Jerusalem (Acts 11:30). On the first missionary journey Paul and Barnabas ordained or appointed elders in Galatia (Acts 14:23), and elders held office in churches not founded by Paul (James 5:14; 1 Peter 5:1).

The exact procedure used in the selection of elders is not clear. In Titus 1:5 it seems that Paul instructs Titus to ordain or appoint elders on his own authority, but this is not altogether certain. In Acts 14:23 the word used for "ordain" or "appoint" can mean "to vote by stretching out the hand." Thus it is possible that Paul and Barnabas were in charge of the meeting at which the congregation selected its leaders. In 2 Corinthians the same verb is used of the churches' selecting a traveling companion for Paul (compare Acts 13:2). The Seven in Acts 6:1–6 were definitely selected by the people and set apart by the apostles. A representative process of government was at work in the New Testament churches (compare 1 Tim. 4:14). This type of process was also at work on a larger scale in the meeting of the Jerusalem Council (Acts 15). Elders were set apart or ordained by the laying on of hands (1 Tim. 4:14; 5:22).

> *Read the list of qualifications of elders given in 1 Timothy 3:1–7 and Titus 1:6–16.*

> *Read the duties of elders found in the following passages: Acts 15:2–35; 16:4; 20:17, 28; 1 Timothy 3:4–5; 4:14; 5:17; Titus 1:9; James 5:14; 1 Peter 5:1–4; Hebrews 13:17.*

After the death of the apostles, the elders gradually took over the formerly more spontaneous duties of other leaders. After New Testament times, the monarchial bishop arose from among the elders, but that is another story.

The office of deacon originated in New Testament times. The word means "servant." The qualifications for deacons are enumerated in 1 Timothy 3:8–13. Their duties are not clearly designated in the New Testament unless the Seven were deacons (Acts 6:1–6; see Phil. 1:1).

In addition to the responsibilities already implicit in the various ministries mentioned previously, the church also assumed the following kinds of responsibilities: the care of widows and orphans (1 Tim. 5:3–16; James 1:27), relief for victims of famine (Acts 11:29–30; Gal. 2:10; 2 Cor. 8:9), visiting Christian prisoners and seeking their release (Heb. 13:3), and showing hospitality to strangers (Heb. 13:2).

Many Christian groups have been wise in recognizing that the reality and existence of the church do not depend on one kind of organization. Clearly the New Testament Christians adapted organization to meet the needs of the situation. Those of the Reformed tradition have been wise in operating on the principle of representative democracy.

Christians in the earliest days worshiped in the Jewish Temple, in synagogues, and in one another's homes. Gradually Christians broke with Judaism entirely. Both the Jewish Sabbath and the Lord's Day were celebrated at first, but gradually the Jewish Sabbath was left behind. The worship of the church grew more liturgical. The Lord's Prayer (very much like a Jewish prayer of Jesus' time) came to play an important part in public worship. The time soon came when a candidate for baptism was given instruction in theology and ethics. Baptism came to be administered with the Trinitarian formula as it continues today. The Lord's Supper came to be separated from the fellowship meal.

## Summary

As we have given ourselves to Paul's witness by letter, we have had the privilege of sitting at the feet of the great Apostle to the Gentiles. He has taught us of justification by faith, the second coming of Christ, the resurrection of the body, the Christian life, the ministry of reconciliation, the stewardship of money, the righteousness of God, Christ the Head of the universe and the church, unity in the cosmic Christ, joy in the midst of adversity, and church organization. We bow our knees unto God in sincere gratitude for Paul's ministry to us.

# The Witness of the Church in Conflict

*B*ecause of human sin and because of the nature of Christian faith, the church is necessarily in conflict within itself and with the world. We now come to a period in the life of the church when conflict becomes increasingly varied and intense.

## Conflict with Judaism

According to the flesh, Jesus was a Jew. Yet one of his major conflicts was with some of his own people. Peter and others ran into conflict with the Sanhedrin. Stephen was stoned to death. Paul first persecuted the Christians and then joined them. He himself experienced conflict from Judaizers within the church and some of his Jewish brethren outside the church. Evidently Herod Agrippa I executed James, the brother of John, to please those Jews who opposed the Christian movement (Acts 12:1). James, the brother of Jesus, was put to death by Jewish leaders. The first Jewish revolt against Rome (66–70 C.E.) was the occasion of the flight of Christians from Jerusalem to Pella and of the destruction of Jerusalem by Titus, the son of the Emperor Vespasian. The persecution of Christians by Jews, however, was short-lived in comparison with the tragic centuries of the persecution of Jews by Christians.

## The Letter of James

The letter begins "James, a servant of God and of the Lord Jesus Christ" (1:1). The question arises at once, Who is James? Tradition answers, the brother of Jesus (see Mark 6:3; Matt. 13:55). This James did not believe in Jesus (John 7:5) until after his resurrection (1 Cor. 15:7). Soon, however, he became the leader of the church in Jerusalem (Gal. 1:19; 2:9; Acts 12:17; 15:13; 21:18). Some think he wrote this letter as early as 45 C.E. Others put the date about 60 because they feel one passage of the letter (2:14–26) reflects an acquaintance with Paul's views. In favor of this identification of the author are allusions to the teachings of Jesus (for example, compare 5:12 with Matt. 5:34–37) and the Jewish approach to ethical concerns.

There are other scholars, however, who think the letter was composed at the end of the first century or the beginning of the second by someone else for the following reasons: (1) The letter was slow in being accepted as a part of the New Testament canon; (2) its Greek is better than many expect from a person who customarily spoke Aramaic; and (3) the author of the letter does not show the concern for ritual that James, the Lord's brother, showed at the meeting of the Jerusalem Council (Acts 15).

*Which side of this fence looks preferable to you? Why?*

The recipients of the letter are described as "the twelve tribes in the Dispersion" (1:1). On the surface this phrase seems to designate Jews rather than Christians, who are scattered here and there in the Roman empire. But James uses this phrase to identify the church in its entirety as God's new Israel. Such a title is especially appropriate from the pen of one who appreciates his Jewish heritage.

The most discussed part of the letter is 2:14–26, because some have maintained that James is attempting to refute Paul's doctrine of justification by faith (Gal. 3; Rom. 3:21–4:25). But this is to misunderstand both James and Paul. Paul used the word "faith" in its dynamic Hebraic sense, meaning a commitment to Jesus Christ as Savior and Lord that issues in the faithfulness of the new life. He insisted that justification cannot come to a person on the basis of observing certain legal requirements. Apparently there were those who had misunderstood Paul and understood faith as only an intellectual assent to certain ideas. James says even the demons have that kind of faith, but they remain demons. A faith that does not work is a dead faith—that is, it is not the genuine article.

In the preceding chapter, we noted that faith is essential throughout the Christian's life. James undergirds this teaching. True faith expresses itself in doing the word, bridling the tongue, showing no partiality to the rich, loving one's neighbor, avoiding covetousness, exercising patience, telling the truth, visiting the sick and praying for them (directed particularly to elders), and leading sinners back from the error of their ways.

James belongs to the literary category of wisdom literature and calls to mind our study of wisdom in chapter 13 of this book. In fact, the word "wisdom" is found in James 1:5; 3:13, 15, 17. A few of the choice wise sayings from the letter include the following:

"But be doers of the word, and not merely hearers who deceive themselves" (1:22).

"For just as the body without the spirit is dead, so faith without works is also dead" (2:26).

"Anyone, then, who knows the right thing to do and fails to do it, commits sin" (4:17).

"The prayer of the righteous is powerful and effective" (5:16).

## Conflict with the State

Technically Jesus was crucified by the Roman government. Paul's persecution at the hands of Jews sometimes brought him into conflict with Roman authorities. Indeed it was this sequence of events that took him to Rome.

The Roman emperors with whom we are here concerned in relation to the persecution of Christians are Claudius (41–54 C.E.), Nero (54–68 C.E.), Domitian (81–96 C.E.), and Trajan (98–117 C.E.). In the time of Claudius Christians were still regarded as Jews by the Roman government. It is probable that conflicts between Christians and Jews were the occasion for the expulsion of the Jews from Rome.

A great fire broke out in Rome in 64 C.E., which lasted for six days. It was reported that Nero himself was responsible for the fire. But he laid the blame on the Christians. The Christians were disliked by many on account of their high moral standards and their allegiance to only one God. Their Christian commitment kept them from participating in the social and religious life of Rome. These facts made it possible for Nero to consider the Christians his scapegoat. Tacitus says that they were clothed in animals' skins, torn in pieces by dogs, crucified, or made into torches to serve as lights by night. It was under Nero that both Peter and Paul were put to death. Fortunately the persecution of Christians was not officially extended to the whole of the empire at this time.

Domitian became increasingly autocratic. Therefore, his antipathy was vented on all who tended to frustrate his self-centeredness in any way. In 89 C.E. he banished philosophers and astrologers from Rome. He was sensitive to any kind of suspected disloyalty from any source. He insisted on being worshiped and called "Lord and God." Apparently Jews and Christians were still thought of as one group by Rome. Neither could give ultimate allegiance to any but God alone. Therefore both suffered and died under Domitian. This persecution probably spread to parts of the empire outside the imperial city itself.

For political reasons Trajan was afraid of secret societies, particularly in Asia Minor. By his time Christians were distinguished from Jews and were regarded as participating in a secret society. He did not hunt for Christians. When a person was accused of being a Christian, however, the chance was given to deny and recant. This meant that the Christian was required to worship the emperor's statue and then renounce Christ. If one refused, one was executed.

## First Peter—A Living Hope

The letter begins "Peter, an apostle of Jesus Christ" (1:1). Some have felt, however, that it was written later than the time of Peter, either in the time of Domitian or in that of Trajan. But there is no need for dating the letter so late. The persecution reflected in it was probably unofficial. For Peter takes essentially the same attitude toward the Roman government (2:13–17) as Paul (Rom. 13:1–7). Moreover, the church later accepted the letter as Peter's. The similarity of its thought and expression to those of Paul may be accounted for by the fact that Silvanus, one of Paul's assistants, actually did the writing for Peter (5:12), and by the fact that all the apostles had much in common.

The letter is addressed "to the exiles of the Dispersion" in Asia Minor (1:1). This designation of the recipients is similar to that in James 1:1. The word "Babylon" in 5:13 is probably a cryptic name for Rome. In other words, at the close of the letter Peter seems to say that the church at Rome sends greetings to the churches of Asia Minor. The position taken here is that Peter wrote this letter from Rome shortly before his death under Nero.

The theme of 1 Peter is the "living hope." And this theme is developed around two chief emphases: the Christian gospel as the basis of hope (1:1–2:10) and the Christian hope as a basis of Christian living (2:11–5:11). While these two emphases are not wholly separated into these two parts of the letter, the major division of the book comes precisely at the point indicated. In part one, Peter enumerates the following aspects of the gospel as the ground of hope: the resurrection of Jesus Christ (1:3–9), the announcements of the prophets (1:10–12), the call to sanctification (1:13–17), the atoning work of Christ (1:18–21), the new birth (1:22–25), "the kindness of the Lord" (2:1–3), and the nature of the church (2:4–10).

*As you read 1 Peter 1:1–2:10 with the aid of this outline, give special attention to the understanding of the church found there (2:4–10).*

*What are the teachings and implications of this passage for the church of our own time?*

In part two, Peter issues a call to Christian living on the basis of the hope he has just delineated. This call deals with abstaining from the passions of the flesh (2:11–12), obedience to the state (2:13–17), the relation of servants to masters (2:18–25), the relation between husbands and wives (3:1–7), unity within the community (3:8–12), reverence for Christ as Lord (3:13–22), purity of life (4:1–6), the ethics of crisis (4:7–11), suffering as a Christian (4:12–19), an exhortation to elders (5:1–5), and commitment to God's care (5:6–11).

*Read the second part of the letter with the help of this outline. Then concentrate on the passages listed below:*

*Christ, the Servant, an Example to Christian servants (2:21–25).* While these words were addressed particularly to Christian slaves, they are in the final analysis addressed to all slaves of Christ. Peter was interpreting Jesus as the Servant of the Lord presented in Isaiah 53. As you read Peter and Isaiah, see how many parallels you can find between them.

*The Prayers of Husband and Wife (3:7).* While Peter is speaking primarily of the husband's prayers, it is implied that the prayer life of husband and wife can realize its potential only if the two are living together harmoniously.

*Stewards of God's Varied Grace (4:7–11).* How may Peter's doctrine of stewardship be applied in specific relationships? What does this kind of stewardship involve?

*Suffering as a Christian (4:12–19).* In what sense is it possible to share Christ's sufferings? When does one suffer as a Christian today?

*Commitment to God's Care (5:6–11).* Memorize verse 7, "Cast all your anxiety on him, because he cares for you." Does this statement bring to mind other statements from the Bible?

## Hebrews—A Call to Steadfastness

Like 1 Peter, Hebrews was written in time of persecution. But unlike 1 Peter, it does not name its author. Paul's name has been placed in the title of the book in some Bibles, but this is not a part of the biblical text. Luther suggested the name of Apollos, and others have suggested Barnabas. The fact is that no one knows who wrote this work. Most are agreed that Paul did not write it.

Strictly speaking the book is a combination of sermon and letter. To use the author's own description of his work, it is a "word of exhortation" (13:22). There is no greeting or thanksgiving as in the Pauline letters. The body of the work is sermonic. The last chapter, however, is similar in form to the last chapters of some of Paul's letters. On the basis of the twenty-fourth verse of this last chapter, it seems that it was written to the church in Rome.

It was certainly written at a time when its recipients were undergoing a severe testing of their faith. The "hard struggle" of "those earlier days" (10:32) may be a reference to the persecution under Nero. If this is correct, the letter may have been addressed to Christians suffering under the persecution of Domitian. In any case, the suffering was so severe that some had "drooping hands" and "weak knees" (12:12). They were tempted to desert the Christian faith. The author exhorts them to remain steadfast in the faith by positive affirmation of Christian truth and by warning against the consequences of apostasy (desertion of the Christian faith). Because the book draws so heavily on Old Testament materials, it is maintained by many that the readers were Christian Jews who were tempted to return to Judaism. We outline the book briefly with comments at selected points.

1. God's revelation by the Son is final and perfect (1:1–4).

2. The Son is superior to angels (1:5–2:18). If transgressors of the Law, which was mediated by angels, were punished, how shall we escape if we neglect the salvation offered in the gospel?

3. The Son is superior to Moses (3:1–19) and Joshua (4:1–13 ). Do not harden your hearts, as your forebears did under Moses, in unbelief and rebellion. The rest (salvation) into which Joshua led the people was not the final rest that God has promised. "Let us therefore make every effort to enter that rest, so that no one may fall through such disobedience as theirs."

4. The Son is High Priest and is superior to the Levitical high priest (4:14–7:28). The Levitical high priest is a sinner and as such has to offer sacrifice for his own sins as well as for those of his people. The Son is sinless and offered himself once for all for the sins of the people.

5. The Son's ministry is superior to the Levitical ministry, and he is the Mediator of a better covenant (chs. 8–10). The sacrifices required by the Law pointed beyond themselves to Christ and his sacrifice, and through Christ's once-for-all sacrifice the new covenant was ratified and the

forgiveness that was promised by Jeremiah (Jer. 31:31–34) was made actual.

6. Faith meant to be faithful (chs. 11–12). "Now faith is the assurance of things hoped for, the conviction of things not seen." This assurance-conviction bore real fruit in the lives of the old covenant's champions of faith. "All of these died in faith without having received the promises"; that is, they did not receive the complete fulfillment of God's promise in this world. If they had, faith would have given way to sight. But life in this world always requires faith. They did not receive the complete fulfillment of God's promise because "God had provided something better so that they should not, apart from us, be made perfect." God's promise includes not only the faithful in ancient Israel, but also God's people in all ages.

*In 12:1–2 we have one of the greatest appeals to steadfastness. Memorize these words and ask for guidance in your application of them.*

The Christian life is pictured as a race (compare 1 Cor. 9:24–27). Attention is first called to the cloud of witnesses, that is, the champions of faith just named. They sit in the amphitheater, so to speak, and see how we perform. Next, our attention is called to ourselves as participants in the race. As the contestants in a race, we are to lay aside all that hinders us in the race of life: every weight and especially sin. Positively speaking, we are to run life's race with perseverance or steadfastness. Finally, our attention is called to Jesus, "the pioneer and perfecter of our faith." In our race of life we are aware of the cloud of witnesses and of ourselves, but our focus must be on Jesus and nowhere else. He is our Pioneer or Leader, alone worthy to set the pace. Jesus is also the Perfecter of faith; that is, the One who really achieved what faith is all about. For faith in his life did not lead to doing nothing. Jesus in faith saw beyond the immediate shame and suffering of the cross to the joy inherent in accomplishing the purpose of his life and death. Indeed Jesus is now seated at the right hand of the throne of God. In spite of all the suffering that we may be called on to endure, we are to remain steadfast in our faith.

Christ endured the hostility of sinners. We as children of God can expect the same. In fact, we should look on our suffering as the discipline of a caring Parent. Through it we are enabled to become what we are called to be. It is therefore time to lift up drooping hands and weak knees, to strive for peace and holiness. Christians do not journey to fearsome Sinai but to the heavenly Jerusalem, where they receive an unshakable kingdom. But be warned against refusing the One who spoke on earth at Sinai and who speaks from heaven today. God consumes that which is out of harmony with the divine will.

7. Christians are to be characterized by Christian living (ch. 13). The author exhorts those who receive the message to show love for one another in a variety of ways, to remember and to obey their Christian leaders, not to be led away by false teachings, to share what they have, to pray for the author and those associated with the author, and to take what has been written seriously. In the midst of these various exhortations, there are at least four well-known statements: "Do not neglect to show hospitality to strangers, for by doing that some have entertained angels without knowing it"; "Jesus Christ is the same yesterday and today and forever"; "For here we have no lasting city, but we are looking for the city that is to come"; and the benediction in verses 20–21.

> *Memorize this benediction and think through the meaning of each phrase and clause. What makes it so appropriate at the end of this particular sermon-letter?*
>
> *This book contains a strong emphasis on warning. Many in our time seem to shrink from giving or receiving warning. Why?*
>
> *Warning is a necessary part of life. Pain warns us that we must see the doctor. Signs at railway crossings warn us to stop, look, and listen. The Bible contains numerous warnings.*
>
> *Study the warnings of Hebrews as found in 2:1–4; 3:7–4:13; 5:11–6:12; 10:26–39; and 12:12–29. What purpose were they intended to serve in the first century? What is God's message through them to us today?*
>
> *How may a warning be communicated so as not to defeat its purpose?*

## Revelation—The Apocalypse of the New Testament

Revelation was probably addressed to a situation in Asia Minor somewhat comparable to the situation faced by the recipients of Hebrews in Rome. The probable occasion of both books was the persecution of Christians by Domitian at the close of the first century. He demanded worship of himself that Christians could render only to God. This means that the purpose of Revelation is essentially the same as that of Hebrews: to encourage the faithful and warn the indifferent.

But the methods employed for achieving this purpose are quite different. The author of Hebrews uses a sermon; the author of Revelation an apocalypse. Daniel is the major apocalypse of the Old Testament, and Revelation is the major apocalypse of the New Testament. You may find it helpful to review what was said about Daniel in Chapter 14.

The word "apocalypse" means "revelation" or "unveiling." Apocalyptic literature, biblical and nonbiblical, is addressed to God's people in time of suffering and is couched in highly symbolic language. Of course all language is symbolic, but apocalyptic language is more so. This is true because it attempts to express the inexpressible. That is, it attempts to deal with the supernatural world in the language of this world. Moreover, it is a kind of code that prevents the persecutor from understanding the message and therefore affords no ground on which to incriminate the author or the recipients. This code includes the symbols of numbers, of animals and birds, and of natural portents.[1] For example, three is the number of the supernatural world, four the number of the earthly world, seven the number of perfection, six the number of imperfection, and twelve the number of God's people. Angels and demons also have an important role in apocalypse.

The author gives his name as John. What John? He does not tell us. An ancient tradition says he was the Apostle John, though he himself makes no such claim. His references to the apostles throw no light on the question (18:20; 21:14). Comparative studies have led many to conclude that the author of Revelation is not the author of the Fourth Gospel. In other words, little can be said about the author of Revelation with certainty.

We do know, however, that John was a Christian brother and prophet who was suffering for Jesus' sake (1:9). We also know that he was well acquainted with the seven churches in the province of Asia and that he addressed them in this book.

In spite of the abuse of this apocalypse at the hands of some interpreters because of failure to understand its symbolic nature, it continues to bring to people, especially those in crisis, the strength of divine assurance. For no matter how bad things may be, the seer reminds us that the victory belongs to God and God's people.

*Introduction (1:1–3)*

John is concerned with "the revelation of Jesus Christ." He "testified to the word of God and to the testimony of Jesus Christ." His message was given to him through vision.

*The Letters to the Seven Churches (1:4–3:22)*

The seven churches are Ephesus, Smyrna, Pergamum, Thyatira, Sardis, Philadelphia, and Laodicea. First, John greets all the churches in a covering letter (1:4–20). The grace and peace of the Triune God are invoked upon them. The Father is the One "who is and who was and who is to come"; that is, he is eternal. The "seven spirits" seems to be an apocalyptic way of speaking of the Holy Spirit in divine perfection. Jesus Christ is "the faithful witness, the firstborn of the dead, and the ruler of the kings on the earth." The word "witness" is the Greek word from which our word "martyr" comes. Some of those to whom this letter would be read would follow Christ in giving a witness through the literal surrender of their lives. But Christ is coming again in power and glory. At the present time Christ is in the midst of the churches. "Lampstands" are symbols of the churches (1:12–13; 2:1). When the risen Christ says, "I am the first and the last," he designates himself in language very much like that used to designate the Father (see vv. 4 and 8). It is Christ who gives John that which he is to write concerning "what must soon take place."

After the general letter, John addresses a particular message to each of the seven churches. These letters include commendation, call to repentance, and judgment.

> *List the name of each church in your notebook and record after it the elements in the message that it received. Note that the letters convey a sense of impending crisis.*

*Visions of Worship in Heaven (4:1–5:14)*

The first vision centers on the worship of God as the Creator (chap. 4). The twenty-four elders who worship may be a combination of the twelve tribes of Israel and the twelve apostles of Christ. That is, they seem to represent the people of God under both the old covenant and the new covenant. The two are one people of God.

The second vision centers in the worship of the Lamb (chap. 5). John sees no one who is worthy to open the scroll of destiny. Therefore, one of the elders tells him that the Lion of the tribe of Judah is able to do this. When John looks, he sees a Lamb (Christ) standing, as though it had been slain. The Lion is a Lamb. This Lamb combines meekness and power. His power is that of self-sacrifice, not that of preying upon others. In the preceding vision the four living creatures (God's servants) and the elders sang the Song of Creation. Here they sing the Song of Redemption. The implication is that the church on earth is to pattern its worship on the worship of heaven. Jesus taught his disciples to pattern their life on earth after the life of heaven.

*The Central Portion of the Book (6:1–16:21)*

This section is composed of four series of sevens: the seven seals (6:1–8:5), the seven trumpets (8:6–11:19), the seven signs (12:1–14:20), and the seven bowls (15:1–16:21). God's judgment and salvation are depicted in many dramatic ways. We consider only two of the series.

The vision of the seven seals sets forth the logic of history as fought out by people in any age. The white horse represents military conquest and triumph with special reference here to the Roman empire. The bright red horse of further strife follows. In turn the bright red horse is followed by the black horse of famine. And the black horse is followed by the pale horse of death. Through the almost two thousand years since John wrote, nations have still not learned the lesson of peace suggested here. Although horses play a small part in modern warfare, conquest still produces the same trilogy of evil: further war, famine, and death. Yet in all times of tragedy the Christian martyrs are under the altar—sacrificed yet protected. The redeemed are sealed unto salvation. And "the Lamb at the center of the throne will be their shepherd, and he will guide them to springs of the water of life, and God will wipe away every tear from their eyes" (7:17). Who better than the Lamb who has been slain is qualified to be the Shepherd of glory? "Earth has no sorrow that heaven cannot heal."[2]

In the vision of the seven signs the first sign is that of "a woman clothed with the sun." She is Israel and a little later the church. The woman gave birth to Messiah, and the great red dragon tried to destroy him but he was caught up to heaven (in the ascension). The second sign is war in heaven between Michael (an angel) and the heavenly host on the one hand, and the dragon and his hosts on the other. The dragon and his hosts are cast out of heaven. The third sign is the pursuit of the woman (the church) and her offspring by the dragon.

The fourth sign is the beast from the sea. To this beast the dragon (devil) gives his power and purpose. In our study of Daniel, we found that certain beasts came from the sea. This sea is the sea of chaos and evil—it gives the theological location of the beast. Here the beast that makes war on the saints is the Roman empire, but, by implication, any government that tyrannizes over the faith and conscience of people is a beast from the sea. The fifth sign is the beast from the earth (13:11–18). It is a wicked and idolatrous priesthood in league with the beast from the sea. The uniting of wicked religion and wicked governments is evil compounded. The number 666 (13:18) may well have referred to a particular person (Nero). In any case, it is the number of imperfection—every beast falls short of divine power and cannot defeat God.

The sixth sign is the Lamb on Mount Zion (14:1–5). Here is a note of hope. With the Lamb are the redeemed. There are 12,000 out of each of the twelve tribes of Israel (7:4–8), which make 144,000. This is a symbolic number for the whole family of the redeemed, including us—that is, the Israel of God (recall the symbolism of numbers).

This message of hope is continued in an interlude (14:6-13). One angel announces the hour of God's judgment, another the fall of Babylon (a cryptic name for Rome), and a third the doom on idolatrous worshipers. The saints are called to endurance and assured of the blessedness that awaits them.

The seventh sign is the "one like a Son of Man" who executes the final judgment (14:14–20).

### The Fall of "Babylon" (17:1–20:15)

Rome ("Babylon") with its seven hills is pictured as a great harlot (17:1-18). She is not only filled with sexual immorality but also with economic corruption, which includes traffic in human souls (18:1–24). Her doom is sure. In the midst of the portrayal of judgment comes a hymn of praise to God as Judge (19:1–5). The victory and blessedness of Christ and the church are presented under the figure of the marriage supper of the Lamb (19:6–10). Christ is the Lamb, and the church is his Bride. As conqueror he is "The Word of God" and the "King of kings and Lord of lords" (19:11–16). The beast (the Roman government) and the false prophet (its false religion) are condemned (19:17–21). Satan is bound and the martyrs reign with Christ a thousand years (20:1–10). It is not possible here to enter into the warm debate concerning the interpretation of this brief passage. The main point is that Christ will give those who have been martyred for his sake special recognition. The scene of the great white throne teaches that the final judgment involves a separation between those whose names are in the book of life and those whose names are not (compare Matt. 25:31–46).

### The New Heaven and the New Earth (21:1–22:5)

In his vision of the new heaven and the new earth, John reaches the climax of his message. The persecuted Christians of the seven churches could face the worst that Rome could do with the assurance that victory belongs to God and God's people. Indeed no government, regardless of its might, can ever usurp the throne of God.

*Conclusion (22:6–21)*

Here John finishes his book in the form of a letter.

## Conflict with False Teaching

The early Christians not only experienced conflict with the Jews and the Roman state but also faced the problem of false teaching. We have already been made aware of this in our study of Colossians and the pastoral epistles. One of the chief sources of false teaching was Gnosticism.[3] This was a system of thought based on esoteric (private) knowledge. The word "Gnosticism" comes from the Greek word for "knowledge."

The Gnostics held that the supreme God did not create the world, but that this was done by a lesser deity. Physical matter was regarded as evil in itself. Since humans have material bodies, it was maintained that salvation consisted in freeing oneself from the body. On the basis of such reasoning the heretics at Colossae were teaching that Jesus was inferior to angels because he had a body of flesh. Gnosticism also had other effects. Some of its adherents tried to free themselves from the body through various ascetic practices. Others went to the other extreme of indulgence of the flesh because they said the physical could not harm the spiritual. An effect with which we are particularly concerned at this time is known as Docetism. The Docetists claimed that Jesus did not really have a physical body but only seemed to have. The word "Docetism" comes from the Latin word that means "seem" or "appear." In other words, this heresy was a denial of the humanity of Jesus.

In our time there are religious groups that have an unhealthy or negative attitude toward that which is material. Have you found such groups in your community? Furthermore, there are some theologians who tend to ignore the historical life of Jesus and so emphasize "the Christ of faith" that they remind others of the Docetists. Some tend to forget that Jesus was truly human. On the other hand, there are others who so emphasize the humanity of Jesus as to have little or no understanding of his deity and consequently no real doctrine of the incarnation. Still others think of religion in terms of knowing certain things with the top of our heads. We sometimes forget that Christianity involves also commitment of the heart. All of these misconceptions of Christianity are in one way or another related to the heresy John was attacking.

## The Gospel of John

The Gospel of John has already been studied briefly in connection with Chapters 15–18 on "God's Mighty Act in Jesus Christ." But it is appropriate that we consider it here also. Review what was said about this Gospel in Chapter 15. John, the Gospel writer, desired to refute Docetism, but even more he desired to evangelize the world for Christ. While all the evangelists wrote their Gospels in the light of the death and resurrection of Jesus, John sought to help people see that what was validated as true by Jesus' death and resurrection was true from the beginning. Unless the Gospel is studied in this light, much of its meaning is overlooked.[4]

### Introduction (1:1–51)

One of the central affirmations of the Prologue (vv. 1–18) contradicts Docetism head-on: "And the Word became flesh." In this Gospel that stresses Jesus' unique Sonship to the Father, we find this strong statement of his humanity also. The remainder of the introduction is composed of the witness to Jesus as Son of God and Messiah by John the Baptist, Andrew, Peter, Philip, and Nathanael.

### Jesus' Power to Give Life (2:1–6:71)

Salvation in the Synoptics is the reign of God; in John it is eternal life. John shows that Jesus has power to give both biological and eternal life, but his emphasis is on the latter. In fact, the former bears witness to the latter.

> As you read these chapters, underline the words "life" and "live" every time they occur. When you have finished, reread the underlined passages. What did you learn by this procedure?

The changing of the water into wine (2:1-11) was probably a sign for John pointing to Jesus' power to give new life to people. At least the miracle is set within the general context of new life. The cleansing of the Temple (2:12–25) was a sign that Jesus was bringing a new community into being, in which he himself would take the place of the Temple.

> Jesus' conversation with Nicodemus and John's interpretation of the conversation are concerned with the new birth and the new life (3:1–21).

> Compare the theology of John 3:16 with that of Ephesians 2:8.

> In the passage on John the Baptist (3:22–36), note especially verse 36.

*Jesus' conversation with the woman at Jacob's well (4:1–42) cen-*
*ters around the "living water" that he can give.*

The healing of the official's son (4:43–54) shows that Jesus has the power
to prevent the loss of biological life. The healing of the lame man on the
Sabbath (5:1–47) is the occasion for calling attention to Jesus' unique
relation to the Father and his ability to give eternal life. The feeding of the
five thousand (6:1–71) is the occasion for the discussion of the Bread of
Life. Jesus is just as essential to eternal life as bread and water are to biological life.

### Light and Darkness (7:1–12:50)

John introduces this theme in the Prologue, and in these chapters he
develops it. The unbelief of Jesus' own siblings (7:1–9) is one illustration
of darkness. Another is the people's division and confusion concerning his
identity (7:10–44). A third is the opposition of the chief priests and the
Pharisees (7:45–52). Notwithstanding, he is the light of the world
(8:12–20 ). Kinship to Abraham is not a matter of biological descent
(8:31–59; compare Rom. 9:6–7). To the man born blind Jesus gives literal
sight and the Light of Life. Life and light are closely related. The Good
Shepherd is willing to die for the sheep, but Jesus' enemies will not
acknowledge him but choose instead to remain in darkness (10:1–42). The
raising of Lazarus (11:1–57) continues the life theme in the midst of the
context of light. Jesus is sought by Mary, certain of the Jews, and
Greeks—this fact indicates that there were those who were seeking the
Light. The cross of Christ gives life and light to people of faith (12:27–36).
Jesus came into this world to be Light and to give life (12:37–50).

### The Meaning of Discipleship (13:1–17:26)

Washing the disciples' feet is the occasion for teaching that they are to
be servants and that they are to love one another as Christ has loved them
(13:1–38). How did Christ love them? How does Christ love us? Christ
promises his disciples a home in the Father's house, power to do God's
work, the Holy Spirit as counselor and guide, and his own personally
communicated peace (14:1–31). The allegory of the Vine and the
Branches (15:1–17) underscores the necessity of abiding in Christ if we
are to produce the proper fruit as Christians. It is in this vital union with
Christ that the capacity for real love is generated. The Christian community is a fellowship of those who share Christ's love. Jesus prepares his
disciples for the time when he will be separated from them (15:18–16:33):

by informing them that the world will hate them, by promising the Spirit who will lead them into all the truth, and by reassuring them of victory—"In the world you face persecution. But take courage; I have conquered the world" (16:33).

Jesus prays for his disciples (17:1–26), which is another way of saying that he prays for the church.

> *As you read this vicarious prayer, look for the definition of eternal life contained therein.*
>
> *Identify each petition Jesus makes.*
>
> *What connection do you see between this prayer and John 15, Ephesians, and 1 Corinthians 1:10–17?*
>
> *Why did Jesus pray for the unity of the church?*

The answer is found in verse 23: "so that the world may know that you [God] have sent me and have loved them [the disciples] even as you have loved me." In other words, God has a purpose for the world, and the church is an instrument of that purpose. It has a mission to the world.

John is very conscious of the world, as shown by his Gospel and the First Epistle. He uses this word for "world" (*kosmos*) more than all the other New Testament writers put together. A few illustrations will suffice to give his emphasis. It was God's love for the world that motivated the gift of the Son (3:16). "Indeed, God did not send the Son into the world to condemn the world, but in order that the world might be saved through him" (3:17). As the Bread of Life Christ gives life to the world (6:33–35). He is the Light of the world (8:12; 9:5). And yet the world is hostile to him.

*Jesus' Passion and Resurrection (18:1–21:25)*

> *You are encouraged to reread these chapters in John.*

It is possible that the words of John's Gospel were written at the time the Roman emperor claimed to be Lord and God. If so, Thomas's confession of the risen Christ (20:28) was exceedingly relevant: "My Lord and my God!"

## The Letters of John

The three Letters of John were probably written from Ephesus toward the end of the first century by the author of the Gospel of John (see Chapter 15). The first two letters reflect the conflict with Docetism. The two most obvious refutations of Docetism in them are these: "Every spirit that confesses that Jesus Christ has come in the flesh is of God" (1 John 4:2); "Many deceivers have gone out into the world, those who do not confess that Jesus Christ has come in the flesh" (2 John 7). But this heresy seems to be in the thinking of John as he pens all three of these letters.

Though 1 John is only five chapters long, it is very difficult to outline satisfactorily. In part this grows out of the fact that the Christian life, with which it deals, cannot be divided into separate compartments. There are at least three key words, however, by which the message of the book may be unlocked: life, light, and love. These three are not wholly distinguishable from one another. In fact they are different handles by which to take hold of the same reality.

> *If you are willing to make the effort, read 1 John three times. On the first reading, concentrate on John's theme of life and mark every occurrence of every word pertaining to life. What does John teach about life? Follow the same procedure with "light" and "love." What is said below about these themes is suggestive, not exhaustive.*

## Life

Life in the Gospel and Letters of John is usually eternal life, whether the adjective is used with the noun or not. Eternal life is that quality of life that God gives to those who have faith in Jesus Christ. It is salvation, which begins now and continues forever. In the introduction (1:1–4) to the letter under consideration, the word "life" occurs three times, one of these with the adjective "eternal." John reacts against Docetism from the start. The life he describes is the *enfleshed* life of God's Son, Jesus Christ, a life that the early witnesses heard, saw, and touched. The disciple's life is made possible by that life. Our new life is brought into being by a supernatural birth: we are born of God (3:9; 5:18; compare John 1 and 3). "Those who have been born of God do not sin" (3:9); that is, the new life given by God is in its nature without sin. The person who has such life is not given over to sin. Sin is the opposite of this new life. Yet when Christians are viewed in their finiteness and weakness, all are sinful (1:8–2:2). But "if we confess our sins, he who is faithful and just, will forgive us our sins and cleanse us from all unrighteousness." We have the assurance that "whatever is born of God conquers the world [evil]. And this is the victory that conquers the world, our faith" (5:4). "God gave us eternal life, and this life is in his Son" (5:11). The letter ends as it began with eternal life (5:20).

*Light*

"God is *light* and in him there is no darkness at all" (1:5). That is, God is by nature self-revealing, and in this self-revealing there is no evil of any kind. In response to God's revelation we are to "walk in the light" (1:7). This means to walk as Jesus walked (2:6). Indeed when he was born, "the true light, which enlightens everyone, was coming into the world" (John 1:9). He is "the light of the world" (John 8:12; 9:5). Even now "the darkness is passing away and the true light is already shining" (2:8). God's revelation has the content of Christ and that content is love. It is those in whom God's love is operative that abide in God's light, for any one who hates another is in darkness (2:9–10). Persons who do not live by the light of love do not even know where they are going (2:11). They are without adequate purpose and guidance.

Response to the Light also involves knowing the truth. Knowing means receiving in faith, and truth means God's revealed dependability. The real knowledge (*gnosis*) is not the so-called knowledge of Gnosticism, but the confession of Jesus as Christ and Son (2:18–25). For knowledge in the biblical sense requires decision, choice.

*Love*

"God is love" (4:8, 16). Such love is not dependent on the worthiness of its object; it is self-giving.

> As you read about love in 1 John, look up the parallel passages in the Gospel of John as they are provided in the NRSV or any other Bible you may have.

The Docetists by reason of their scorn of the physical nature of human beings failed in the ethic of Christian concern for human bodily needs. The beliefs one holds are determinative of life.

God revealed divine love for us by sending the Son to make atonement for our sins (3:16; 4:9–10). This means that we are the children of God (3:1). In response to God's love, we are also to love. "We love, because he first loved us" (4:19). God's love for us is our motivation for loving others (4:7–21). Loving others means that we are abiding in the light (2:10). In fact, "we know that we have passed from death to life because we love one another" (3:14). The Docetists may think that loving God is all that matters, but the fact is "those who do not love a brother or sister whom they have seen [with their *physical* eyes], cannot love God whom they have not seen" (4:20). Loving that is taken out in well-wishing is not enough. We must love in deed and in truth (3:18). The real test of love is obedience to God (2:5; 5:2). And all God's commandments spell "love." Jesus has given us the incarnate pattern of this love (3:16; John 13:1; 15:13).

## Jude and Second Peter

Jude and Second Peter belong together since they are general letters dealing with the same kind of false teaching—Gnosticism. We have already noted that Gnosticism sometimes issued in asceticism and at other times in immoral indulgence. These letters are addressed to the latter form of the problem in particular. Whatever the underlying causes may be, we are obviously living in an age of great immoral indulgence, and the message of Jude and 2 Peter applies.

When Jude speaks of contending for the faith (v. 3), he means that the church is not to tolerate false teaching and the immorality to which it leads. He points out that God judged people for their sins in time past and that God still judges today. The New Testament writers consistently demand self-discipline and consistently repudiate immoral behavior. Jude not only exhorts readers to build themselves up in the faith but also to keep others from falling into the trap of false teaching (20–23). Note how very appropriate his benediction is for the situation about which he has written (24–25).

Second Peter is longer than Jude and shows dependence on Jude in the second chapter. At the earliest, the Letter of Jude must be dated after the death of Peter. Thus, this dependence and other factors have led most scholars to date this letter after the time of Peter. Some of the early church leaders had questions about its authorship and the church was slow to admit it into the New Testament canon. At a much later time John Calvin was a bit uncertain as well about the Petrine authorship of the epistle. The writer refers to Paul's letters as being among "the other scriptures" (3:16). Paul's letters were not regarded as authoritative scripture until long after the time of Peter. If this evidence is taken seriously, it means that the author wrote between 100 and 150 C.E. a message he was confident Peter would address to the situation at hand.

The believers are called to be more zealous in confirming their call and election (chap. 1), warned against the same kind of problem faced by the author of Jude (chap. 2), and reminded that the Lord will yet come (chap. 3). There was an expectation in the early church that the Lord would return soon. The seeming delay had been the occasion of mocking on the part of some. But 2 Peter states, "with the Lord one day is like a thousand years, and a thousand years are like one day" (3:8).

*In what kinds of conflict is the church involved today at home and abroad?*

## The Canon of the New Testament

Like the Old Testament canon (see Chapter 14), the New Testament canon was slow in formation. For the earliest Christians the Old Testament was the only Bible. In the days of his flesh, Jesus was a living authority for his disciples. After his ascension many of his remembered sayings helped to guide the young church. Between 60 and 95 C.E. the four Gospels were written. Each was read publicly, copied, and circulated. They were the first group of books to have a revered place in the life of the Christian community. Paul's letters, however, were written, at least for the most part, before the Gospels, and they carried a certain degree of apostolic authority from the beginning. Eventually they were grouped together and accorded a special place in the life and worship of the community. Other groups of books went through a similar process. By the latter part of the second century most of the books of the New Testament-to-be had been accepted as authoritative by the church. Those whose status was still undecided were Hebrews, James, Jude, 2 Peter, 2 John, 3 John, and Revelation. In 367 C.E. Athanasius of Alexandria listed the twenty-seven books of our present New Testament as canonical. This same list was accepted by the Council of Hippo in 393 and by the Council of Carthage in 397.

One purpose of canon formation was to exclude from authoritative status various books that did not measure up to the Christian faith as it was understood in the early church. The false teaching, to which we have just given our attention, was another motivating influence. The church needed an authoritative, new-covenant scripture. The use of particular works in the community and their association with the apostles were important factors in the process of canon formation. We should be grateful to God for the guidance given to the early church in this crucial selection of New Testament books.

# PART SEVEN

# GOD'S COMING ACTS OF CONSUMMATION

23

# Chaos—Opposition to God's Purpose

*W*e have now come to the last major division of our study together, "God's Coming Acts of Consummation." These acts have not been ignored as they have been proclaimed here and there by the biblical writers. Here, however, we focus our attention on them in a special way in order to see that to which our Christian hope points. To do this in proper context, we must also present the account of opposition to God's purpose. "Chaos" is the word that best represents this opposition.

*Look up each biblical reference.*

## Cosmic Evil

### In the Old Testament

At the very beginning of our study of creation, we encountered the idea of chaos. Genesis 1:2 may be literally translated: "The earth was a formless void and darkness covered the face of the deep, while a wind from God swept over the face of the waters." By God's creative power, order was brought out of chaos. The words "formlessness," "chaos," "darkness," and "deep" all have negative connotations. It is only by the power of God that the created world (*kosmos*, in Greek) is prevented at any moment from returning to chaos (see Ps. 46:1–3). Chaos may, therefore, be thought of as representative of all forms of evil; that is, everything that is out of harmony with the purpose of God.

The allusions of various Old Testament writers to the ancient Near Eastern story of the dragon suggest a recognition of the cosmic dimensions of evil (compare chap. 3). In Psalm 74:12–17 are combined a reference to the Babylonian story of creation and the Canaanite story of Baal. According to the Babylonian story, the god Marduk conquered the "dragon" goddess Tiamat and from her divided carcass made heaven and earth. According to the Canaanite story, Baal crushed the sea-dragon Yam, also called Tannin, Lothan (Leviathan), "the winding Serpent," and "Shalyat of the seven heads." The Babylonians and the Canaanites believed their stories to be true, but the psalmist did not. The psalmist uses some of their language in referring to the LORD in order to state symbolically God's power as the One True God in creation and history. In other words, God's mighty acts in creation are combined with the mighty acts of dividing the Sea of Reeds, overcoming the Egyptians, providing food and water for the people in the wilderness, and creating a dry place in the Jordan for Israel to pass over. In any case, the psalmist's primary interest is in God's power, which is adequate to save Israel under the present circumstances in history.[1]

Isaiah 51:9–11 contains a somewhat similar use of the dragon story. On this occasion the story is used to portray symbolically God's deliverance from the dragon Egypt. In other words, the ancient story has been historicized, that is, made to serve the purpose of interpreting history. Moreover, we read in Isaiah 27:1, "On that day the LORD with his cruel and great and strong sword will punish Leviathan the fleeing serpent, Leviathan the twisting serpent, and he will kill the dragon that is in the sea." Here there is an anticipation of God's final overthrow of God's enemies, though the language is still symbolic. Yet, in these three passages (Ps. 74:12–17; Isa. 51:9–11; and Isa. 27:1) as well as in other Old Testament passages, there is at least a hint that evil is more than that which is found in evil people and nations.

Satan appears in the Old Testament as the accuser (Zech. 3:1–2), tester (Job 1–2), and tempter (1 Chron. 21:1) of mortals. But these three passages are the only ones in which Satan is mentioned by name in the Old Testament. The serpent of Genesis 3 was only first identified as Satan in the apocryphal Wisdom of Solomon 2:24. In the Old Testament itself, however, Satan is not identified with the dragon, or Rahab, or Leviathan, or the serpent.

## In the New Testament

In the Persian and intertestamental periods demonology became more highly developed in Jewish theology probably because of the influence of the Persians. And in the New Testament, the devil and his demons have a rather prominent place. This is notably true in the Gospels, where Jesus is tempted by the devil and casts out demons. But it is by no means confined to the Gospels. For example, Paul could say, "Put on the whole armor of God, so that you may be able to stand against the wiles of the devil. For our struggle is not against enemies of blood and flesh, but against the rulers, against the authorities, against the cosmic powers of this present darkness, against the spiritual forces of evil in the heavenly places" (Eph. 6:11–12). And John could say, "The whole world [*kosmos*] lies under the power of the evil one" (1 John 5:19). In Revelation 12:7–9, the dragon, the serpent, the devil, and Satan are all identified with one another. That which was metaphor and symbol in the Psalms and Isaiah is perhaps here united and identified with a personal devil.

It can hardly be doubted that the devil of the Gospels and "the god of this world" (2 Cor. 4:4) were considered as the same evil personality in New Testament times. Of course there are those who say this belief is a dispensable aspect of the "time-conditioned framework" of the New Testament—in other words, that the idea of a personal evil force, while inevitable in those days, has no place in our modern thought forms. But does this fit in with all that we know? Or is this belief rather a profound understanding of the cosmic nature of evil? The New Testament writers keep us reminded that the mystery of evil cannot be eliminated by our oversimplifications and that evil is so much stronger than we are that we must look to God, not to ourselves, for our salvation.

Another aspect of cosmic evil often overlooked is the groaning of the whole creation set forth by Paul in Romans 8:18–25. Behind Paul's thought in Romans lies the close connection between humanity and nature in the Old Testament and in the Judaism of his own time. The close connection between humankind and the soil is presented in Genesis 2:7—"then the LORD God formed man from the dust of the ground." But human disobedience resulted in the impairment of that bond (see Gen. 3:17). The relation of humankind to nature is also seen in such passages as Hosea 4:1–3 and Isaiah 11:6–9. Furthermore, the anticipation of the new heaven and the new earth (Isa. 66:22) implies that the old heaven and the old earth leave something to be desired. Genesis 3:17 was interpreted by some in Paul's day to mean that the fall of humankind involved the fall of the universe as well.

In Romans 8:18–25, the key words in Paul's view of nature's condition are "futility," "bondage to decay," and "groaning in labor pains." "We know that the whole creation has been groaning in labor pains together until now." In other words, Paul sees the need for a cosmic redemption. Note the following comment on verse 22:

> We observed above Paul's sensitiveness to the pathos of nature's plight of subjection to futility; here he alludes more particularly to the *sorrow* of nature. He thinks of the sufferings of animals—the weak devoured by the strong—of the ruthless destruction of plant life, of natural catastrophes of all kinds; he listens, it is not too fanciful to suggest, to the cryings of the wind and the sea; and he receives an impression that all of nature is "groaning in travail together," i.e., in all its parts. The whole created world is crying for release from pain, as a woman cries in childbirth; but it does so with hope for that which will give meaning to all the pain and turn it into joy.[2]

Shall we take Paul's words seriously, or are they just figurative decoration? Paul apparently meant them in all seriousness, and we should take them in all seriousness. The whole of God's creation stands in the need of redemption. We as humans are tied up with God's universe, and God's purpose is bigger than our egos.

## Human Sin[3]

Throughout our study much attention has been given to human involvement in the problem of evil. For example, Chapter 3 was devoted entirely to this subject. According to Genesis 3, sin, suffering, and death are interrelated. Much of Israel's suffering was the judgment of God on sin. In the New Testament, Satan is related to sin, suffering, and death. He is the tempter. People often succumb to temptation, and this means sin. And "the wages of sin is death" (Rom. 6:23). It is the devil who has the power of death (Heb. 2:14). Satan's relation to suffering is implied in these words from Luke 13:16—"And ought not this woman, a daughter of Abraham whom Satan bound for eighteen long years, be set free from this bondage on the sabbath day?" Satan's causative relation to suffering is also implied in the ministry of Jesus as he cast out demons (Luke 11:20). According to the Revelation to John, the dragon (Satan) is the power behind a corrupt government in its persecution of the saints (Rev. 13:4). Satan yet assumes many alluring forms in our world today.

Human sin remains, however, the heart of the problem of evil so far as humans are concerned. The devil cannot make one sin against one's will, and neither will God force one to do right. People must accept responsibility for their response to God. To Jesus, sin was primarily a matter of inner spirit (Mark 7:20–23). He dealt more tenderly with those guilty of sexual immorality than with the self-righteous. Sin places people in the category of the lost, and Jesus "came to seek out and to save the lost" (Luke 19:10). Sin is giving first place to anything less than the Kingdom of God ( Matt. 19:16–22; Luke 12:13–21). It is neglecting to use the talents that God has given us (Matt. 25:14–30). It is forfeiting one's relationship to God (Luke 15:11–32). It is social as well as personal (Matt. 11:20–24).

In his letters Paul stresses the fact that all, Jew or Gentile, are unrighteous and cannot save themselves. Sin is communal (that is, a characteristic of the entire human race from its first representatives) as well as personal. Sin came into the world of humans through the first Adam and death (as we know it) came through sin, "and so death spread to all because all have sinned" (Rom. 5:12–21). Christ is the last Adam (1 Cor. 15:45). "For as all die in Adam, so all will be made alive in Christ" (1 Cor. 15:22). All humans were in Adam as father of the human race and are therefore the extension of Adam just as the Old Testament writers thought of all Israelites as being in Jacob and as becoming the extension of Jacob. To be in Adam is to be in the realm of death; to be in Christ is to be in the realm of life.

The church as the body of Christ is the new humanity in which all worldly distinctions are abolished. It is the creation of God by redemption. To be in Christ is to be a new creation (Gal. 6:15; 2 Cor. 5:17; Col. 3:9–11). The image of God is being renewed in the Christian (Col. 3:10). The first Adam was grasping and wanted to be God (Gen. 3), and every succeeding Adam except One has followed in the first Adam's footsteps. Christ, the last Adam, was not grasping "but emptied himself, taking the form of a slave" (Phil. 2:5–11).

John presents the problem of sin and the remedy for sin in strong contrasts:

| The World | John 18:36; 1 John 2:15 | The Kingdom |
| Unbelief | John 3:16–18; 6:64; 1 John 5:12 | Faith |

| Bondage | John 8:31–38 | Freedom |
| Darkness | John 1:5; 8:12; 1 John 1:5; 2:9 | Light |
| Death | John 5:24; 3:16 | Eternal Life |
| Hate and Fear | John 15:18–19; 1 John 4:18–20 | Love |
| Lawlessness | 1 John 3:4–6 | Abiding in God |

*Read the references cited in each part of the table and write down in your notebook the relation between each of the pairs as John presents that relation.*

In the Letter to the Hebrews, sin is unbelief, stubbornness, or hardening of the heart (3:1–19). It is neglect of "so great a salvation" (2:3). In James it is yielding to temptation, laziness, omission of doing good, and indifference to the needs of others. In Jude it is active hostility to God. The most generally used word for sin means "to miss the mark." Regardless of what words are used to designate sin, it is always a missing of the mark that God has set for us. Any thought, word, deed, attitude, or feeling contrary to the Spirit of Christ is sin. That is, the New Testament writers recognize specific sins as well as sin in general. Basic human alienation from God expresses itself in many ways. Both the alienation and its many expressions are regarded as sin.

In the light of the cross, sin is that which puts to death the best that God can do. The teaching about the devil and human corruption are never used anywhere in the New Testament to excuse humans from their responsibility. These teachings confront us with the seriousness of our predicament and our need of God's salvation. Apart from Christ we are lost sinners, but through Christ we may become redeemed saints.

# Consummation—The Final Victory

*T*he final word is with God, not with the opposition. This final word, however, is not unrelated to the first word and all succeeding words. Past, present, and future enter into the one inseparable message of the Bible.

## The Old Testament Expectation

God's people have always lived in hope. God promised Abraham and Sarah descendants, a land, and a blessing. Indeed Abraham himself would be a channel of blessing to all nations. The promise was only partially kept in Old Testament times. God promised to make David a house. The messianic hope was bound up with God's covenant with David. In time the figure of the Son of man was united with that of Messiah. There was also the anticipation of the servant of the LORD. No wonder the messianic expectations among first-century Jews were quite varied.

There was also the promise of a new covenant with the people of God—a covenant that would center in the heart, in the knowledge of God, and in the forgiveness of sin. This covenant, therefore, involved a new life. This new life was to be the gift of God. The Spirit of God would be poured out on all sorts of people. The Day of the LORD would come in judgment and in mercy. Ultimately God would overthrow all God's enemies. There would be a new heaven and a new earth.

## The Fulfillment of the Promise

The New Testament records the fulfillment of the promise. In other words, there is what has been called a "realized eschatology," a fulfillment of certain aspects of God's purpose with finality. The messianic kingdom began to dawn in Jesus' Person and work. His healing ministry was evidence that the power of the new age was at work in him. The new covenant became a reality through him. His death and resurrection are central in the proclamation of the gospel.

At the new Pentecost the promise concerning God's Spirit was kept. The disciples were endowed with power to become "the witnessing community." Eternal life is the new life generated by the Holy Spirit in the new birth. This quality of life begins now in the life of the believer. The Christian lives in Christ, and Christ lives in the Christian. In fact, the Christian is already a new creation in Christ. The power of the new age is now at work in us.

In Chapters 15–22, we have spent much time in studying the working out of the promises. We were right in doing this, for the New Testament writers have much to say about what God has done and is doing in Christ and through this church. But intermingled with this emphasis is also the vibrant expectation of the completion of God's purpose. And this expectation is more than an incidental concern.

## The Consummation Yet to Come

Just as there is a realized eschatology, there is also an unrealized eschatology. All people, including Christians, are daily confronted by the fact of evil in various forms. Jesus and the writers of the New Testament looked forward to the consummation of the kingdom. And this consummation is united with what is usually called the "second" coming of Christ. We look back to what God has already done in Christ and forward to what God will yet do in him.

### The Second Coming

Though the word "second" is nowhere used with the word "coming" in the New Testament, the idea is present. One of the clearest statements of the idea is found in Hebrews 9:28: "Christ, having been offered once to bear the sins of many, *will appear a second time*, not to deal with sin, but to save those who are eagerly waiting for him." Of course we may speak of Jesus as coming back from the dead in his resurrection, as coming in the Spirit at the new Pentecost, as coming in the crises of history and personal life, but none of these comings is what the New Testament writers intend when they speak of Christ's final coming in a variety of ways.

The hope of the second coming was based on Jesus' own teaching. The apostles included the return of Christ as Savior and Judge in their earliest preaching of the gospel (Acts 3:20; 10:42). The Lord's Supper anticipates it (1 Cor. 11:26). And it occurs as a continuing theme throughout the New Testament. It means that God will consummate the kingdom through the same Jesus Christ through whom the kingdom was inaugurated and who is present in the lives of God's people today. The Christ who is to come is the Christ who was to come, who did come, and who is present with us. His first coming was in humiliation; his second coming will be in glory.

*The second coming is interpreted by its associations in the New Testament. Read each of the passages listed below.*

### The Day of the Lord (1 Thess. 4:13–5:11)

*Review what was said about the Day of the Lord in Chapter 14.*

The passage from 1 Thessalonians indicates that the ancient announcement of the Day of the Lord is to be consummated by the coming of Jesus Christ again. This means his coming will be a time of judgment and mercy. It is also called "the day of Christ" (Phil. 1:10; 2:14–18). The early church thought of it as imminent (compare 1 Peter 4:7). Paul's mention of the clouds in writing to the Thessalonians called to mind the covenant with Noah (Gen. 9:13), the covenant at Sinai (Exod. 19:9–16), God's presence at the tent of meeting (Exod. 40:34–38), God's presence at the transfiguration (Mark 9:2–8), Jesus' departure in the ascension (Acts 1:9), and the coming of the Son of man (Dan. 7:13; Mark 13:26–27; compare Rev. 1:7).[1] Paul's emphasis is on Christ's immediate presence with his people.

### Christian Ethics (1 John 3:2; 1 Peter 1:3–9)

The second coming is used by John in his First Letter as an incentive to purity of life and by Peter as an encouragement under trial. The book of Revelation makes both emphases.

### The Resurrection (1 Thess. 4:16; 1 Cor. 15:23, 51–57; Phil. 3:20–21)

There is a sense in which one is raised from the death of sin when one becomes a Christian (Rom. 6:1–11). On the basis of Philippians 1:19–26, it is sometimes said that a person is raised from literal death at the time of death. Paul says, "For to me, living is Christ and dying is gain." But we must admit that Paul does not use the word "raise" or "resurrection" in this connection. In this world Paul lived *in* Christ, and in the other world he expected to live *with* Christ. Second Corinthians 4:16–5:10 is understood by some to refer to what happens immediately after death and by others to the time of the second coming. However one may interpret the time element in this particular passage, the passages listed in the parentheses above all refer to the resurrection at the time of the second coming.

Paul thought as a Jew in terms of the unity of a person. This final resurrection means that the Christian shares in God's redemptive work in behalf of the whole creation (Rom. 8:18–25). As "bodies" (Rom. 8:23) we are creatures akin to the rest of creation—and we are included in God's cosmic purpose. There are three stages in the Christian's resurrection: (1) the resurrection (or rebirth) in the present time, (2) the transfer from life in Christ to life with Christ after death, and (3) the resurrection at the end of the present world order.

### A Glorious Surprise (1 John 3:2)

John, who places great stress on eternal life as a present reality, does not neglect the second coming (compare John 5:28–29; 6:44; 12:48). In fact, he whets our anticipation for the glorious surprise awaiting us: "Beloved, we are God's children now; what we will be has not yet been revealed. What we do know is this: when he is revealed, we will be like him, for we shall see him as he is."

### The Millennium (Rev. 20:1–10)

The millennium is the thousand-year binding of Satan mentioned in Revelation 20:1–10. These ten verses have been the subject of endless debate. When students seek to relate the second coming of Christ to the millennium, they usually divide into three schools of interpretation (though these are not the only schools). Premillennialists believe that Christ will return *before* (pre-) the millennium, or thousand-year period of peace and righteousness. Postmillennialists believe that he will return *after* (post-) a period of righteousness and peace. And amillennialists believe that Christ will return apart from any millennium at all, that the term is symbolic and refers to the whole period between the first and second coming.

### Scoffing (2 Peter 3:3–15)

By the time 2 Peter was written, there were scoffers who said he would not come at all. But the writer reminds them that "with the Lord one day is like a thousand years, and a thousand years like one day" (3:8). Unfortunately there are those who still scoff at the second coming as if their faith is superior to that of the New Testament writers. On the other hand, there are many who have abused the doctrine by claiming to know the unknowable and by neglecting the application of Christian ethics to certain aspects of life here and now. There is an analogy between the first coming of Jesus and his second coming; otherwise we could not speak of "first" and "second." Just as his first coming enriches the hope that anticipated him, so his second coming will exceed and enrich all our expectations. We have every reason to believe this, for the New Testament hope of his second coming is even clearer and stronger than the Old Testament hope of his first coming.

## The New Creation

The ancient prophet had already anticipated God's creation of a new heaven and a new earth (Isa. 65:17; 66:22). We have seen that Paul was conscious not only of human suffering but also of the groaning of the whole creation (Rom. 8:18–25). While he did not use the expression "a new heaven and a new earth," he did say, "the creation itself will be set free from its bondage to decay and will obtain the freedom of the glory of the children of God" (v. 21). And John gives us the vision of the new heaven and the new earth (Rev. 21:1–22: 5; compare 2 Peter 3:13). This is some of the most exalted language in all Holy Writ. Heaven and earth are both involved in God's consummation of the divine purpose. The new Jerusalem is not the result of human schemes; it is the gift of God. In one sense it is the church as the bride of Christ. It stands for God's dwelling with God's people, for the end of sin, weeping, pain, and death. The eternal city is built on historical foundations, for on its gates are inscribed the names of the twelve tribes of Israel and on the foundations of its walls the names of the twelve apostles of the Lamb. The two twelves together symbolize the old-covenant people of God and the new-covenant people of God as one community.

But in contrast to those who have accepted God's gift of salvation stand those who have refused God's grace (v. 8). The statement of the consequences of such rejection here is, along with many other New Testament passages, a solemn warning to the disobedient.

> *For example, consider the following statements: Matthew 25:41–46; Mark 9:42–48; John 3:16, 36; and Romans 2:5; 5:9.*

God does not wish "any to perish, but all to come to repentance" (2 Peter 3:9), yet no one is forced to accept God's salvation.

In the final analysis the city will be in the realm of the Spirit, for in it there will be no need for a temple. "Its temple is the Lord God the Almighty and the Lamb," and the glory of God is its light. Nations shall walk by the light of the city and kings shall bring their glory into it, reminding us that God's salvation extends beyond near horizons.

The Bible begins with the story of humans in a garden and ends with the story of humans in a city, but the city is a "garden city"; and in this garden city there is a river of the water of life and the tree of life. That from which the flaming cherubs barred sinful humans (Gen. 3:24) is now available forever. The leaves of the tree are for the healing of the nations.

Is this a symbol of heaven or of earth? It is a symbol of both, as the eternal redeems the temporal. For those in whose heart is the new Jerusalem and whose heart is in the new Jerusalem, the song of the redeemed is already a reality, but one day that song will be sung without a single discordant note. Like the Old Testament, the New Testament ends on a note of hope and expectation. God who has acted mightily in history, and supremely in Christ, will through that same Christ accomplish the new creation.[2]

# Conclusion—The One Story of the Bible

*O*ur journey through the Bible together is completed. It is impossible to say again all that has been said already. It is our purpose simply to restate the story of God's mighty acts in a very abbreviated form, in order that it may be seen in its overall unity.

The Bible begins with a recitation of *God's mighty acts of creation*. God created the universe and all things therein. God created humankind in the divine image with a likeness to God that no other creature in this world shares. People were therefore intended by God to be God's responsible representatives. While closely related to the earth and the rest of creation, humans are those living beings who were designed to have fellowship with God and to work happily in God's world.

But humans are not only creatures made in the image of God; they are also suffering and dying sinners standing in the need of a salvation that they themselves cannot provide. All of us have yielded to the temptation to try to be God. As humans, we are estranged from God, from our neighbors, and from ourselves. The effects of sin have permeated all aspects of life. The stories of Adam and Eve, Cain and Abel, the Flood, and the Tower of Babel, all bear their witness to the human predicament, and our own lives confirm it.

God is not only Creator; God is also Redeemer. By *covenant acts of redemption* God was made known to God's ancient people as Redeemer. Onto the scene of human need God brought Abraham and Sarah and the other patriarchs and matriarchs, and with them made a covenant of grace. This divine covenant was essentially a promise. God promised Abraham to make of him a great nation, to bless him, and to make him a blessing.

Our ancestors were far from perfect, but God used them, ruling and overruling in the affairs of their lives.

Some of the Hebrews went down to Egypt in the days of Jacob and later were enslaved by a pharaoh who did not know Joseph. God called Moses to be the instrument of their deliverance and revealed to him the divine name, the LORD. God redeemed the people from the Egyptian bondage, and by this act these people and their descendants forever after knew the LORD as the God of redemption. At Sinai God's choice of the people was given the form of a covenant, of which the Law was made an expression. God made a commitment to the people and the people pledged themselves to God.

A land was a part of the covenant promise to Abraham. The people of Moses' generation, however, did not inherit the promise on account of unbelief. Joshua led the next generation in the initial conquest of the land. Under his leadership the covenant was renewed at Shechem, when other people closely related to the Israelites probably joined the covenant for the first time. After Joshua God gave the people judges to deliver them from their oppressors.

Samuel was the chief leader in the transition from the period of the Judges to the establishment of the monarchy. He was the last of the judges, the first of the prophets after Moses, and a priest. It was he who anointed Saul the first king of Israel. While Saul did some things to pave the way for the greatness of David, he was essentially a troubled man.

David was the founder of a house and a city (Jerusalem). It was God's covenant with David that laid the foundation for the messianic hope. David sinned grossly and later repented of his sin. Nevertheless, the consequences of his sin were tragic in the life of his family and the kingdom. Yet God's grace was greater than David's sin, and in time God made him a house of far greater dimensions than David ever imagined.

Solomon, in spite of all his wisdom, mimicked the oriental despots of his time. His most famous undertaking as a builder was the Temple in Jerusalem. The support of his court, his many wives and concubines, his army, and his building program induced him to make taxes high and to make use of the hated corvée (forced labor). The judgment of God was pronounced on him particularly for the support of the cults of his foreign wives.

Indeed, God's covenant acts of redemption were followed by his *righteous acts of judgment*. Solomon's policies issued in the judgment of division between the North and the South. Jeroboam, who led the ten northern tribes to rebel against Solomon's son Rehoboam, established a sanctuary at Dan and another at Bethel, setting up a bull calf at each, and came to be known as the king who sinned and "made Israel to sin." The house of Jeroboam was extinguished by Baasha. The next dynasty to be established in the Northern Kingdom was that of Omri. It was during the reign of Omri's son Ahab that Elijah challenged the Phoenician Baalism of Queen Jezebel.

The second great act of judgment was the fall of the Northern Kingdom to Assyria in 721 B.C.E. Earlier in the eighth century Amos and Hosea saw the moral and spiritual rot that was to result in captivity. Most of Judah's leaders and the people also left much to be desired when measured by God's righteousness and love. Isaiah's message to Judah centered about the holiness of God, faith in God, the remnant, and the coming Davidic king. Micah's message included the famous summary of eighth-century prophecy: "to do justice, and to love kindness, and to walk humbly with your God."

The third great act of judgment was the fall of the Southern Kingdom to Babylon in 587/586 B.C.E. From 697 to 587 Judah had seven rulers. The worst was the idolatrous Manasseh, and the best was the reforming Josiah. The discovery of the Book of the Law in the Temple encouraged and guided Josiah in his attempt to abolish idolatry from Judah. But Josiah was killed in 609 B.C.E. by Pharaoh Neco of Egypt. Josiah's reformation had not penetrated to the hearts of the people, so the fall of Judah and the dynasty of David was inevitable.

The period was rich in prophetic voices warning the people of the consequences of disobedience. Zephaniah announced the coming Day of the LORD. It is probable that the Book of the Law that was found in the Temple was Deuteronomy or a part of it. Many Judeans had accepted the Davidic covenant as an unconditional promise of God's favor and had ignored the covenant made at Sinai with its demands on the people. The book of Deuteronomy is a series of three sermons on the Sinaitic covenant and was providentially made available in the time when it was greatly needed. Nahum announced the coming destruction of Nineveh, the capital of the bloody Assyrian Empire. Habakkuk was disturbed about the exercise of God's justice within Judah and between Judah and Babylon. It was in the midst of his dialogue with God that God told Habakkuk, "The righteous live by their faith." Jeremiah was called "to pluck up and to break down" and "to build and to plant." In his ministry of breaking down, he told the people that they had been unfaithful to the covenant, that the Temple could not save them, that their prophets were false, and that the destruction of the nation was certain. In his ministry of building, he proclaimed the salvation of a remnant, the coming of the new David, and the making of the new covenant of the heart.

God's righteous acts of judgment were followed by *gracious acts of renewal*. The exiles were comforted through God's chosen instruments. Ezekiel was preeminently the prophet of God's glory. Before the destruction of Jerusalem, his message of judgment on the sinful nation was presented as the departure of God's glory from the Temple and the city. After the destruction, however, he comforted his people with the assurance that the glory of God would return, thereby making possible a new life. The poems of Lamentations brought cleansing and release from despair. Comfort from Obadiah came through the reassurance he brought that God controls all history in justice. The prophets of the exile (Isa. 40–55; 56–66) brought comfort to the people through their glorious presentation of the One Incomparable God, the election of Israel to be God's witness to the nations, the promise of the Suffering Savior, and the anticipation of the new creation.

God restored the remnant. The Persian period was a time both of fulfillment and of frustration for the Jews. Cyrus permitted the exiles to return home. Some of them did return immediately. The foundation of the Temple was laid, but work on God's house was interrupted until 520 B.C.E. In response to the preaching of Haggai and Zechariah, the Temple was rebuilt between 520 and 515 B.C.E., though not without opposition. In a sense the Psalter may be called "the hymnbook of the Second Temple," though this is an oversimplification. It is the faith of the Old Testament set to music.

Malachi and Joel seem to present the condition of the struggling Jewish community at the time Nehemiah came to Jerusalem. Nehemiah was a dedicated layman who supervised the rebuilding of the walls of Jerusalem and the reorganization of Jewish life. Ezra was a conscientious priest and scribe who read the Law to the people and served as a leader in renewing the covenant. The work of both Nehemiah and Ezra issued in a spirit of exclusivism and lack of missionary outreach. The story of Ruth lifted the eyes of those who heard or read it to wider horizons. The book of Jonah challenged the restored remnant to be God's servant in witnessing to the nations. The book of Esther confronts God's people in any age with the question of how their loyalties are to be interrelated.

The wisdom movement in Israel did not begin or end in the postexilic era, but this is the best point at which to consider it. It deals with the affairs of everyday life in a prudential manner and wrestles with the great problems of human experience. The chief examples of wisdom in the Old Testament are Proverbs, Job, Ecclesiastes, and to some degree the Song of Solomon. Wisdom literature keeps us mindful of the fact that the down-to-earth matters of our lives (such as anxiety, suffering, doubt, and sex) are of concern to the Creator.

God's gracious acts of renewal include the encouragement of hope. In the second century B.C.E. the religious practice of Jews was outlawed by Antiochus Epiphanes of Syria. The military response to this situation was the Maccabean rebellion, and the literary response was the book of Daniel. This book was designed to bring hope to God's people in these tragic times. Chapters 1–6 call them to faithfulness and a responsible ministry in the midst of adversity. Chapters 7–12 assure them that God will give the kingdom to the "one like a human being," who represents both the people of God and their Leader. The Jewish hope embraced the expectation of the Day of the LORD as a time of judgment and salvation, a varied anticipation of a messianic deliverer, and a belief in the resurrection of the dead.

The Old Testament is an essential part of God's written word, but it is only a part. The New Testament provides witness to God's continuing faithfulness in *the mighty act of God in Jesus Christ.* Though Jesus came into the Greco-Roman world of the first century, his main heritage was Jewish. Yet he cannot be identified with any one Jewish party. His life, death, resurrection, and ascension preceded the proclamation of the gospel. And the proclamation of the gospel preceded the writing of the Gospels.

Jesus was born in Bethlehem and grew up in Nazareth. He was baptized by John the Baptist. He was tempted to be an economic messiah, a marvelous messiah, and a political messiah; but he remained true to his calling to be the Servant-Messiah. Much of his ministry was carried on in Galilee. People responded to it in both acceptance and opposition. Jesus set his face steadfastly to go to Jerusalem to accomplish God's will there. Though his last days in Jerusalem led to the cross, they issued in the victorious resurrection.

Jesus performed a ministry of the spoken word, the mighty deed, and the given life. By the ministry of the spoken word he proclaimed and taught the good news of the reign or kingdom of God. He was the Master-Teacher who embodied perfectly what he taught, distinguished the important from the trivial, and spoke with authority. The kingdom, he said, is both present and future. To enter the kingdom requires the response of repentance and faith. The ethic of the kingdom is the ethic of love— love even for one's enemy. The mighty deeds of Jesus are as truly a part of his ministry as anything he ever said. He ministered to the whole person. Miracle reminds us that God deals with us in a person-to-person relationship. Jesus' entire ministry was a ministry of the given life, which reached its climax on Calvary. Through this given life he made atonement for our sin.

Jesus made an impact on people and on the world that no one else has ever made. The Old Testament prepared for his coming. The New Testament speaks of him as the One who did come, as the One who is with his people, as the One who was preexistent, and as the One who is yet to come.

The books of the New Testament also tell us of *God's transforming acts through the church*. The risen Christ promised his disciples: "You will receive power when the Holy Spirit has come upon you; and you will be my witnesses in Jerusalem and in all Judea and Samaria, and to the ends of the earth." The first two parts of this program of witness are recorded in the first twelve chapters of Acts. The witness "in Jerusalem" was inaugurated by the events of the new Pentecost: the outpouring of the Spirit, the witnessing in tongues, the preaching of Peter, and the response to the gospel. The community of believers worshiped God and put love in dynamic action. They faced opposition from the authorities boldly, and Peter even preached to the court. The Seven were appointed to assist the apostles. And Stephen became the first Christian martyr. The persecution that arose in connection with Stephen's death was used by God in taking the witness "in all Judea and Samaria" through the ministry of Philip the evangelist, Peter's ministry in Gentile territory, and the establishment of the church in Syrian Antioch. The ministry of the early church was patterned on the ministry of Jesus.

The latter part of Acts and parts of Paul's letters tell the story of Paul's witness by life. Paul was prepared for his ministry as the Apostle to the Gentiles by his combined Jewish and Greek heritage, by his conversion and call on the road to Damascus, and by the period of orientation following the conversion. He and Barnabas were commissioned as world missionaries by the church at Syrian Antioch. The story of his life is largely the story of his three missionary journeys and his journey to Rome. Severe opposition inside the church and outside the church could not deter him from his commitment. He had wanted to go to Rome but had not, at first, expected to go as a prisoner of the Roman government. In Rome he bore witness to both Jews and Gentiles. It is probable that he was released from this imprisonment in Rome and that he carried on a further ministry in Asia, Macedonia, Spain, Crete, and Greece. According to tradition he was put to death by Nero. Paul's ministry was also one of the spoken word, the mighty deed, and the surrendered life.

But Paul's ministry included as well a ministry of the written word. His witness by letter is a major part of the New Testament. He teaches us of justification by faith, the second coming of Christ, the resurrection of the body, the Christian life of faith and love, the ministry of reconciliation, the stewardship of money, the righteousness (salvation) of God, Christ the Head of the universe and the church, the church as the body of Christ, unity in the cosmic Christ, joy in the midst of adversity, and church leadership and organization. Truly God was mightily at work through the life and letters of this devoted servant.

The church encountered conflict with the Roman government and with false teaching, yet continued to bear its witness. The Letter of James exhibits the kind of concern for Christian ethical behavior that might be expected from a devout Jewish Christian. First Peter, Hebrews, and Revelation were written against the background of persecution by the Roman government. Apparently the persecution had not yet become intense when 1 Peter was written. Peter says that the Christian gospel is the basis of hope and that the Christian hope is the basis of Christian living. It is one thing to suffer for being a Christian; it is quite another thing to suffer as an evildoer. Hebrews was written as a call to steadfastness when Christians were tempted to defect from the faith. The book of Revelation was addressed to Christians in the provinces of Asia who were facing persecution and martyrdom. The author sought to encourage the faithful and to warn the indifferent.

The Gospel and Epistles of John and the Letters of Jude and 2 Peter were addressed at least in part to the problem of false teaching. The writings of John suggest conflict with that form of Gnosticism known as Docetism, a denial of the humanity of Jesus. John insists that the incarnation was real. His three key words are "life," "light," and "love," whose meanings overlap. The Docetists, who despised the body, failed in showing Christian love to others. But "those who do not love a brother or sister whom they have seen, cannot love God whom they have not seen" (1 John 4:20). The Gnosticism that was faced by Jude and 2 Peter was producing immoral conduct, for the Gnostics said that what one does with one's body cannot affect one's soul.

The biblical writers not only announced God's mighty acts in the past, they also *promised coming acts of consummation*. But this was not done without taking the total opposition (cosmic evil as well as human sin) into consideration. The Old Testament focuses on an expectation to be fulfilled beyond the borders of its own time. The New Testament records the keeping of the promise in the Person and work of Jesus and in the coming and working of the Holy Spirit in the life of the believer and the church.

Nevertheless, the full promise is yet to be consummated. The final coming of Christ in judgment and mercy is keenly awaited. This hope is wrongly conceived when it leads to inactivity in the present time and divisive speculation. Rightly understood, it is an incentive to Christian living and faithfulness in the midst of testing. The vision of the new heaven and the new earth means that God's purpose for humankind and for the whole creation shall have been accomplished through Jesus Christ.

There is nothing comparable to the biblical story in all the world. It is God's invention, not ours. Yet we are included in it. We are grateful for God's mighty acts in our behalf and pledge ourselves anew to undertaking the responsibility of our privilege. Indeed we count the responsibility itself a joyous privilege and an undeserved favor.

# Notes

## CHAPTER ONE

1. See G. Ernest Wright, *God Who Acts,* Studies in Biblical Theology (London: SCM Press, 1966). Since the first printing of *The Mighty Acts of God,* much has changed. Currently there is a greater emphasis on the diversity of biblical tradition, the challenge the Bible presents to church doctrine, and the reality of pluralism. This revision seeks to incorporate some of the current discussion while presenting the integrity of the biblical story that was a high priority of the original. For an assessment of the current situation, see Walter Brueggemann, *Theology of the Old Testament* (Minneapolis: Fortress Press, 1997), 61–114.

2. Diagrams similar to this one have been used by various teachers in presenting the story of redemption. Amos N. Wilder, for instance, used this in a class at the University of Chicago as he interpreted Oscar Cullmann's view of the biblical message.

3. Arnold B. Rhodes, "The Message of the Bible," in *Introduction to the Bible,* The Layman's Bible Commentary, vol. 1, ed. Balmer H. Kelly (Richmond: John Knox Press, 1959), 73–74.

4. "For All the Saints," *The Presbyterian Hymnal,* No. 526.

5. *The Mighty Acts of God* was originally published in 1964 as part of the Covenant Life Curriculum of the Associate Reformed Presbyterian Church, Cumberland Presbyterian Church, Moravian Church in America, Presbyterian Church in the United States, and Reformed Church in America.

## CHAPTER TWO

1. For additional reading on the relation of Genesis 1 to natural science, see H. H. Ridderbos, *Is There a Conflict Between Genesis 1 and Natural Science?* trans. John Vriend (Grand Rapids: Wm. B. Eerdmans Publishing Co., 1957); William M. Logan, *In the Beginning God* (Richmond: John Knox Press, 1957); and Terence E. Fretheim, "The Book of Genesis," in *The New Interpreter's Bible,* vol. 1 (Nashville: Abingdon Press, 1994), 337–38.

2. Emil Brunner, *The Christian Doctrine of Creation and Redemption* (*Dogmatics,* Vol. 2), trans. Olive Wyon (Philadelphia: Westminster Press, 1952), 46–88, deals with this subject.

## CHAPTER THREE

1. B. Davie Napier, *From Faith to Faith: Essays on Old Testament Literature* (New York: Harper & Brothers, 1955), 45–59; and Gerhard von Rad, *Genesis, A Commentary,* trans. John H. Marks (Philadelphia: Westminster Press, 1972), 102–55, are useful materials on this theme.

2. See Herbert E. Ryle, *The Book of Genesis,* The Cambridge Bible for Schools and Colleges (Cambridge: Cambridge University Press, 1921), 96–91, and Terence E. Fretheim, "Book of Genesis," in *The New Interpreter's Bible,* vol. 1, 388–89.

## CHAPTER FOUR

1. John Bright, *A History of Israel,* 3rd ed. (Philadelphia: Westminster Press, 1981), 92.

2. See Gerhard von Rad, *Genesis, A Commentary,* trans. John H. Marks (Philadelphia: Westminster Press, 1972), 237f.

3. The later Levitical law prohibited the marriage of sisters to the same man (Lev. 18:18).

4. Von Rad, *Genesis,* 351–52.

5. Ibid., 376.

6. Ibid., 439.

## CHAPTER FIVE

1. John Bright, *A History of Israel,* 3rd ed. (Philadelphia: Westminster Press, 1981), 134, n. 69.

2. Arthur Gabriel Hebert, *When Israel Came Out of Egypt* (Richmond: John Knox Press, 1961), 83.

3. F. S. Bodenheimer, "The Manna of Sinai," *The Biblical Archaeologist* 10 (February 1947): 2–6.

4. Bright, *History of Israel,* 155.

5. J. Coert Rylaarsdam, "The Book of Exodus," in *The Interpreter's Bible,* vol. 1 (New York and Nashville: Abingdon Press, 1952), 985.

6. See H. H. Rowley, *The Growth of the Old Testament* (London: Hutchinson's University Library, 1950), 15–46, and Joseph Blenkinsopp, "Introduction to the Pentateuch," in *The New Interpreter's Bible,* vol. 1 (Nashville: Abingdon Press, 1994), 308–14, for a more detailed presentation of the documentary hypothesis.

7. See particularly Blenkinsopp, "Introduction to the Pentateuch," 315–18, and R. N. Whybray, *The Making of the Pentateuch* (Sheffield: JSOT Press, 1987).

8. See Edward J. Young, *An Introduction to the Old Testament* (Grand Rapids: Wm. B. Eerdmans Publishing Co., 1958), 41–50, for a more complete documentation of this position.

9. Ibid., 50.

CHAPTER SIX

1. G. Ernest Wright, *Biblical Archaeology* (Philadelphia: Westminster Press, 1957), 71.

2. See the summary by John Bright, "The Book of Joshua," in *The Interpreter's Bible,* vol. 2, 584.

CHAPTER SEVEN

1. Chester Charlton McCown, *The Ladder of Progress in Palestine: A Story of Archaeological Adventure* (New York: Harper & Brothers, 1943), 239.

2. G. Ernest Wright, *Biblical Archaeology* (Philadelphia: Westminster Press, 1957), 132–36.

CHAPTER EIGHT

1. W. F. Albright, *From the Stone Age to Christianity,* 2d ed. (Baltimore: Johns Hopkins Press, 1957), 298–301.

2. John Bright, *A History of Israel,* 3rd ed. (Philadelphia: Westminster Press, 1981), 233–34.

3. From Paul J. Achtemeier, ed., *HarperCollins Bible Dictionary,* rev. ed. (San Francisco: HarperCollins, 1996), 182.

4. Norman H. Snaith, "The First and Second Books of Kings," in *The Interpreter's Bible,* vol. 3, 194.

CHAPTER NINE

1. Jacob M. Myers, *Hosea, Joel, Amos, Obadiah, Jonah,* The Layman's Bible Commentary, vol. 14, 113.

2. Ibid.

3. Ibid., 122.

4. See Norman H. Snaith, *The Distinctive Ideas of the Old Testament* (Philadelphia: Westminster Press, 1946), 167–182.

5. One presentation of this general point of view has been made by Professor William Sanford Lasor of Fuller Theological Seminary in a pamphlet entitled "Isaiah 7:14—'Young Woman' or 'Virgin'?" See also J. B. Taylor, "Virgin," in *The New Bible Dictionary,* 2d ed., J. D. Douglas, ed. (Wheaton, Ill.: Tyndale House, 1982), 1237–38; Gerald T. Sheppard, "Isaiah 1–39," in *Harper's Bible Commentary* (San Francisco: Harper & Row, 1988), 555–56.

CHAPTER TEN

1. John Bright, *A History of Israel,* 3rd ed. (Philadelphia: Westminster Press, 1981), 324.

2. Adapted from Arnold B. Rhodes, "The Message of the Bible," in *Introduction to the Bible,* The Layman's Bible Commentary, vol. 1, 89–90.

3. Howard T. Kuist, *Jeremiah, Lamentations,* The Layman's Bible Commentary, vol. 12, 47.

## CHAPTER ELEVEN

1. See John Bright, *A History of Israel,* 3rd ed. (Philadelphia: Westminster Press, 1981), 336–59, for a more detailed coverage.

2. See Carl G. Howie, *Ezekiel, Daniel,* The Layman's Bible Commentary, vol. 13, and Walther Eichrodt, *Ezekiel, A Commentary* (Philadelphia: Westminster Press, 1970), 1–48, for especially helpful treatments of Ezekiel.

3. See H. H. Rowley, *The Growth of the Old Testament* (London: Hutchinson, 1964), 89–100, if you want to read further on the theory of multiple authorship of Isaiah; see Edward J. Young, *An Introduction to the Old Testament* (Grand Rapids: Wm. B. Eerdmans Publishing Co., 1958), 215–25, if you wish to read further on the theory of single authorship.

4. Adapted from Arnold B. Rhodes, "The Message of the Bible," in *Introduction to the Bible,* The Layman's Bible Commentary, vol. 1, 93–94.

## CHAPTER TWELVE

1. From Otto Weber, *Ground Plan of the Bible,* trans. Harold Knight (London: Lutterworth Press, 1959), 78.

2. James H. Gailey, Jr., *Micah, Nahum, Habakkuk, Zephaniah, Haggai, Zechariah, Malachi,* The Layman's Bible Commentary, vol. 15, 101.

3. See Arnold B. Rhodes, *Psalms,* The Layman's Bible Commentary, vol. 9, 21–27 and J. Clinton McCann, Jr., "The Book of Psalms," in *The New Interpreter's Bible,* vol. 4, 644–52, for a more complete discussion of the classification of the Psalms.

4. Ibid., 157–58.

5. See Balmer H. Kelly, *Ezra, Nehemiah, Esther, Job,* The Layman's Bible Commentary, vol. 8, 9–10, for further information.

6. Carl Heinrich Cornill, *The Prophets of Israel,* trans. Sutton F. Corkran (Chicago: The Open Court Publishing Co., 1895), 170.

7. H. H. Rowley, *The Growth of the Old Testament* (London: Hutchinson, 1964), 114–15.

8. "Esther," *HarperCollins Bible Dictionary,* 309.

## CHAPTER THIRTEEN

1. See James B. Pritchard, ed., *Ancient Near Eastern Texts Relating to the Old Testament* (Princeton: Princeton University Press, 1950), 405–52.

2. John F. Genung, *The Epic of the Inner Life* (Boston and New York: Houghton, Mifflin and Co., 1891).

## CHAPTER FOURTEEN

1. Adapted from Arnold B. Rhodes, "The Kingdoms of Men and the Kingdom of God," *Interpretation* 15 (October 1961): 411–30. The details of this period may be found in First and Second Maccabees, and Bright, *A History of Israel,* 428–31.

2. Adapted from Rhodes, "The Kingdoms of Men and the Kingdom of God," and from Rhodes, "The Book of Daniel," *Interpretation* 6 (October 1952): 436–50. For a different point of view, see J. C. Whitcomb, "Daniel, Book of," *The New Bible Dictionary,* 262–65.

3. Edward J. Young, *An Introduction to the Old Testament* (Grand Rapids: Wm. B. Eerdmans Publishing Co., 1958), 380–93.

## CHAPTER FIFTEEN

1. Otto Weber, *Ground Plan of the Bible,* trans. Harold Knight (London: Lutterworth Press, 1959), 94.

2. "Sanhedrin," *HarperCollins Bible Dictionary,* 971–72.

3. See W. H. Brownlee, "John the Baptist in the New Light of Ancient Scrolls," in *The Scrolls and the New Testament,* ed. Krister Stendahl (New York: Harper & Brothers, 1957), 33–53, and Millar Burrows, *More Light on the Dead Sea Scrolls* (New York: Viking Press, 1958), 56–63, for details concerning this theory.

4. See Edwin Basil Redlich, *Form Criticism, Its Value and Limitations* (New York: Charles Scribner's Sons, 1939) and Howard Clark Kee, *Understanding the New Testament,* 5th ed. (Englewood Cliffs, N.J.: Prentice-Hall, 1993), 406–8.

5. Eusebius, *The Ecclesiastical History,* trans. Kirsopp Lake, Loeb Classical Library (Cambridge, Mass.: Harvard University Press, 1949), iii. 39.15.

6. From Archibald M. Hunter, *Introducing the New Testament,* 3rd ed. (Philadelphia: Westminster Press, 1972), 54.

7. Eusebius, *The Ecclesiastical History,* trans. Kirsopp Lake, Loeb Classical Library (Cambridge, Mass.: Harvard University Press, 1949) iii. 39. 16.

8. From Edward W. Bauman, *The Life and Teaching of Jesus* (Philadelphia: Westminster Press, 1960), 208.

9. From Floyd V. Filson, *Opening the New Testament* (Philadelphia: Westminster Press, 1952), 61.

## CHAPTER SIXTEEN

1. See Donald G. Miller, *Luke,* The Layman's Bible Commentary, vol. 18, 87.

2. Ibid., 101–31.

3. Edward W. Bauman, *The Life and Teaching of Jesus* (Philadelphia: Wesstminster Press, 1960), 99.

4. Vincent Taylor, *The Life and Ministry of Jesus* (New York and Nashville: Abingdon Press, 1955), 201.

## CHAPTER SEVENTEEN

1. Gunther Bornkamm, *Jesus of Nazareth,* trans. Irene and Fraser McLuskey with James M. Robinson (London: Hodder & Stoughton, 1960), 57.

2. See Archibald M. Hunter, *The Work and Words of Jesus* (Philadelphia: Westminster Press, 1956), 45, n. 1.

3. Paul S. Minear, *Mark*, The Layman's Bible Commentary, vol. 17, 95.

4. Hunter, *The Work and Words of Jesus,* 75.

5. Ibid., 54.

6. H. H. Farmer, *The World and God* (London: Nisbet & Co., 1948), 122–27.

7. James S. Stewart, *A Faith to Proclaim* (New York: Charles Scribner's Sons, 1953), 81.

8. Based on D. M. Baillie, *God Was in Christ* (New York: Charles Scribner's Sons, 1955), 157–202.

9. Isaac Watts, "When I Survey the Wondrous Cross," *The Presbyterian Hymnal,* No. 101.

## CHAPTER EIGHTEEN

1. Vincent Taylor, *The Names of Jesus* (London: Macmillan & Co.; New York: St. Martin's Press, 1953), 17.

2. See F. J. Taylor, "Mediator," in *A Theological Word Book of the Bible,* ed. Alan Richardson (New York: Macmillan Co., 1950), 141.

3. Ibid.

4. Francis W. Beare, "The Epistle to the Colossians," in *The Interpreter's Bible,* vol. 11, 168–69.

## CHAPTER NINETEEN

1. For this chapter, see especially Albert C. Winn, *Acts of the Apostles,* The Layman's Bible Commentary, vol. 20.

2. See "Pentecost," *HarperCollins Bible Dictionary,* 826.

3. Winn, *Acts of the Apostles,* 29.

4. See G. H. C. Macgregor, "The Acts of the Apostles," in *The Interpreter's Bible,* vol. 9, 87–91.

5. Winn, *Acts of the Apostles,* 64.

6. Ibid., 73.

## CHAPTER TWENTY

1. Albert C. Winn, *Acts of the Apostles,* The Layman's Bible Commentary, vol. 20, 67.

2. Benjamin W. Robinson, *The Life of Paul* (Chicago: University of Chicago Press, 1918), 74–76.

3. Archibald M. Hunter, *Galatians, Ephesians, Philippians, Colossians,* The Layman's Bible Commentary, vol. 22, 19–25.

4. Winn, *Acts of the Apostles,* 103.

5. Ibid., 107.

6. Robinson, *Life of Paul,* 216.

## CHAPTER TWENTY-ONE

1. Floyd V. Filson, *Opening the New Testament* (Philadelphia: Westminster Press, 1952), 91.

2. Clarence Tucker Craig, "The First Epistle to The Corinthians," in *The Interpreter's Bible,* vol. 10, 213.

3. Kenneth J. Foreman, *Romans, 1 and 2 Corinthians,* The Layman's Bible Commentary, vol. 21, 97.

4. See John Knox, "The Epistle to the Romans," in *The Interpreter's Bible,* vol. 9, 534–78, for a valuable treatment of these chapters.

5. Filson, *Opening the New Testament,* 175, endorses this theory.

## CHAPTER TWENTY-TWO

1. See Julian Price Love, *1, 2, and 3 John, Jude, Revelation,* The Layman's Bible Commentary, vol. 25, 42–44, for more details.

2. "Come, Ye Disconsolate, Where'er Ye Languish," *The Hymnbook,* No. 373.

3. See "Gnosticism," *HarperCollins Bible Dictionary,* 380–81.

4. Compare "John, the Gospel, According to," *HarperCollins Bible Dictionary,* 533–36.

## CHAPTER TWENTY-THREE

1. From Arnold B. Rhodes, *Psalms,* Layman's Bible Commentary, vol. 9, 110.

2. John Knox, "The Epistle to the Romans," in *The Interpreter's Bible,* vol. 9, 521.

3. From Arnold B. Rhodes, "The Message of the Bible," *Introduction to the Bible,* Layman's Bible Commentary, vol. 1, 114–15.

## CHAPTER TWENTY-FOUR

1. See Paul S. Minear, *Christian Hope and the Second Coming* (Philadelphia: Westminster Press, 1954), 119–24.

2. Adapted from Arnold B. Rhodes, "The Message of the Bible," *Introduction to the Bible,* Layman's Bible Commentary, vol. 1, 117–18.

# Study Aids

## THE BIBLE

*The HarperCollins Study Bible*. New Revised Standard Version. New York: HarperCollins, 1993.

*The Holy Bible*. New Revised Standard Version. New York: Oxford University Press, 1989.

*The New International Version*. London: Hodder & Stoughton, 1996.

*The New Jerusalem Bible*. New York: Doubleday, 1999.

## CONCORDANCES

Kohlenberger, John R., III. *The New Revised Standard Version Concordance*. Grand Rapids: Zondervan Publishing House, 1991.

Young, Robert. *Analytical Concordance to the Bible*. New York: Funk & Wagnalls Co., n.d.

## COMMENTARIES

Barclay, William. *The Daily Study Bible*. 17 vols. Philadelphia: Westminster Press, 1957–61.

Buttrick, George, ed., *The Interpreter's Bible*. 12 vols. New York and Nashville: Abingdon Press, 1952–57.

Keck, Leander, ed., *The New Interpreter's Bible*. 12 vols. (not all complete). Nashville: Abingdon Press, 1994–.

Kelly, Balmer H., ed. *The Layman's Bible Commentary*. 25 vols. Richmond: John Knox Press, 1959–64.

Mays, James L., ed. *Harper's Bible Commentary*. San Francisco: Harper & Row, 1988.

Newsom, Carol A., and Sharon H. Ringe, eds. *The Women's Bible Commentary*. Louisville, Ky.: Westminster/John Knox Press, 1992.

## INTRODUCTIONS TO THE BIBLE

Alter, Robert, and Frank Kermode, eds. *The Literary Guide to the Bible*. Boston: Harvard University Press, 1987.

Anderson, Bernhard W. *Understanding the Old Testament,* 4th ed. Englewood Cliffs, N.J.: Prentice-Hall, 1986.

Beker, J. Christiaan. *The New Testament: A Thematic Introduction.* Minneapolis: Fortress Press, 1994.

Brueggemann, Walter. *The Bible Makes Sense.* Rev. ed. Minneapolis: Christian Brothers, 1997.

Ehrman, Bart D. *The New Testament,* 2d ed. New York: Oxford University Press, 2000.

Kee, Howard Clark. *Understanding the New Testament.* 5th ed. Englewood Cliffs, N.J.: Prentice-Hall, 1993.

Kelly, Balmer H., ed. *Introduction to the Bible.* The Layman's Bible Commentary, vol. 1. Richmond: John Knox Press, 1959.

## HISTORY OF ISRAEL

Bright, John. *A History of Israel.* 3d ed. Philadelphia: Westminster Press, 1981.

## BIBLICAL ARCHAEOLOGY

Cornfield, Gaalyah, and David Noel Freedman. *Archaeology of the Bible: Book by Book.* San Francisco: Harper & Row, 1976.

Wright, G. Ernest. *Biblical Archaeology.* Philadelphia: Westminster Press, 1962.

## BIBLE ATLASES

Aharoni, Yohanan. *The Macmillan Bible Atlas.* New York: Macmillan Publishing Co., 1993.

Pritchard, James B., ed. *The HarperCollins Concise Atlas of the Bible.* San Francisco: HarperCollins, 1997.

## BIBLE DICTIONARIES

Achtemeier, Paul J., ed. *HarperCollins Bible Dictionary.* Rev. ed. San Francisco: HarperCollins, 1996.

Buttrick, George Arthur, ed. *The Interpreter's Dictionary of the Bible.* 4 vols. Nashville: Abingdon Press, 1962.

Crim, Keith, ed. *The Interpreter's Dictionary of the Bible,* Supplementary Volume. Nashville: Abingdon Press, 1976.

Freedman, David Noel, *The Anchor Bible Dictionary.* 6 vols. New York: Doubleday, 1992.

# Index of Scripture Passages

This Index includes only those passages that you have been requested to study in some special way. It does not include all the passages that have been interpreted or referred to in the book, or all the passages it is hoped you will read. The page reference usually indicates the place at which the discussion of a given passage begins. Somewhere within this discussion you will find suggestions for your special study. Sometimes, however, there is no discussion of the passage. In such a case the reference is to the page on which the suggestions for study occur.

## Old Testament

# New Testament